MW01001340

A History of Genocide in Africa

A History of Genocide in Africa

TIMOTHY J. STAPLETON

Praeger Security International

An Imprint of ABC-CLIO, LLC
Santa Barbara, California • Denver, Colorado

Library of Congress Cataloging-in-Publication Data

Names: Stapleton, Timothy J. (Timothy Joseph), 1967– author.
Title: A history of genocide in Africa / Timothy J. Stapleton.
Description: Santa Barbara, California : Praeger, an Imprint of ABC-CLIO, LLC, 2017. | Includes bibliographical references and index.
Identifiers: LCCN 2016054577 (print) | LCCN 2016055865 (ebook) | ISBN 9781440830518 (hardcopy : alk. paper) | ISBN 9781440830525 (eBook)
Subjects: LCSH: Genocide—Africa—History. | Genocide (International law) | Civil war—Africa. | Africa—Politics and government—1960–
Classification: LCC DT30.5 .S74 2017 (print) | LCC DT30.5 (ebook) | DDC 364.151096—dc23
LC record available at https://lccn.loc.gov/2016054577

ISBN: 978-1-4408-3051-8
EISBN: 978-1-4408-3052-5

21 20 19 18 17 1 2 3 4 5

This book is also available as an e-book.

Praeger
An Imprint of ABC-CLIO, LLC

ABC-CLIO, LLC
130 Cremona Drive, P.O. Box 1911
Santa Barbara, California 93116-1911
www.abc-clio.com

This book is printed on acid-free paper ∞
Manufactured in the United States of America

Contents

Acknowledgment

This history of genocide in Africa was initially meant as a coauthored book involving a historian of Africa and a scholar of genocide studies. The latter was Berthe Kayitesi who had survived the 1994 genocide against the Tutsi in Rwanda when she was a teenager and later completed a doctorate in genocide education at the University of Ottawa. Through extensive public speaking and the publication of her memoir *Demain ma vie* (*Tomorrow My Life*), she had become a strong advocate for Rwandan genocide survivors and for preserving the memory of that horrific event. While Berthe was involved in the conceptualization of this book and drafting the proposal, she did not get a chance to write any of the content. She passed away in June 2015. She was 36 years old. The circumstances around her death serve as a cautionary tale about the potentially overwhelming power of the concept of genocide. In the troubled months leading up to Berthe's death, some suspected that she was suffering from post-traumatic stress related to her experience of genocide while others who were awestruck by her heroic survival story encouraged her to believe that nothing was wrong with her. Neither view was correct. She died of multiple brain aneurysms.

Introduction

The mid-20th-century emergence of the concept of genocide and its international legal definition had little to do with Africa, which, at the time, was a colonized continent with almost no autonomous representation in the global community. In 1933 at an international criminal law conference in Madrid, Spain, a Polish lawyer, Raphael Lemkin, presented a paper proposing that international law recognize the extermination of national groups as a crime distinct from war crimes, which had already been recognized through a series of earlier conventions. However, Lemkin struggled with coining suitable terms. His proposal to call the destruction of human groups "barbarism" and the destruction of human cultural heritage "vandalism" was not well received. During the Second World War (1939–1945), Lemkin fled to the United States where, as a law professor at Duke University, he collected information on Nazi atrocities in Europe, which included the murder of many of his own family who were Jews. In an August 1941 radio broadcast, British prime minister Winston Churchill famously highlighted the inadequacy of existing legal terminology in describing Nazi outrages in Europe by referring to them as "a crime without a name." This void in vocabulary was filled by Lemkin. In 1944 he published a book entitled *Axis Rule in Occupied Europe,* in which he devised the term "genocide" by combining the Greek "genos" for race or people with the Latin "cide" for murder. In doing this, Lemkin was building on existing and widely used terms such as "homicide," "fratricide," and "regicide." When he coined the term, Lemkin understood genocide as "a coordinated plan of different actions aiming at the destruction of essential foundations of the life of national groups, with the aim of annihilating the groups themselves."[1] As will be discussed throughout this book, the concept of genocide would have an enormous impact on Africa and Africans.

With the circulation of films showing the liberation of Nazi concentration camps at the end of the Second World War, Lemkin's term genocide became popularized in a short time. Although the 1945 Nuremberg trials of defeated German Nazi leaders did not officially employ the notion of genocide, they influenced the creation of new international law that did. In December 1946, the United Nations (UN), a new international body originally consisting of the victorious powers of the Second World War but which quickly expanded to include others, passed a resolution that affirmed genocide as a crime under international law and invited member states to reflect this way of thinking in their national legal codes. Authored by Lemkin, the definition presented in the initial UN resolution stated that "genocide is a denial of the right of existence of entire human groups, as homicide is the denial of the right to live of individual human beings."[2] Furthermore, the resolution explained the scope of genocide to include the extermination of groups of people defined by "religious, racial, political or any other grounds."[3] National interests dominated the subsequent two-year-long UN debate over which precise legal definition of genocide that nations would adopt. A number of countries—including the Soviet Union, given Stalin's purges of political enemies—objected to the inclusion of political or social groups as targets of genocide. Similarly, the United States, Canada, and South Africa opposed the concept of cultural genocide, given their histories of settler dispossession of indigenous people. Eventually, in December 1948, the UN adopted the Convention on the Prevention and Punishment of the Crime of Genocide, which defined genocide as "acts committed with intent to destroy, in whole or in part, a national, ethnical, racial or religious group."[4] Those acts included killing, causing serious physical or mental harm, imposing conditions of life meant to bring about physical destruction, imposing measures to prevent births, and forcibly transferring children of one group to another group. The 1948 convention defined genocide, conspiracy to commit genocide, incitement of genocide, attempted genocide, and complicity in genocide as international crimes. At that time, only four African members of the UN existed. Of those, Ethiopia, Egypt, and Liberia signed the convention, whereas South Africa, which had just elected a racially segregationist apartheid government, did not. The UN genocide convention came into effect in 1951, which was a time when European policy toward colonial Africa was on the cusp of a dramatic change. While European colonial powers had no intention of withdrawing from Africa at the start of the 1950s, within a decade most African colonies would become independent states and have to interact with the recently established international legal concept of genocide that they had nothing to do with creating.[5]

Since its inception, the 1948 international legal definition of genocide has been the subject of much criticism and debate. For instance, the convention gives no indication of the number of deaths that might be needed to qualify an incident of mass violence as genocide. In the popular imagination, any violent process that results in large numbers of fatalities is often but inaccurately called genocide. In addition, one of the most problematic aspects of the 1948 legal standard is the issue of intent. What type of evidence proves that a regime, organization, or individual intended to commit genocide? Must there be such specific written plans or instructions as the extermination order issued by the German commander in South West Africa (today's Namibia) in 1904, or, in the absence of written plans, can genocidal intent be inferred from such systematic massacres as witnessed in Rwanda in 1994? The relation between war and genocide is also controversial. It is often difficult to differentiate between the tragic death of civilians as a result of war, which is now euphemistically called "collateral damage," and a purposeful attempt to exterminate a specific racial, ethnic, or religious group. Confusion often arises when discussing counterinsurgency campaigns or conventional military operations aimed at suppressing regional secessionist movements that can be seen as targeting people based on ethnicity or regional origin. As will be discussed, there are many instances of this in postcolonial African history. Such problems with the UN convention have inspired debates over redefining genocide.

Some scholars have proposed narrowing the definition of genocide, while others have sought to broaden it. For some, a campaign to exterminate a group "in part," as stated in the 1948 convention, should not be included in the category of genocide, because it trivializes the crime and degrades the victims and survivors of well-known total genocides. In this view, genocide should refer only to cases in which perpetrators desire the complete elimination of a group such as the Holocaust of the Jews during the Second World War or the methodical killing of Tutsi in 1994 Rwanda.[6] Conversely, with the expansion of genocide studies as an academic discipline in the 1980s and 1990s, many scholars saw a need to widen the legal and intellectual meaning of genocide to go beyond the Holocaust model. Many alternative definitions have been put forth. For instance, Frank Chalk and Kurt Jonassohn completely open up the definition of target groups and scale of extermination by stating that "Genocide is a form of one-sided mass killing in which a state or other authority intends to destroy a group, as that group and membership are defined by the perpetrator."[7] Critics of broadening the definition of genocide point out that doing so will mean that almost any instance of mass violence could be seen as genocide, which will result in the term losing its specific legal and analytical usefulness. As such, this book will employ the existing international legal definition of genocide.

While most countries that created national laws against genocide stuck closely to the wording of the 1948 UN convention, several created broader legal frameworks. Ethiopia, the first country to deposit the 1948 genocide convention officially with the UN secretary-general, promulgated its own genocide law during the 1950s that ignored the objections of other UN member states and defined target groups as "national, ethnic, racial, religious *or political*."[8] During the early 1990s, the Eastern European countries of Poland, Latvia, and Lithuania, reflecting their recent history of Soviet domination from which they had just emerged, changed their laws to extend the scope of genocide targets to include political and sometimes social groups—and in some cases added deportation and torture to the list of genocidal acts.[9] In March 1994, ironically just days before the beginning of genocide in Rwanda in which French forces would be implicated, France's new Penal Code adopted a definition of genocide that is similar to the 1948 UN convention but added two new features: "the enforcement of a *concerted plan* aimed at the partial or total destruction of a national, ethnic, racial or religious group or *a group determined by any other arbitrary means*." While this definition creates a more "objective criterion" for establishing genocidal intent, which must be seen as a part of a "concerted plan," it significantly expands the scope of potential target groups.[10]

In the late 1950s and early 1960s, most of Europe's African colonies became independent states and, as such, were admitted into the UN. African states became subject to international law regarding genocide and had to promulgate their own national laws on the subject, which generally repeated the existing international standard. During the immediate post-decolonization period of the 1960s, which also represented the height of the global Cold War that was now superimposed on Africa, areas of Africa became the scene of fears and accusations relating to genocide. That was particularly the case when newly sovereign African governments reacted to the emergence of regional separatist movements, often in areas with valuable natural resources and with foreign encouragement. Since the newly independent countries of Africa generally inherited the political borders European colonial conquerors imposed on them during the late 19th century and which tended to ignore geographic and ethnic realities, people in some areas objected to their inclusion in the new states and demanded self-determination. In 1960 Patrice Lumumba, the first prime minister of the Democratic Republic of Congo (DRC), was accused by the UN secretary-general of orchestrating genocide against the Luba people of the breakaway and diamond-rich region of South Kasai. The government of oil-rich Biafra justified its 1967 secession from Nigeria as a reaction to what it called the genocide of its people (primarily the Igbo). Around the same time, southern Sudanese separatists charged that the northern-dominated Sudanese government's counterinsurgency campaign amounted to genocide. The sudden adoption of Western-style democracy also resulted in power shifts that occasionally led to accusations of genocide. In early 1964, international observers condemned the new Hutu majority government of Rwanda for conducting genocide against the country's formerly dominant Tutsi minority. Racism was also equated with genocide. International revulsion over the imposition of apartheid in South Africa, heightened by the Sharpeville massacre of 1960, led to discussions of the term genocide.

In 1967 the UN Commission on Human Rights suggested that the South African system of apartheid may have represented a violation of aspects of the 1948 genocide convention. Although the UN moved away from associating apartheid with genocide, those discussions ultimately led to the 1973 International Convention on the Suppression and Punishment of the Crime of Apartheid, which criminalized the domination and oppression of one racial group by another. With the rising anticolonial sentiments of the 1950s and 1960s, some scholars began to apply the term genocide to earlier instances of European colonial conquest on the continent. Lemkin used the word genocide in the 1950s to describe Leopold II's already infamous conquest and exploitation of the Congo Free State at the turn of the 19th and 20th century and in 1966, East German historian Horst Drechsler used the term with reference to the 1904–1907 German military campaign in Namibia.[11] Although a wave of genocide allegations were made involving Africa in the tumultuous 1960s, there were almost no legal ramifications, and as was the case elsewhere no one was ever formally indicted for genocide crimes.

During the 1970s and 1980s, with Africa mostly divided between authoritarian regimes allied either to the United States or Soviet Union and the continent becoming the scene of Cold War proxy conflicts, the employment of genocide rhetoric seemed to decline. At the same time, vicious regimes such as those of Idi Amin in Uganda, Jean-Bedel Bokassa in the Central African Republic (CAR), and Mengistu Haile Mariam in Ethiopia embarked on mass murder—the scale of which was unprecedented on the continent. Though actions that could arguably be defined as genocide continued and accusations of genocide did not disappear entirely, the international community or media did not appear to take them seriously with regard to Africa, and other parts of the world as well. For example, there was almost no international reaction to the 1972 mass killing of educated Hutu and Hutu students in Burundi, which some were quietly calling genocide. Underlying this general disinterest in genocide was the old and still evolving myth that Africans are inherently violent people engaging in tribal warfare, which could not be explained in rational terms.

Beginning in the 1990s, the mobilization of genocide accusations in and concerning Africa was resuscitated and dramatically expanded. The immediate stimulus was the international horror caused by events in Rwanda in 1994, but the general instability created by the end of the Cold War provided the broader context. Superpower-backed dictatorships collapsed, many countries experienced civil war, a few became "failed states," and armed groups that could no longer gain external sponsorship by espousing obsolete ideologies instead turned to securing natural resources for the world market. At the same time, revolutionary developments in global media and communications through 24-hour television news channels and particularly the Internet, which grew exponentially during the early

2000s, popularized interest in genocide prevention, mostly among North Americans and Europeans. Developments in media provided a venue for international activists, who began focusing their attention on the increasing number of dire conflicts in Africa. Africans also engaged with the rising global media, and some African leaders sought to manipulate it. Given its absolute failure in Rwanda, the UN suddenly renewed its commitment to genocide investigation and prevention. The UN founded a special court to deal with genocide crimes committed in Rwanda in 1994, and a series of UN committees began to investigate genocide allegations in other parts of Africa. A 1996 UN report stated that killings of Tutsi in 1993 in Burundi had amounted to genocide, and another 1998 UN report concluded that the predominantly Tutsi Rwandan military had arguably conducted genocide during its pursuit of Rwandan Hutu refugees across the DRC.

During the mid-2000s, the release of many books, feature films, documentaries, and Web sites related to the 1994 tragedy in Rwanda fueled Western obsession with genocide in Africa. That focus influenced the 2004 establishment of the Save Darfur campaign, which emerged from established Holocaust education institutions and attracted attention through celebrity activism in the United States and that eventually morphed into a wider antigenocide movement. While the United States government and the European Union described Sudan's counterinsurgency campaign in Darfur as genocide, a 2005 UN report disagreed on the use of that term, though it recognized that grave crimes had been committed. Around that time, Western countries such as Belgium and Canada began using new laws that extended their legal jurisdiction when addressing genocide and crimes against humanity to prosecute Rwandan immigrants accused of crimes during the 1994 genocide in their country of origin. Characteristic of this period and informed by international guilt over Rwanda, an awarding-winning 2002 book by Samantha Power, later the U.S. ambassador to the UN, urged the United States government to look beyond national interests and to use its capabilities to intervene forcefully in other countries to prevent genocide.[12] In 2005 the UN general assembly unanimously adopted the principle of "responsibility to protect" (R2P), which theoretically limited sovereignty by obliging states to shield their citizens from genocide, ethnic cleansing, crimes against humanity, and war crimes and empowered the international community to intervene when national governments failed in this regard. Critics of the new policy warned that it would compromise national sovereignty, would only be applied to poor countries such as those in Africa, and might unintentionally worsen conflicts.[13] Not surprisingly in this environment, allegations related to genocide in Africa multiplied exponentially. Many Congolese began to claim that the invasion of the DRC by Rwanda and Uganda from 1998 to 2002, in a conflict that arguably claimed several million lives, represented not only a massive theft of resources but also genocide. It appeared that international guilt over genocide had given Rwanda the right to carry out atrocities in neighboring DRC. The language of genocide was picked up by various sides in eastern DRC's local conflicts. During the first half of the 2000s, Ituri Province was the scene of genocide finger-pointing between Lendu and Hema militias, and the long-marginalized Twa minority complained of genocide. In the late 2000s and early 2010s, Congolese Tutsis in the Kivu region rebelled against a new DRC government, citing the need to protect themselves from potential genocide by Hutu rebels from Rwanda. In the mid-2000s international indigenous rights activists accused the government of Botswana, a country that has not experienced a war in its postcolonial history, of conducting a genocide of the Basarwa (Bushman) minority. Fears of state-sponsored genocide against the historically marginalized Tuareg people of the Sahara arose during rebellions in Mali and Niger during 2006–2009 and in Mali in 2012–2013. In 2013 violence in the CAR and South Sudan incited international concerns over possible genocide.

Many old genocide accusations were given new life. The resurrection of Biafra separatism in southwest Nigeria during the 2000s prompted a return of genocide accusations related to the civil war of the late 1960s. Following Namibia's independence from South Africa in 1990, there were calls for newly unified Germany to pay reparations to the Herero and Nama, and those requests intensified during the next two decades. With the rise of Zimbabwe's first significant political opposition during the 2000s, charges that the long-ruling and authoritarian Mugabe regime had committed genocide against the Ndebele minority during the 1980s were rediscovered and promoted. Southern Cameroon separatists and other critics of Cameroon's long-time French-sponsored state accused the French of having committed genocide there in the late 1950s and 1960s and claimed that the current government was continuing the process. When Kenya's disputed 2007 election led to violence between politicized ethnic communities, Kenyan politicians blamed each other for harboring genocidal intent, and those accusations were eagerly repeated by the international media. In 2006 a long trial in Ethiopia concluded with the conviction of many members of the country's former military regime, including exiled leader Mengistu Haile Mariam, for genocide of political opponents during the late 1970s.

In general, the rhetoric of genocide has had destructive consequences for postcolonial Africa. As others have noted, the genocide concept creates a moral hierarchy of perpetrators and victims that has been manipulated in contests over power and wealth. Those who stand accused of genocide allegedly have committed the "crime of crimes," and, given the obvious association with the Nazis who perpetrated the Holocaust, they are labeled as evil and inhuman. By extension, those killed become the honored and memorialized dead, and those who survive are often venerated and granted saint-like status. Supposed agents of genocide are seen as the bad guys, whereas their victims and opponents are the good guys. Conflicts in postcolonial Africa, unfortunately, have not usually been that simple. In addition, those who question the veracity of genocide accusations are often themselves vilified as "genocide deniers," which equates them to wacky conspiracy theorists, Holocaust deniers, and neo-Nazis. That complication can make the critical study of genocide intimidating, and, within Rwanda, even the most basic questions about genocide can result in criminal convictions and prison terms. Over the past two decades, genocide-prevention campaigners—mostly from Western countries—have popularized moralistic genocide identities and narratives with reference to Africa. While antigenocide activism pursues a "never again" goal, such discourse has often and unfortunately prolonged wars in post-colonial Africa. Genocide rhetoric gained international support for the separatist Biafra regime, which it would not have otherwise enjoyed and therefore prolonged the Nigerian Civil War and led to many more deaths. Much the same could be said for the more recent conflicts in Sudan's Darfur region and eastern DRC. Negotiated settlements are unlikely in conflicts in which some leaders face international indictment for genocide or other crimes against humanity and in which others have successfully mobilized antigenocide language to rally international sympathy and support. In looking at those cases, it might seem as if Africans would have been better off had Lemkin never coined the term genocide, but one cannot un-ring that bell. Of course, not all genocide accusations related to Africa have been cynical or opportunistic, and some episodes of terrible mass violence can be accurately described as genocide under the 1948 convention. To illustrate the ambiguities surrounding terminology, some instances of mass violence in African history that cannot be appropriately understood as genocide involved greater loss of life and destruction than those that clearly fall under the international legal standard.

This book provides an historical overview of how the concept of genocide has been deployed with reference to Africa. As an empirical history, it will not offer theoretical models to predict when and where genocide could occur or analyze imagined stages of genocide. In addition, it will not dwell on the perceived "banality of evil" or mention the devil or hell. It examines the historical context of six African countries that have experienced conflict and in which the term genocide has been vigorously applied: Namibia, Rwanda, Burundi, the DRC, Sudan, and Nigeria. This information is supplemented by a conclusion that discusses other parts of Africa in which genocide claims have been made but which are either obviously problematic or remain largely uninvestigated. The main point of the book is that relatively few of the many instances of mass violence in African history can be considered genocide under the existing international legal definition, which is the only definition that truly matters. Where genocide has occurred in Africa, there seems to have been a common history of the imposition of racial ideology—the idea that certain groups of people are biologically superior to others—on state and society during the colonial era. In early-20th-century Namibia, the Germans engaged in what they saw as a race war against indigenous people, while in late-20th-century Rwanda and Burundi the legacy of colonial Social Darwinism and Hamitic theory turned deadly. That sort of colonial racial ideology was different and applied in far fewer places than the ethnic divide-and-rule policies that were common throughout much of colonial Africa. The concept of ethnicity is based on language, culture, and region of origin rather than claims concerning biology. Ethnicism or tribalism, about which exists a huge Africanist literature, and regionalism often influenced the development of dreadful postcolonial violence in which genocide claims were sometimes made but which rarely met the international legal standard. As will be addressed, that was the case with the Congo Crisis and the Nigerian Civil War of the 1960s, as among other examples. Clearly, not every instance of racial ideology and domination in colonial Africa translated into genocide. The specific situation and context of each time and place was central. In Namibia, the German extermination order was facilitated by the relatively small size of the Herero and Nama populations and the harsh desert environment. Rwanda and Burundi are unusual among African countries in that they are small, have high population densities, and people of different racialized (not ethnic) identities live among each other rather than in different regions or homelands. In Sudan, a racial hierarchy overlapped with identities related to religion and way of life.

There are several reasons to focus on the history of genocide as it relates to Africa. Although there is incredible human and geographic diversity in Africa, the continent shares a generally common history of European colonization that began in the late 19th century, caused dramatic social and economic change, and was followed by a sudden transition to independence around the 1960s. This book assumes that something can be learned in placing genocide within the specific context of African history. Several scholars have indicated that there is limited utility in comparing genocides that took place in Africa to events that happened elsewhere, including the Holocaust in Europe or the genocides that took place in Armenia and Cambodia.[14] The historical context is too different. In a recent study of why genocides did not take place in certain postcolonial African countries that experienced conflict, Scott Straus makes a convincing argument that it is useful to look at African examples because there are common factors such as the relative newness of African states, a political history that has moved from one-party rule to multiparty democracy, a low-income economy based on resource export and sometimes international aid, and interaction with each other.[15] Furthermore, it is obvious that some genocide-studies literature could benefit from improved contextualization when it comes to Africa. That genocide-studies encyclopedias describe the early-19th-century expansion of the Zulu Kingdom as a genocide that killed 1 million people and that depopulated the interior of what is now Southern Africa betrays a shockingly superficial knowledge of the region's history. Although the origins and expansion of the Zulu Kingdom has been hotly debated, no serious historian of Southern Africa would describe it as genocidal or as resulting in a million deaths; the "empty land" theme was debunked years ago as a colonial and apartheid myth meant to justify the dominance of later white settlers.[16] Similarly, the claim that the British invasion of the Zulu Kingdom in 1879 represented genocide against the Zulu people lacks any basis in reality.[17] While genocide-studies scholars will benefit from learning more about the history of Africa, it may also be useful for historians of Africa to think more broadly about how the mounting rhetoric of genocide has affected African conflicts. What does genocide mean and has the term been applied accurately with reference to episodes from Africa's colonial and postcolonial history?

CHAPTER 1

Namibia

GERMAN COLONIALISM AND THE SCRAMBLE FOR AFRICA

As a collection of relatively small central European states unified in 1871, Germany was a newcomer to the quest for colonies in Africa. Although founding German Chancellor Otto von Bismarck wanted to focus on acquiring territory in Europe and opposed what he considered irrelevant and costly overseas empire building, he eventually succumbed to pressure from German merchants and missionaries with interests in Africa who wanted direct support from their home government. In 1884 Germany abruptly declared control over territories in every region of Sub-Saharan Africa: Togoland and Cameroon in West Africa; German East Africa, which consisted of what is now the mainland of Tanzania as well as Rwanda and Burundi; and German South West Africa, which is present-day Namibia. Germany's rush to acquire colonies was also linked to its ambition to develop a world-class navy to rival Britain and to the belief that the status of such great powers as Britain and France was linked to possession of overseas territories. To some extent, the sudden German claim to parts of Africa prompted other older European colonial powers to formalize control of their hitherto loosely understood spheres of influence out of fear of losing them. It was not a coincidence that Germany hosted the Berlin Conference of 1884–1885, at which, without any Africans in attendance, representatives of European powers planned the partition and conquest of Africa. Previously confined to coastal colonies in Africa, European powers conquered most of the continent over the next two decades, except for the independent African American republic of Liberia in West Africa and the powerful kingdom of Ethiopia, which defeated Italian invasion in 1896. Scholars have put forth various theories to explain this European "Scramble for Africa" with the main debate revolving around economic motives such as the search for new investment opportunities and the desire to extract raw materials versus the perceived need to secure strategically important points such as the Suez Canal and the Cape.[1] Of course, other factors such as extreme nationalism and white racism were important. The conquest itself was facilitated by fairly recent European technological innovations such as rapid-firing and more accurate firearms, which granted military superiority; telegraphs, which provided fast communication; and steam ships and railways, which sped up transportation and enhanced economic exploitation of colonies. Given their narrower geographical vision, African leaders were divided in their response to European invasions. In addition, most of the foot soldiers of the European-led armies in Africa were local people from older coastal colonies and allied groups.[2]

Since Germany did not have a history of administering colonies, its approach to colonial rule and the development of colonial economies in Africa tended to mirror other European powers in neighboring territories. Therefore, in West and East Africa, the Germans copied the British and French regional practice of sending small numbers of administrators and soldiers to administer large African populations who were encouraged through a mixture of coercion and taxation to produce raw materials for export. By contrast, the Germans perceived South West Africa as a colony for European settlement with an economy based on mining and cattle ranching in which African people became a servile class engaged in migrant labor in neighboring territories. This policy was informed by Southern Africa's early and distinct history of European settler colonization, which had been facilitated by relatively low levels of tropical disease and which had largely kept settlers out of the rest of Sub-Saharan Africa. The Cape Colony had been established by the Dutch East India Company in 1652 and was seized by the British at the turn of the 18th and 19th century. When the Germans arrived in South West Africa in 1884, Southern Africa was dominated by such well-established settler states as the internally self-governing British Cape Colony and the colony of Natal on the coast, and the Boer republics of the Orange Free State and Transvaal in the interior, which had recently secured autonomy from Britain. Relations between the British and Boers were strained because the Transvaal had successfully rebelled against Britain in 1880–1881. Indeed, concern over possible collusion between the Germans and the Boers prompted London, in 1885, to formalize relations with indigenous Tswana leaders, who agreed to come under colonial rule within the framework of the Bechuanaland Protectorate (today's Botswana) that lay between South West Africa and the Transvaal. Furthermore, during the 1880s, Southern Africa was experiencing the beginning of its Mineral Revolution; the diamond fields of the Northern Cape had been operating for over a decade, and gold would be discovered in the Transvaal in 1886. Across the region, the settler states were conquering the remaining independent African groups, and African people were being transformed into landless, impoverished, and low-paid migrant workers for the mines. In the 1890s, informed by the context of the scramble and the search for new mineral resources, Cecil Rhodes, the wealthy mining magnate, British imperialist, and Cape premier, arranged for the colonial conquest of the area immediately north of the Transvaal, which became the white settler colony of Southern Rhodesia (present-day Zimbabwe). Escalating tensions between the British and Boers eventually led to the South African War (or Second Anglo-Boer War) of 1899–1902, in which the Boer republics were conquered by Britain. That conflict resulted in the 1910 formation of the Union of South Africa as a settler-ruled British dominion consisting of the Cape, Natal, and the two former Boer republics.[3]

GERMAN COLONIZATION IN SOUTH WEST AFRICA

Near the Atlantic coast of Southern Africa, the arid grassland between the Kalahari and Namib deserts was dominated by various Khoisan-speaking Nama groups who had moved north from the Cape, where they had been dispossessed by Dutch settlers who were expanding during the 18th century. With horses and guns acquired in trade from the Dutch settlers of the Cape Colony, the nomadic Nama raided cattle, mostly from the Bantu-speaking pastoralist Herero, who lived near present-day Windhoek, and the agricultural Ovambo further north. During the 1860s, the Herero increasingly challenged the Nama with firearms obtained from European traders seeking cattle to feed miners in the diamond fields. In 1878 the British, encouraged by Herero requests for protection against Nama raids, annexed the important Atlantic trading outlet of Walvis Bay, which was placed under the administration of Britain's Cape Colony. During the 1880s and 1890s, Nama leader Hendrik Witbooi, who had been converted to Christianity by missionaries and who was inspired by religious visions, sought to unite the Nama groups and lead them north; this resulted in years of guerrilla warfare with the now stronger Herero. By the end of the 1880s, Witbooi was the dominant leader among the Nama, in what is now southern Namibia.

In 1884 Germany declared a protectorate over the Atlantic coast and hinterland from the Orange River in the south to the Cunene River in the north, except for the British enclave of Walvis Bay. While Herero leader Maherero initially accepted German protection, he renounced it in 1888 as the Germans proved unable to stop Nama attacks that seized cattle and destroyed settlements. In January 1889, a small German military detachment led by Captain Curt von Francois landed at the port of Swakopmund and constructed a fort about 200 kilometers inland at Tsaobis. The next year, with reinforcements, the Germans constructed another fort farther east at Windhoek, which became the colonial capital. Given the gradual colonial penetration, Maherero renewed his agreement with the

Germans just before his death in 1890, but Witbooi stubbornly rejected colonial rule.

Witbooi's resistance led to the German-Nama War of 1893–1894. In April 1893, German commander Francois led an attack by 200 German troops on Witbooi's camp at Hoornkranz during which 150 Nama were killed, including many women and children. Witbooi abandoned the camp with approximately 250 armed and mounted Nama. Based in the Naukluft Mountains, Witbooi's army grew to around 600, of whom 400 had guns and 300 had horses. They waged a guerrilla war against the Germans by raiding colonial outposts and supply wagon trains. With reinforcements from Germany, Francois attempted to surround the elusive Nama who attacked his rear areas. On February 1 and 2, 1894, the Germans engaged the Nama in the Onab Valley, but once again the Nama melted into the nearby hills. In early 1894, Major Theodor Leutwein, who had been instructed to establish a German colonial administration in the territory, took over as German commander, and while awaiting additional reinforcements, he isolated Witbooi by turning other African groups against him. In late August, Leutwein's force swept the Naukluft Mountains, capturing waterholes and observation points and surrounding Witbooi's Nama, who yielded in early September and accepted a protection treaty that allowed them to retain their weapons and ammunition.

In the 1890s, a Herero civil war broke out between the followers of the late Maharero's sons, Nikodemus and Samuel. In 1896 Leutwein directed German forces against the supporters of Nikodemus, some of whom were hanged and had their land and cattle confiscated. With German support, Samuel Maherero became the principal Herero leader and agreed to German settlement in the southern part of Herero territory. In mid-1896, the arrival of 400 more German troops consolidated colonial control of German South West Africa (SWA) south of Ovamboland. With its dry climate and lack of tropical disease, Berlin saw SWA as a place for European settlement similar to neighboring British colonies and Boer republics in which Africans would provide labor for cattle ranches and mines. By 1897 there were 2,600 Europeans, some of whom were German military veterans who had been granted land, living in the colony. Reflecting the colony's settler orientation and open geography, the German colonial military, or Schutztruppe, in SWA was almost entirely European and consisted of nearly 700 mounted infantry. In German tropical African colonies such as Cameroon or German East Africa, a small number of Europeans led the local colonial military but the majority were African soldiers. Leutwein officially became governor of SWA in 1898, and although his policies undermined indigenous groups like the Nama and Herero, the emerging settler community criticized him for not acting aggressively enough and for failing to provide them with enough land. In 1896 Leutwein warned against a more antagonistic approach, which he thought would result in a "war of extermination against the Herero" that would deprive the colony of its source of African labor.[4]

THE HERERO REBELLION (1904)

At the turn of the 19th and 20th century, several developments put increased pressure on the Herero and Nama. The European population increased as Boers, displaced by the British conquest of their republics during the South African War (1899–1902), moved to SWA. Colonial recruitment of migrant labor for the region's mines also caused tension. In 1903 the German government announced plans to facilitate white settlement by building a railway though Herero territory and relocating the Herero to reserves. Many Herero and Nama, rendered destitute by the rinderpest cattle plague of 1896–1897, which had spread across the subcontinent, transferred land to settlers and became indebted to European merchants. The 1903 announcement by the colonial administration that it would cancel the African debts to prevent conflict had the opposite result. European merchants hired off-duty German soldiers to collect what they were owed all at once, which led to mass seizures of livestock and other property from the Herero. That response ignited the Herero rebellion, which began in mid-January 1904 with a surprise attack on European settlers. Approximately 150 European men were killed. Seeing the German colonial state as his enemy, Herero leader Samuel Maherero instructed his fighters to spare Boer and British men and all European women and children.

At the start of 1904, there were between 7,000 and 8,000 Herero combatants, half of whom were armed with guns and a limited supply of ammunition. The German force consisted of nearly 800 regular soldiers, the same number of reservists, 400 armed settlers, and 250 African scouts. The German force was also supported by five field guns and five machine guns. When the rebellion began, Governor Leutwein and most of the Schutztruppe were in the territory's far south suppressing a rebellion by the small Bondelswart community. Since the Herero had no experience attacking fortified positions defended by rapid-firing rifles and machine guns, the Germans gained time to respond. In late January and early February, the Germans relieved the besieged posts at Okahandja and Windhoek, and several companies of German marines landed on the coast. During February and March, a major expeditionary force of 1,500 men with 1,000 horses, 10 artillery pieces, and 6 machine guns arrived from Germany. With 2,500 troops under his command, Leutwein organized two columns that attempted to surround the Herero during March and April. However, Leutwein later withdrew the soldiers because of the spread of disease and concerted Herero attacks, which came close to encircling the Germans.

In June 1904, Lieutenant General Lothar von Trotha, who had fought against the Hehe in East Africa and the Boxers in China, arrived in SWA with yet more reinforcements. Replacing Leutwein as governor, he rejected possible negotiation with the rebels in favor of complete military subjugation. Von Trotha answered directly to Kaiser Wilhelm II, who had given him a free hand to crush the rebellion. Colonial officials were sidelined, and SWA was entirely administered by the German military. With a colonial force that was now 10,000 strong supported by over 30 artillery pieces, von Trotha launched an offensive against the Herero, who took refuge in the northeast on the Waterberg Plateau on the western edge of the Omaheke region of the Kalahari Desert. As the railway had not yet been extended farther inland than Windhoek, it took German forces three months to reach the Waterberg. Before engaging the rebels, German forces constructed a stockade for 8,000 possible captives, which some historians believe indicated that they did not intend to exterminate the Herero at Waterberg. However, there were around 50,000 Herero present, and therefore the camp may have been meant for survivors who would be used as slave labor. In mid-August, six German columns, with a total of 1,500 soldiers equipped with machine guns and cannon, converged on the Herero, who consisted of 4,000 to 6,000 men with rifles and thousands more noncombatants. Advancing from the south, under von Trotha, the main German column overcame stiff Herero resistance to capture the important waterholes at Hamakari and bombarded Herero positions. Consequently, the next day, Samuel Maherero led his people east through an opening in German lines and into the Omaheke Desert. It is possible that the gap was purposely created by von Trotha as a strategy to channel the Herero into the desert, but it also could have been created inadvertently by the late movement of a German column. Nevertheless, the Herero were driven into the desert and set out to march 320 kilometers to seek refuge in British-ruled Bechuanaland (today's Botswana).[5]

EXTERMINATION OF THE HERERO AND NAMA (1904–1907)

On October 2, 1904, von Trotha, who saw the conflict as a race war, issued an extermination order in which he instructed his soldiers to kill any Herero men, women, and children remaining in German colonial territory. He declared that "The Herero people must leave this land. If they do not, I will force them to do so by using the great gun (artillery). Within the German border every male Herero, armed or unarmed, with or without cattle, will be shot to death. I will no longer receive women or children but will drive them back to their people or have them shot at. These are my words to the Herero people."[6] On the same day, von Trotha also wrote of the Herero that "I believe that the nation as such should be annihilated."[7] In turn, a military cordon was established to keep the Herero away from water sources, and German soldiers, in keeping with the above proclamation, were instructed to shoot all Herero men and drive women and children into the desert, where many died of thirst. In Germany, a military publication celebrated victory in the campaign by stating that "Like a wounded beast the enemy was tracked-down from one water-hole to the next, until finally he became the victim of his own environment. The arid Omaheke (desert) was to complete what the German army had begun: the extermination of the Herero nation."[8]

The day after von Trotha proclaimed the extermination order, Witbooi's Nama rebelled—amid the German brutality against the Herero, rumors that they would be disarmed, threatening movement of German soldiers into Nama territory, and Christian millenarian prophecies. Von Trotha disarmed the Nama scouts working for the German army, and in April extended his extermination order to Witbooi's people. Avoiding the sort of pitched battle that had gone badly for the Herero at Waterberg, some 1,000 to 2,000 Nama horsemen fought a guerrilla war of over 200 minor engagements against 15,000 German troops, who resorted to scorched-earth tactics. Although Nama resistance began to wither after 80-year-old Witbooi was killed in late October 1905, the Germans continued operations until March 1907, and some fighting continued for another year. Colonial concerns of eliminating the supply of African labor for the colonial economy and the damage to Germany's international reputation caused the German imperial government to rescind von Trotha's extermination order at the end of 1904, but the restriction of the Herero to the desert was not lifted until the end of 1905. Leutwein, who had been replaced by von Trotha, disagree with the annihilation policy stating, "I do not concur with those fanatics who want to see the Herero destroyed altogether . . . I would consider such a move a grave mistake from an economic point of view. We need the Herero as cattle breeders . . . and especially as labourers."[9]

Although the retraction of von Trotha's order meant that German soldiers began taking prisoners instead of forcing Herero and Nama into the desert, the extermination continued by other means. The Germans in SWA copied the concentration camp system that had been employed by the British during the South African War (1899–1902) and in which approximately 25,000 Boers and 20,000 of their African servants had perished from disease. However, the Germans added new and horrific elements. Beginning in 1905, Herero and Nama prisoners were herded into concentration camps, where they became slave workers on railway construction or victims of medical experiments. By March 1907, some 7,600 Herero and 2,000 Nama had died in camps which contained a total of 17, 000 inmates. At Shark Island, called Death Island by its German commander and located in Luderitz Bay, between 1,000 and 3,000 Herero and Nama died from cold, starvation, disease, violence, and exhaustion between 1905 and 1907. There were also cases of German guards forcing female inmates into sexual slavery. Island inmates were used as slave labor in the extension of a railway from coastal Luderitz inland to Aus and the building of Luderitz harbor facilities. Decapitated heads of dead inmates were studied by race obsessed German scientists including Eugen Fischer whose work would later influence Nazi ideology in Germany. Another German scientist, Dr. Bofinger, conducted experiments on prisoners suffering from scurvy and then autopsied the corpses. He later wrote a paper blaming high mortality in the camps on the poor hygiene of the inmates. Shark Island was perhaps the world's first extermination camp. As the island's reputation spread, some prisoners in other parts of SWA committed suicide rather than accept transfer there. Initially, Herero prisoners were sent south to Shark Island, and Nama prisoners were sent north to concentration camps near Windhoek. However, complaints from the German residents of Windhoek concerning the number of prisoners in the area prompted the administration, in 1906, to use railway cattle cars to dispatch several thousand Nama to Shark Island. Reports of those atrocities reached Cape Town, where they were published in the local press. Some Nama prisoners were deported to the West African German colonies of Togo and Cameroon, where most died of tropical disease to which they had little resistance.[10] Though the numbers have been debated, it is likely that roughly 60,000 Herero, which represented as much as 80 percent of their population, and 10,000 Nama, which amounted to about 60 percent of their population, died during the conflict. Given that the postrebellion situation was called "the peace of the graveyard," the related labor shortage in SWA incited the Germans to extend their rule north over the Ovambo.[11]

GERMANY'S LOST COLONIES

During the First World War, the German colonies in Africa were cut off from the mother country. Isolated from each other and surrounded by enemies, they were eventually invaded and occupied by British, French, and Belgian forces. While the initial objective of the Allied invasions of German colonies was to secure such strategic assets as wireless stations and harbor facilities, the campaigns quickly turned into a race to conquer more African territory in what became a second "Scramble for Africa." At the outset of the war, London invited the Union of South Africa—its main ally in Southern Africa, which was also anxious for territorial expansion—to invade neighboring German SWA. Although delayed by the outbreak of a Boer or Afrikaner mutiny within the union, the South African occupation of SWA took place fairly quickly during 1915; the Germans put up token resistance, which meant that the total fatalities in the campaign was relatively low, numbering in the hundreds. The territory was then governed by a South African military administration. As part of the postwar settlement, Germany was stripped of its overseas colonies, which were given to the war's victorious powers, to be administered as mandates of the new League of Nations. Theoretically, those mandated territories were meant to be prepared for independence, though in Africa they were generally seen as unofficial colonies and spoils of war. Most of Togoland and Cameroon were taken by the French, with small slices of territory added to the adjacent British territories of Gold Coast (today's Ghana) and Nigeria, respectively. German East Africa was divided, with most of it becoming British-administered Tanganyika, and Rwanda and Burundi coming under Belgian rule. In 1920 South Africa gained formal control of SWA; it treated it as a new province and moved in Afrikaner settlers. During 1917 and 1918, South African officials in SWA conducted an investigation into the events of the 1904–1907 rebellion by interviewing some 50 African survivors and consulting official German documents. The subsequent Blue Book "Report on the Natives of South West Africa and Their Treatment by Germany" revealed the horrors of the German extermination campaign, which justified the removal of Germany's colonies and contributed to South Africa gaining a mandate over South West Africa. In response, the post–First World War republican German government produced a White Book in 1919, which outlined the atrocities of other colonial powers in Africa, claiming that Germany had been no different. Furthermore, the German settlers who remained in SWA denied the charges made by the Blue Book. Ultimately the Blue Book became inconvenient for the South Africans and British. In 1926 the new exclusively white territorial legislative assembly in SWA ordered the destruction of all copies of the Blue Book as part of a program to unify the territory's established German and new Afrikaner settlers as a dominant white minority in a majority black territory. By 1935 all copies in SWA had been destroyed, and, with the resurgence of Germany as a major power, surviving copies in other parts of the empire were centralized in the British Foreign Office and placed under restricted access.[12]

During the 1920s, the German Colonial Society emerged to challenge the accusation that Germany had been a particularly brutal colonial power and to lobby for the restoration of the country's lost overseas territories. One of the most prominent leaders of that movement was Heinrich Schnee, the last governor of German East Africa, who served as a member of the German parliament during the Weimar Republic and Nazi era, and wrote a series of articles and books promoting German colonial revisionism. In 1926 he tried to distance the former German imperial government from atrocities committed in SWA:

> The British Blue Book misrepresents the facts to such a degree as to make it appear that the Herero tribes had been persistently and cruelly oppressed by the German colonists and that the crushing of the rebellion had been a mere war of extermination. These charges have been completely refuted by the before-mentioned German White Book, which, nevertheless, does not attempt to conceal the fact that at times military methods were adopted in combating the revolt which were not

sanctioned by the German government and were formally repudiated. These measures may be explained, if not excused, by the bitterness occasioned by the massacre of the German settlers.[13]

In 1932 the Nazi movement adopted the colonial cause and celebrated the supposed achievements of German colonial rule at a festival addressed by Nazi leader Hermann Goring whose father, Heinrich Goring, had been the first governor of German South West Africa during the 1880s. Shortly after the Nazis came to power in 1933, the German Colonial Society was incorporated into the German government under the leadership of General Franz Ritter von Epp, who had commanded a company of German colonial troops in SWA during the 1904–1907 rebellion. Von Epp had led the emerging Fascist movement in Bavaria immediately after the First World War, during which time he mentored future Nazi leaders, including Ernst Roehm and Adolph Hitler, and became Nazi commissioner of Bavaria during the 1930s.

THE FIRST GENOCIDE OF THE 20TH CENTURY

After the Second World War, the West German government continued to celebrate the supposed achievements of German colonialism and rejected accusations of atrocities in SWA, for which the newly coined term "genocide" seemed to fit very well. At the same time, in West Germany it became a criminal offence to deny the Holocaust. During the 1960s and 1970s, anyone in West Germany who challenged the positive image of German colonialism faced intimidation from the foreign office and even death threats. However, historians on both sides of the Berlin Wall did just that. At the start of the 1970s, West German historian Helmut Bley published a book that identified the suppression of the Herero-Nama rebellion as a precursor to the Holocaust. In communist East Germany, which officially repudiated Germany's colonial history, historian Horst Drechsler used the colonial archive in Potsdam during the 1960s to reveal the brutality of German colonial rule in SWA and to demonstrate that the campaign of 1904–1907 constituted genocide. On the other hand, West German authors Karla Poewe and Gerd Sudbolt, who had been active in a German cultural group in SWA, denied that the German military operations of 1904–1907 amounted to genocide by claiming that von Trotha's use of the term "extermination" had been misinterpreted, the numbers of Herero dead had been exaggerated, camps had been built to accommodate prisoners, and the extermination order had been meant to frighten the rebels into not attacking German positions. Neither Sudbolt nor Poewe had access to the Potsdam archive. In 1985 the United Nations Whitaker Report on the prevention and punishment of genocide, which had resulted from the stagnation of the 1948 convention, described the attempted extermination of the Herero and Nama as one of the earliest instances of genocide in the 20th century. In 1989, on the eve of Namibia gaining independence from South Africa after a long liberation war, Brigitte Lau, chief archivist of the National Archives of Namibia, provoked an intense debate by claiming that the 1904–1907 conflict could not be considered genocide because the numbers of dead had been exaggerated.[14] Critics of Lau pointed out that her material came entirely from Sudbolt and Poewe, and that the issue of a perpetrator's intention to exterminate rather than the total of fatalities was central to determining if the term "genocide" was applicable.[15]

With the independence of Namibia and the reunification of West and East Germany in 1990, some began to call on the new German government to provide reparations to the descendants of the survivors of the Herero and Nama genocide. In 1998 Herero leaders confronted German President Roman Herzog during a state visit to Namibia and demanded compensation. Although he expressed regret over the events of 1904–1907, he did not accept responsibility by issuing an apology. In 2001 the Herero community filed a lawsuit in a U.S. court against the German government, Germany's largest bank, and several German companies that had used slave labor during the rebellion, seeking $2 billion in compensation. However, the German government, once again expressing remorse over the event, rejected the claim, citing that international rules protecting civilians during war did not exist in that period. During a 2004 ceremony to mark the centenary of the rebellion, the German minister for international development, Heidemarie Wieczorek-Zeul, apologized and accepted German responsibility for what she described as genocide. However, she also stated that Germany would not pay reparations, though it would continue providing US$14 million per year in development funding to Namibia. Subsequently, the German government claimed that the minister spoke in her personal capacity and that her statement did not represent an official apology, which would lend support to the legal action. In 2006 the Namibian National Assembly voted to support the demand of genocide reparations from Germany. At the invitation of Herero traditional leaders, descendants of Lothar von Trotha visited Namibia in 2007, where they expressed sorrow over the actions of their ancestor but refused to be drawn into the reparations issue. Proponents of reparations point out that the modern Herero and Nama continue to suffer the effects of German-imposed land alienation, political marginalization, and population reduction and that Germany's actions in the early 1900s clearly violated existing international agreements that provided for reparations to the survivors of atrocities.

The centenary of the Herero-Nama rebellion and the legal and diplomatic controversy over reparations sparked renewed scholarly interest in the event, with several books confirming that the German campaign amounted to genocide. A book written by a law professor involved in the legal action against Germany claimed considerable circumstantial evidence showed that Kaiser Wilhelm II approved von Trotha's extermination policy, which some have argued were the actions of a rogue general.[16] Some scholars fleshed out Bley's contention that the genocide of the Herero and Nama represented a source of inspiration for the later racial ideas of the Nazi movement and the Holocaust of the Second World War era. The connection between what happened in SWA and the Nazis was explained in terms of broad concepts, including Social Darwinism, eugenics, fears of race mixing, racial war, and Lebensraum (living space), as well as such specific actions as the use of death camps like Shark Island, the actions of individuals such as Fischer and von Epp, and even the adoption of the old colonial brown uniform by Nazi paramilitary units.[17] Critics of this approach point out that links between German colonial rule in SWA and the later Nazi regime were limited, and that the vast majority of colonial soldiers and officials who served in Africa had nothing to do with the later Holocaust.[18]

Following a German television documentary on the genocide, former Namibian ambassador to Germany Peter Katjavivi orchestrated the return of 20 skulls of Namibians that had been taken to Germany as scientific specimens after the rebellion and kept at several academic institutions, including Freiburg University. In 2011, at a ceremony in Berlin, those skulls were formally returned to a Namibian delegation while Namibian protestors called on the German government to pay reparations. The German government refused to officially welcome the Namibian delegation, and during the ceremony German Foreign Minister Cornelia Pieper declined to acknowledge the genocide and left the venue without listening to the Namibian presentations. The return of the skulls prompted members of Namibia's white German-speaking community, a small but relatively wealthy minority, to send letters to a local German-language newspaper, denying that genocide had taken place in 1904–1907 and blaming the Herero massacre of Germans for bringing about colonial retaliation: no different, it was claimed, from other colonial wars in Africa. In March 2012 the German parliament rejected a motion by left-wing opposition members to recognize German colonial crimes in SWA as genocide, to issue a formal apology, and to provide reparations. Some observers wondered if the German government, in defeating the motion, was hesitant to alienate its European partners and former colonial powers—France, Britain, and Belgium—by agreeing to hand over millions in compensation and setting a legal precedent.[19] In Namibia, anger over the German denials provoked removal of a celebratory colonial-era German monument to the 1904–1907 war from public space, with President Hifikepunye Pohamba declaring that he would not object to it being shipped back to Germany. In responding to Germany's acknowledgment of the Armenian genocide of the First World War, the Turkish government criticized Berlin's failure to accept the genocide its colonial forces had conducted in Namibia. In July 2016 the German government, which had long accepted responsibility for the Holocaust, issued a formal statement saying that it would finally recognize the German campaign against the Herero and Nama as genocide and make a formal apology.[20]

CONCLUSION

The German response to the Herero and Nama rebellion of 1904–1907 represents one of the clearest cases of genocide, albeit applied retroactively, as defined by the 1948 international convention. It is a rare instance in the history of genocide in which a single document—von Trotha's extermination order—proves genocidal intent, in this case on the part of the German military administration of SWA. Debates concerning the kaiser's knowledge or lack thereof seem irrelevant, as authority had been delegated to von Trotha to act on behalf of imperial Germany. In addition, the scope of the genocide was total. Although the Herero and Nama communities were relatively small because of the arid nature of their homeland, a large percentage of those populations were killed by German forces or died from being driven into the desert or imprisoned in concentration camps. The Herero and Nama were dispossessed, their land taken by white settlers, and the ancestors of the Herero who made it to Botswana live there to this day. Finally, it is obvious from von Trotha's order and the subsequent actions of the German military that the Herero and Nama were targeted because of their ethnic and racial identity. Although other colonial wars of conquest in Africa were just as or even more deadly than the 1904–1907 German campaign in SWA, it was highly unusual for a colonial regime to embark on the extermination of its subject population, as their labor was needed for economic exploitation. In Namibia, German ideas of racial warfare and a particularly aggressive military approach combined with local demographic and environmental factors to produce modern Africa's first genocide.

CHAPTER 2

Rwanda

In 1994 an incredibly fast genocide took place in the small, impoverished, and hitherto internationally obscure African country of Rwanda. Since many people around the world first heard of that country during the shocking events of that year or through subsequent books and movies about them, the name "Rwanda" has almost become synonymous with the horror of total genocide. Within 100 days, roughly 800,000 people were slaughtered, mostly by state-sponsored mobs wielding simple weapons like machetes and clubs. Although there were no mechanized means of mass murder such as gas chambers or strategic bombers, modern communication methods—particularly the radio—played an important role in orchestrating the deadly campaign. That episode was one of the most appalling and infamous incidents of mass violence in the late 20th century. It was also strongly consistent with the 1948 international legal definition of "genocide," as there was an intentional and planned program of murder meant to exterminate a distinct section of the Rwandan population completely, based solely on their Tutsi identity. Of course, many other people were killed. Why did that terrible event happen? In answering that question, the international media often fell back on racist stereotypes of Africa and offered easy but inadequate explanations of innate ethnic hatred and "tribal warfare." While some academics have suggested that Rwandans had been psychologically conditioned to become particularly obedient people who responded to terrible orders, others have pointed to intense overpopulation and competition over land as a contributing factor.[1] An important point to remember is that the 1994 event was not the first genocide to have taken place in the history of Rwanda. There was an earlier and much less well-known massacre of Tutsi in 1963–1964, seen as a genocide by international observers at the time, which strongly foreshadowed the events of 30 years later. This chapter will discuss the historical context of the two genocides against the Tutsi that took place in postcolonial

Rwanda. It will look at a combination of elements that made Rwanda's history distinct from other African countries and perhaps contributed to those terrible events. Those factors include a long history of violence, a culture of fear and state control that dates from the precolonial era, and the rise of a colonial racial hierarchy that combined with such other issues as the country's small geographic size and population density.

PRECOLONIAL HISTORY

By the time of colonial conquest in the late 19th century, the Great Lakes region of east-central Africa was dominated by a series of centralized states, including Buganda, Bunyoro, Nkore, Burundi, and Rwanda. Given the limited nature of African oral tradition and the lack of documentary sources, little is known of the detailed history of those hinterland states before roughly 1800. Archaeological evidence broadly illustrates that people in the region had been practicing settled agriculture and metallurgy for several millennia. Furthermore, archaeological evidence also suggests that roughly a thousand years ago cattle keeping became increasingly popular and that a relatively sudden change in pottery style across the region seems to indicate the arrival of immigrants from another area. However, the lack of impact on local Bantu languages suggests that this group of important newcomers may have been somewhat small and eventually absorbed into local communities. During the 1400s and 1500s CE, within the context of Later Iron Age developments associated with state formation, the people of the Great Lakes formed the area's first-known organized kingdoms, with some focusing on cultivation and others on pastoralism, depending on local environmental conditions. Much earlier, between around 200 BCE and 1000 CE, Nilo-Saharan-speaking (commonly called Nilotic) pastoral people from northwest of Lake Turkana, in what is now South Sudan and southern Ethiopia, had gradually moved southward into the Great Lakes region. Their arrival may have been related to the changes discussed above. That process accelerated during the 1400s and 1500s CE, as other groups of Nilo-Saharan-speaking pastoralists of similar origin, probably reacting to drought, also moved south. Some of those pastoralists moved east near Lake Victoria to form the basis of well-known East African pastoralist communities such as the Karamojong of Uganda and the Maasai of Kenya and Tanzania, who pushed Bantu-speaking cultivators off the grasslands and into the highlands of the Great Rift Valley. Other Nilo-Saharan pastoralists, Luo-speakers from what is now South Sudan's Sudd floodplains, also moved south around the same time and broke into small groups, with some settling northeast to establish Luo communities in what is now western Kenya and others moving west around Lake Victoria. It is well known that the last element of Luo migrants was instrumental in the creation of such centralized states as Bunyoro and Buganda on the northwest side of

Lake Victoria in the 1500s and 1600s. In this area, the Luo merged with the preexisting population of cultivators. Historians have long recognized that similar Luo pastoralists may have also formed the nucleus of the distinct pastoralist minorities who came to dominate cultivating communities in the highlands between Lake Victoria and Lakes Edward and Kivu and eventually formed the states of Nkore, Burundi, and Rwanda. Since the historic origins of the Tutsi have become a controversial topic (particularly within Rwanda), it is important to remember that the southward movement of Nilo-Saharan pastoralists is a well-established feature of East African history and certainly affected the Great Lakes region.

The precolonial Kingdom of Rwanda (often called the Nyiginya Kingdom after the name of the royal clan) represented a compact but militarily powerful state located in the southern portion of the modern country of Rwanda. By 1700, the kingdom had developed an effective, centralized royal court with control over land and labor and a permanent army, which was a rare and potent institution in precolonial East and Central Africa. Although there is no doubt that Rwanda's Tutsi, Hutu, and Twa identities existed when the first German colonists arrived in the mid-1890s, the origins and nature of those categories has been contested. The lack of certainty mostly relates to the nature of historical evidence, as there was no literature concerning Rwanda before the advent of German colonial rule. As in most of the rest of precolonial Sub-Saharan Africa, Rwanda was a non-literature society, in which information was passed orally from person to person and generation to generation. Rwandan oral traditions recorded in the 1950s, more than half a century after colonization, relate strongly to the Tutsi-dominated traditional kingdom that still existed at that point and, as all oral sources, are malleable and symbolic. As such, there is almost no direct evidence regarding the history of the Tutsi, Hutu, and Twa identities before 1895. In discussing postcolonial genocide, one may ask why the precolonial origin of those identities matter as they clearly existed in people's minds and were the subject of Rwandan state policy in the early 1990s. As will be discussed below, however, the Tutsi, Hutu, and Twa identities have a long and dynamic history in Rwanda (and Burundi) and are thus deeply rooted in that society. Understanding that history, as Mahmood Mamdani explains, serves to contextualize popular participation in the genocides against the Tutsi that took place in 1963–1964 and 1994 and helps clarify "how the unthinkable becomes thinkable."[2]

A basic narrative of Rwanda's early precolonial history was initially put forth in literature written during the colonial era. It explains that Twa hunter-gatherers were the original inhabitants of the area, which was subsequently settled by Bantu-speaking and iron-using Hutu farmers at some point in the distant past. Then, perhaps no more than 500 years ago, Tutsi pastoralists arrived and used their military prowess and systems of patronage created by loaning out cattle to the existing inhabitants to gradually establish the centralized Nyiginya state. In the colonial view, different regional origins meant that members of each group were believed to possess stereotypical physical characteristics: the Twa who were short, the Hutu who were of medium height and stocky build with round facial features, and the Tutsi who were tall and thin with sharp facial features. Although colonial scholars believed that those identities and their associated traits had always existed, more recent historians point out that the names Tutsi, Hutu, and Twa probably crystallized over time, especially as new groups moved into the area and began to make distinctions between themselves and others. For example, the ancestors of late-19th-century Hutu probably did not always call themselves by that name and only came to do so as they fell under the rule of the Rwandan kingdom. Jan Vansina, an eminent historian of Central Africa who conducted extensive original research on precolonial Rwandan history in the 1950s and 1960s, believes that this process happened over a long time. Choosing his words carefully, Vansina explains that "there is no doubt that present-day Rwandans really encompass three different biological 'populations' and that whichever scenario is adopted to account for this fact, the differences among the groups run so deep that they must extend back millennia rather than centuries."[3] Vansina proposes that the polarization of Tutsi and Hutu identities may have begun within the 18th-century Rwandan military as warriors were recruited from elite cattle-herding families called Tutsi and noncombatant support personnel originated from less-prestigious agricultural families and were referred to as Hutu, which meant that they were servants. Eventually, those terms and their hierarchical pastoral and agricultural connotations spread within the broader society. Precolonial marriage practices and artificial selection may also have contributed to the rise of those identities and their concomitant physical traits. Twa hunter-gatherers were long shunned by other groups, married and reproduced among themselves, and took to making pottery as a niche economic activity. As the Nyiginya state expanded during the 1700s, the pastoralist Tutsi imitated their royal family and avoided marrying into less-respected agricultural lineages.[4] In the 19th century, that practice became much stricter, resulting in the emergence of a recognizable hierarchy of three social identities—Tutsi, Hutu, and Twa—which was clearly observed and recorded by the first Europeans who visited Rwanda at the turn of the 19th and 20th centuries. Similar processes happened in neighboring kingdoms such as Burundi to the south with the Tutsi/Hutu/Twa division and Nkore in the northeast with Hima pastoral warriors who dominated Iru cultivators.

Since the terrible events of 1994, it has become popular to reject the idea that Rwanda's historic Tutsi, Hutu, and Twa identities originated with the movement of different groups into the area at different times, which is criticized as a divisive colonial theory. As such, Rwanda is often presented as the ancestral home of all its people. It follows then, that the three identities must have emerged from a single community because of local factors, or perhaps later colonialists either invented them entirely or changed them in some way to facilitate divide-and-rule. In the early 1970s, Walter Rodney, a polemical historian of the transatlantic slave trade, speculated that different diets may have caused the development of dissimilar physical traits among the Tutsi, Hutu, and Twa. In other words, the pastoral Tutsi grew taller because of their protein-rich diet of milk and meat, whereas the Hutu and Twa did not enjoy such luxuries. Rodney presented no evidence to support this view.[5] In the 2004 Hollywood film *Hotel Rwanda,* which is about the 1994 genocide, several Rwandan characters tell visiting foreign journalists that the Tutsi and Hutu identities were simply made up by the Belgian colonial rulers. In a book on the military in Rwanda, former Rwandan Patriotic Front (RPF) officer Frank Rusagara presents the Tutsi, Hutu, and Twa identities as irrelevant in the country's precolonial history.[6] In contemporary postgenocide Rwanda, the common-origin theory has become the official history of the country and is enforced by antigenocide ideology laws that limit freedom of expression, especially around issues of identity and history. The Tutsi, Hutu, and Twa identities do not officially exist, yet they are forever on people's minds. The common-origin version of history is mobilized to promote national unity and reconciliation in a postconflict society. It is also a useful mechanism of control, given that the ban on discussing identities serves to obscure the fact that many top government officials are from the Tutsi minority and thus might not be seen as representing the interests of the majority.

Several realities of contemporary Rwandan culture seem to support the common-origin theory. There does not appear to be obvious linguistic evidence that different groups moved into the country from other areas, because today every Rwandan speaks the same language, Kinyarwanda. In a lengthy theatrical performance entitled *Rwanda 1994,* an authoritative Belgian commentator presents a long lecture on the history of Rwanda, in which he states categorically that the ancestors of the Tutsi could not have come from outside the country, as no foreign conqueror, in all human history, has ever adopted the language of the conquered. Of course, there are many examples from world history (particularly China) that contradict that sweeping statement. One only has to look as far as Malawi to see that the Ngoni people, who conquered part of that area in the middle 1800s, have now almost lost their original Nguni language in favor of the Chinyanja language of their former subjects. If the movement of new groups into what is now Rwanda took place millennia ago, then other languages that were present there may well have been replaced by a broad common language. Today's Kinyarwanda does have such variations as the slight difference between the language spoken in the north and south of Rwanda, and the distinctive accent of the Twa. It is also important to note that Kinyarwanda, historically, is not a language that is only associated with the precolonial Kingdom of Rwanda as mutually intelligible versions such as Kirundi (the language of Burundi) are spoken by people in neighboring areas. Another fact presented in support of the common-origin theory is that every Rwandan is a hereditary member of one of 18 different clans, each of which includes people of Tutsi, Hutu, and Twa identities. However, the 18 clans may have originated as Tutsi institutions into which their subjects and servants were incorporated.[7]

In contextualizing Rwanda's two postcolonial genocides, it is often forgotten that precolonial Rwanda had a particularly violent history in comparison to other African states and societies. The legendary founder of Rwanda, Ruganzu Ndori, is said to have spent most his life fighting in different military campaigns, and, after he died from a battle wound to his eye, his spirit was believed to inhabit the royal Kalinga drum that became the state's symbol. Ndori created Rwanda's military system, which allowed for something like a standing army and represented a major advantage over the kingdom's neighbors. In another distinct military innovation, many armies had matching and named "cattle armies," which functioned as a commissariat and consisted of livestock from warriors' families and war booty. According to Vansina, "The deepest effect of this new military organization was the institutionalization of militarism and martial violence that finally permeated the whole of Nyiginya culture as the armies became the foundation of the administrative structure of the realm."[8] Successful warriors, who cut off the testicles of their victims to show that they had killed men, were revered and displayed symbols of their violent accomplishments. Killing 7 men in combat earned a warrior an iron necklace with bells; after 14 total kills, he was given an iron and brass bracelet; and 21 resulted in a mountaintop ceremony during which he became a national hero.[9] During the 1700s and 1800s, Rwanda was embroiled in almost-constant warfare, including attacks on neighbors meant to reduce them to tributary status and expansionist campaigns west toward Lake Kivu and north toward the volcanoes. There were also terrible internal conflicts between rival claimants to kingship, as there was never a peaceful transition of power. Relations with Burundi to the south were intensely violent over a long period. By the 1790s, the Nyiginya Kingdom had organized 30 armies and could field about 12,000 combatants, which made it a principal regional military power. Between 1800 and 1870, Rwanda doubled its size. This history of warfare inspired local sayings such as "Rwanda attacks, it is not attacked," and "Tutsi share blood, not milk." Although Rwanda began to engage in increasing regional trade in the 1850s, the state remained somewhat isolationist, as Swahili/Arab caravans protected by gunmen and carrying goods from the East African coast were banned from its borders. As such, the kingdom's arrogant pastoralist warriors did not show much interest in acquiring newly arriving firearms.

Perhaps the most aggressive precolonial ruler in the history of Rwanda and potentially the entire Great Lakes region was Kigeri IV Rwabugiri, who led the kingdom from his coming of age in 1875 to his death in 1895. He launched an average of two major military campaigns per year, which, for a precolonial African state, was extremely ambitious. Given the pressure that this put on the kingdom's primarily Hutu farmers to feed the ever-expanding and active armies, Rwabugiri had to crush three major provincial rebellions and many smaller insurrections. Furthermore, he formed eight new armies and altered the kingdom's military system so that he gained more authority and a greater share of loot taken during those wars. It is likely that Rwabugiri's increased centralization of the Rwandan state and the concentration of cattle into the hands of a small number of wealthy pastoralist families furthered the division between Tutsi pastoralists and Hutu farmers.[10] Recognizing this history should not be seen as a vilification of Rwanda or Rwandans (many countries have a violent history) but as a reminder that extreme violence was not new and did not end with the beginning of colonial rule. It is often said that Rwanda had a peaceful history up until 1994, but that is simply not true.

GERMAN COLONIAL CONQUEST (1895–1914)

During the early 1890s, as the European Scramble for Africa was in full swing, the Kingdom of Rwanda was weakened by drought and locusts that ruined crops, rinderpest and foot-and-mouth disease that killed cattle, and small pox and jiggers that affected people. At that time, Rwanda was positioned between three expanding colonial powers. To the east and southeast, the Germans had taken control of a portion of the East African coast and were moving inland through what is now Tanzania; to the west, the Belgians of Leopold II's Congo Free State were establishing their authority over the vast Congo River Basin; and to the north the British had intervened in the Buganda civil war and were creating the colony of Uganda. In May and June 1894, a German colonial expedition under Gustav Adolf von Gotzen entered Rwanda and visited Rwabugiri, who was embroiled in a war with neighboring Nkore in what is now Uganda and attempting to quell resistance in the subordinate area of Bushi in what is now the Democratic Republic of Congo (DRC). On leaving Rwanda, the German expedition used its firepower to repel a surprise attack by some of the kingdom's warriors, though it is unclear if Rwabugiri had ordered the action. With the sudden death of Rwabugiri in September 1895, the territories he had conquered, including Ijwi Island in Lake Kivu and Bushi, rebelled and threw off Rwandan dominance. The next year, after Rwabugiri's son, co-ruler, and heir, Mibambwe IV Rutarindwa, ordered what turned into a disastrous attack on a Belgian colonial post at Shangi on the south end of Lake Kivu, violence broke out at the royal residence of Rucunshu, in which hundreds were killed and the ruler committed suicide.

In February 1897, Kanjogera, a widow of the late Rwabugiri and a rival of Rutarindwa, emerged victorious from the Rucunshu massacre and arranged for her teenage son Yuhi V Musinga to become king, followed by a purge of potentially disloyal military commanders. Since this coup represented the rise of Kanjogera's Bega clan over that of the royal Nyiginya clan, the new regime would struggle with legitimacy. The next month, a German expedition with 300 soldiers under Captain Hans von Ramsay arrived from Lake Tanganyika, and Kanjogera and Musinga accepted a German protectorate over Rwanda in exchange for military support against internal rivals and other external forces like the Belgians. Almost immediately after the Germans left, Kanjogera and her supporters had to contend with a series of rebellions led by rival claimants to the kingship and by Hutu in the north who had been recently conquered by the late Rwabugiri and wanted to reclaim their independence. In suppressing those uprisings, Kanjogera's warriors devastated many communities, including some that had not rebelled, and many people fled into the hills. In 1900 the mostly French-speaking Catholic missionaries of the White Fathers arrived in Rwanda. The royal court secured the loyalty of the Tutsi by initially forbidding them from attending missionary instruction, but many Hutu flocked to the newcomers, whom they saw as offering protection against the exploitive kingdom. Some began to refer to missionaries as the "kings of the Hutu." At that point, the Germans exerted little authority in Rwanda, as their only military post was in the far south of the country, and their regional headquarters was in Bujumbura in Burundi. In 1901, at the request of Musinga's court, a German military detachment moved up from Bujumbura to suppress a rebellion in the eastern region of Gisaka. Many dissident leaders fled to exile in Burundi. In April 1904, the Bega faction that controlled the court consolidated its power by slaughtering a large number of rivals from the Nyiginya clan. Around the same time, the White Fathers, leading armed groups, pushed into the mountainous northern frontier, where they raided local Kiga communities to compel them into providing workers for building missions. At that point, the term "Kiga" (plural Bakiga) referred to the people of the mountains who were not Tutsi or Hutu, as they were not yet under the control of the Rwandan state. In 1904 a German military expedition led by Werner von Gravert toured Rwanda to impress the royal court and ventured north to inflict terrible vengeance on the Kiga for attacking a mission.

After Musinga came of age in 1905, he relied increasingly on German colonial troops to suppress rebellions and to extend his rule northward into agriculturally rich and previously autonomous areas in which Kiga farmers were subjugated by the Rwandan kingdom and therefore became known as Hutu. The Germans were eager to cooperate with Musinga because they were being challenged elsewhere in German East Africa by the Maji Maji Rebellion, and they had few personnel on the ground in Rwanda. The Germans also began to force Rwandans to cut and transport timber for the construction of a new colonial capital called Kigali in the center of the territory. Furthermore, Musinga gradually emerged from the dominance of his mother's Bega clan and began to reestablish the primacy of his paternal Nyiginya clan.

Violence plagued Rwanda's northern frontier as several interrelated rebellions challenged the advancing dominance of Musinga and the Germans. In the early 1900s, the prophetic Nyabingi movement led by Muhumuza, a woman who claimed to be a widow of the late Rwabugiri, fought a guerrilla war against Musinga's rule in Ndorwa, as well as against German, Belgian, and British colonial rule in what became a colonial tri-border zone. In 1908 the Germans imprisoned Muhumuza for two years, and in 1911 a British expedition captured her and exiled her to Uganda. Between 1905 and 1912, a force of Twa led by Basebya used the forest and swamps of northern Rwanda as a staging area for guerrilla war against the Rwandan and German forces sent into the region. In 1910 Rukara, a Hutu and leader of the Barashi, the strongest Kiga group in the north, killed a European missionary and rebelled against Musinga. At the start of 1912, Ndungutse, who had previously been involved with Muhumuza's activities and similarly claimed royal links to the late Rwabugiri, led a rebellion in north-central Rwanda that encouraged Kiga to refuse demands for labor and tax from the Rwandan state and to expel its agents. Ndungutse became popular with the newly defined Hutu of northern Rwanda and posed a significant threat to Musinga's rule. In April 1912, a detachment of German soldiers and 3,000 of Musinga's warriors moved north, where they stormed the rebel leader's stronghold and killed him. The soldiers then conducted a reign of terror in the north by destroying homes and crops, seizing livestock, taking hostages, and conducting massacres. A missionary wrote, "The war continues; the batutsi massacre, are without mercy, half of the population of Bumongo [a neighboring region] will be destroyed. Groups of women are led away and will become the booty of the Great Chiefs." It was at that time that the Twa leader Basebya was captured and executed by a German patrol. Rukara was also captured by the Germans, and, although he was shot to death while trying to escape on his way to the gallows, his corpse was hanged to dissuade further Kiga resistance. In the aftermath of this reign of terror, Musinga sent more officials, mostly Tutsi, to administer the north, including some areas never before under his kingdom's authority. A victory celebration was held at Musinga's capital of Nyanza, where the king, given his dependence on colonial support, was compelled to parade his royal cattle before a German official as a sign of his submission.[11]

BELGIAN COLONIAL RULE (1916–1959)

During the First World War, Musinga cooperated with the Germans as Kiga resistance in the newly conquered north resurfaced. In 1916, as part of a general invasion of German East Africa, Belgian colonial troops from neighboring Congo occupied Rwanda and Burundi. Initially, the Belgian occupation forces seemed to undermine the central court by interacting directly with subordinate Tutsi officials and Hutu commoners to acquire resources for the war effort. However, within a year, the danger of anarchy prompted the Belgians to adopt the German system of governing indirectly through Musinga's court. In the north, Belgians and Tutsi court officials gradually suppressed the decentralized resistance of the Kiga, which furthered their transformation into Hutu subjects of the Rwandan state.

With the end of the global conflict in 1918, the League of Nations divvied up defeated Germany's former colonial territories to the victorious powers as mandates that were theoretically meant to one day become independent countries; in practice, those mandates were treated like other African colonies. Within this context, Belgium formally took over the administration of Rwanda and Burundi in the early 1920s. Immediately after the war, the Belgians adopted the contradictory policies of ruling Rwanda indirectly through the traditional kingdom—as the British did in parts of neighboring Uganda—and simultaneously "civilizing" its society through the promotion of Christianity and individual rights. Since the royal court was hostile to Christianity, the Belgian administration introduced secular education for Tutsi young men at the king's capital of Nyanza in the south. Hutu who sought education attended mission schools. In the mid-1920s, the Belgian administration began to strip the royal court, which was divided between traditionalist and pro-European factions, of its power to appoint officials, collect tax, and settle judicial cases. As the Belgians became more influential, members of the Tutsi court became more interested in Western education, and many converted to Christianity, which, given the existing network of patron-client relations, led to the popularization of schools and churches throughout the country. At the same time, the colonial capitalist economy developed through the mining of tin and growing of coffee for export.

To govern and exploit Rwanda more efficiently, the Belgians simplified the administrative system, creating a hierarchy of Tutsi chiefs and subchiefs who reported to them. In 1926 the Belgians eliminated Rwanda's existing administrative structure, in which each hill community had three chiefs—one for each the land, people, and cattle—and in which Hutu and Tutsi could occupy those positions. A new and much more authoritarian system was created, whereby each hill was under one chief, who was always Tutsi. The Hutu were completely deprived of avenues for advancement and redress of grievance. Without the legitimacy of the historic monarchy, the Belgians emphasized racial myths, whereby the supposedly intelligent Tutsi were seen as natural rulers and the allegedly less-intelligent and submissive Hutu were seen as natural workers. The new system provoked resistance. Anxiety was also worsened by a famine in the late 1920s that was caused by drought and colonial labor demands that hindered agriculture and led to the deaths of at least 40,000 people. In 1928 the Kiga in northern Rwanda rallied around a leader called Semaraso and attacked Tutsi officials, killing about a dozen and seizing cattle. After colonial troops and Tutsi warriors easily suppressed the rebellion by killing and jailing several dozen people and destroying the shelters and crops of around 1,000 more, Semaraso fled into Uganda. In other parts of the country, anti-European millenarian movements such as Nyabingi gained popularity among the Hutu and were repressed by Belgian authorities.

In November 1931, Belgian officials, with approval from their superiors, deposed the traditionalist Musinga, who had subtly resisted Westernization, Christianization, and growing colonial authority.[12] The Catholic Church, led in Rwanda by Bishop Leon-Paul Classe, a longtime advocate of Tutsi racial supremacy, supported the removal of Musinga, because he had been making contacts with rival Protestants and Seventh-day Adventists. Musinga was immediately replaced by his son, Mutara III Rudahigwa, who had always been interested in European ways and who, upon his baptism in front of his subordinate chiefs, became the first Christian king of Rwanda. This transition prompted a final wave of religious conversion throughout the country, which further enhanced the power of the Catholic Church. Seen by many as the "King of the Whites," Rudahigwa became a mostly symbolic ruler and a model of Christian values. Tutsi officials and overseers enforced intensified and individualized taxation, obligatory labor on the building of infrastructure such as roads and terracing, and the compulsory growing of certain crops under antifamine and development policies through corporal punishment against Hutu peasants. As such, colonial Rwanda was turned into "a vast forced labour camp" geared toward the production of agricultural exports that profited Belgian businesses.[13]

A colonial racial hierarchy was imposed. In 1933 and 1934, the Belgians conducted an official census in Rwanda that categorized all inhabitants as Tutsi, Hutu, or Twa and required people to carry identity cards on which their status was inscribed. Any flexibility in the application of those identities was lost. With privileged access to Western education and exemption from forced labor, the Tutsi minority were transformed from the historic pastoralist-warrior elite into the new colonial intellectual-administrative elite tied to the Catholic Church. The Hutu majority, subject to coercion and taxation, became the peasant producers of cash crops. As in precolonial times, the Twa minority continued to be reviled, although now this low status was reinforced by European racial ideology. The categorization of Rwandans in the census was based on personal information provided by the Catholic Church—physical appearance and ownership of cattle. Contrary to popular belief, the census did not classify any Rwandan with ten cows or more as a Tutsi.

Colonial racial theories such as Social Darwinism—the idea that human societies had experienced a process of natural selection and evolution—were applied to the history of Rwanda to explain the development of this hierarchy of identities. Although the European application of those ideas to Rwanda dated back to the late 19th century, they now became incredibly influential within Rwandan colonial society. The Twa were seen as the almost subhuman original inhabitants of the country, who had been conquered by the agricultural Hutu, who were understood as biologically and technologically similar to other Bantu-speaking Africans of sub-equatorial Africa. In turn, the Twa and Hutu were subjugated by the supposedly racially superior Tutsi pastoralists, who were believed to have originated from somewhere outside of Africa. In the colonial mind, the Tutsi were seen as evidence of the Hamitic theory, which postulated that indigenous Africans were incapable of organizing complex states and thus the existence of precolonial kingdoms could only be explained by the arrival of mysterious non-African outsiders termed "Hamites" (named after the son of Noah from the Bible) at some point in the remote past. The defining feature of colonial rule in Rwanda became race. The Hutu were imagined as the inferior, indigenous Bantu race, and the Tutsi as the alien and superior Hamitic race. Unlike many other colonies in Africa in which indirect rule was imposed, the inhabitants of Rwanda were not broken down into different ethnic groups with separate traditional political structures and customary laws. The Europeans taught colonial ideas about race and history in Rwanda, which were accepted by the emerging Tutsi intelligentsia, who attended a special Tutsi school in Astrida (Butare), as proof of their superiority. With separate educational streams, Tutsi students were taught in French and prepared for administrative careers, whereas the few Hutu students were given an inferior education in the broad East African language of Kiswahili.[14]

In the 1950s, the ideology of "Hutu Power" emerged to challenge the Tutsi-minority domination of Rwanda. The context was provided by the Second World War, which saw the global circulation of powerful ideas about national self-determination and democracy. The authors of Hutu Power were from Rwanda's small but nascent Hutu counter-elite, who had managed to gain Western education and access to publication venues through the Catholic Church, in which there was new interest in social justice issues. Some of the first Rwandans to express interest in Christianity were Hutu, and in 1919 the first group of Hutu priests were ordained. The new Hutu Power movement of the 1950s reinterpreted colonial ideas about race and history. From their perspective, the Tutsi were presented as foreign usurpers and decadent exploiters of the hardworking and pious Hutu majority. A leading member of the new Hutu elite was teacher and former Catholic seminarian Gregoire Kayibanda, who attended a Catholic youth conference in Belgium in 1950. In 1953 Kayibanda became the first lay editor of a Catholic monthly magazine called *L'Ami* (the friend), and in 1955 he was promoted to the editorship of the Catholic Kinyarwanda weekly newspaper *Kinyamateka* (about history). In March 1957, Kayibanda and Swiss-born Catholic Archbishop Andre Perraudin published the ten-page "Bahutu Manifesto" that explained the problems of Rwanda in terms of the racial division between Hutu and Tutsi and called for the emancipation of the Hutu and the implementation of racial quotas in education and employment that would clearly favor the majority. Several months later, in June, Kayibanda was instrumental in forming the Muhutu Social Movement (MSM), which advocated for the general improvement of conditions for the Hutu majority. In November 1957, while Kayibanda was again visiting Belgium to build contacts with Catholic politicians and labor leaders, the extremist anti-Tutsi activist Joseph Gitera formed the Association for the Social Promotion of the Hutu Masses (APROSOMA) in the south of Rwanda. Around the same time, conservative Tutsi launched their own political grouping that, in 1959, transformed into the Rwandan National Union (UNAR). Within the broad context of decolonization discussed below, the emerging African political parties of Rwanda were clearly divided along Hutu and Tutsi lines.[15]

DECOLONIZATION AND THE FIRST GENOCIDE AGAINST THE TUTSI (1959–1963)

Across Africa, during the late 1950s, the moderate Westernized associations of the interwar years morphed into modern mass nationalist movements that demanded immediate independence from the colonial masters. The new and growing cities of Africa, which had swelled during the Second World War, provided a consolidated venue for nationalist leaders to spread their message and rally support, often among the unemployed and disappointed. The subsequent and rapid decolonization of Africa in the late 1950s and 1960s happened for many reasons. Those reasons included the spread of international anticolonial sentiment, the failure of British and French military intervention in Egypt in 1956, anticolonial insurgencies in Kenya and Algeria, the domination of global politics by two officially anticolonial superpowers, and the decolonization of Asia in the late 1940s, which created a growing anticolonial block within the new United Nations. As such, Britain granted independence to Ghana in 1957, and at the same time, negotiations were underway for the independence of Nigeria, which took place in 1960. Belgium came under increasing pressure, both internationally and within the Congo, to move toward similar decolonization. Reluctant to abandon its interests in Africa, the Belgian government attempted to grant independence quickly to unprepared and friendly African regimes that Brussels could control. As such, the vast Belgian Congo, with just six months of preparation, became independent in 1960. The country rapidly broke down through a mutiny by African soldiers against Belgian officers who were still in charge and through declarations of independence by separatists in the regions of Kasai and Katanga, which resulted in civil war.

In late-1950s Rwanda, Belgian officials began to see that the emerging Hutu political leadership were potentially more cooperative postcolonial partners than the Tutsi intellectual and administrative elites. As in other parts of Africa, many members of the established, Westernized, educated elite of Rwanda—who were mostly Tutsi—had embraced anticolonialism, African nationalism, and aspects of socialism. The predominantly Tutsi UNAR seemed to represent those ideals that were seen as threats to continuing Belgian interests. On the other hand, the small Hutu leadership was deeply Catholic, strongly anticommunist, and could convincingly claim to represent the majority in a future democratic system. This fear of socialism and communism must be understood within the international Cold War context in which Belgian officials, businesspersons, and church leaders worried about losing influence to future postcolonial African regimes friendly to the Soviet Union or Communist China. In early 1959, the Belgian government, copying what it was trying to do in Congo, announced that elections for a territorial government would take place in Rwanda toward the end of the year. Such embryonic Hutu and Tutsi political associations as APROSOMA began to declare themselves as formal political parties that would run for electoral office. When King Mutara Rudahigwa was suddenly admitted to hospital in Burundi and died of an apparent cerebral haemorrhage, many Tutsi believed that he had been murdered by the Belgians. Subsequently, they launched UNAR and demanded immediate independence under the existing Tutsi-dominated monarchical system. Around the same time, some moderate Tutsi formed the Rwandan Democratic Rally (RADER), which advocated cooperation with the Belgians and the Hutu, but it quickly became marginalized in the extremist environment. In October 1959, Kayibanda transformed MSM into the Party for the Emancipation of the Hutu (PARMEHUTU). Its manifesto called for the end of Tutsi colonialism and feudalism, rejected hostility toward Europeans, thanked the missionaries for their educational endeavors, advocated gradual democratization rather than immediate independence, and supported private property rights and a constitutional monarchy.[16]

Violence was triggered when Belgian authorities attempted to depose three Tutsi chiefs who were also UNAR supporters. At the beginning of November 1959, a Hutu subchief who was active within PARMEHUTU was attacked by UNAR enthusiasts because he refused to condemn the dismissal of the three Tutsi chiefs. Within a week, violence spread across most of the country, with Hutu mobs burning Tutsi homes and the newly installed King Kigeri V Ndahindurwa forming a monarchist/UNAR militia that counterattacked and killed Hutu leaders. In mid-November, Belgian Governor Jean-Paul Harroy declared a state of emergency and placed Colonel Guy Logiest—commander of a Force Publique colonial military detachment in neighboring Congo—in charge of the territory. Troops from eastern Congo had already begun to occupy Rwanda and used their firepower to restore order in a way that favored the Hutu gangs. Preferring the idea of a future independent Hutu republic to a Tutsi monarchy, Logiest replaced more than half of the Tutsi chiefs with Hutu ones, many of whom were PARMEHUTU members. Although UNAR activists were prosecuted for crimes committed during the violence, supporters of APROSOMA and PARMEHUTU were not. Given the violence, Belgian officials rescheduled local government elections for June 1960, despite objections from a UN delegation, which witnessed Tutsi homes being burned and which called for negotiation between all major parties before a vote could proceed. PARMEHUTU won a stunning electoral victory, taking 160 out of 229 legislative seats, with the Tutsi-oriented parties, including UNAR, winning just 19. In turn, local officials of the new Hutu government took power from the chiefs, and periodic violence against Tutsi continued into the next year. The deposed King Kigeri fled the country in July. Since Congo became independent in June 1960, the Force Publique withdrew from Rwanda and Burundi, and the Belgians replaced it with the new, locally recruited Territorial Guard of Ruanda-Urundi (GTRU). Although this new military in Rwanda was supposed to reflect the population by consisting of 14 percent Tutsi and 86 percent Hutu, in practice it was almost entirely Hutu and led by Belgian officers. Ignoring further UN protests, Belgium granted independence to the Republic of Rwanda in July 1962, with Kayibanda as the country's first president and PARMEHUTU in control of the legislature. Characterized by a dramatic reversal of power relations, the decolonization process in Rwanda between 1959 and 1962 would be celebrated by the new Hutu regime as the "social revolution."

From 1959 to 1964, some 336,000 people, mostly Tutsi, fled Rwanda to escape violence and settled as refugees in neighboring Burundi, Tanganyika (Tanzania from 1964), Uganda, and Congo, all of which were in the middle of a decolonization process. Since it had a similar Tutsi monarchy that was eventually replaced by a Tutsi-dominated military regime, Burundi was the most welcoming to the Rwandan Tutsi refugees. In 1961 some of those refugees began to form armed groups, bent on retaking power at home. The exiled movement's leadership was plagued by internal quarrels between monarchists such as Francois Rukeba, socialists like Gabriel Sebyeza, and apolitical military activists. Some Rwandan exiles went to Communist China for guerrilla warfare training, and the Chinese provided the movement with money to buy weapons. More arms were stolen from a police station in Tanganyika, and a training camp was established at Kigamba in Burundi that became independent in 1962. Given that the guerrillas operated at night, the Rwandan government called the Tutsi rebels *inyenzi*, or cockroaches, which eventually became a dehumanizing term for all Tutsi. In March 1962, as revenge for a series of cross-border raids by exiles in which some police and civil servants were killed, Rwandan state forces slaughtered 1,000 to 2,000 Tutsi civilians in the northern area of Byumba. The victims' homes were burned, and their land and possessions were given to local Hutu residents. In late November 1963, some 1,500 Rwandan exiles in Burundi, armed mostly with spears and bows and arrows, marched toward the Rwanda border but were intercepted and disarmed by Burundian authorities.

In late December 1963, the disorganized exiled leadership launched a poorly planned offensive, partly meant to take advantage of problems within Rwanda's Hutu government. The Rwandan National Guard (GNR), Rwanda's Belgian-led and almost exclusively Hutu military, was waiting for them. Some 600 insurgents crossed the border from recently independent Uganda and were stopped by the GNR, which killed 300 and handed the rest over to the Ugandan army. Another force from eastern Congo, where the exiles were allied with local Simba rebels, crossed the southern border near Cyangugu and was defeated by the GNR, which executed 90 prisoners. The anticipated contingent from Tanganyika did not show up. A unit of 200 to 300 insurgents crossed the Burundi border at Nemba, captured a police station where they seized weapons and ammunition, and advanced to Nyamata, where they were welcomed by Tutsi inhabitants of a refugee camp. By the time the force arrived at Kanzenze Bridge, just 15 kilometers south of Kigali, it had grown to 1,000 poorly armed people, who the GNR easily gunned down and dispersed. The attempted invasion had failed.

Rwanda's Kayibanda administration responded to the incursions by organizing Hutu civilian militias that carried out a wave of reprisals against the Tutsi population. The regime encouraged violence by promoting an atmosphere of panic about further Tutsi incursions. Although the Rwandan government claimed that 750 people were killed in this period, other sources put the figure at around 10,000 to 14,000 victims, and some claim it was as high as 20,000. Among the dead were all the moderate Tutsi political leaders still inside the country, who were arrested and taken to Ruhengeri in the north, where they were executed. The most intense violence took place in the Gikongoro district in the south, which included the old royal capital of Nyanza, where between 5,000 and 8,000 people were killed, who represented between 10 and 20 percent of the district's Tutsi population. The prefect of Gikongoro reputedly told a meeting of mayors and PARMEHUTU supporters that "we are expected to defend ourselves. The only way to go about it is to paralyse the Tutsi. How? They must be killed."[17] The UN remained mute; Burundi, given its sympathy for the exiles, was the only state to protest. The violence prompted more Tutsi to leave Rwanda, and, by 1990, around 1 million Rwandans lived in exile. In 1966 the Tutsi exile movement launched a few more raids from Burundi but collapsed shortly thereafter amid leadership quarrels. Many of its members became caught up in the insurgency in eastern Congo that was eventually suppressed by American-sponsored mercenaries and Belgian paratroopers. Within Rwanda, the exile raids allowed the Kayibanda government to overcome internal divisions and bolstered the reputation of the GNR as the heroic defender of the nation. As Mamdani has noted, the elimination of the Tutsi leaders within the new regime meant that the PARMEHUTU government could portray itself as "a native post-revolutionary republic in which the Tutsi would be tolerated only so long as they remained outside of the political sphere."[18]

Although there was no official international protest, the massacres of Tutsi in Rwanda during late 1963 and early 1964 inspired comparisons with the Holocaust of the Second World War and were repeatedly described as genocide. In January 1964, two UN officials working in Rwanda resigned because they could no longer remain in a country "which is practising genocide."[19] In early February, a British newspaper reported that British subjects who had visited Rwanda and were staying in Nairobi, Kenya, had made "allegations that the Rwanda Government is engaged on a deliberate policy of genocide against the country's former rulers."[20] A few days later, prominent British philosopher Bertrand Russell, writing for a French newspaper, described the killing as "the most horrible and systematic massacre since the extermination of the Jews by the Nazis."[21] Around the same time, Vatican Radio broadcast that "since the Genocide of the Jews by Hitler, the most terrible systematic genocide is taking place in the heart of Africa."[22] A British newspaper reported that "local observers, who can move around fairly freely, consider that genocide is not too strong a word to describe what is going on."[23] Margery Perham, a British pioneer of African history, urged that "at least Rwanda should be expelled from the United Nations for such an appalling breach of the convention on human rights and genocide."[24] Of course, that did not happen. There were also those who believed that it was inappropriate to categorize the massacres as genocide. The Kayibanda government accused its critics of slander and neocolonial agendas.[25] Thomas Jamieson, the director of field operations for the UN High Commission for Refugees (UNHCR), thought that the reports of killings in Rwanda were exaggerated.[26] Burundian prime minister Pierre Ngendandumwe, who was trying to calm the situation and convince the new Organization of African Unity (OAU) to convene a conference on the matter, called Russell's statement an "inaccurate generalization" and claimed "that while the majority of those being killed were

Watutsi, many Wahutu had also been killed because the massacres were directed primarily at the opposition UNAR party [National Rwandese Union]."[27] The next year, Ngendandumwe, the first Hutu prime minister of Burundi, was assassinated by a Tutsi refugee from Rwanda. In retrospect, the massacres of Tutsi in 1963–1964 would seem to correspond to the international legal definition of genocide; they were intentional and aimed at the extermination of at least part of a group defined along racial lines.

POSTCOLONIAL REGIMES AND EXILES (1962–1990)

In newly independent Rwanda, President Kayibanda became a secretive and authoritarian ruler who demanded the same unquestioning obedience as the old monarchy and ruled by manipulating divisions within the dominant elite. Kayibanda generally favored Hutu elites from the southern part of the country and played them against those from the north. During the middle-to-late 1960s, a potential rival political faction was eliminated when the southern Hutu leaders of APROSOMA were gradually pushed out of government. Ultimately, Kayibanda depended increasingly on a small circle of supporters from his hometown of Gitarama in central Rwanda. The PARMEHUTU regime promoted an official ethos of strong Catholic faith and pride in the hardworking but penurious life of the Hutu peasantry. The president led by example through his austere personal lifestyle—unusual among African heads of state. Popular support among the Hutu was garnered through the abolition of forced labor and the redistribution of pasture land formerly controlled by the old royal court and now devoted to cultivation, which increased food production and ended famine. The colonial system of local administration through chiefs was replaced by a hierarchy of elected officials. Some academics celebrated the majoritarian gains of the revolution, which had overturned Tutsi colonialism. At the same time, Kayibanda's government continued the racial system of the Belgian colonial rulers: Rwandan citizens were required to carry identity cards that indicated a racial status of Tutsi, Hutu, or Twa, and the regime adopted a quota system whereby a racial group's percentage of the total population determined their access to civil service jobs and public education. Allocated 9 percent of the quota, Tutsi opportunities were limited. Tutsi could be active in church, business, and education sectors and in the civil service, but they were excluded from politics and portrayed as essentially foreign. Kayibanda's regime saw Rwanda as an indigenous Hutu nation with a Hutu republic. Within the region, Rwanda became isolated during the late 1960s and early 1970s; it stayed out of the civil war in eastern Congo, feared the Tutsi military government in Burundi, and could not credibly engage in the anticolonial rhetoric of Julius Nyerere's Tanzania. Rwanda's main external sponsor remained Belgium, the former colonial power, and it developed ties with Christian nationalist politicians in West Germany. Known as the "Hermit of Gitarama," Kayibanda rarely left Rwanda. At the time, Rwanda was one of the poorest countries in the world, and its economy was extremely vulnerable to fluctuations in the world price of its coffee and tea exports.

Events in the adjacent countries of Burundi and Rwanda have often influenced each another with tragic results. In April 1972, an incursion by Tanzanian-based Hutu insurgents into Burundi was defeated, which led to the Burundian Tutsi military regime and its militias killing between 100,000 and 200,000 Hutu citizens. As a result, several hundred thousand Burundian Hutu refugees fled to neighboring countries, including Rwanda, which, given its Hutu government, was obviously seen as sympathetic. Kayibanda attempted to use the situation to address several internal problems faced by his regime. For a few years, there had been discontent among Hutu students who saw that, despite government regulations, Tutsi still dominated the educational sphere, amid the increasing number of Hutu school graduates who could not get jobs because the government racial quotas did not apply to the private sector. In late 1972 and early 1973, the increasingly out-of-touch Kayibanda tried to exploit the Burundian refugee situation to recreate the anti-*inyenzi* fervor of 1963: he launched a government campaign to enforce the 9 percent quota on the Tutsi for government jobs and school placements. Many people were expelled from the civil service, and, at the National University of Rwanda in Butare, students' family histories were scrutinized to determine if they were truly Hutu. Radio broadcasts incited the Hutu to defend themselves, and extremists called for a final solution to the Tutsi problem. The oppressive campaign, which resulted in around 750 deaths, led to another major exodus of fearful Tutsis from the country. Kayibanda's plan backfired, however, as violence between rival Hutu factions broke out in rural areas. The regime seemed to be losing control.[28]

In early July 1973, Major General Juvenal Habyarimana, commander of the Rwandan military, staged a coup that seized political power and restored order. Kayibanda was imprisoned and probably starved to death. Hutu from the southern and central parts of the country were removed from government and replaced by Hutu from the north, Habyarimana's home region. The new military regime abandoned the old rhetoric of racial ideology, which was anathema to most independent African countries and portrayed the Tutsi, Hutu, and Twa identities in terms of the familiar concept of ethnicity. The Tutsi were no longer seen as a foreign race but as a previously advantaged minority ethnic group that had to be restricted for the benefit of others, while at the same time protected. In the same vein, northern Hutu were seen as a previously disadvantaged majority who became the beneficiaries of affirmative action. As such, the identity cards and quota system were retained, though not as rigidly supervised as before, and a very few Tutsi were given posts within the central government and diplomatic corps. However, Tutsi were almost completely excluded from local government and the military, where Hutu officers were forbidden to marry Tutsi women. An unofficial understanding developed whereby the Tutsi stayed out of politics and were allowed to prosper in private business and rise to prominence in the Kigali social scene. Although it seems ironic now, some referred to Habyarimana as the "protector of the Tutsi."

In 1978 Habyarimana transformed his military regime into a civilian one-party state under the National Revolutionary Movement for Development (MRND), which all citizens, regardless of ethnicity, were required to join. The new constitution was modeled on that of Tanzania, which, like many other African countries at the time, employed a one-party system. In the Rwandan elections of 1983 and 1988, Habyarimana was the only presidential candidate and was reelected with over 99 percent support. Some critics of the regime quietly disappeared, but there were no massacres. Under the guise of a traditional practice called Umuganda, the state reintroduced a version of forced labor that obliged citizens to engage in several days of work per month on public projects, which sometimes included estates owned by government elites. In terms of local administration, the MRND returned to the practice of the colonial state, with the central government appointing local officials who held dictatorial power over their communities, including the right to call for Umuganda. Internationally, the hitherto isolationist Rwanda joined the French-sponsored Economic Community of the Great Lakes Countries (CEPGL) in 1976 and the World Bank–backed Kagera River Basin Organization in 1977, and the amount of foreign aid money and expatriate aid workers increased substantially. The country's economic, health, and educational systems all improved. In 1978 Habyarimana signed a defense agreement with France, which was seeking to bolster its alliance of Francophone African countries, mostly former French colonies, against imagined encroachment by their Anglophone neighbors. Habyarimana became a close ally of Mobutu Sese Seko, the similarly anticommunist and notoriously corrupt dictator of Zaire (formerly the Belgian Congo), who had also shifted from Belgian to French sponsorship. Although elements of Habyarimana's regime such as the one-party state, the rhetoric of ethnic cooperation, compulsory communal labor, and select political murder were common in postcolonial Africa of the 1970s and 1980s, the degree of social control in Rwanda was unusual for a noncommunist country.[29]

RWANDAN EXILES (1959–1990)

During the Kayibanda and Habyarimana eras, a large and growing refugee population of mostly Tutsis developed outside the country. By the end of 1964, they numbered around 360,000, with 200,000 in Burundi, 78,000 in Uganda, 36,000 in Tanzania, and 22,000 in Congo. By the end of the 1980s, the total figure had increased to around 500,000 and may have been as high as 700,000, with diasporic communities in Europe and North America. There are disagreements over the total number of Rwandan refugees at different times, because they were sometimes confused with other people who had left Rwanda as labor migrants during the colonial era and who had assimilated into such countries as Zaire and Uganda. In addition, not all Rwandan exiles were officially registered as refugees in host countries, which made counting them difficult. The number of exiles was also exaggerated by refugee activists who wanted to vilify the Kigali regime for excluding so many of its citizens and by the successive Rwandan governments who wanted to make it seem impossibly difficult to accommodate so many returnees. Both the Kayibanda and Habyarimana regimes refused to address the exile issue. Throughout the 1970s and 1980s, Rwandan exiles, many of whom had been spirited out of Rwanda as small children or were born in other countries, developed their own identity through a network of associations and periodic publications and promoted a fantasy of Rwanda as a paradise from which they had been expelled.[30]

During the 1960s, the postcolonial government of Milton Obote and his Uganda People's Congress (UPC) discriminated against Rwandan refugees in Uganda. Many Rwandan refugees lived in Uganda's Nkore (Ankole) area, which shared a border with Rwanda, where they became involved in familiar political disputes between local Hima pastoralists, who had been favored by the outgoing British colonial regime, and Iru agriculturalists, who were coming to dominate local government. Whereas the Iru mostly supported the UPC, the Rwandan exiles, who were mostly Tutsi, sided with their Hima counterparts and backed the Uganda's Democratic Party (DP), which became the opposition after Uganda's 1962 independence. Hostility from both the new Obote central government and the Iru majority of the border region meant that the armed movement among Rwandan exiles in Uganda was greatly restricted. By 1969, Prime Minister Obote was planning to conduct a survey that would be used to exclude Rwandan exiles from Ugandan politics and eventually to eject them from the country. Therefore, Rwandan exiles welcomed the military coup that brought Idi Amin to power in 1971 and Amin appeared to favor them as an anti-Obote group. However, while a few Rwandan exiles served in Amin's notorious secret police, they still faced discrimination and obstacles to citizenship.[31]

Among the many people who fled Amin's brutal dictatorship in Uganda during the 1970s were some of Rwandan origins, who joined the Tanzania-based Front for National Salvation (FRONASA), led by Yoweri Museveni, who was from a Nkore Hima background. As such, Rwandan exiles were among the Ugandan exiles who participated in the 1979 Tanzanian invasion of Uganda that vanquished Amin. Nevertheless, after Obote's return to power in 1980, his new regime engaged in active repression against the Rwandan community. In 1982 some 40,000 people in southern

Uganda were driven toward the Rwandan border, with thousands caught in no-man's-land for many months. A few thousand more Rwandans were driven into Tanzania. Those evictions overlapped with continuing tensions within the Ugandan Nkore area, in which Iru, who were supporters of Obote, sympathized with Rwandan Hutu aspirations, and Hima, who were associated with Rwandan Tutsi exiles, were similarly victimized. In 1979 Rwandan exiles in Uganda formed the Rwandese Refugee Welfare Association (RRWA) to assist those who were victimized after the fall of Amin. The next year, the group changed its name to the Rwandese Alliance for National Unity (RANU), which reflected a more militant political stance, including the ambition of an eventual return to Rwanda. However, the restoration of Obote's administration in Uganda meant that in 1981 RANU had to relocate to Nairobi, Kenya, where it remained until 1986. The Kenya-based RANU facilitated the recruitment of Rwandan exiles into Museveni's new National Resistance Movement/National Resistance Army (NRM/NRA), which waged a guerrilla struggle against the Obote regime in southern Uganda during the first half of the 1980s. Famously, Museveni personally led the small NRA unit that launched the campaign in 1981, and the unit included Rwandan exiles Fred Rwigyema and Paul Kagame. Obote's denunciation of the NRA as a foreign Rwandan group—which included the portrayal of Museveni as a Rwandan invader because of his pastoral Nkore Hima heritage and the victimization of Uganda's Rwandan refugees, many of whom languished at border camps because Rwanda would not admit them—encouraged more exiles to join Museveni. Although the Habyarimana government grudgingly agreed to accept some Rwandan exiles to relieve pressure on the Uganda border camps, it is unclear how many were actually resettled, and Obote's security forces continued to harass the refugees. When the victorious NRA seized Kampala in January 1986, its 14,000 personnel included some 4,000 Rwandans, many of whom were now experienced military leaders and soldiers. In 1987 RANU headquarters returned to Kampala with the popular Rwigyema as the group's president. It recruited more Rwandan exiles from across the region and changed its name to the Rwandan Patriotic Front (RPF), which illustrated an even greater militancy that sought to overthrow the Habyarimana regime and to repatriate Rwandan refugees. The next year, a world congress of Rwandan exiles in Washington, D.C. passed resolutions about a "right of return," a term borrowed from Israel, which were communicated to Rwanda's Habyarimana government.

Within Museveni's new NRM administration in Uganda, the upper strata of the military contained a disproportionally high number of officers of Rwandan origin, as they had risen to prominence and gained combat experience during the insurgency. These included Major-General Rwigyema, who was both deputy defense minister and deputy army commander-in-chief; Major Kagame, who was head of military intelligence;

Peter Bayingana, who was head of medical services; and Major Chris Bunyenyezi, who was a brigade commander. While it initially appeared that Museveni would grant citizenship to Rwandan exiles as a reward for their contribution in the liberation of Uganda from a series of bloody regimes, rising xenophobia among Ugandans and the NRM quest for political legitimacy made this difficult. Furthering the problem was the accusation that two Rwandan NRA officers, Bunyenyezi and Stephen Nduguta, had committed atrocities during counterinsurgency operations in marginalized northern Uganda in the late 1980s. In the south, economic competition between incoming Rwandan exiles and local people also became a factor. As a result, Museveni began to remove Rwandans such as Rwigyema and Kagame from important positions. Although many long-term Rwandan refugees in Uganda had resolved to stay in that country, the reemergence of local hostility toward them stimulated a dramatic move to reclaim a lost homeland. It was an opportune time to strike, as a recent decrease in world coffee prices had hurt the Rwandan economy, rendering the country vulnerable to attack. Furthermore, Habyarimana had just announced plans to allow more exiles to return, which meant that the RPF had to act quickly before their grievances lost legitimacy.[32]

WAR IN RWANDA (1990–1994)

During September 1990, Rwigyema, using the cover that he was organizing a Ugandan Independence Day parade, gathered Rwandan members of the Ugandan army near the Rwanda border. On October 1, 1990, some 2,500 out of 4,000 Rwandan NRA soldiers, led by Rwigyema and other senior officers, seized the border post at Kagitumba and invaded Rwanda. Calling themselves "Inkotanyi," or "those who struggle together," the newly constituted RPF army was equipped with small arms, heavy weapons, and communications vehicles taken from the Ugandan army. They had no armored vehicles or heavy artillery, which would have been difficult to acquire surreptitiously, and carried limited fuel and ammunition because they expected to seize Kigali quickly. Although Habyarimana's 5,200-strong Rwanda Armed Forces (FAR) possessed armored cars, artillery, and helicopters, they had no recent combat experience and were caught off guard by the incursion. As such, the RPF quickly advanced 60 kilometers south of the border to capture the town of Gabiro. However, the RPF's problems mounted: supply lines from the Ugandan border became overstretched; the Ugandan government erected roadblocks to block other NRA Rwandan soldiers from joining the expedition; and civilian Rwandan refugees, trying to return home, flooded the roads near the border. On the second day of the operation, given a dispute over tactics, Majors Bunyenyezi and Bayingana murdered Rwigyema. They were later arrested and returned to Uganda, where they were executed. During October, the FAR staged a phoney RPF attack on Kigali as pretext to arrest thousands of suspected rebel sympathizers, most of whom were Tutsi, and FAR soldiers massacred Tutsi civilians.

France quickly intervened, given its defense agreement with the Habyarimana regime. French authorities attempted to discredit and vilify the RPF by calling them "Khmer Noir" (Black Khmers), a reference to the genocidal Khmer Rouge in 1970s Cambodia, and portrayed them as part of a broad plan to expand Anglophone, particularly American, influence in the region. Paris sent heavy weapons to the FAR and launched Operation Noroit (North Wind), in which over 500 French paratroopers were dispatched to Rwanda. Habyarimana put the head of the French military mission, Lieutenant-Colonel Gilles Chollet, in charge of operations, which effectively made him the unofficial FAR commander. Some 400 Belgian troops were sent to Rwanda to protect Belgian citizens, but they were soon withdrawn. Mobutu directed 1,000 elite Zairean soldiers to help his ally in Rwanda, but their looting, raping, and brutalizing of civilians turned them into a liability, and they were sent home. Supported by French-piloted attack helicopters, an FAR counteroffensive began on October 7, and, by the end of the month, the leaderless RPF, enduring heavy casualties and desertions, had been pushed back to Akagera National Park in the northeast.

The repulsed RPF consolidated and continued its struggle. In late October, Kagame returned from a military course in the United States, took command of the beleaguered RPF forces, and gained permission from Museveni to lead his men through Ugandan territory to the Virunga Mountains in northern Rwanda, where they regrouped. Colonel Alexis Kanyarengwe, a Hutu former FAR officer exiled after a failed coup attempt in 1980, was appointed RPF chairman to reduce the appearance that the movement was predominantly Tutsi. Recruits from the Rwandan diaspora flocked to the RPF—at first mostly from Burundi, but eventually from Zaire, Tanzania, Europe, and North America. The RPF grew from 5,000 in early 1991, to 12,000 at the end of 1992, to 25,000 in April 1994. Museveni's administration looked the other way as Ugandan army officers supplied their former colleagues with ammunition, weapons, and equipment. Funded by the Rwandan diaspora and facilitated by Uganda, the RPF also purchased bargain-price ammunition and weapons from recently independent and penniless former Soviet republics.

As the war dragged on, the FAR was dramatically expanded from 5,200 in October 1990, to 30,000 by the end of 1991, to 50,000 by the middle of 1992. The recruits were mostly landless Hutu peasants or unemployed youth, who were given just 15 days training before deployment. The lack of training meant that French military advisors had to adopt an active role in combat. Additionally, the war drained the resources of the Rwandan state. Although Rwanda received a credit of $41 million (U.S.) from the

International Monetary Fund in 1991 and imposed a special tax to pay for the war, by the end of the 1991 financial year, there was a budget deficit of $188 million (U.S.).[33]

In January 1991, the RPF launched a guerrilla campaign with a raid on a prison in the northern town of Ruhengeri; the raid was embarrassing to Habyarimana and his inner circle as that was their home area. The Rwandan state replied by massacring between 300 and 1,000 Tutsi civilians in the northwest. Based in the north, the RPF closed the road to Uganda, which meant land-locked Rwanda's imports and exports had to be transported via the longer and more costly route through Tanzania. Both sides lacked commitment to negotiations and cease-fires; the FAR was confident in French military assistance, and the RPF believed it could not be dislodged from its Virunga mountain sanctuary. After the failure of an FAR offensive at the end of 1991, the RPF launched its own offensive in early 1992, which took control of the agriculturally rich Byumba area. Mutinous and ill-disciplined FAR soldiers undertook massacres of Tutsi, separate from state-ordered actions. At the same time, Hutu peasants feared revenge by the Tutsi and fled RPF-occupied territory, which revealed the movement's lack of popular support.

In April 1992, Habyarimana introduced multiparty democracy, which was influenced by both the immediate Rwandan conflict and political reforms sweeping across post–Cold War Africa. In Rwanda, that democracy resulted in the emergence of anti-Tutsi extremist parties such as the Coalition for the Defense of the Republic (CDR) and pushed the RPF into serious negotiations because it could no longer claim to be fighting a one-party dictatorship. During 1992, Hutu Power groups formed "civil defense" militias such as the ruling MRND's Interahamwe (those who work together) and the CDR's Impuzamugambi (those with a common purpose) trained by French military advisors. Negotiations in Arusha, Tanzania, produced an unstable cease-fire that lasted from July 1992 to February 1993 and was monitored by a Neutral Military Observer Group (NMOG) with personnel from Francophone and Anglophone African countries outside the region (Senegal, Nigeria, Zimbabwe, and Mali) and that reported to an Organization of African States (OAU) joint military-political commission in Ethiopia. The negotiations enraged Hutu extremists, including many within the government and military, who disapproved of their president's engagement with the Tutsi enemy, with whom they might have to share power. It was likely at that point, perhaps sometime in early 1992, that Hutu extremists began discussing the possibility of a mass slaughter of the Tutsi to avoid that eventuality. Within the Rwandan state, shadowy Hutu extremist organizations were formed such as the Zero Network, which focused on assassination and those known as "bullets" within the army who believed the war was not being waged with enough intensity. In November 1992, Leon Mugesera, an MRND official in Gisenyi, told party supporters that "the fatal mistake we made in

1959 was to let them get out . . . They belong in Ethiopia and we are going to find them a shortcut to get there by throwing them into the Nyabarongo river. I must insist on this point. We have to act. Wipe them all out!"[34]

A breakdown in the Arusha negotiations led to the January 1993 killing of 300 Tutsi civilians in northern Rwanda. In early February, as a result, the RPF mounted a successful offensive in which it captured Ruhengeri, doubled the territory under its control, and advanced to within 23 kilometers of Kigali. On February 20, the RPF unilaterally declared a cease-fire, as it did not want a direct confrontation with French forces defending the capital, and a major battle over Kigali would unite the city's inhabitants behind Habyarimana and scuttle the chance of a negotiated settlement. Almost the entire population of the areas newly occupied by the RPF—some 800,000 people—fled south to avoid what the state claimed was a return of Tutsi feudal oppression. In retaliation for previous massacres, the RPF killed local Hutu officials and their families. In April, both sides returned to the Arusha negotiations; Habyarimana's forces had been largely defeated, and the RPF was under pressure from the UN, which intervened in the crisis for the first time. The RPF agreed to withdraw from the territory it had conquered in February, which was designated a demilitarized zone (DMZ) and initially patrolled by NMOG, and the small UN Observer Mission to Uganda-Rwanda (UNOMUR) tried to ensure that the RPF was not being supplied via the Uganda border.[35]

Both sides in the war employed print and radio propaganda, but Hutu Power media had a much greater impact. In 1987 a newspaper called *Kanguka* (wake up), launched by a Tutsi businessman in Rwanda, began to criticize the Habyarimana government and openly sympathized with the RPF, even after it had invaded the country. In 1990, shortly after the initial RPF invasion, Habyarimana's MRND funded a French and Kinyarwanda newspaper called *Kangura* (wake others up) as a foil to *Kanguka*. In December of that year, *Kangura* published the "Hutu Ten Commandments." The commandments discouraged Hutu men from associating with Tutsi women; prohibited Hutu from doing business with Tutsi; claimed all important government and administrative positions for Hutu; demanded the majority of educational jobs be occupied by Hutu; emphasized that all military personal must be Hutu and that soldiers must not marry Tutsi; warned Hutu not to have mercy on Tutsi; urged Hutu to unite; and insisted on the proselytizing of the Hutu ideology of the 1959–1962 social revolution. Once the CDR was formed, *Kangura* and its funders shifted toward that more-extreme movement and criticized Habyarimana for betraying the Hutu cause in negotiations. From its inception, *Kangura* published articles hinting at or directly calling for the extermination of RPF sympathizers, who were generally assumed to belong to the Tutsi identity, and, in January 1993, it predicted that Habyarimana would be assassinated in March. In mid-1991, the RPF established Radio Muhabura (leading the way) in Uganda, which encouraged armed resistance to the Rwandan state, read official statements by RPF leaders, encouraged FAR soldiers to desert, accused Habyarimana's military and militia of committing massacres, and denied RPF involvement in atrocities. However, the station's impact was limited, given its vague reporting, its inability to broadcast as far as southern Rwanda, and its use of English language. Radio Muhabura generally avoided the terms "Hutu" and "Tutsi," and, when it responded to the January 1993 massacre of Tutsi by stating that "the Kigali regime has now embarked on genocide," it did not specify whom the genocide was targeting. In July 1993, a radio station called Radio-Television Libre des Mille Collines (RTLM, or Thousand Hills Radio-Television) was established in Rwanda to broadcast anti-RPF and anti-Tutsi propaganda. With some of the same Hutu extremist funders as *Kangura*, it condemned the Habyarimana government for participating in the Arusha process and the UN for supposedly siding with the Tutsi.[36]

In early August 1993, Habyarimana's regime, moderate-opposition groups, and the RPF signed the Arusha Accords, in which they agreed to form a transitional government of all political parties, allow the return of hundreds of thousands of refugees, and create integrated security forces. Since the RPF-occupied area was in the north and thus removed from the capital, its representatives in Kigali's transitional parliament were protected by a 600-strong RPF battalion. Some 2,500 peacekeepers of the UN Assistance Mission for Rwanda (UNAMIR), commanded by Canadian Lieutenant-General Romeo Dallaire, would supervise implementation of the agreement and monitor the DMZ. Woefully unprepared, UNAMIR lacked an intelligence unit, had no ability to investigate violence, and maintained only two combat-capable infantry battalions—one Belgian and another Ghanaian. Dallaire had not heard of Rwanda before he was sent there, and he arrived in the country with only a tourist map and no staff. In October 1993, as UN peacekeepers began to arrive in Rwanda, the Tutsi-dominated army in Burundi murdered the democratically elected Hutu president and massacred tens of thousands of Hutu, which forced approximately 200,000 Hutu refugees into Rwanda. For Rwanda's Hutu radicals, that act demonstrated the dangers of a possible Tutsi-RPF takeover. As stipulated in the Arusha agreement, France's Operation Noroit concluded in December with the withdrawal of the main French intervention force, but French military advisors and mercenaries remained with the FAR. In January 1994, Dallaire reported to UN headquarters in New York that an informant had told him of a Hutu militant plan to assassinate members of the transitional government and eliminate the Tutsi population, and he outlined a plan to seize weapons caches and requested reinforcements and additional equipment for UNAMIR. However, given the lack of strategic interest in Rwanda by Western powers and the recent disastrous American intervention in Somalia, the UN head of peacekeeping and later secretary-general Kofi Annan ignored the warning and forbade UNAMIR from taking action. That would turn out to be a catastrophic mistake.[37]

THE SECOND GENOCIDE AGAINST THE TUTSI (1994)

During the early evening of April 6, 1994, Rwanda's presidential jet—carrying Habyarimana and Burundian president Cyprien Ntaryamira—was approaching Kigali airport when it was destroyed by a surface-to-air missile. The identity of the assassins has been contested hotly. From the time the incident took place, Hutu Power advocates accused the RPF of shooting down the plane in a bid to restart the war and take over the country. A decade later, in 2004, French judge Jean-Louis Bruguiere, who investigated the incident as a result of the deaths of the aircraft's French crew, accused nine RPF leaders, including Kagame—by that time president of RPF-ruled Rwanda—of complicity in the destruction of the aircraft. In 2006 the same judge issued international arrest warrants. The RPF strongly denied those claims and attributed the accusation to an attempt by the French state to conceal its complicity in the 1994 genocide, which is discussed below. Indeed, that dispute prompted Kagame's government to break diplomatic ties with Paris in 2006. However, another French judge later criticized Bruguiere's report for relying too heavily on the testimony of a small number of former RPF soldiers, who subsequently changed their stories. In 2010 Rwanda's RPF government issued the findings of its own investigation, which concluded that Hutu Power supporters within the FAR shot down Habyarimana's aircraft. France's reestablishment of diplomatic links with Rwanda that year seemed to indicate its acceptance of the report. Another French investigation, the results of which were released at the start of 2012, stated that the missile could not have been launched from the RPF base in Kigali but that it had come from the FAR's Kanombe barracks, which was the home of Habyarimana's presidential guard. In response, former high-ranking members of the RPF, now exiled from Rwanda and involved in opposition politics, stated that they knew back in 1994 that Kagame had indeed ordered the downing of the plane.[38]

It seems most likely that the assassination of Habyarimana represented the start of a Hutu extremist coup within the Rwandan state and military led by ministry of defense official Colonel Theoneste Bagosora. After the aircraft was destroyed and the killing of Tutsi began, some fighting broke out between FAR units, as not all officers were party to the conspiracy that seemed to mostly involve those from the north—the home area of Habyarimana's inner circle. Within a week of the assassination, the conspirators formed a transitional government that implemented a policy of eliminating the Tutsi population to avoid power sharing through the Arusha Accord. Almost immediately after Habyarimana's death, Hutu militias and FAR units erected roadblocks in Kigali and began the systematic slaughter of Tutsi civilians. The process was facilitated by the identity card system, which indicated a person's status as Tutsi, Hutu, or Twa. Radio broadcasts by RTML encouraged the killings and announced the names and addresses of potential victims as well as suspected hiding places. The massacres quickly spread to other parts of the country, and, over the next three months, almost one million people, mostly Tutsi, were murdered. Neighbors killed neighbors, and killing was often conducted in public. While some have claimed that a high percentage of the adult male Hutu population took part in the murders, a specialized study by Scott Straus maintains that only around 200,000 people were involved, and, among those, only a small minority conducted most of the killings. In addition to the established militias, killers were organized through the Umuganda communal labor system, which had been implemented in the 1970s, and the murderers often referred to killing as "work." Among the murderous mobs, there was a variety of motivations: a few were hard-line Hutu radicals, eager to kill; others feared retribution if they did not participate; some saw opportunities for looting property or grabbing land, and freely flowing beer removed inhibitions. The weapons were generally cheap, everyday objects used in an agricultural society—the most infamous of which was the machete. Rape and other kinds of sexual assault became common and were influenced by the particular hatred that the Hutu Power groups reserved for Tutsi women, who had been seen in the colonial mind as possessing superior beauty. There were not many places to hide or escape in small, densely populated, and highly controlled Rwanda. Some people survived by concealing themselves among corpses, taking shelter with a sympathetic neighbor or relative willing to take a massive risk, or fleeing into wilderness areas, where some were pursued by mobs with hunting dogs. There were ambiguous situations in which people who were engaged in killing also acted to save a relative, friend, or even a stranger for whom they felt momentary pity.[39]

During the unfolding genocide, many Tutsi sought protection at local churches, which facilitated massacres, as the victims were concentrated and trapped. Since the Catholic Church had a long association with state power in Rwanda, many priests and nuns participated in the killings. For example, in April 1994 Father Athanase Seromba, parish priest at Nyange in western Rwanda, persuaded 2,000 Tutsi civilians to hide in his church. He then urged local militia members to burn the building, and he personally shot people who tried to escape and ordered the church's remains crushed with a bulldozer. Leaders of Protestant denominations were also involved in massacres. However, a few clergy and nuns worked against the genocide, including Hutu nun Felicitas Niyitegeka, who concealed Tutsi in a church facility in Gisenyi, smuggled some into nearby Zaire, and insisted on dying with them when they were discovered. Since Sister Felicitas's brother was a senior army officer, she could have avoided retribution.[40]

On April 7, the day after Habyarimana's death, the FAR presidential guard disarmed, tortured, and killed 10 Belgian UNAMIR soldiers assigned to protect interim Prime Minister Agathe Uwilingiyimana, a moderate Hutu who had been prevented from going to the radio station to address the country and who was also murdered. The killing of the Belgian soldiers precipitated the sudden withdrawal of the Belgian contingent from UNAMIR, and, despite Dallaire's request for a 5,000-strong force to stop the massacres, the UN ordered the mission reduced to just 270 personnel. Nevertheless, Ghanaian Brigadier Henry Kwami Anyidoho, UNAMIR deputy commander, and the Ghanaian battalion of 456 troops remained in Kigali, where they protected UN headquarters and several thousand people who sought safety at Amahoro Stadium and escorted humanitarian relief convoys. Another factor that prevented more robust action by UN peacekeepers was that some of their unarmed colleagues, who were spread out in small detachments across the country, became virtual hostages.[41]

On April 8, French advisors with the FAR cleared vehicles from the Kigali airport's runway to allow the nighttime landing of a French transport aircraft carrying a 544-strong intervention force. Over the next two days, about 500 Belgian paracommandos and a company of Italian paratroopers landed at the Kigali airport and were joined by the Belgian battalion that had left UNAMIR. Called Operation Amaryllis by the French and Operation Silverback by the Belgians and Italians, the action was meant to evacuate European civilians quickly. Despite French influence among Rwanda's Hutu politicians and military officers and the popularity of French soldiers among the Hutu militia, those French forces did little to save Tutsi people from violence. By April 14, when RPF forces began mortaring the airport, French, Belgian, and Italian forces had flown out with 2,000 civilians, including Agathe Habyarimana, the late president's widow and a central figure in the coup, and her entourage.[42]

The United States was one of a few countries in the world that possessed the military capability to intervene decisively to stop the unfolding genocide in Rwanda. However, from early April, the Clinton administration decided against intervention, given Rwanda's lack of strategic importance and fear that American troops might get involved in fighting as they had in Somalia the previous year. Despite later claims that they were not immediately aware of the scale of the killing, classified documents reveal that senior officials of the Clinton administration had accurate and timely information on what was happening. Almost from the moment it began, the administration privately discussed the "genocide" and the "final solution" in Rwanda, and the president and vice president were informed. However, in late May, Washington officials played word games by publically describing events in Rwanda as "acts of genocide" to prevent the American public from demanding action. At a press briefing, journalist Alan Elsner asked State Department spokesperson Christine Shelley, "How many acts of genocide does it take to make genocide?" Shelley could not respond. Furthermore, the Clinton administration used its position within the UN Security Council to block the reinforcement of UNAMIR and refused to use American technological capability to disrupt the RTML radio broadcasts that were encouraging and directing the death squads.[43]

The war between the Rwandan state and the RPF resumed immediately after the downing of Habyarimana's aircraft. On April 7, the RPF detachment in Kigali left parliament and established a defensive position along the northern route into the city, from where they repelled an FAR attack. The next day, the main RPF force in northern Rwanda launched a three-pronged offensive. One element moved west to Ruhengeri, where it engaged the FAR and protected the right flank of the main southward advance. A second element moved down the eastern frontier, encountered little resistance, and reached the Tanzanian border on April 22, which secured the main force's left flank. The principal RPF force moved south, and, by April 11, its vanguard had begun to encircle Kigali, while the RPF battalion already there threatened the airport. Consequently, Rwanda's interim government fled to Gitarama. The RPF forced the closure of the Kigali airport on May 6, cut the Kigali-Gitarama road on May 16, and captured the Kigali airport and military camp on May 22. Attempting to relieve pressure on its new headquarters at Gitarama, the FAR launched a counteroffensive south of Kigali on June 6 that the RPF easily defeated. With the subsequent capture of Gitarama on June 13, the RPF mounted an offensive against Kigali from the northern, eastern, and southern suburbs, with heavy fighting continuing until July 3, when the FAR, its ammunition spent, withdrew from the city, along with most of its civilian inhabitants. During June, the RPF's eastern prong reached the southeastern corner of Rwanda, turned west to push FAR units along the Burundi border, and, at the start of July, captured Butare. With Kigali secured and the FAR routed, Kagame turned his main force north to seizure Ruhengeri and Gisenyi in mid-July. In late May, with 15,000 of its 20,000 to 25,000 troops engaged in the battle for Kigali, the RPF had begun to recruit young Tutsi genocide survivors and exiles from Burundi, who were eventually blamed for revenge killings of Hutu.[44]

In mid-May, UN authorities reversed their decision to downsize UNAMIR and ordered its expansion to 5,000 personnel. However, it would take time to assemble international troops and transport them to Rwanda, where the genocide continued. As such, the UN approved a French interim measure called Operation Turquoise, which was launched on June 23 and aimed, at least officially, to create a refugee sanctuary in southwestern Rwanda. The Turquoise zone was occupied by a force of 2,550 French soldiers and 500 others from Francophone African countries, who were flown into a staging area at Goma in neighboring Zaire by the French Air Force, who rented transport aircraft. The United States refused to provide airlifts. The establishment of the Turquoise zone blocked the RPF's westward advance along the Burundian border. Among the hundreds of thousands of refugees who passed through the French-occupied area en route to eastern Zaire were retreating FAR elements, complete with weapons and equipment, Hutu Power militia, and senior planners of the genocide. Indeed, the genocide continued within the Turquoise zone, with some French troops assisting Hutu militia to locate hiding Tutsi. In late June, a French reconnaissance detachment arrived at Bisesero near the western town of Kibuye, where they convinced Tutsi, who had used bows and arrows, spears, and clubs to fight off Hutu militias, to come out of their forest and hillside hiding places. The French troops then abruptly left the area and returned three days later to find between 1,000 and 2,000 Tutsi murdered. In late August, the French and their allies withdrew and were replaced by Ghanaian UNAMIR peacekeepers, who watched the RPF complete their occupation of the country. Although Operation Turquoise saved between 10,000 and 17,000 people, the small and poorly armed UNAMIR rescued twice as many.[45]

In mid-July, with the genocide effectively suppressed, the RPF and the Republican Democratic Movement (MDR), the main opposition party under the old regime, and a number of smaller moderate parties formed a government of national unity in the spirit of the Arusha Accords. Pasteur Bizimungu, a Hutu RPF member, became president; Kagame became vice president/minister of defense; and Faustin Twagiramungu, a Hutu MDR member, became prime minister. In the initial cabinet, the RPF held 8 positions, which represented the largest of any party, and there were 15 Hutu and 6 Tutsi ministers. The RPF morphed into the Rwandan Patriotic Army (RPA), the new Rwandan military, which meant that Kagame directly controlled the coercive means of the state. Tensions quickly developed within the government when ministers such as Seth Sendashonga, a Hutu RPF member, began to ask questions about allegations that the RPF was terrorizing the population through massacres and select assassinations.

In April 1995, the Kibeho camp, located in the south of Rwanda and home to 150,000 internally displaced people who were afraid to return home, was forcefully dismantled by two RPA battalions that fired into the crowd. While the new government stated that 338 people had been killed in the massacre, Australian UN peacekeepers present at the camp put the figure at around 5,000. That attack would serve as a model for a subsequent and much deadlier RPA campaign against refugee camps inhabited by Rwandan Hutu in eastern Congo, which will be discussed in another chapter. The Kibeho massacre enflamed tensions within the unity government, which effectively broke down in August with the dismissal of Twagiramungu, Sendashonga, and three other cabinet ministers. In

2000 the politically impotent Bizimungu resigned the presidency, which was assumed by Kagame, who had always been the real power behind the throne. Bizimungu, who formed an opposition party that was hastily banned, was imprisoned for inciting violence and corruption. During the 2003 election, the first under a new constitution, Kagame represented the RPF and gained a remarkable 95 percent of the vote, while his main competitor, Twabiramungu, whose MDR party had been outlawed, gained just under 4 percent. The authoritarian RPF state tolerated the existence of token opposition groups and orchestrated the assassination of exiled political leaders such as Sendashonga, who had moved to Kenya.[46]

POSTGENOCIDE JUSTICE

Shortly after coming to power, Rwanda's RPF-led government formulated new laws for the prosecution of genocide-related offenses. The initial approach emphasized retribution. In 1998 the Rwandan state publically executed 22 people for genocide crimes, with some having been condemned by summary trials without legal assistance. By 2000, there were around 130,000 suspected genocide perpetrators in overcrowded Rwanda prisons awaiting trails that could take over a century to complete within the established Western-style legal system inherited from the colonial era. Compounding the problem was the fact that Rwanda's postgenocide legal system was in tatters, as many judges and lawyers had been killed or fled the country.

In 2001 the RPF regime instituted the Gacaca system, which was based on Rwandan traditional law and represented a new approach to the issue of genocide-related justice. The principle of revenge was replaced with reconciliation. Gacaca involved just over 12,000 community courts throughout the country that would hear 1.2 million cases. In addition to accelerating the justice system, the Gacaca courts were meant to discover the truth of what had happened in 1994, including finding the location of victims' remains, eliminating impunity, and encouraging reconciliation and national unity. While the alleged leaders of the genocide and those accused of rape remained in prison, awaiting trial by ordinary courts, the Gacaca system dealt with people accused of murder, attempted murder, torture, assault, and property offenses. Councils consisting of nine elected members had the authority to impose prison sentences ranging from 30 years' imprisonment for murder to community service for property crimes. The many criticisms of the Gacaca process included complaints of the defendants' lack of right to legal representation, whereas the councils were advised by professional state prosecutors; allegations that some of the untrained and unpaid councillors engaged in corruption; suspicions that some of the councils included suspected genocide perpetrators; and the prohibition on discussing crimes allegedly committed by the RPF during 1994. Some genocide survivors disliked Gacaca, as it seemed like a way for perpetrators to avoid punishment by seeking forgiveness, and they believed the RPF government was sacrificing justice for political expediency to cultivate legitimacy among the Hutu majority.[47]

In November 1994, the United Nations established the International Criminal Tribunal for Rwanda (ICTR), which began work in Arusha, Tanzania, the following year. It was mandated to judge people accused of genocide, crimes against humanity, and war crimes in Rwanda during 1994 and developed as a trial venue for those considered to have been leaders of the genocide. In 1998 the ICTR found Jean-Paul Akayesu—mayor of Rwanda's Taba commune during 1993 and 1994 who had been extradited from Zambia in 1996—guilty of nine counts of genocide and crimes against humanity and sentenced him to life imprisonment. The trial was significant in a number of ways: it was the first instance in which a court enforced the 1948 UN Convention on the Prevention and Punishment of the Crime of Genocide; genocide was clearly distinguished from violations of the Geneva Convention, which regulates warfare; and sexual assault within this context was included among acts of genocide. In 2003 three men involved with RTML broadcasts were convicted of genocide and incitement to genocide and crimes against humanity; they were sentenced to some 30 years' imprisonment. By May 2015, the ICTR, much criticized for its slowness, had indicted 93 people and completed 55 trials involving 75 accused.[48]

Since many genocide perpetrators had fled Rwanda in 1994, the justice systems of other countries became involved in the issue. Under the recently adopted principle of "universal jurisdiction," which extends the ability to prosecute beyond national borders, trials of suspected genocide criminals from Rwanda were held in Belgium, Switzerland, Germany, Canada, Finland, Norway, Sweden, the Netherlands, and France. In the United States, alleged Rwandan genocide perpetrators were tried for immigration offenses, which usually involved gaining access to the country based on false statements. In 2001 a Belgian court convicted two Catholic Rwandan nuns of murder and war crimes for their participation in burning to death some 5,000 people who had taken refuge at their convent in southern Rwanda in 1994. They were sentenced to 15 and 12 years imprisonment, respectively. Both were released after serving half their sentences, which is not unusual in the Belgian justice system, and returned to their Belgian monastery. In 2009 a Canadian court convicted Desire Munyaneza—a shopkeeper in Butare in 1994, who had later fled to Toronto—of genocide, war crimes, and crimes against humanity and sentenced him to life imprisonment with no possibility of parole for 25 years. In Germany in February 2014, Onesphore Rwabukombe, a former mayor in Rwanda, was found guilty of aiding and abetting genocide and sentenced to 14 years in prison. Since France harbored many genocide planners and perpetrators, including Agathe Habyarimana, it was notable when, in March 2014, Pascal Simbikangwa, former intelligence head in the Habyarimana regime, was prosecuted by a new war crimes department, found guilty of genocide and complicity in crimes against humanity, and imprisoned for 25 years. In 2007 Rwanda abolished the death penalty to facilitate the extradition of suspected genocide perpetrators from other countries in which capital punishment did not exist. In 2011 the ICTR transferred its first case to Rwanda, and the same year a decision by the European Court of Human Rights allowed genocide suspect Sylvere Ahorugeze to be extradited from Sweden to Rwanda. In January 2012, after a long legal struggle that went to the Supreme Court of Canada, academic Leon Mugesera was deported to Rwanda, where he was to stand trial for a 1992 speech, partly quoted above, which encouraged the extermination of the Tutsi. The Mugesera case was significant because he had left Rwanda before the 1994 genocide.[49]

MEMORIALS AND DENIALS

In 2008 the RPF government of Rwanda created a National Commission for the Fight against Genocide to coordinate commemoration activities, develop strategies for fighting genocide and genocide ideology, counter genocide denial and trivialization, and assist genocide survivors. Beginning in 1996, the RPF regime developed a network of officially recognized genocide memorial sites across the country. In 2004 a national genocide memorial and museum was opened at Gisozi in Kigali and was funded and designed by a British-based organization called Aegis Trust, which was involved in Holocaust education. Throughout Rwanda, genocide memorials are often located at former churches or schools in which victims had gathered to seek safety only to be trapped and killed. They often feature various displays of human remains, ranging from neatly piled bones in an ossuary basement at a church in Nyamata to rows of lime-covered desiccated corpses laid out on tables at a former school in Murambi. Those sites became venues for annual memorial ceremonies held every April and have become "dark tourism" attractions for visitors to the country. Advocates for the exhibition of human remains argue that it provides irrefutable proof that the genocide happened—which is important, given genocide denial—and represents an essential element of ensuring that it will never happen again. Critics of the practice point out that it violates the dignity of the dead, has no precedent in Rwandan culture, and presents an obstacle to reconciliation, as the Hutu majority is constantly reminded of its collective guilt. While the Tutsi-led RPF government banned the Tutsi, Hutu, and Twa identities in favor of a broad Rwandan national identity, the memorials and events associated with them serve to remind people of those divisions. Furthermore, the RPF regime stands accused of using the memorials and related events to create an historical narrative that legitimizes and entrenches its power. Western countries are reminded that, given their failure to intervene to stop the 1994 genocide, they do not have the moral authority to criticize the RPF. Similarly, the stark nature of the memorials enables the RPF to portray its critics on such issues as human rights and freedom of speech as dangerous genocide deniers seeking to return Rwanda to the horrific days of 1994. Rwanda has been compared to Israel, which is seen as using the memory of the Holocaust to justify repression of the Palestinians and to silence critics. Indeed, President Kagame has used annual genocide commemoration ceremonies to disparage political opponents and international critics of the RPF, and even to boast about the assassination of a former colleague in South Africa.[50]

Survivors of Rwanda's 1994 genocide became active in forming organizations to pursue their interests. Rwandan communities in different parts of the world were central to the effort. In August 1994, survivors and relatives of victims living in Belgium formed an organization called Ibuka (remember) to commemorate the victims, seek prosecution of perpetrators, and assist survivors of the genocide. In May 1995, a similar group formed in Switzerland. The Rwandan-based version of Ibuka launched in November of 1995 and eventually developed into an umbrella organization for different branches and similar groups in Rwanda and others in countries such as France and Canada. Although Ibuka initially cooperated with the ICTR in Tanzania, the relationship deteriorated in the late 2000s over concerns for the safety of witnesses, the acquittal of some suspects, and the reduction of some sentences on appeal. Within Rwanda, Ibuka champions the interests of the roughly 300,000 genocide survivors, who, as a minority within a population of around 12 million, are seen as vulnerable and sometimes feel ignored by the government in the pursuit of national unity. A number of more-specialized survivor groups were also formed. The Association of Widows of the Genocide: Consolation (AVEGA Agahozo) was established in 1995 and by 2002 had 25,000 members and 49 employees. It facilitates medical and psychological treatment and legal assistance and raises money for housing and small-business projects. Other survivor groups include the Association of Orphan Household Heads (AOCM), which was founded in 2000 and had 6,000 members by 2006, and the Association of Student Survivors of Genocide (AERG) formed at the National University of Rwanda in 1998, with graduates then establishing the Group of Former Student Survivors of Genocide (GAERG) in 2002.[51]

The 1994 genocide in Rwanda has become one of the most written about and filmed events related to modern African history. It represents the subject for an ever-growing literature that includes specialized academic studies, accounts by eyewitnesses and survivors, and even some fictional novels. Furthermore, there are many films relating to the genocide in Rwanda, including several dozen documentaries (some based on books) and more than half a dozen feature films, some of which include internationally acclaimed actors. A number of those films appeared in the mid-2000s, near the tenth anniversary of the genocide. Some of those films have been criticized for inaccurate portrayals: in particular, Hollywood's 2004 *Hotel Rwanda*, which tells the supposedly true story of a Hutu hotel manager in Kigali, Paul Rusesabagina, who heroically offered sanctuary to potential victims. However, it has now become known that Rusesabagina—who later denied that there had been a genocide against the Tutsi—allegedly extorted money from those he was protecting, and that the hotel residents were spared because of media attention and the nearby UN presence. Other films such as *Shooting Dogs* and *Sometimes in April*, both released in 2005, have been received more positively.[52]

Despite overwhelming evidence from eyewitnesses that the 1994 genocide in Rwanda targeted people of Tutsi identity, several alternate and often far-fetched theories have been put forth. Those claims have been called "genocide denial." A very few people, including former UN representative to Rwanda Jacques-Roger Booh-Booh, have claimed that no genocide took place and that the massacres were greatly exaggerated. A few others maintain that the predominantly Tutsi RPF shot down President Habyarimana's aircraft and then embarked on a genocide against the Hutu, which was subsequently covered up by the U.S. government, which sought to install a friendly regime in Rwanda. As such, it is claimed that most of the hundreds of thousands of corpses that littered the streets and countryside of Rwanda were not really Tutsi but Hutu. Of course, that represents a ridiculous conspiracy theory for which there is no proof. Another view accepts that a genocide took place against the Tutsi, but provocatively blames the mainly Tutsi RPF for purposefully provoking it as part of its strategy to gain power.

There is also a "double genocide" theory that claims that, although Hutu Power extremists did attempt to exterminate the Tutsi population in 1994, the almost-simultaneous RPF counteroffensive represented another genocide against the Hutu. Statements to that effect were made in the press in 1994 by French foreign minister Alain Juppe and French president Francois Mitterrand, key allies of the Habyarimana regime, and subsequently became a common theme in the legal defense of alleged genocide perpetrators before various courts, including the ICTR. The total number of deaths during the genocide has also raised controversial questions about the nature of the genocide. According to a 1991 Rwandan government census, 600,000 Tutsi lived in Rwanda at that time. To use rough figures, if around 350,000 Tutsi survived the genocide, that means somewhere around 250,000 must have been killed. It followed then, that if around 800,000 or more people in total were killed in the genocide, as many sources indicate, the remaining 550,000 victims were not Tutsi. Is it possible that they were Hutu massacred by the RPF? That line of thinking is based on the assumption that the 1991 census was accurate, and it seems entirely possible that the Habyarimana government underestimated the size of the internal Tutsi population to minimize their claims to political representation. It is also likely that the total number of genocide victims has been overstated, with the figure of about 500,000 advanced by some. While it seems certain that RPF elements conducted revenge massacres of Hutu during the fighting in Rwanda in 1994, that cannot be labelled genocide under the international legal definition, as there is no evidence of an RPF plan to exterminate part or all of the Hutu population.[53] However, as discussed in the next chapter, there is a possibility that RPF killings of Rwandan Hutu refugees in eastern Congo in 1996 constituted genocide.

CONCLUSION

The genocides that occurred in Rwanda in 1963–1964 and 1994—similar events though different in the scale of killing—were the result of a combination of factors, some of which date back to the precolonial era. The country has a long history of violence and warfare that intensified during the rule of late-19th-century leader Rwabugiri and continued through the periods of German and Belgian colonial rule. The history of violence was important, because it created an historical memory of terror that was exploited by postcolonial regimes. A series of paranoid and manipulative regimes imposed tight controls: the Nyiginya monarchy, the Belgian colonial rulers, and the two postcolonial Hutu republics. Arguably, the post-1994 RPF regime has continued the tradition. In a way that was distinct from most of the rest of colonial Africa, in which ethnic and regional divide-and-rule became the norm, Belgian officials and missionaries imposed the concepts of race and racial hierarchy on the long-existing Rwandan identities of Tutsi, Hutu, and Twa. The binary of an alien Tutsi minority and an indigenous Hutu majority—the former favored in colonial times and then oppressed by postcolonial states—came to dominate Rwandan society and politics through most of the 20th century and beyond. The genocides of the late 20th century were certainly avoidable and were the result of decisions made by specific leaders. However, those choices were heavily influenced by a dangerous combination of historical factors, including violence, control, fear, and racial ideology within the context of a small and densely populated country. Such a mixture of elements was rare in colonial and postcolonial Africa, which is likely why there are few comparable cases of such clearly defined and total genocide in the continent's history.

CHAPTER 3

Burundi

Although it has been described as postcolonial Africa's first genocide,[1] the extermination of educated Hutu and Hutu students in Burundi in 1972 is still a little-known event among both academics and the general public. It has attracted relatively little scholarly attention, especially when compared to the large volume of academic literature on the 1994 genocide in neighboring Rwanda. The dearth of knowledge is partly the result of the Burundian Tutsi military regime's successful denial of the genocide and also stems from a complete lack of interest on the part of the international community and media when it happened. Furthermore, the relatively recent scholarly and popular focus on genocide in Rwanda has drawn attention away from and obscured similar events in the history of neighboring Burundi. The many books, speaking tours, and films devoted to the 1994 genocide in Rwanda have created a set of widely held stereotypes, in which the Tutsi are seen as the "good guys" of the story usually cast in the role of tragic victims or heroic survivors, and the Hutu are perceived as the "bad guys": those who perpetrated crimes against humanity. The history of postcolonial Burundi, however, appears to uncomfortably reverse those roles and is therefore often avoided in general discussions of genocide in Africa. At the same time, the memory of the 1972 massacres has remained strong in Burundi and has influenced subsequent conflict and mass violence in that country into the present.

PRECOLONIAL HISTORY

The origins of the Kingdom of Burundi, located on the highlands overlooking the north end of Lake Tanganyika, can be traced back at least several centuries. As in precolonial Rwanda, a flexible and complex social structure developed in which pastoralists called Tutsi were generally wealthy and exercised some dominance over cultivators called Hutu and hunter-gatherers called Twa. In the early 1800s, the centralized state of Burundi emerged as one of the major powers in Africa's Great Lakes region. Ruling from around 1800 to 1850, Ntare Rugamba (Battle Lion) established a professional cadre of warriors recruited from the sons of aristocrats, court advisors, and provincial governors. During war, this mostly Tutsi force formed the core of an expanded army made up of temporary levies from different communities. As the new army expanded Burundi's territory, Ntare Rugamba organized a new administrative system in which royal sons (Ganwa) and their wives and retainers were sent to control newly conquered lands in which existing powerful families were undermined and tribute collected in the name of the central court. It is believed that tensions among the Ganwa led the monarchy to seek support beyond the Tutsi pastoralists and build alliances with Hutu commoners, some of whom occupied important positions as court ritualists and local officials.

At that point, Burundi's primary rival was neighboring Rwanda. In 1770 an army from Burundi invaded Rwanda but was defeated. Throughout the first half of the 1800s, almost-constant warfare occurred between Rwanda and Burundi, with each state launching several major but ultimately disastrous invasions of the other. Postcolonial tensions between these neighbors, discussed elsewhere in this book, are not entirely new.

A civil war between royal factions in Burundi during the 1850s led to the appointment of Mwezi Gisabo, the late Ntare's youngest son, as king, under the regency of his older brother Ndivyariye. During the late 1860s, Mwezi Gisabo came of age and led a successful military campaign against the forces of his regent, who was unwilling to relinquish power. Around 1881, Rwanda—under expansionist ruler Rwabugiri—staged an ambitious incursion into Burundi called the War of Rito, which failed partly because of royal intrigue among the invaders. As a result, Rwanda and Burundi engaged in a long negotiation that produced a nonaggression pact at the end of the 1880s. With the northern frontier relatively secure, Mwezi Gisabo and his armies could fend off new dangers associated with the growing East African slave trade, including numerous raids by Swahili-Arabs linked to the coast and an attack by the Nyamwezi of what is now central Tanzania in 1884. At the same time, internal conflict continued, as Mwezi Gisabo sought to replace independent-minded Ganwa who had been appointed by his father with his own sons, who became subordinate provincial rulers. Between 1879 and 1881, European Catholic missionaries of the White Fathers established a mission on the north shore of Lake Tanganyika, but it was abandoned after conflict with a local leader. Although the mission was not within Burundi's territory, Mwezi Gisabo saw its proximity as a threat and worked to undermine the missionaries.

COLONIAL CONQUEST AND RULE

In 1896 the Germans established a military post at the trading town of Bujumbura on the north end of Lake Tanganyika and claimed nearby Burundi as part of their developing East African colony. In 1899 a German military expedition under Captain Heinrich von Bethe marched into Burundi and attacked communities under a local ruler who had ordered the burning of a new Catholic mission. At that time, Mwezi Gisabo accepted German authority, perhaps because he was intimidated by colonial firepower, with which Burundi had very limited experience. In 1902 continuing violence in Burundi between territorial rulers and the king, who now seemed to reject German supremacy, prompted Captain Friedrich Robert von Beringe, the German commander at Bujumbura, to organize a punitive expedition. The German force that converged on Mwezi Gisabo's capital killed 200 men and suffered only 3 dead. Mwezi Gisabo surrendered, recognized German sovereignty, promised to refrain from attacking trade caravans and missionaries, granted independence to rebellious subordinates who had assisted von Beringe, and provided over 400 cattle as reparations. Since Beringe had disobeyed explicit instructions from German East Africa Governor Gustav Adolf von Gotzen to avoid conflict, he was replaced by Captain Werner von Grawert. Gotzen then reversed Beringe's policy of divide and rule with strong support for Mwezi Gisabo as a central ruler. The Germans applied the same approach to Musinga's regime in Rwanda. Assisted by a 1905–1906 German expedition under Grawert that included machineguns, Mwezi Gisabo reasserted his authority over rebellious local leaders, including those who had supported Beringe, and extended his influence into new territory. Exploiting old rivalries, both the Beringe and Grawert expeditions in Burundi employed allied warriors from Rwanda.[2]

The Germans established the foundations of colonial rule in Burundi. They built an administrative headquarters at Gitega, the existing capital of the kingdom, and a series of outposts around the territory, which was earmarked for integration into German East Africa. The death of Mwezi Gisabo in 1908 and the installation of the young Mutaga Mbikije as king, weakened the state and prompted many members of the royal court to appeal to the Germans for support. Taxation was introduced to facilitate the growth of a colonial capitalist economy that would produce cash crops to be exported via a new railway line under construction from Kigoma on the eastern side of Lake Tanganyika.

During the First World War, Belgian forces from the Congo occupied Burundi where Mutaga died under mysterious circumstances and was replaced by his son Mwambutsa Bangiricenge, who was still a toddler. Granted a League of Nations mandate over Burundi in 1924, the Belgians empowered elements of the central royal family and alienated regional rulers and ritualists, who were sometimes subdued by force. In 1929 the Belgians introduced a series of administrative reforms, similar to those undertaken around the same time in Rwanda, which consolidated many of the hitherto autonomous regional authorities. During the 1930s, a three-tier system of indirect rule was created, with a few Belgian officials supervising a hierarchy of Burundian chiefs, subchiefs, and administrators. Within this new system, the number of Hutu chiefs declined from 27 in 1929 to 3 in 1933 to none in 1945. Chiefly positions were split between the royal Ganwa and the broader Tutsi, whom the Belgians saw as racially superior. Supporting this system, missionaries focused Western educational efforts on Christian royal princes and members of prominent Tutsi families who constituted the colonial elite symbolized by King Mwambutsa and his family. Previously flexible identities now became fixed as the small elite was associated with the Tutsi concept (though some saw the royal Ganwa as distinct from the general Tutsi), and the majority, who mostly produced coffee and tea for export, were labeled Hutu. As in Rwanda, identities were enshrined and enforced through an identity card system.

Since the beginning of German colonial rule and continuing into the Belgian period, violent protest in Burundi had adopted an increasingly anti-Tutsi tone. At the start of the 20th century, the regional leader Kilima rebelled against the central court of Mwezi Gisabo and was initially supported but then suppressed by the Germans. People often referred to Kilima as "the butcher of the Tutsi." At the beginning of the 1920s, a rebellion occurred in the eastern area of Buyenzi, where a cattle disease was devastating local herds and a new Ganwa official had imposed compulsory coffee growing and mobilized forced labor on road building and marshland reclamation. The uprising was led by a man named Runyota-Kanyarufunzo, who was of Hutu origin, who was possibly linked to a clan associated with important ritualist duties, and who foretold the coming of a new, more just order. In 1934 another rebellion broke out in the predominantly Hutu area of Ndorwa in northwest Burundi, where the new Ganwa chief had brought in Tutsi from the south to enforce lower prices for cash crops and collect taxes. Those tensions were enflamed by the outbreak of typhus. An elderly Hutu woman called Inamujandi, who prophesized the arrival of a new king who would restore justice and spit on the Tutsi and Europeans, directed Hutu and Twa rebels, who burned 300 huts and 10 mission schools. Such rebellions were quickly suppressed by colonial troops.[3]

DECOLONIZATION

In the uncertain and expectant decolonization atmosphere of the late 1950s, Burundi's elites formed a number of political parties. It should be remembered that at that time the Hutu revolution occurring in adjacent

Rwanda, and supported by Belgian authorities, further polarized Hutu and Tutsi in Burundi, which was also moving toward self-government and independence. As in Rwanda, the post–Second World War Burundian Tutsi had benefited from greater access to Western education and therefore tended to gravitate toward anticolonial, socialist, and nationalist ambitions. Led by Crown Prince Louis Rwagasore, the Union for National Progress (UPRONA) demanded immediate independence from Belgium, promoted national unity, and urged Burundians to boycott Belgian businesses and stop paying tax to the colonial state. The charismatic Rwagasore enjoyed broad appeal. He impressed both traditionalists and Westernized intellectuals, he showed concern for the impoverished majority through the development cooperatives he had initiated a few years earlier, his physical appearance resembled the Hutu rather than Tutsi stereotype, and he was said to have married a Hutu woman to serve as an example of national unity. However, Rwagasore's UPRONA had political competition. The Christian Democratic Party (PDC) was led by a rival faction of the Ganwa/Tutsi royal family that feared losing power in a democratic system dominated by the Hutu majority. The party was sponsored by the local Belgian administration, who wanted to see a friendly group in power in postcolonial Burundi. The Party of the People (PP), inspired by the recent Hutu revolution in Rwanda, was blatantly pro-Hutu and supported by some Belgian officials and settlers who wanted to see Burundi become a Hutu majoritarian republic. In the subsequent electoral campaign, Jean-Paul Harroy, the last Belgian governor-general of Rwanda and Burundi, patently favored PDC, providing it with money, vehicles, and technical support while demonizing UPRONA as a radical, dangerous, and pro-Communist party. However, his efforts only served to bolster Rwagasore's nationalist and anticolonialist credentials. In late 1960, while the Belgians briefly imprisoned Rwagasore, the PDC won Burundi's first elections, which led to their brief domination of a transitional government. At the insistence of the United Nations, Rwagasore and other UPRONA political prisoners were released, and legislative elections, meant to create the first independent Burundian government, were set for 1961.

In September 1961, to the great surprise and disappointment of Belgian officials and PDC leaders, UPRONA won a massive victory in the legislative elections, which meant that Rwagasore became Burundi's first prime minister in preparation for independence in the next year. However, in October, Rwagasore was assassinated at the behest of PDC leaders, who seemed to have acted with the tacit approval of Belgian authorities. The death of Rwagasore is often seen as a central event in the history of postcolonial Burundi as it established a tradition of political murder and robbed the country of a unique leader who seemed determined to work toward national unity. Politics became racialized and violent. In January 1962, six months before independence, Tutsi members of the UPRONA youth wing burned houses and killed some Hutu Christian trade unionists and PP supporters in the Kamenge section of Bujumbura.[4]

THE RISE OF A TUTSI MILITARY REGIME

Although Burundi became an independent constitutional monarchy at the start of July 1962, King Mwambutsa became increasingly authoritarian, appointing and dismissing a series of prime ministers and taking direct control of the military, police, and radio stations. The legislature was paralyzed, as it was hopelessly divided between Tutsi and Hutu members. As emerging Hutu political leaders began to realize their potential power within a Western-style democratic system, the king's government recognized Communist China in order to gain support from a non-democratic state. At the same time, the 1963–1964 genocide against the Tutsi in Rwanda and the arrival of tens of thousands of mostly Tutsi refugees from there heightened tensions and fears within Burundi. The Rwandan Tutsi refugees saw the establishment of a Tutsi regime in Bujumbura as the best way to further their interests of overthrowing the Hutu Republic in Kigali, and the Tutsi in Burundi welcomed their support against local Hutu aspirations. In January 1965, Pierre Ngendandumwe, Burundi's first Hutu prime minister, who had been appointed just three days earlier, was assassinated by a Tutsi refugee from Rwanda. Burundi became the staging area for rebels from eastern Congo and exiled Rwandan Tutsi rebels, both of which were supported by the Chinese.

In May 1965, King Mwambutsa refused to recognize elected Hutu candidates, and in July he declared an absolute monarchy. As a result, in October, some Hutu soldiers and police staged an unsuccessful coup that included the murder of Prime Minister Leopold Biha, who was a prominent Ganwa. The mutiny's failure prompted Hutu to kill hundreds of Tutsi in the Muramvya area, which was a center of both historic royalist politics and more recent pro-Hutu politics. In turn, in late October, the army, led by Captain Michel Micombero, a Tutsi of modest origins, arrested and executed over 100 Hutu military officers and politicians in Bujumbura. The next month, the army and militias slaughtered perhaps 5,000 Hutu in Muramvya. With all the leading Hutu politicians dead, a group of Tutsi military officers and UPRONA youth wing leaders and politicians formed an alternative government. In July 1966, Micombero orchestrated the replacement of Mwambutsa, who had fled to Europe, with his son Charles Ndizeye, who was installed as King Ntare V. However, King Ntare and Micombero, who was prime minister and minister of defense, clashed, which motivated the latter to abolish the monarchy and declare a republic.

A Tutsi military regime was created. Micombero banned all political parties save UPRONA, which he co-opted and ruled through a National Revolutionary Council of 17 military officers, of whom 12 were Tutsi. Hutu were quickly excluded from power: within several years, only one of nine provincial governors was Hutu, very few town mayors were Hutu, and the upper ranks of the army were mostly Tutsi. Furthermore, Micombero strongly favored members of his own traditionally lower status Tutsi-Hima group from the south, particularly Bururi Province, and excluded the higher status Tutsi-Banyaruguru from the north (particularly those from Muramvya) and the Ganwa royals. In the late 1960s, prominent government officials from the Tutsi-Bururi faction criticized their Tutsi-Muramvya rivals for being too soft on the threat posed by the Hutu who might rally behind and attempt to restore the monarchy. The regime's "discovery" of a Hutu coup plot in 1969 led to the arrest of 30 Hutu army officers and government officials and the execution of dozens of Hutu soldiers. After that, only a few Hutu retained cosmetic positions within the state. The 1969 killings impelled a few Hutu students and one former government representative to flee to the bush to organize armed resistance against the Tutsi state. Within the army, where the rank-and-file consisted mostly of Hutu, a system of physical requirements for recruits was imposed with a view to excluding Hutu. In 1968 Belgian military advisors were sent home because of their interference with this recruiting system. By the end of the 1960s, given the fallout from the coup crisis, all levels of the military were increasingly dominated by Tutsi-Hima. In 1971 and early 1972, within the context of criticism of the government over the failing economy, the Micombero regime arrested some prominent Tutsi-Banyaruguru officials and military officers for treason and sentenced them to death or life imprisonment. However, local and international censure of the sham trial meant that none of the condemned were executed and a few were freed.[5]

THE GENOCIDE AGAINST THE HUTU (1972)

Little is known about the activities of the very few Hutu elites who took to the bush in 1969 to launch an armed struggle against Burundi's Tutsi military regime. They traveled to neighboring Tanzania and recruited fighters from among the growing Burundian Hutu refugee community. It also appears that they established networks among Hutu teachers and Hutu merchants, whose activities were being frustrated by the Tutsi regime, in the far south of Burundi in an area where Hutu groups had a long history of autonomy until the advent of colonial rule. Furthermore, the recent history of rebellion in nearby eastern Congo made it relatively easy to acquire weapons and enlist assistance from defeated Congolese insurgents. Infighting among Burundi's Tutsi elites in early 1972, which created a climate of instability and fear, provided an opportunity for the exiled Hutu rebels to strike.

On April 29, 1972, somewhere between 300 and 500 Hutu insurgents based in Tanzania crossed into southern Burundi. Their numbers were bolstered by rebels from eastern Congo (recently renamed Zaire), who had been paid to participate until more Burundians could be recruited. The insurgents seized the state armories at the lakeside towns of Rumonge and Nyanza Lac and mobilized groups of Hutu, armed with spears and machetes, to slaughter any Tutsi they could find and any Hutu who refused to participate. Somewhere between 2,000 and 3,000 people were killed over the next few days. Most of the members of the Rumonge provincial government were killed when rebels surprised them during a meeting. The rebels, their numbers enlarged to 1,000 or 2,000, eventually declared a short-lived people's republic in Bururi, which was also the home area of leading figures in the Tutsi military government. Furthermore, on the same day that the rebels crossed the southern border, a rebel attack took place in Cankuzo in eastern Burundi, and a group of around 50 rebels tried to seize the radio station in Bujumbura but were dispersed by the military. On the evening after the rebellion began, King Ntare, who had recently returned from exile only to be placed under house arrest at Gitega, was murdered by members of the Micombero regime, who saw him as a potential rallying figure for Hutu peasants or the rival Tutsi-Banyaruguru faction. The king's death was blamed on the Hutu insurgents. Micombero dissolved the government and declared martial law.

On April 30, the army began an offensive that crushed the rebellion within a few weeks and simultaneously embarked on a campaign to eliminate any potential Hutu political leadership. Some Hutu who helped put down the uprising were then killed by the military. The few Tutsi who objected to the massacres were arrested and executed. Within the security forces, some 750 Hutu soldiers and 300 Hutu police were quickly murdered. Initially assisting the military in the south, the UPRONA youth wing called Rwagasore Revolutionary Youth (JRR) became an independent force as the killings spread to Bujumbura and the north. Radicalized Tutsi refugees from Rwanda were also involved in the violence. Prompted by reports that Zairean (Congolese) rebels were involved in the fighting, the neighboring Mobutu regime in Kinshasa supported Micombero by sending 200 paratroopers to secure the Bujumbura airport. That assistance freed up Burundian military units for deployment elsewhere.

Educated Hutu, including students, became the main targets for elimination. State radio broadcasts encouraged people to "hunt down the python in the grass," which was interpreted by Tutsi across the country as sanction to murder all educated Hutu, which included secondary and even sometimes primary school students. Military units seized privately owned trucks and drove them to schools where Tutsi pupils were required to make lists of their Hutu teachers and classmates, who would then be taken away, never to be seen again. In Bujumbura, Gitega, and Ngozi, all Hutu civil servants, drivers, clerks, and semiskilled workers were taken to local jails, where they were beaten to death or shot. The killings were mostly done out of public view. One third of the students at the University of Bujumbura disappeared. At one Bujumbura secondary school, 300 out of 700 students were killed or fled, and, at another school in the Bujumbura suburb of Ngagara, 100 out of 315 students went missing. Furthermore, Hutu Catholic priests and Protestant ministers were murdered. One of those was Father Michel Kayoya, whose personal courage and calls for forgiveness inspired his fellow prisoners before their execution. There was little resistance to the massacres, and some obedient Hutu actively assisted in rounding up other Hutu, and subsequently all were killed. Tutsi killers were also motivated by material gain, murdering their Hutu neighbors to acquire their land, cars, furniture, and money. Although senior army officers were involved in orchestrating the massacres, the overall director of the genocidal campaign was civil servant and former foreign affairs minister Arthemon Simbananiye, who was a Tutsi-Hima from Bururi Province. By late August, when the violence stopped, between 200,000 and 300,000 people had been killed, and hundreds of thousands had fled to neighboring Zaire, Rwanda, and Tanzania. Almost all Burundi's educated Hutu were dead or exiled.[6]

There was almost no international reaction to the massacres that took place in Burundi in 1972. One reason for that was the lack of media coverage, as no international journalists were present. Another was that the perpetrators of the mass killing remained in power for many years and built a narrative that the state had reacted to an incursion by Hutu insurgents bent on committing genocide against the "people of Burundi." Manufactured evidence and coerced confessions were produced in support of this idea. For example, the regime claimed to have captured a rebel map of Burundi that showed a large shaded area in which the insurgents supposedly planned to exterminate the Tutsi. Based in Bujumbura, U.S. diplomat Michael Hoyt sent repeated messages to Washington reporting on the massacres, which he described as genocide. Although President Richard Nixon was outraged by those reports, he felt he could do little given the State Department's unwillingness to act decisively in Africa and the lack of interest among the American public. Other international leaders appeared oblivious to the killing. The secretary-general of the United Nations, Kurt Waldheim, commenting on a special UN mission sent to Burundi in June during the massacres, expressed hope that stability would return so that the country could continue striving toward the organization's development goals. Diallo Telli, first secretary-general of the Organization of African Unity (OAU), visited Burundi in May 1972 and expressed solidarity with the president, government, and people of Burundi. Ironically, a few years later, the OAU also failed to react when Telli, then serving in the government of his home country of Guinea, was accused of plotting a coup, tortured, and starved to death.[7]

The few scholars who have studied the 1972 massacres of Hutu in Burundi have disagreed on the extent to which it represented genocide.

Rene Lemarchand initially described it as a "selective" or "partial" genocide, as compared to the "total" genocide that happened during the Holocaust or in Rwanda in 1994. He later categorized it as a "retributive genocide," enacted to eliminate a real or perceived threat. Jean-Pierre Chretien and Jean-Francois Dupaquier, while emphasizing the myth of a grand Hutu plot to exterminate the Tutsi, which prompted the latter to defend themselves, hesitantly categorized the 1972 massacres of Hutu as genocide on the basis of the bureaucratic character of the killing.[8] In another work, Chretien admitted that it represented a "genuine genocide of Hutu elites."[9] However, scholars working on genocide in Rwanda, where the role of victim and perpetrator is reversed, often downplay the significance of the 1972 violence in Burundi. For example, David Leonard and Scott Straus clearly differentiate between the "organized massacres" in 1972 Burundi and the "genocide" in 1994 Rwanda.[10] It is clear that the murder of perhaps 200,000 or more Hutu in Burundi in 1972 corresponds with the international legal definition of genocide, which includes the "intent to destroy, in whole or *in part* a national, ethnical, racial or religious group" (italics added for emphasis). The fact that Burundian soldiers showed up at educational institutions with prepared lists of Hutu students demonstrates intent by the state, and targeting of the educated element of the Hutu population shows that the aim was to destroy a definite "part" of a group commonly understood in Burundi to constitute an ethnicity or race. Furthermore, the Tutsi military and militia campaign went far beyond the suppression of a minor regional rebellion—which the state exaggerated to provide an excuse for the massacres—with defenseless people slaughtered across the country.

HUTU EXILES

Burundian Hutu had been fleeing the country since the rise of the Tutsi military regime in the second half of the 1960s, and, as mentioned above, some formed a rudimentary armed resistance movement based in Tanzania, which was becoming a haven for many African liberation movements. The outflow of Hutu refugees from Burundi increased dramatically with the 1972 genocide. During the late 1960s and 1970s, Burundian students in Belgium formed a leftist group called the Movement of Progressive Students of Burundi (MEPROBA), which criticized the Micombero regime. The efforts of some MEPROBA members to assist Burundian refugees following the 1972 genocide prompted the formation of an exiled political organization. In 1978 they formed Tabara (come to my rescue), which sought to forge an alliance of workers, peasants, and intellectuals to overthrow the regime in Bujumbura. However, in 1979 the Tabara leadership was expelled from Rwanda, because they were getting too close to local Hutu extremists, who criticized President Habyarimana's more moderate approach, and their activities endangered the delicate relations between Kigali and Bujumbura. Having fled to Tanzania, the Tabara leadership fell out over strategy.

In April 1980, the Party for the Liberation of the Hutu People (PALIPEHUTU) was formed by Remy Gahutu, a former Tabara leader, in a Burundian refugee camp in Mishamo, Tanzania. Gahutu wrote a book entitled *Persecution of the Hutu of Burundi,* in which he described the Hutu as a people with an inferiority complex who needed liberation from Tutsi domination. During the middle 1980s, the Tanzanian-based PALIPEHUTU established an armed wing called the National Forces of Liberation (FNL) that planned to overturn minority-Tutsi domination in Burundi. PALIPEHUTU-FNL established offices in Denmark, Belgium, Switzerland, and Germany, and, unlike previous small Burundian Hutu exile groups, it developed a populist ideology that appealed to refugees in the Tanzanian camps. Gahutu became an effective and active spokesman for the Burundian Hutu cause until he was imprisoned in Tanzania and murdered by agents of the Burundian government in 1990. Hutu refugees in Tanzania developed a view of Burundi's history that saw the Tutsi as innately cruel foreign invaders who, in precolonial times, had conquered the long-established and basically peaceful Hutu, who now had to fight to recover their country. The exiled Burundian Hutu also saw 1972 as the moment of their political awakening; before that point, they believed themselves to have been naively unaware of the reality of the situation in their homeland. The refugees saw the 1972 genocide as an attempt by the Tutsi to change their minority status and thereby gain greater political legitimacy by equalizing the Tutsi and Hutu populations.[11]

THE MILITARY REGIME AND THE 1988 MASSACRES

Burundi's Tutsi-Hima military regime was greatly strengthened by the successful 1972 genocide against the Hutu. The leadership and core of any potential Hutu opposition was either dead or in exile, and the surviving Hutu majority had been terrorized into accepting a subservient role. Given the perception of a common Hutu threat created by the 1972 rebel incursion, the previously critical Tutsi-Banyaruguru elites fell in line behind Micombero's Tutsi-Hima dominated state. By 1985 Tutsi composed some 96 percent of the Burundi Armed Forces (FAB) and two-thirds of students at the University of Bujumbura. The Tutsi-Hima officers who controlled the government favored their home area of Bururi in terms of education, which meant that their children followed them into the officer corps, and they dominated the FAB for many years. The Tutsi military regime within Burundi denied the existence of different identities within the country and explained the Hutu-Tutsi problem as a result of illegitimate colonial divide-and-rule policies and nefarious neocolonial conspiracies.

Although the 1972 mass murder of Hutu had benefited the Tutsi military state, it ultimately tarnished Micombero, who became an international embarrassment to his own regime. As such, in 1976 he was removed from power by a military coup led by his cousin and National Revolutionary Council chairman Colonel Jean-Baptiste Bagaza. Speaking of national reconciliation and unity, Bagaza introduced universal adult suffrage and land reforms, outlawed forced labor, and directed the building of infrastructure like roads. However, he also continued the UPRONA one-party state, stood unopposed in elections, and brutalized critics. References to ethnic identity were banned and could bring criminal charges of inciting "racial hatred." While the establishment of the common local language of Kirundi as the exclusive medium of instruction in primary and secondary schools was explained as a way of promoting unity, in practice it meant that Hutu children often did not learn enough French to access white-collar jobs and thus became a permanent underclass. The children of Tutsi elites often attended French-language private schools, which were expensive. Better academic preparation and blatant discrimination meant that Tutsi students more easily accessed secondary schools and university. In the countryside, people living in small villages were forcibly relocated to larger settlements, supposedly to increase agricultural production, in a manner also envisioned by the simultaneous Ujamaa scheme in Tanzania, and their relocation conveniently facilitated government supervision and control. The secular Tutsi military regime was hostile to the Catholic Church, as it was well aware of its role in the 1959 Hutu revolution in Rwanda and was threatened by church efforts to offer education and venues for organization to Burundi's Hutu peasants. The Bagaza regime imposed increasingly severe restrictions on Catholic and Protestant church activities, including a 1977 ban on religious radio programs; a 1979 ban on church gatherings outside official parish buildings, which took aim at hilltop prayer meetings; the closure of church newspapers and radio stations; and the expulsion of several hundred foreign missionaries. In 1985 the government ordered religious activities confined to Saturday afternoons and Sundays. The next year, all church secondary schools and even seminaries were taken over by the state, and catechism schools for children were banned. Of course, that prompted international criticism and diplomatic rows with predominantly Catholic Belgium and France. The instability created by the repression of the Church and corruption scandals involving government officials incited a 1987 coup in which Bagaza, while attending an international conference in Canada, was deposed by Major Pierre Buyoya, another Tutsi-Hima military officer from Bururi Province. Although the new ruling Military Committee of National Salvation (CMSN) was similar to the old regime in that it consisted entirely of Tutsi, most of whom were from Bururi, it reversed all the restrictions on church activity.

Changes implemented by the new Buyoya administration, which included the release of many political prisoners, inspired hope among the Hutu majority and resentment among Tutsi extremists. In 1988 violence broke out in Burundi's northern areas of Ntega and Marangara, which, given the proximity of the border with Rwanda, were exposed to Hutu Power propaganda coming from the regime in Kigali and were inhabited by Rwandan Tutsi refugees who hated Hutu. Fears of a repeat of 1972 prompted Burundian Hutu peasants in those areas to form self-defense groups, arm themselves with hoes, machetes, and bows and arrows and to sabotage bridges to prevent vehicles from accessing their communities to round up potential victims. The state responded by dispatching a Tutsi military unit, which only served to confirm the worst fears of local Hutu. In mid-August 1988, gangs of Hutu killed a particularly unpopular Tutsi businessman who had been involved in the 1972 killings, in addition to 300 other Tutsi across Ntega and Marangara, and proceeded to burn homes of Tutsi. The army responded by launching an operation, supported by helicopters and armored vehicles, that killed 20,000 Hutu and drove over 50,000 people into neighboring countries. Given increased concern about human rights, international reaction to the 1988 massacres was more robust than it had been in 1972. Harrowing reports by Burundian Hutu refugees in Rwanda were published in the international press, and Western governments, including Belgium, Canada, and the United States, engaged in diplomatic protest against Burundi. Since protests jeopardized the flow of international aid money, Buyoya appointed a new Council of Ministers and a commission of inquiry into the violence, both of which consisted of equal numbers of Hutu and Tutsi. Of course, while Tutsi extremists might have seen equal representation as a radical concession, the Hutu represented over 80 percent of the general population. The commission's report repeated the Tutsi military regime's well-established position that Burundi had been a historically united nation until colonialism caused the Tutsi-Hutu division, and it also ignored the 1972 genocide against the Hutu.[12]

LIBERALIZATION AND GENOCIDE

Given the context of the end of the Cold War and the wave of democratization sweeping Africa, Buyoya's political reforms led to the creation of a national unity government in 1991, with 12 Hutu and 12 Tutsi ministers—though the key posts of defense, foreign affairs, and the interior remained with the latter. While discrimination against the Hutu in the education system no longer occurred, the Tutsi military refused similar changes. Subsequently, the army suppressed several minor Hutu uprisings, especially along the Rwandan border, and some conservative Tutsi army officers staged several failed coups. Political liberalization led to a national election in June 1993, in which the new Front for Democracy in Burundi (FRODEBU), moderate and predominantly Hutu, defeated Buyoya's UPRONA. The charismatic leader of FRODEBU, Melchior Ndadaye, became Burundi's first Hutu president with a strong majority of the vote. Like many Hutu students, Ndadaye had escaped the 1972 genocide by fleeing to Rwanda, where he attended university and organized Burundian exiles before continuing his education in France. Although Ndadaye appointed a Tutsi prime minister and formed a cabinet that was one third Tutsi, many Hutu gained government posts previously denied them. Efforts to reduce Tutsi control of the security forces, which had been entrenched since the 1960s, caused worry that the Tutsi minority would not be protected from a potentially vengeful and genocidal Hutu majority. The issue of returning Hutu refugees prompted fear among Tutsi that they would lose their land, some of which had been taken from Hutu during the 1972 genocide, and then sometimes subsequently sold to other Hutu, and a newly free press enflamed tensions in the country. In July, resentment over the reforms led to a failed coup attempt.

In October 1993, disgruntled elements of the Tutsi-dominated army assassinated Ndadaye and other prominent Hutu politicians and members of their families. That act plunged Burundi into many years of civil war. News of the murder announced over the radio incited Hutu FRODEBU supporters, outraged by the murder of the country's first Hutu president and fearful of a repeat of the 1972 genocide against the Hutu, to undertake revenge killings of some 25,000 Tutsi around the country. The killings were conducted by Hutu rural peasants using machetes, spears, and clubs, and many of their victims were covered in kerosene and burned to death. In one terrible incident at Kibimba, around 70 Tutsi children were immolated at a petrol station. Despite the horror of those killings, there is no evidence that they were part of a planned national campaign of extermination against the Tutsi. In turn, the Tutsi-controlled army and militias moved to stop the massacres and carried out reprisal killings of Hutu. Tutsi in rural areas fled to the army-controlled towns, and Hutu in the towns escaped to rural areas or crossed the border. In late 1993, a total of perhaps 50,000 to 100,000 Burundians perished, as many as 600,000 became internally displaced, and perhaps 700,000 fled to neighboring countries. Many Hutu refugees, perhaps 350,000, flooded into Rwanda, which heightened pressures within that country's Hutu regime, which was about to enter a power-sharing agreement with the predominantly Tutsi RPF rebels.[13]

Several years later, a UN commission of inquiry, likely influenced by the terrible events of 1994 in Rwanda, visited Burundi to investigate the massacres that had been associated with the Ndadaye assassination. While its report recognized that Burundi's Tutsi army had slaughtered tens of thousands of Hutu, the 1972 extermination of educated Hutu was not called genocide. Furthermore, the report concluded that "acts of genocide against the Tutsi minority were committed in Burundi in October 1993."[14] The report created resentment among Hutu, while confirming Tutsi fears of future genocide and providing an excuse for the Tutsi military to cling to power at all costs. In the wake of the 1993 mass violence, several extremist Tutsi organizations were formed such as PA Amesekanya (Power of Self-Defense) and AC Genocide (Action against Genocide), which strongly claimed that the killings of Tutsi constituted genocide comparable to what happened in Rwanda in 1994, while denying that the 1972 massacres of Hutu in Burundi should be seen in the same light.

CIVIL WAR

Post–Cold War Burundi experienced over a decade of insurgency and counterinsurgency. In April 1994, Cyprien Ntaryamira, a Hutu who had succeeded Ndadaye as president of Burundi, was killed in the same downed aircraft as Rwandan President Habyarimana. Burundi's first two Hutu presidents had been killed within less than a year. Over the next few weeks, thousands of Rwandan Tutsi escaped genocide by crossing into Burundi. Over the next two years, in what has been called a "creeping coup," elected FRODEBU officials in Burundi were rendered powerless by intimidation and violence from the Tutsi security forces and Tutsi extremists. In early 1994, street gangs in Bujumbura became polarized between Hutu and Tutsi, and allied themselves with the racialized political and military leadership. In April 1994, a Hutu militia called Intagoheka (those who do not sleep) began attacks on the Tutsi army. In June, frustrated FRODEBU leaders founded the National Council for the Defense of Democracy (CNDD), with an armed wing called Forces for the Defense of Democracy (FDD) that vowed to fight until the army was restructured and there were internationally supervised negotiations. In early 1995, the FDD began attacks on the army, particularly in Cibitoke and Bubanza provinces, where they installed alternative local governments and collected taxes. Between March and June 1995, the army "ethnically cleansed" Bujumbura by driving masses of Hutu into the nearby hills and across the border into Zaire. From July to September 1995, PALIPEHUTU's armed wing massacred Tutsi civilians in Cibitoke, which provoked army retaliation against Hutu. While most of the 15,000 to 25,000 civilians killed during 1995 were Hutu murdered by the Tutsi army or militia, the number of Tutsi soldiers and civilians killed by the rebels increased in the second half of the year. In early 1996, there were attacks on military posts and Tutsi civilians in the south and southwest, probably by the small National Liberation Front (FROLINA) that had split from PALIPEHUTU. From February 1996 to the middle of the next year, the army resettled 300,000 (some say 600,000) rural Hutu in concentration camps to deprive the rebels of support. Given that people died of hunger and disease in the remote camps, this once again raised the spectre of the 1972 genocide and pushed Hutu peasants to back the rebels. By the middle of 1996, 11 out of Burundi's 15 provinces were experiencing civil war, the army was under severe pressure, and FRODEBU President Sylvestre Ntibantunganya was impotent.

In July 1996, Buyoya returned to power in another military coup. This had been motivated by the slaughter of some 300 Tutsi by Hutu rebels in Bungendana and the Tutsi military's desire to forestall regional international military intervention. Although the army's noncommissioned officers and radical Tutsi militia had wanted the more militant Bagaza to take over, army officers backed the relatively moderate Buyoya, who was seen as more internationally acceptable. However, as a result of the coup, international aid to Burundi was suspended, and its neighbors imposed economic sanctions. Around the same time, the Rwandan military intervention in eastern Zaire destroyed CNDD-FDD bases in South Kivu, which led to increased violence in Burundi's south as retreating rebels passed through en route to Tanzania. That meant that during 1997 and early 1998, Burundi's western provinces that bordered Tanzania were the most affected by the war. It appears that during 1997, some 5,000 to 10,000 civilians were killed by the army and rebels. The minister of defense, Colonel Firmin Sinzoyiheba, declared that all Hutu males of military age were the enemy. On New Year's Eve 1997, CNDD-FDD rebels attacked Bujumbura airport and the nearby Gakumbu military camp, and the army responded by massacring 500 Hutu civilians. Buyoya pursued both military and diplomatic means to end the war. He introduced one-year obligatory military service for secondary school and junior university students, though in practice the only ones enrolled were Tutsi. The Burundi army grew from 13,000 personnel in 1993 to 30,000 in 1996 and 45,500 in 2002. With almost half the national budget spent on the military, a war tax was imposed on civil servants and farmers.

International sanctions on Burundi were lifted in 1998, when Buyoya agreed to engage in negotiations initially supervised by former Tanzanian President Julius Nyerere, who Burundian Tutsi did not like, as Tanzania had been a staging area for Hutu rebels. Held in Arusha, Tanzania, the talks involved two coalitions of extremely small political parties, the Hutu one called the G8 and the Tutsi one called the G10, and dragged on, given that the representatives did not want to see an end to their generous expense allowances. An August 2000 peace agreement facilitated by South Africa's Nelson Mandela, who was criticized by Tutsi for comparing the situation of Burundian Hutu to South African blacks under apartheid, stipulated that Buyoya would rule for 18 months, followed by 18 months under FRODEBU's Domitien Ndayizeye. However, that was rejected by the armed wings of CNDD and PALIPEHUTU, which demanded their own representation in negotiations. The agreement committed the parties to form a new integrated National Defense Force (FDN), in which Hutu and Tutsi would each have no more than 50 percent representation. Hutu rebel leaders asked why the Tutsi should have 50 percent control of the government when they amounted to 15 percent of the population. In October, 700 South African troops arrived in Burundi to protect exiled leaders returning to participate in the peace process.

Violence continued: in late December 2000, FNL rebels stopped a bus outside Bujumbura, separated Hutu and Tutsi passengers, and killed 20 of the latter plus a British aid worker. Between October and December 2000, the army mounted a successful offensive against the FNL in Tenga forest near Bujumbura. Nevertheless, in February 2001, the rebels regrouped and renewed attacks on the capital, to which the army responded with another offensive with artillery and aerial bombardment in December, which, according to the government, killed 500 insurgents. The peace process in Burundi was delayed by officials in Kinshasa allowing the CNDD-FDD to reestablish staging areas in South Kivu, and the rebel groups fought each other and were internally split between moderate and radical leaders. The main difference between the two principal rebel organizations was that CNDD-FDD had external bases and support and wanted democratic reform, whereas PALIPEHUTU-FNL was largely based within Burundi and pursued a more radical, pro-Hutu agenda.

In December 2002, FDD leader Pierre Nkurunziza, a former university lecturer whose father had been killed in the 1972 genocide, agreed to a cease-fire that led to his CNDD becoming a political party and integrating its fighters into the army. That was accomplished within the context of regional peace talks aimed at ending external intervention and civil war in the neighboring Democratic Republic of Congo (DRC). With the UN averse to sending peacekeepers to Burundi because it was not clear if there was peace to keep, the African Union (until recently the OAU) embarked on its first peacekeeping mission in April 2003, called the African Union Mission in Burundi (AMIB) with 3,300 troops mostly from South Africa, Ethiopia, and Mozambique. The AMIB protected the transitional government, secured demobilization centers, and enabled displaced people to return home. Ndayizeye assumed power in May 2003, which led to the signing of a peace agreement in Pretoria in October. However, the war continued in the predominantly Hutu area outside Bujumbura, as the radical FNL of Agathon Rwasa refused to enter the peace process. In August 2004, FNL insurgents massacred 153 Congolese Tutsi (Banyamulenge) refugees at Gatumba on the DRC border and began to rely heavily on child soldiers. Given the peace agreement, in June 2004 AMIB was absorbed into the UN Operation in Burundi (ONUB), which grew to 4,500 troops and 1,000 civilians by 2005, and, within a year, those forces had demobilized some 20,000 Burundian fighters.

In 2005 CNDD won Burundi's first elections in over a decade, and Nkurunziza became president. The next year, FNL agreed to the cease-fire.

Although there was a brief battle between the army and FNL in Bujumbura in April 2008, the rebels eventually entered a disarmament, demobilization, and reintegration process and dropped the name PALIPEHUTU, as the use of racial or ethnic names in political parties had been outlawed. In 2005 the process of incorporating former soldiers and rebels into the new FDN began, and mixed units were formed quickly. Belgium and the Netherlands provided officer training, and the involvement of Burundian soldiers in fighting Islamist militants in Somalia resulted in limited American support.[15]

In 2010 Nkurunziza won a second term in office after the withdrawal of opposition parties, who complained about intimidation and suspected vote rigging, from the election. Now a prominent opposition leader working within the political system, former Hutu rebel leader Rwasa was temporarily forced into hiding. In 2015 violent protest erupted when Nkurunziza declared that he would exploit a loophole in the wording of the new constitution to run for a third presidential term, despite this being illegal. After a failed coup by elements of the military, the election took place, and the president was returned to office amid international objections. Fearing a reoccurrence of ethnic killing, tens of thousands of mostly Tutsi Burundians fled to Rwanda and Tanzania, and the Nkurunziza administration accused neighboring Rwanda of organizing exiled Burundian rebels. Murders of government officials, army officers, and opposition leaders inspired international concern over possible mass violence against the Tutsi minority, but the violence did not seem to follow that pattern. Proposals for an African Union (AU) or UN peacekeeping force were scuttled when Nkurunziza declared that his state would resist what he saw as foreign invasion. Although Nkurunziza agreed that a very small contingent of UN police could be dispatched to Burundi to monitor the situation, disagreements continued over its deployment. In late 2016, a report by a federation of international human rights groups warned of impending genocide against the Tutsi in Burundi. The report also claimed that the memory of the 1972 massacres of Hutu, which it seemed to doubt constituted a genocide, served as an excuse for continued state repression of Tutsi. While the same human rights federation launched a media campaign based on a mock movie trailer entitled "Genocide in Burundi: A Film You Don't Want to See," the government of Burundi responded with a social media account named "This is my genocide" that highlights a positive view of the situation in the country.[16]

Although Burundian politicians have discussed the formation of a Truth and Reconciliation Commission, similar to the one held in South Africa in the late 1990s, to address crimes committed in the past such as the massacres of 1972, 1988, and 1993, it has not become a reality. No one has ever faced local or international prosecution for genocide or other crimes against humanity that took place in postcolonial Burundi. The current crisis makes it unlikely that this will happen in the near future.

CONCLUSION

Many of the same factors that contributed to genocide in Rwanda were also present in neighboring Burundi: a history of violence, control, and fear, and the imposition of a colonial racial hierarchy in a small and densely populated country. A political culture of assassination and impunity quickly emerged in postcolonial Burundi. The influence of Rwanda was also important. In Burundi, the Tutsi-dominated military acted to prevent the rise of a majoritarian Hutu Republic, like the one that existed north of the border. The first genocide against the Tutsi minority in Rwanda during 1963–1964 served as a powerful example of what could happen in such a situation; it is no coincidence that Burundian Tutsi army officers seized power shortly thereafter and jealously held it for most of the next 40 years. Central to the longevity of that Tutsi minority military regime was the successful 1972 genocide against the Hutu, which deprived the subject majority of potential leaders and terrorized the rest into submission. The 1972 genocide also became a central event in the development of Burundian Hutu political consciousness, because it motivated an exiled, armed liberation movement and created anxiety among the Hutu within Burundi that the same thing would happen again. Both sides feared genocide. A vicious circle developed in which the Tutsi minority regime clung to power to avoid falling victim to the Hutu majority, who themselves eventually engaged in mass violence to prevent a possible repeat of 1972, which only served to confirm Tutsi worries.

CHAPTER 4

Democratic Republic of Congo

The Democratic Republic of Congo (DRC) has a particularly tragic history. Since the late 19th century, this vast territory has been dominated by a succession of predatory colonial and postcolonial states that have focused on the extraction of valuable resources for personal profit and ignored the welfare and aspirations of the people. National political institutions and economic and social infrastructure were not developed in any meaningful way. Employed both retrospectively and contemporaneously, the rhetoric of genocide has featured prominently in the violent history of DRC. There are at least five periods in Congo's history in which the term "genocide" has been mobilized: the colonial conquest of the late 19th and early 20th centuries, the Congo Crisis of the early 1960s, the First Congo War of 1996–1997, the Second Congo War of 1998 to 2002, and the post-2002 violence in the eastern part of the country. In most instances, however, the use of the term genocide with reference to the DRC has clearly failed to measure up to the 1948 international legal definition. In many cases, accusations of genocide in DRC, which proliferated after 1994, have represented cynical ploys to demonize enemies and justify violent actions in pursuit of power and wealth.

PRECOLONIAL HISTORY

Comprising the Congo River Basin in western equatorial Africa, the DRC covers well over 2 million square kilometers and is Sub-Saharan Africa's largest state. The center of the country is dominated by a massive lowland rainforest, the world's second largest, and characterized by many rivers. On the forest periphery is a savannah in the south and southwest, mountains in the east and west, and grassland north of the Congo River. It is important to remember that the current borders of the DRC, like those of most African countries, were imposed by late-19th-century European colonialism and meant little to the people who were already living there.

People have inhabited this enormous area for thousands of years, with those living around the forest edge tending to form centralized states. By the start of the 1400s, the Kingdom of Kongo had emerged among Iron Age farmers and fishers close to the Atlantic coast on the south side of the Congo River, which served as an avenue for trade. In 1483 Portuguese mariners established contact with Kongo, and in 1506 a faction of the royal family who had converted to Catholicism took power in a civil war. As Portugal's primary ally in west-central Africa, the Kongo Kingdom engaged in wars to capture an increasing number of African slaves, who were exported to the Atlantic trade and often to the Portuguese colony of Brazil. The shifting of the slave trade south in the late 1500s to the new Portuguese colony at Luanda on what is now the Angolan coast weakened Kongo, which fell into a period of civil war and decline in the 1600s and 1700s.

To the south, on the border between the forest and savannah, farming and fishing communities around Lake Kisale merged into the Luba Kingdom during the 15th century. Those people had long exported dried fish and copper crafts in exchange for iron and salt from the north and copper from the south. During the 1700s, Luba conquered decentralized and populous groups along the upper Congo, Luvua, and Luapula River valleys and the western shore of Lake Tanganyika. A civil war delayed this expansion in the late 1700s but the process was renewed in the early 1800s. Around 1500, conflict among the Luba royals resulted in a disaffected faction moving west, where they established a large centralized state known as Lunda, which ruled the many small groups east of the upper Kasai River. Lunda expansion during the 1600s and 1700s was facilitated by the adoption of American crops, particularly drought-resistant cassava, which had been brought to the coast by the Portuguese and served to increase food production and population growth in the interior. Since Lunda had plenty of land but not enough people, its expansion was characterized by raiding armies sent out to seize captives, who were taken back to the capital area, where they worked in agriculture and were eventually incorporated into Lunda society. As its frontier became too far away to bring prisoners to the center, Lunda established satellite states that expanded in the same manner and sent tribute to the parent kingdom. In the 1700s, Lunda pushed westward to gain greater access to the Atlantic coast, where it exported slaves captured in raids against Luba in the northeast. Around the same time, a Lunda army established what would become the semiautonomous and powerful state of Kazembe to the east on the southern shore of Lake Mweru, near what is now the DRC/Zambia borderland. Located between the Luba and Lunda states, Kanyok farming and fishing communities on the southern forest edge experienced a process of militarization and state formation during the 1600s and 1700s.

During the 19th century, Lunda and Luba declined in the face of new aggressive raiders equipped with firearms. Originating from Angola, where they had engaged in slave raiding, which was now declining, bands of Chokwe elephant hunters with guns moved northeast and challenged Lunda. The growth of a slave and ivory trade along East Africa's Indian Ocean coast brought Swahili-Arab and Nyamwezi gunmen into the area. In the 1850s, the Yeke, a Nyamwezi group under Msiri, pushed into the central African interior and carved out a copper-rich territory from the western part of Kazembe, the southern part of Luba, and the eastern part of Lunda. In the 1860s, Swahili-Arab leader Tippu Tip established a raiding state on the Lualaba River west of Lake Tanganyika. His slave- and ivory-trading empire stretched from Luba in the south, which he significantly weakened, to the westward bend of the Congo River in the north.

In the dense forest of Central Africa, people lived in decentralized communities and change occurred slowly. Over a long period, Bantu-speaking fishing and farming communities with Iron Age technology entered parts of the forest where they absorbed the existing bands of Twa (called pygmies in colonial times), Stone Age hunter-gatherers, or developed a symbiotic relationship with them. By the mid-1500s, northern Teke groups living around the junction of the Congo and Kasai Rivers began to move eastward to escape Kongo slave raiding or to search for their own victims.

At the northern forest fringe, after around 1600, Savannah raiders with horses and swords pressed south along the Ubangi River to capture slaves who were then sent north along the Trans-Saharan trade routes. Along the Uele River on the northeast forest frontier, in what is now the DRC's northeast corner, the Mangbetu developed a strong agricultural foundation by growing plantain, maize, and cassava, and their skilled ironworkers produced weapons such as spears and a range of swords prized among their neighbors. During the 1800s, several new Mangbetu states fought against but were ultimately dominated by Arab slavers from Khartoum to the north (see chapter 5). In the late 1700s, Azande states expanded east toward the north part of the Congo and Nile watershed in what is today the border area of South Sudan and the DRC. They were motivated by the desire to incorporate subject peoples into their society and gain new land, rivers, and hunting areas. Although the Azande expanded rapidly, they did not centralize, but instead constantly established new and usually rival groups. By the 1870s, a number of powerful Azande states were almost constantly at war with ivory and slave traders probing south from Khartoum.[1]

THE CONGO FREE STATE: HOLOCAUST OR HECATOMB?

In the late 19th century, Belgian King Leopold II engaged in private empire building, as his country's constitutional government was uninterested in the Scramble for Africa. During the early 1880s, Leopold, using his International African Association as a front, organized the personal conquest of the vast Congo River basin, which was euphemistically named the Congo Free State. Although the goals of Leopold's association supposedly involved scientific study and the abolition of slavery, his regime in the Congo became one of colonial Africa's most brutal as it ruthlessly extracted rubber and ivory for profit. Leopold never visited Africa and hired famous Anglo-American explorer Henry Morton Stanley to orchestrate the initial occupation, which focused on gaining control of the Congo River itself. The Congo Free State was not a Belgian colony, but rather Leopold's personal fiefdom.

In 1881 Stanley mobilized Congolese people to carry a steamboat in pieces some 400 kilometers from the Congo River's mouth on the Atlantic coast to Malebo (later Stanley) Pool, a stretch of river rendered unnavigable by rapids and falls, where it was assembled and proceeded upriver. Later, during the 1890s, Leopold's regime constructed a railway from the river port of Matadi near the Atlantic coast to Malebo Pool, which became the site of the colonial capital of Leopoldville and was renamed Kinshasa after independence. Between 1886 and 1896, the Congo Free State expended half its revenue to develop a fleet of steamers that patrolled from Leopoldville, some 1,400 kilometers northeast up the Congo River, to Stanley Falls, eventual site of the town of Stanleyville, which is now Kisangani, and then another 800 kilometers south up the Lualaba River to what would become Katanga Province. Leopold hired Canadian-born British mercenary William Stairs to lead an expedition that travelled from Zanzibar on the Indian Ocean coast to the south end of Lake Tanganyika, where, in December 1891, they killed the Yeke ruler Msiri and incorporated Katanga into the Congo Free State. Leopold was prompted to dispatch this expedition to Katanga given the threat of British colonial expansion north from what was becoming Northern Rhodesia (today's Zambia).

To enforce his rule in the Congo Free State, Leopold created a private army called the Force Publique, which consisted of European officers and local African soldiers and quickly gained a reputation for cruelty, pillaging, and ill-discipline. It became an instrument of state terror. The conquest of the Congo Free State coincided with a dramatic increase in the price of rubber on the world market because this product was needed to manufacture new inflatable tires for bicycles and motor vehicles. If a community in the Congo Free State failed to produce a set quota of rubber for export, Force Publique troops flogged people and cut off hands or heads to prove to their officers that bullets had not been wasted. In many cases, villages and crops were burned, and livestock seized. The Force Publique also put down resistance. In 1887 Tippu Tip, the Swahili-Arab slave and ivory dealer who dominated the western shore of Lake Tanganyika, agreed to become Leopold's governor of the eastern Congo Free State. However, when Tippu Tip retired to Zanzibar in 1891 conflict developed between Leopold's burgeoning regime and the remaining Swahili-Arab leaders, who resented restrictions on their ivory and slave trading. During the Arab War of 1893–1894, the Force Publique used its control of the river system to conquer the Swahili-Arabs and impose colonial rule on eastern Congo. In addition, some of the most serious resistance to Leopold's state came from within the Force Publique, in which African soldiers rebelled against poor treatment. Between 1895 and 1897, mutineers from the Force Publique fought their former superiors in the Kasai region, with guerrilla warfare continuing until 1908. In 1896 a Force Publique expedition sent to seize the headwaters of the Nile in what is now South Sudan was abandoned when a large number of its troops mutinied, and fighting continued until 1900, with the flight of the rebels into the German territories of Rwanda and Burundi.

Even when European colonial conquest and exploitation in Africa were common, the horrors of Leopold's regime were outrageous and inspired an international outcry in Western Europe and North America. The Congo Reform Association, led by E. D. Morel, severely criticized Leopold in a series of newspaper articles, pamphlets, and books, including some by such celebrated authors as Joseph Conrad, Arthur Conan Doyle, and Mark Twain. There were also calls for Leopold to be put on trial for his crimes and then executed. Leopold mobilized his own counter-propaganda, but it failed to convince. A damning 1904 official report by British diplomat Roger Casement, who visited Leopold's Congo, was later confirmed by an independent Belgian commission. In 1908 Leopold was compelled to relinquish the territory to the Belgian government. The Congo Free State became the Belgian Congo. It has been estimated that about half of the Congo's population died during the 23-year reign of the Congo Free State (1885–1908), though some areas were more affected than others. Although there was no census conducted in the Congo until 1924, some historians have claimed that the death toll amounted to between 5 and 10 million people. The causes of death included violence, hunger, disease, and displacement.[2]

The vast number of deaths attributed to Leopold's Congo Free State has tempted scholars to compare those events to later genocides such as the Holocaust. However, the colonial regime's intention, which seems to have been focused on extremely ruthless resource extraction, has led to some debate. Raphael Lemkin, who invented the term "genocide," wrote an unpublished manuscript in the early 1950s that claims that the Congo Free State experienced "an unambiguous genocide." He also believed that up to 75 percent of Congo's population had died, though he blamed the violence on what he saw as the savagery of African colonial troops.[3]

According to Adam Hochschild, whose successful 1998 book popularized awareness about atrocities committed in Leopold's colonial state:

> Although the killing in the Congo was of genocidal proportions, it was not, strictly speaking, a genocide. The Congo state was not deliberately trying to eliminate one particular ethnic group from the face of the Earth. Instead . . . Leopold's men were looking for labor. If, in the course of their finding and using that labor, millions of people died, that to them was incidental.[4]

In an overview of Congo's history, Georges Nzongola-Ntalaja agrees with that assessment, but reminds readers that the Congo Free State caused "a death toll of Holocaust proportions."[5] For international legal scholar Thomas W. Simon, Leopold's regime did not display the type of "corporate intent" that would be needed to characterize those deaths as genocide.[6] Human rights' scholar Rhoda Howard-Hassmann, although she discusses events in the Congo Free State in terms of a colonial genocide, admits that "technically speaking, this was not genocide even in a legally retroactive sense. The Congolese were not systematically murdered because of their race, ethnicity, religion or nationality, the four categories set out in Article II of the 1948 United Nations Convention on the Crime of Genocide."[7] Holocaust historian Robert G. Weisbord, in looking at the role of Pope Pius X in endorsing Leopold's regime, disagrees and maintains that the relevant UN convention considers that "an endeavour to eliminate a portion of a people would qualify as genocide."[8] Such genocide accusations against Leopold's activities in the Congo have become common. For conflict scholar Jeanne Haskin, it was "one of the worst genocides due to colonization."[9] A recent multiauthored history of Western exploitation in the DRC explains its relatively low population in the early 20th century "as a legacy of the genocide of the 1890s."[10] In the most extreme version of this view, Yaa-Lengi M. Ngemi talks of "the genocide of over 10 million Congolese by Leopold II."[11]

Belgian historian Guy Vanthemsche disagrees with comparisons to the Holocaust and questions the estimates of the population of late-19th-century Congo, and hence the number of fatalities brought about by Leopold's regime.[12] A recent best-selling history of the Congo suggests the use of another term to describe the tragedy of the Congo Free State:

> It would be absurd in this context of speak of an act of "genocide" or a "holocaust"; genocide implies the conscious, planned annihilation of a specific population, and that was never the intention here, or the result. And the term Holocaust is reserved for the persecution and annihilation of the Jews during World War II. But it was definitely a hecatomb, a slaughter on a staggering scale that was not intentional . . . a living sacrifice on the altar of the pathological pursuit of profit.[13]

Those who easily apply the term genocide to Leopold's regime seem to do so purely on the basis of its obvious horror and the massive numbers of people who may have perished. Of course, under the international legal definition, the number of murders has nothing to do with defining an episode of mass violence as genocide. Furthermore, no evidence has ever been put forward to prove that Leopold intended to exterminate even a portion of the Congolese population. That said, the impact of Leopold's state on parts of Congo may have caused more loss of life than other incidents throughout Africa's colonial history that could be accurately described as genocide: for instance, the 1904–1907 German campaign against the Herero and Nama in what is now Namibia. The Congo Free State might not have been genocidal, but it certainly was murderous, criminally negligent, and deeply greedy and corrupt. Tragically, Leopold's state would have much in common with subsequent regimes in the Congo.

GENOCIDE AS MURDER ALIBI: THE CONGO CRISIS (1960–1965)

During the 1950s, the era of decolonization in Africa, Belgian colonial rulers failed to prepare Congo for independence. Whereas the British devoted the better part of a decade to the transition in Ghana and Nigeria (which was still problematic), the Belgians gave the Congo six months. Few Congolese, despite the Belgian colonial rhetoric of assimilating Africans into Western civilization, had achieved anything beyond the most rudimentary Western education. The Belgian colonial administration, compared to that of other European colonial powers, had employed a high proportion of Belgian officials in Congo, which meant that almost no Congolese gained experience with running the state. Furthermore, the Belgians had never ruled the vast territory as a single colony: large regions were effectively rented out to multinational companies engaged in resource extraction. As such, the African political movements that emerged in the Belgian Congo in the late 1950s were based on regional and ethnic affiliations and ambitions. When the Belgians finally decided to decolonize in 1959, they provided extremely short notice, intending for a weak, independent Congo to be reliant on their technical assistance for the foreseeable future.

At the end of June 1960, the Congo's first independent government represented a coalition led by Prime Minister Patrice Lumumba, a Pan-Africanist of the Congolese National Movement (MNC) based in the northeast around Stanleyville, and President Joseph Kasavubu of the ethnic irredentist Bakongo Alliance (ABAKO), centered in Leopoldville in the west. In early July, African soldiers mutinied against their Belgian officers, who arrogantly behaved as if independence had not taken place, which led to attacks on Belgian civilians throughout the country. Within a few days, the colonial Force Publique had been renamed the Congolese National Army (ANC); Belgian officers were replaced by rapidly promoted and poorly trained Africans, including former soldier and journalist Joseph Mobutu, who suddenly became a colonel; and the aspirations of the rank-and-file were addressed by promoting all personnel one rank. Some Belgian officers were retained as advisors, and order was restored to the military garrisons at Leopoldville and at Thysville in the west. Within the ANC, Mobutu cultivated a personal power base by channeling money from the U.S. Central Intelligence Agency (CIA), UN, and Belgium to favorite officers and exiling unreliable units to remote locations.

The army mutiny provided an opportunity for Congo's regional separatists. Albert Kalonji proclaimed himself emperor of the diamond-mining area of South Kasai, which he imagined as an autonomous region within a federal Congo. In the mineral-rich southern province of Katanga, Moise Tshombe's Confederation of the Tribal Associations of Katanga (CONAKAT) declared full independence, supported by Southern African and Western mining concerns. Belgian commercial and political interests supported both secessions. In Katanga, Belgian soldiers disarmed ANC units and organized a Katanga military that included white mercenaries from Belgium, France, South Africa, and Rhodesia. In mid-July 1960, Belgian troops intervened in Leopoldville, Elisabethville, Luluabourg, and other towns to protect Belgian civilians, which led to Congolese and wider African claims that they were recolonizing the country. Demanding Belgian withdrawal, Prime Minister Lumumba called for UN assistance and warned that if it failed he would turn to the Soviet Union. As a Pan-Africanist, Lumumba was also influenced by connections with diplomats from newly independent Ghana and Guinea, who were not friendly to Western interests. In late July, Belgian troops were replaced by multinational peacekeepers of the UN Operation in the Congo (ONUC), which undermined Lumumba's authority by seizing the country's airports, disarming soldiers loyal to him, and refusing to crush Katanga separatism, which was seen as an internal affair. In August, Lumumba asked for Soviet military support that, given the Cold War context, prompted the Americans and Belgians to begin planning his assassination.[14] The CIA station chief in Leopoldville at the time later wrote that another American agent "had come to the Congo carrying deadly poisons to assassinate Lumumba, and I was to do the job."[15] As it turned out, others would act to eliminate the Congolese prime minister.

The history of Kasai was central in providing context for Lumumba's murder. During the colonial period, Belgian officials in the province of Kasai had created an imagined ethnic division between the Luba and Lulua people, who spoke the same language. The Luba people were originally from the southeast of Kasai and had moved into the Lulua River area in the late 19th century to escape Swahili-Arab slave raids. As displaced people, they were more easily recruited by newly arrived colonial labor agents and missionaries, who cultivated a favorable stereotype of them as industrious and hardworking. On the other hand, the people originally from around the Lulua River were categorized as Lulua by colonial officials, who saw them as lazy because they preferred to work their own land and stuck to older agricultural methods. However, in the 1950s, the Luba elite, given their relatively greater access to Western education and therefore exposure to ideas about freedom and democracy, began to challenge Belgian rule and racism. That response prompted the Belgians, as they were doing in Rwanda, to abandon their former favorites and foster the growth of a Lulua counter-elite, who were more conservative and compliant. In 1959 Belgian plans to resettle the Luba to their ancestral but impoverished homeland of southeast Kasai led to violence between Luba and Lulua, and the ethnic cleansing of the former from some areas.

In forming his independent government in 1960, Lumumba appeared to side with the Lulua in appointing one of them as provincial leader in Kasai. Discussions over the creation of a new province called South Kasai, in which the Luba would have greater influence, morphed into Luba leader Kalonji declaring the Autonomous State of South Kasai in early August 1960. Kalonji was supported by Tshombe's secessionist regime in Katanga, and the former made his declaration of autonomy from Elisabethville, the Katanga capital. On the other hand, Luba people who lived in Katanga generally did not support independence for that province. For Congo's central government based in Leopoldville (Kinshasa), it made sense to deal with Kalonji's secession first, as a military base in nearby Luluabourg (later renamed Kananga) would provide a staging area for military operations and the main railway to Katanga passed through South Kasai. At the end of August, ANC soldiers used Soviet-supplied vehicles and aircraft to move into South Kasai to crush the rebellion there before moving on to Katanga. Congolese National Army (ANC) soldiers and local Lulua militants massacred thousands of Luba civilians, including many who had taken refuge in a Catholic cathedral in the mining town of Bakwanga (now Mbuji-Mayi), capital of the secessionist state. Lacking logistical support, ANC troops pillaged local communities for food and loot. Some 3,000 Luba were killed.[16] Despite those atrocities, the ANC incursion into South Kasai failed to crush Kalonji's autonomous regime. Furthermore, ANC forces then left Kasai and made a poorly organized foray into Katanga, where mostly Swedish UN peacekeepers refused to act against Tshombe's secessionist regime and the Congolese troops were repelled by the white mercenary-led Katanga army.

United Nations secretary-general Dag Hammarskjold was worried that Lumumba would undermine the UN and turn Congo into a Soviet ally. As such, the secretary-general sought to vilify Congo's first prime minister by comparing Lumumba to Hitler, and his ideology of Pan-Africanism to fascism. Taking those analogies further, particularly Hitler's association with the Holocaust, Hammarskjold also warned of an "incipient genocide" and later described the killing of Luba people in Kasai as "characteristic of the crime of genocide."[17] Academics and right-wing journalists repeated the accusations. An American anthropologist who conducted fieldwork in the Congo in 1960 wrote that the Lulua demand that the Luba accept their chiefs or leave South Kasai led to "one of the bloodiest genocide campaigns in African history." He also stated that Lumumba sent "his troops to join the Lulua in their campaign to exterminate the Luba of Luluabourg."[18] While there has been little research conducted on the ANC massacres of Luba in Kasai, no evidence has been presented that Lumumba or anyone else planned to exterminate part or whole of any group. The rhetoric of genocide deployed against Lumumba was simply meant to justify his elimination.

In early September 1960, President Kasavubu cynically used the pretext that Lumumba had been responsible for "genocide" in South Kasai to dismiss him as prime minister. Lumumba rejected that claim as an unconstitutional neocolonial conspiracy by Belgium and France and responded by dismissing the president. In October 1960, Mobutu, conspiring with U.S. and Belgian officials, used the Congolese military to place Lumumba under house arrest in Leopoldville. After trying to escape to his home area of Stanleyville, where his armed loyalists were rallying under Deputy Prime Minister Antoine Gizenga, Lumumba was recaptured, publically beaten, and detained at the military camp in Thysville. The ousted prime minister was bundled onto an aircraft bound for South Kasai, where he was supposed to face charges of genocide, but, at the last minute, the plane was mysteriously diverted to Katanga. In January 1961, Lumumba was killed by a firing squad commanded by a Belgian mercenary working for Tshombe, who was in direct contact with Belgian officials. Lumumba's corpse was dissolved in acid. The unsubstantiated charge of genocide was used not merely to justify Lumumba's dismissal but his murder. At the start of February, Tshombe, who knew Lumumba was dead, "expressed his astonishment at the concern shown by the United Nations with regard to the transfer to Katanga . . . of the ex-Prime Minister, despite the fact that he had been recognized as guilty of genocide by the United Nations."[19] When asked by journalists about the fate of the missing former prime minister, "Tshombe reminded his audience that the United Nations had already accused Mr. Lumumba of genocide."[20] Several weeks later, the accusations of genocide were reversed, when Tshombe's forces confronted Katanga Luba, who were supporters of the murdered prime minister. After Katangese troops were reported to have destroyed Luba villages and shot fleeing residents, UN head of operations in the Congo and Indian diplomat Rajeshwar Dayal warned Tshombe "that the behavior of his troops contains the elements of genocide."[21]

Given that Kalonji shared the pro-Western and anti-communist view of Mobutu and Kasavubu, the fall of Lumumba renewed the life of the autonomous South Kasai state. Indeed, the Congolese regime sent many supporters of Lumumba there for execution. With revenue from diamond sales, Kalonji's Luba-dominated state became increasingly militaristic and victimized minorities such as the Kanyok. The secession ended in September 1962, when a section of the South Kasai army, encouraged by Leopoldville, rebelled against Kalonji.[22]

In February 1961, the UN, prompted by the now-apparent death of Lumumba and accusations of genocide against Tshombe's regime, authorized ONUC to prevent civil war in Congo by crushing the Katanga secession. In Katanga, Tshombe's mercenary-led forces also fought the ANC and allied Luba fighters. On his way to negotiate a cease-fire in Katanga, Hammarskjold was killed on September 18 when his plane crashed in Northern Rhodesia (now Zambia). Although the official Rhodesian and UN inquiries ruled that the incident had been caused by pilot error, many questions remain about the crash, which some see as an assassination by powers or commercial interests that did not want the Katanga succession to fail. In October 1961, elements of Mobutu's ANC passed through Kasai to invade Katanga but were repulsed and during their retreat sacked Luluabourg. While the U.S. Eisenhower administration had tolerated Katanga as an anti-communist redoubt, the new Kennedy administration saw it as a neocolonial embarrassment and shifted policy toward supporting a friendly regime in the entire Congo. After a series of aggressive operations by UN forces, Tshombe surrendered in January 1963, and Katanga was reintegrated into Congo.[23]

With the suppression of separatist Katanga, ONUC withdrew from Congo, which provided an opportunity for alienated supporters of the murdered Lumumba, now seen as a martyr, who formed the National Liberation Council (CNL), based in neighboring and leftist Congo-Brazzaville. In January 1964, Pierre Mulele led a rebellion in the western area of Kwilu, and Gaston Soumialot established an insurgent staging area in Burundi, from which he recruited exiled Tutsi fighters from Rwanda (see chapter 2) and obtained arms from Communist China. During May and June, Soumialot's rebels, called "Simba," which means lion in Kiswahili, invaded eastern Congo and took the towns of Uvira and Fizi and the Lake Tanganyika port of Albertville. In August, they captured the northeastern city of Stanleyville. The CNL proclaimed the People's Republic of Congo, which was recognized by the Soviet Union, Cuba, and China. Tshombe, now strangely the prime minister of Congo, received support from the U.S. CIA and Belgium to recruit white mercenaries from South Africa, Southern Rhodesia, and France and from among Cuban exiles in the United States. They bolstered the ANC in its campaign against the CNL rebels. By April 1964, the rebellion in Kwilu was crushed. In November, Belgian paratroopers, dropped by U.S. aircraft, and mercenary-led ANC ground forces recaptured Stanleyville and other centers in the east. Although a small Cuban contingent under Ernesto "Che" Guevara arrived in eastern Congo in April 1965 to assist the rebels, the insurgency had been reduced to isolated pockets and was essentially over by the end of the year.[24]

In November 1965, ANC commander Mobutu overthrew Kasavubu and Tshombe and established a U.S.-sponsored anti-communist dictatorship. Mobutu's one-party state created a cult of personality to compensate for lack of legitimacy and competence. As such, it imposed an "authenticity" campaign, which included renaming the country Zaire, replacing colonial place names with African ones, outlawing European personal names and Western attire, and changing his own name to Mobutu Sese Seko Kuku Ngbendu Wa Za Banga (The all-powerful warrior who goes from victory to victory leaving fire in his wake). At the same time, Mobutu had political opponents tortured and murdered and created such a thoroughly corrupt regime that it inspired political scientists to coin the term "kleptocracy." Foreign allies helped overcome serious threats. With air transport provided by the United States and training by Israel, Mobutu's forces overcame a late 1960s mutiny in eastern Congo by white mercenaries whose contracts had expired and did not want to give up control of the area. During the Angolan Civil War, which had been prompted by the departure of the colonial Portuguese in 1974, Mobutu backed the National Front for the Liberation of Angola (FNLA), which was led by his brother-in-law, Holden Roberto. That backing alienated the Zairean dictator from the Popular Movement for the Liberation of Angola (MPLA), which seized power with Soviet and Cuban support. In 1977 exiled Katangese separatists based in Angola invaded Shaba Province (the new name for Katanga) but were eventually repelled by Zairean forces supported by Moroccan allies. Since the U.S. Carter administration had balked at helping Mobutu given his poor human rights record and Belgium resented his nationalization of mines, Zaire entered France's network of francophone allies in Africa. In 1978 French and Belgian airborne operations, supported logistically by the United States and the United Kingdom, defeated another Katanga separatist invasion of Shaba that threatened Western mining interests. In 1984 and 1985, Zairean forces repelled amphibious raids on Moba, a port on the western shore of Lake Tanganyika, by exiled rebels based in Tanzania.[25]

GENOCIDE OF RWANDAN REFUGEES IN CONGO (1996–1997)

Mobutu lost his long-standing U.S. and French support in the early 1990s, given the end of the Cold War. Faced with international and domestic demands for democratization, he clung to power in Zaire by engaging in proposed political reforms that went nowhere as the economy and state crumbled. In eastern Zaire's North Kivu and South Kivu provinces, violence flared over citizenship and control of land. Several groups originally from Rwanda had settled in eastern Zaire, including Tutsi pastoralists called Banyamulenge (people of Mulenge) who had moved there during the 19th century; Hutu and Tutsi laborers called Banyarwanda (people of Rwanda) who had been sent there as a labor force by Belgian colonial rulers during the 1930s; and mostly Tutsi refugees from Rwanda's 1959 social revolution and the 1963–1964 genocide. While Congo's Banyamulenge Tutsi had initially joined the Simba rebellion of the mid-1960s, the slaughter of their cattle by insurgents caused them to change allegiance to Mobutu, who rewarded them with administrative positions. In addition, many of the 1959-era Tutsi refugees were financially better off than locals and could afford to buy land and open businesses. Their prosperity led to bitter resentment, and, from 1963 to 1966, there was a wave of violence by "indigenous" Nande and Hunde people in North Kivu against anyone of "foreign" Rwandan origins, regardless of Hutu or Tutsi affiliation. Beginning in March 1993, with economic crisis and hunger, tensions resurfaced in North Kivu, with "indigenous" groups attacking "Rwandan" Hutu and Tutsi. Around 1,000 people from each of the "indigenous" and "immigrant" communities were killed, and tens of thousands were displaced. The arrival of Mobutu's dreaded security forces calmed the situation, and a series of meetings in late 1993 and early 1994 restored order.

As the primarily Tutsi Rwandan Patriotic Front (RPF) took control of Rwanda in June and July 1994, over 2 million mostly Hutu refugees poured out of the country, with over half going to Zaire's eastern provinces of North Kivu and South Kivu. Among them were elements of the former Rwandan military and Interahamwe militia, who began to reorganize and collect a war tax from civilian refugees to buy back weapons confiscated from them by Zairean forces. They worked through the Mobutu regime and France to have new weapons delivered to Goma. In early 1995, exiled Rwandan Hutu fighters based in eastern Zaire refugee camps began to infiltrate western Rwanda, particularly around the towns of Cyangugu, Kibuye, and Gisenyi, where they ambushed buses and raided schools. At the same time, the influx of Rwandan refugees in North Kivu prompted xenophobic attacks against people of Rwandan origin including some, like the Tutsi Banyamulenge, who had lived there for generations. In August 1995, the Zairian government ordered the expulsion of all refugees and immigrants from Rwanda and Burundi, including the Banyamulenge. In early 1996, violence in North Kivu escalated when Hutu militias attacked Hunde and Tutsi, and Hunde militias attacked Hutu and Tutsi. Many people of Tutsi identity fled to Rwanda. Several operations by Zairean security forces failed to stop the violence and even contributed to it: some units, their personnel not having been paid in some time by the collapsing state, received bribes to support such factions as the Banyamulenge, Hunde, or Rwandan Hutu. In South Kivu, despite the arrival of 200,000 refugees from Burundi in 1993 and 500,000 from Rwanda in 1994, the situation remained somewhat stable until June–July 1996, when attacks began on the Banyamulenge, who subsequently took up arms.[26]

The presence of exiled Rwandan Hutu Power groups and the oppression of the Tutsi Banyamulenge in eastern Zaire prompted Rwanda's new

RPF regime to intervene, resulting in the First Congo War of 1996–1997. In 1995 the RPF began to train and arm Banyamulenge fighters in Rwanda and Burundi, and, the following year, they began to infiltrate eastern Zaire along with Rwandan troops. In October 1996, the Mobutu administration officially accused Rwanda and Burundi of invading its territory. The undisciplined and unpaid Zairean soldiers simply ran away as the Banyamulenge rebels and RPF troops captured the key towns of Uvira and Bukavu. Backed by the allied states of Rwanda and Uganda, the Alliance of Democratic Forces for the Liberation of Congo (AFDL) was formed as a coalition of Zairean anti-Mobutu groups, with the Banyamulenge rebels as its nucleus and the long-exiled 1960s revolutionary Laurent Kabila as its leader. The objective of the Rwandan Patriotic Army (RPA, the name for the RPF-led Rwandan military) in supporting the AFDL rebellion was to eliminate the refugee camps in both South and North Kivu that represented a security threat to Rwanda as they housed exiled Rwandan Hutu Power fighters. As discussed in chapter 2, RPA attacks on refugee camps had started back in April 1995 at Kibeho in southern Rwanda. In September 1996, the RPA bombarded refugee camps across the border in eastern Zaire. In late October, RPA units, using armored vehicles and mortars, attacked the camps, in which some civilians were killed and others forced to flee further from the Rwandan border. By the end of October, some 600,000 people had assembled at Mugunga camp, 20 kilometers west of Goma in North Kivu, making it the largest-known refugee concentration in history. Genocide rhetoric was quickly deployed. Given the atrocious living conditions in the camps, UN secretary-general Boutros Boutros-Ghali referred to the situation as "genocide by starvation" and a physician from Doctors without Borders told a reporter that it amounted to "genocide by disease."[27] The RPA advanced into Zaire. In early November, the RPA occupied Goma, and in early December, it captured the Bukavu-Goma road junction. In mid-November, given international talks about dispatching a UN peacekeeping force to protect the camps, the RPA forcefully and quickly dismantled the remaining camps, including Mugunga. Hundreds of thousands of refugees returned to Rwanda, others fled deeper into Zaire, pursued by the AFDL and RPA for several thousand kilometers; it is likely that large numbers were massacred.

Several other neighboring states invaded Mobutu's beleaguered country. Units of the Uganda People's Defense Force (UPDF) invaded Zaire's northeastern Orientale Province on the pretext of pursuing exiled Ugandan rebels of the Alliance of Democratic Forces (ADF) and also assisted the AFDL in securing the town of Bunia. The Burundian military, in September 1996, made a foray into South Kivu, where they attacked exiled Burundian Hutu rebels of the Forces for the Defence of Democracy (FDD) and Burundian refugees. Mobutu's regime collapsed as Angolan forces, seeking to end Zaire's support for Angolan rebels, advanced across the southern border, and AFDL/Rwandan fighters pushed from the east. It appears that the United States may have provided intelligence, communications, air transport for supplies, and perhaps Special Forces advisors to the AFDL and its Rwandan and Ugandan sponsors. Although Zairean forces mostly abandoned or sold their weapons and withdrew, the retreating Rwandan exiles of the former FAR/Interahamwe fought the AFDL/RPA until late February and early March 1997, when some fled west to other countries, including the Republic of Congo (Congo-Brazzaville) and Cameroon, and others hid in isolated pockets of vast eastern Zaire. Western guilt over failing to intervene in Rwanda to stop the 1994 genocide against the Tutsi and the RPA's banning of journalists from the war zone meant that there was very little international protest over the invasion of Zaire. In May, a sickly Mobutu fled the country, and Kabila declared himself president, changed the name Zaire to Democratic Republic of Congo (DRC), and accompanied victorious AFDL forces into Kinshasa.[28]

Some have claimed that the killing of Rwandan Hutu refugees in Zaire by the RPA and its allies should be understood as genocide. Of course, the RPF regime in Kigali denied (and continues to deny) this, claiming that its forces were fighting exiled Hutu Power extremists and fugitive perpetrators of the 1994 genocide against the Tutsi in Rwanda who represented a threat to their new state. While credible eyewitness accounts state that Rwandan Hutu fighters were present in Zaire, it is clear most of the Rwandan victims of the RPA were unarmed and fleeing civilian refugees. In some cases, the RPA enlisted unwitting humanitarian workers to lure the refugees to a central location in the hopes of receiving aid, but instead they were killed. In May 1997, on the eve of Kabila's seizure of power, AFDL forces under command of Rwandan officers massacred hundreds of unarmed Rwandan Hutu refugees at Mbandaka and the nearby village of Wendji as they were waiting to cross the Congo River into the neighboring Republic of Congo. The fact that Mbandaka is about 1,200 kilometers west of Rwanda undermines the RPF argument that those operations were important for the security of their country. Indeed, the concerted effort by the RPA to attack Rwandan Hutu refugee camps across Zaire and pursue those who escaped might be interpreted as evidence of intention to exterminate a specific group based on national or ethnic origin. Later, in early 1998, a UN team investigated those attacks on Rwandan refugees in Zaire, but its activities were ended prematurely, given lack of cooperation by the recently established Kabila regime, which, at the time, was dependent on Rwandan military support. The UN team reported that it had identified 40 massacre sites and that there was evidence of planned efforts to remove bodies from mass graves and dispose of them elsewhere. The report recommended further investigation and concluded that "one possible interpretation of this phase of the operations carried out by the AFDL with Rwandan support is that a decision was taken to eliminate this part of the Hutu ethnic group as such. If proved, this would constitute genocide."[29] It has been estimated that around 230,000 Rwandan Hutu refugees disappeared in Zaire/DRC during 1996 and 1997. No one has ever been held accountable. For political scientist Emizet Kisangani, "In light of the evidence, the killing of the Hutu refugees was a calculated and premeditated course of action, which started in eastern Congo and continued to the western part where refugees crossed the border. According to Article 2 of the 1948 Genocide Convention, such acts qualified as genocide."[30]

AFRICA'S WORLD WAR (1998–2002)

The new Kabila regime in Kinshasa quickly fell out with its regional backers. Although the new Congolese Armed Forces (FAC) contained many Congolese Banyamulenge and Rwandan Tutsi and its chief of staff was RPA Lieutenant Colonel James Kabarebe, the Rwandan and Ugandan governments believed it was not committing enough troops to control exiled rebel groups in the eastern border region. Beginning in October 1997 and continuing into 1998, former FAR/Interahamwe, known as the Army for the Liberation of Rwanda (ALIR), used eastern Congo as a staging area for guerrilla attacks inside Rwanda. Consequently, the RPA launched an aggressive counterinsurgency campaign within Rwanda. Although the RPA officially withdrew from eastern DRC in September 1997, it returned in December, and the next year soldiers from Rwanda and Burundi began patrolling the Congolese towns of Uvira, Fizi, and Bukavu. Looting by Rwandan troops who locals mockingly called "Soldiers without Borders" prompted the formation of Congolese Mai Mai self-defense militias. Tutsi and non-Tutsi elements of the FAC fought each other, and non-Tutsi FAC soldiers refused to cooperate in the RPA's war against the ALIR (former FAR/Interahamwe). In December 1997, FAC soldiers, firing their weapons into the air to simulate a battle, allowed hundreds of ex-FAR Hutu fighters to pass through Bukavu en route to Rwanda. In July 1998, Kabila, under criticism for his increasingly harsh regime and for letting foreigners control the country, dismissed Kabarebe and ordered all Rwandan military personnel out of the DRC. At the start of August, FAC units in eastern DRC mutinied with the support of the RPA and adopted the name Rally for Congolese Democracy (RCD), which aimed at overthrowing Kabila. Around the same time, 1,200 RPA soldiers under Kabarebe commandeered civilian airliners at Goma airport in eastern DRC and flew to Kitona in the west of the country, which threatened the nearby capital of Kinshasa. In September, Rwandan and Ugandan forces invaded and occupied parts of eastern DRC. In northern DRC's Equateur Province, the Ugandan army sponsored a new rebel group known as the Movement for the Liberation of Congo (MLC), led by Jean-Pierre Bemba, who had links to the old Mobutu regime, which had derived its support from that region.

Since the Kabila regime had recently joined the Southern African Development Community (SADC), it was able to call on military assistance from Zimbabwe, Angola, and Namibia. Zimbabwe wanted to secure business deals with Kabila; Angola wanted to continue its support for Kabila to obstruct the activities of Angolan rebels in the DRC; and Namibia supported its long-time ally Angola. Other SADC members, including South Africa, Botswana, and Zambia, were not eager to intervene in support of the unelected Kabila. Within the DRC, the Angolan military quickly destroyed the RPA expeditionary force near Kitona, as Zimbabwean forces secured Kinshasa, where mobs killed suspected rebel infiltrators and anyone who looked like a Tutsi. However, Congolese rebels and Rwandan and Ugandan troops quickly took control of key towns in eastern DRC. Other African countries became involved. Since Uganda was backing rebels in southern Sudan, the Sudanese government convinced Chad to send an expedition to support Kabila, and those troops were transported on Libyan aircraft. Sudan also recruited Rwandan former FAR/Interahamwe and sent them to fight in the DRC. Kabila and his allies mobilized exiled Rwandan and Burundian Hutu fighters to pit against the RPA. Kabila's regime enlisted former FAR/Interahamwe from such neighboring countries as the Central African Republic and the Republic of Congo, gave them weapons and training, and sent them to fight in the east and north. Burundian FDD fighters were recruited from refugee camps in Tanzania, trained and equipped in Zimbabwe, and sent to their new base in Lubumbashi in southern DRC. During the first half of 1999, the Rwandan-led RCD/RPA alliance advanced through Kasai and North Katanga toward the diamond-mining center of Mbuji-Mayi, but Zimbabwean troops halted their progress. The fighting around Mbuji-Mayi also involved some 8,000 ex-FAR/Interahamwe flown in on Angolan and Zimbabwean aircraft. The involvement of so many countries and exiled groups in the DRC inspired U.S. assistant secretary of state Susan Rice to dub the conflict the first "African World War."

The war stalemated with a static "frontline"—in reality a series of pockets in which enemy forces opposed one another rather than a continuous war zone—running from Mbandaka in the northwest through Kananga (formerly Luluabourg) and Mbuji-Mayi to Pweto in the southeast. The DRC was effectively partitioned, with areas occupied by various state forces and rebel groups. In Equateur Province, Bemba's MLC remained popular as locals anticipated the return of a northern-dominated regime and disciplined Ugandan troops behaved well. However, in the east, the RCD lacked legitimacy: it was seen as a puppet of Rwanda, its leadership quarreled, and RCD/RPA troops victimized communities in a continuing conflict with enclaves of Mai Mai and ALIR fighters. Many Tutsi Banyamulenge leaders now felt that Rwanda was cynically using them for its own reasons, opposed the RPA occupation, and rejected the RCD. In early 1999, some Banyamulenge rebels began fighting the RPA and eventually allied with their old Mai Mai enemies. In August 1999 and May–June 2000, soldiers from Uganda and Rwanda, along with their respective rebel clients, fought each other in Kisangani. The RCD split into rival factions, consisting of pro-Uganda RCD-Kisangani (RCD-K) and pro-Rwanda RCD-Goma (RCD-G). As the war continued, most external forces began to steal and illegally export DRC mineral resources such as diamonds, coltan, and cassiterite. The swelling of the global electronics industry fueled demand and increased profits for some of those resources. A UN investigation revealed that the armies of Rwanda, Uganda, and Zimbabwe were involved in theft of DRC minerals.

In July 1999, all major actors in the war agreed to a cease-fire and peace process called the Lusaka Agreement, which was meant to be supervised by the new UN Mission in the Democratic Republic of Congo (MONUC). However, Kabila's stubbornness and Western international sympathy for Rwanda and Uganda delayed the deployment of UN peacekeepers, which meant the war resumed. In late 1999, both major rebel groups and their supporters attempted to advance down different rivers toward Kinshasa, with the MLC/Ugandans on the Ubangi and the RCD-G/Rwandans on the Tshuapa. That action was blocked by FAC and Zimbabwean troops, but a counteroffensive launched by Kabila proved disastrous. With their failure to advance down the Tshuapa, the Rwandans abandoned the goal of establishing a new puppet government in Kinshasa and focused on securing the mineral wealth of Kasai and Katanga. When Kigali, where the RPF's Paul Kagame had recently become president, announced in August 2000 that it would withdraw its troops 200 kilometers from the frontline, the diplomatically incompetent Kabila exploited the opportunity by initiating an offensive in northeast Katanga in which FAC units were supplemented by former FAR/Interahamwe and Burundian FDD. The RCD-G and RPA immediately staged an effective counterattack that pushed south to grab the much-contested town of Pweto at the start of December. The RCD-G/RPA was prevented from moving on the city of Lubumbashi by Zimbabwean reinforcements that were flown right up to the frontline at Lake Mweru.

In January 2001, Kabila was assassinated by his own bodyguards and swiftly replaced by his son, Joseph Kabila, who was more open to negotiation. The new Bush administration in the United States, less burdened by guilt for failing to act against the 1994 genocide in Rwanda than its predecessor, appeared less sympathetic to Kigali and insisted it honor the Lusaka Agreement. The foreign powers involved in the DRC war were now looking for an exit, as the expensive and internationally embarrassing conflict could no longer be paid for by looted minerals. Throughout 2001 and 2002, the young Kabila attended a series of international meetings that resulted in foreign forces withdrawing from the frontline. In April

2002, at Sun City in South Africa, the Kabila regime and the MLC rebels signed an agreement to form a unified, multiparty government and hold elections, but their negotiations were rejected by RCD-G. At the end of July, Kinshasa and Kigali signed the Pretoria Accord, in which the former promised to dismantle and disarm ex-FAR/Interahamwe groups in eastern DRC and the latter agreed to extract its forces. The September Luanda Agreement followed, in which the DRC and Uganda made peace, and the latter committed to bring its soldiers home. By late October 2002, most foreign forces had left the DRC, except the Ugandans, who withdrew in June 2003. In mid-December 2002 in South Africa, all the major DRC parties, consisting of the Kabila regime, MLC, three RCD factions, Mai Mai militias, and civil society representatives signed the Global and Inclusive Accord (AGI), in which they agreed to form a shared government with Kabila as president, to integrate the armed groups into a new national military, and to hold elections within two years. The settlement was ratified by all parties at another meeting in Sun City in April 2003. The renewal of negotiations meant that the number of MONUC peacekeepers in the DRC increased from just 200 in December 2000 to 2,400 by October 2001 and 4,200 by the end of 2002.[31]

The number of people who died as a result of "Africa's World War" has been hotly debated. Given the inaccessibility of the area during the conflict, it is not possible to calculate precise fatality figures, and estimates are based on demographic studies that extrapolate from small local surveys. During the conflict, the International Rescue Committee (IRC), a long-established international humanitarian organization, regularly studied and reported the mounting death toll. It ultimately concluded that between August 1998 and November 2002 some 3.3 million people had died as a result of conflict in the DRC, which made it the world's deadliest conflict since the end of the Second World War. Extending the period from 1998 to 2004 resulted in a figure of 3.9 million war-related deaths, and a further expansion from 1998 to 2007, given the continuation of violence in the DRC, resulted in a figure of 5.4 million deaths attributed to conflict. It was noted that the vast majority of those deaths were not caused by direct violence but by disease and hunger related to population displacement and state collapse. Those extremely high fatality figures were used to convince the UN to dispatch and maintain the world's largest peace-keeping force in the DRC.[32] They also resulted in widespread accusations from Congolese that they were the victims of genocide initiated in 1998 by the U.S.-backed Rwandan and Ugandan invaders. Many Congolese maintained that they had not been involved in the 1994 genocide in Rwanda but were paying the price for it, as the RPA invaded the Congo and looted its resources on the pretext of ensuring Rwanda's security. For example, Yaa-Lengi M. Ngemi cites the IRC fatality figures when he accuses US President Bill Clinton of "supporting Rwanda, Uganda and Burundi in their invasion and occupation of part of the Congo, and in their carrying this genocide against the Congolese people, with the Congo's minerals and other resources being stolen from the occupied areas by both these three countries and the American and European corporations operating there."[33] However, more recently, the Canadian-based Human Security Report Project (HSRP) has criticized IRC research methodology for underestimating the peacetime death rate in the DRC and thus dramatically inflating its estimate of war-related deaths. For the HSRP, which acknowledges the gravity of the conflict in the DRC, many of the millions of Congolese who died during the war would have perished regardless, given the country's historically poor living conditions. As such, it is possible that in reality several hundred thousand people—not millions—died from war-related causes in the DRC during Africa's World War of 1998 to 2002 and that the figure increases to around 800,000 for the longer period of 1998 to 2007.[34] To some extent, arguments over death totals and related accusations of genocide are similar to claims made concerning the impact of early colonization on the Congo. For some, the higher number of deaths, the more appropriate it is to employ the term genocide. As previously discussed, however, that is a fallacy; the international legal definition of genocide makes no mention of number of deaths. Intention is the key point, and in the case of Africa's World War, there is no indication that anyone planned to exterminate part or all of the Congolese population. Lack of intention should not be seen as a vindication of the powers who were involved in the war. Just like Leopold II a century earlier, the Congolese and foreign leaders who joined in what might be called the "Scramble for Congo" from 1998 to 2002 cannot be described as genocidal, but they were certainly bent on greedily looting the country's natural resources and did not care about the people who suffered and died in the process.

CONTINUING VIOLENCE AND ACCUSATIONS OF GENOCIDE (2003–2013)

Violence in eastern DRC continued after the formal withdrawal of foreign forces in 2002–2003. Accusations of genocide and genocidal intentions increased as local groups had seen how effectively the RPF government of Rwanda and its sympathizers had employed such rhetoric in previous years. Foreign occupation had created a deadly legacy in the DRC. In 1999 the Ugandan military occupying Congo's northeastern Orientale Province created a separate local administration for the eastern portion, which became the new Ituri Province. That action enflamed existing tensions between the area's Hema pastoralists and Lendu cultivators, as the Ugandans appeared to favor the former. The Belgian colonial rulers and Mobutu's regime had also favored the Hema, who formed a local, administrative, land-holding, and economic elite. Tensions in Ituri worsened during 2001 with the split of RCD-K into a supposedly pro-Hema RCD-ML (Liberation Movement) and the allegedly pro-Lendu RCD-K. While each side expressed growing fear of genocide perpetrated by the other, control of the province's rich mineral resources (particularly gold) provided a material motivation for conflict. Ugandan officers justified their continued occupation of Ituri as necessary to prevent genocide among those groups. Around 2002, with Ugandan withdrawal imminent, Hema militias accepted military support from Rwanda, which wanted to gain access to the mineral wealth of the area and counter Ugandan influence. Hema leaders compared themselves to Rwanda's Tutsi and their local Lendu enemies to the Hutu. A Hema chief stated that the Tutsi leaders of Rwanda "had lived through a genocide so they knew what it was like. They understood me and provided us with weapons and logistics." On the other hand, Lendu militias began to accuse Uganda and Rwanda of trying to establish a Tutsi-Hema empire in the region that would exterminate other groups.[35]

During the first half of 2003, the Ugandan military withdrawal from Ituri Province resulted in heightened violence between Hema and Lendu militias. At the same time, representatives of the historically marginalized Mbuti Twa (pygmy) minority reported to the UN Indigenous People's Forum that their community had become subject to genocide and cannibalism by various factions, particularly the MLC in 2002 and more recently by local Ituri militias.[36] In April 2003, MONUC deployed an 800-strong Uruguayan battalion in Bunia, but this force, although it saved many lives, was insufficient to stop the fighting. In June, Lendu militias and the Hema Union of Congolese Patriots (UPC), led by Thomas Lubanga—who had formerly been under the protection of Uganda but now was supported by Rwanda—fought each other over Bunia, resulting in thousands of civilians fleeing to the local MONUC headquarters and airport. Both Hema and Lendu militias massacred civilians of the opposite ethnicity. At the end of August, UN envoy Iulia Motoc, a Romanian scholar of international law, visited Bunia and declared that genocide and other war crimes and crimes against humanity may have been committed in Ituri and urged an international investigation.[37] The rhetoric of genocide was powerful enough to prompt the European Union to undertake its first autonomous military operation (Operation Artemis) outside Europe. With UN approval, an Interim Emergency Multinational Force (IEMF), consisting mostly of French troops, arrived in Bunia in June and secured the town but did nothing to disarm the ethnic militias. In September, the IEMF was replaced by MONUC's new Ituri brigade. which imposed a weapon-free zone on Bunia. However, violence resumed in October and continued into the next year. In 2005 MONUC launched aggressive cordon and search operations against the Ituri militias. By late June, a UN ultimatum to surrender weapons or join the integrated national army resulted in the disarming of 15,600 out of an estimated 20,000 fighters. In February 2007, the Lendu Nationalist and Integrationist Front (FNI) became the last Ituri militia group to begin handing in weapons to UN officials. However, over the subsequent years, new armed groups involved in mineral smuggling clashed with DRC government forces trying to exert control over the province. No one has ever been charged with the crime of genocide for events in Ituri. In March 2005, the UPC's Lubanga, who was detained by the DRC interim government, became the first person ever arrested on an International Criminal Court (ICC) warrant. The Hema militia leader was sent to The Hague in the Netherlands and eventually found guilty of conscripting child soldiers and sentenced to 14 years imprisonment. Pro-Lendu militia leaders Germain Katanga and Mathieu Ngudjolo Chui were handed over to the ICC by the DRC authorities in 2007 and 2008, respectively, and charged with crimes against humanity and war crimes for massacres of Hema people in 2003. Chui was released in 2012, given lack of evidence, and Katanga was convicted two years later.[38]

The 2002 Pretoria Agreement failed to end conflict between Rwanda and exiled Rwandan Hutu groups based in the eastern DRC provinces of South Kivu and North Kivu. While Rwanda had defeated the ALIR during its 1998 invasion of the DRC, the 2001–2002 peace process allowed former FAR/Interahamwe elements who had been mobilized by the Kabila regime to reestablish themselves in that region as the Democratic Forces for the Liberation of Rwanda (FDLR). When the DRC government halted official support for the FDLR as part of the wider 2002 peace process, Hutu rebels obtained weapons and ammunition from the local Mai Mai militia and corrupt Congolese military commanders. While the Rwanda Defence Forces (RDF—the new name of the RPA) officially evacuated the DRC in September 2002, it left behind a small covert presence to combat exiled Hutu militants and acquire valuable resources. The Rwandan government convinced some important FDLR officers to join the RDF, and some 7,000 Hutu fighters returned home between 2003 and 2007 as part of a reconciliation project. However, the continued presence of 5,000 FDLR insurgents in eastern DRC provided Kigali with an ongoing excuse to intervene across the border in pursuit of the dreaded *genocidaires*.

With encouragement from Rwanda, some Congolese Tutsi Banyamulenge officers from RCD-G refused to integrate into Congo's new armed forces and claimed to protect local Tutsi civilians from the FDLR. In May 2003, General Laurent Nkunda, a Congolese veteran of the 1994 RPF campaign in Rwanda, led mutinous Congolese Tutsi troops from Goma in North Kivu to Bukavu in South Kivu, where they killed several hundred loyalist troops and civilians and raped and looted as MONUC peacekeepers stood by. Given diplomatic pressure from the UN, the United States, and Britain, the Kigali government encouraged Nkunda's forces to leave Bukavu, and the returning Congolese army took revenge on local Banyamulenge, with

3,000 fleeing to Rwanda. In late 2004, Rwandan troops crossed the border to attack the FDLR and supplied weapons to Nkunda's fighters, which enabled them to repel a Congolese army offensive with over 100,000 civilians displaced in the violence. The media-savvy Nkunda, at the time of the tenth anniversary of the Rwandan genocide, claimed to be fighting to prevent another genocide of Tutsi in the DRC. At the end of March 2005, following a MONUC demand for FDLR to disarm, the group's chairman, Ignace Murwanashyaka, renounced the 1994 genocide and violence and requested to return to Rwanda to participate in politics, but that request was dismissed by Kigali. In 2005 and 2006, UN and Congolese forces conducted offensive operations against the FDLR, which simply moved deeper into the bush. In 2006 Nkunda's mutineers enlarged their territory in North Kivu and sought legitimacy by forming the National Congress for the Defence of the People (CNDP), which claimed to protect minorities. The implication was that Congolese Tutsi needed to retain their weapons to protect themselves from genocide by the Hutu FDLR.[39]

After defeating another Congolese army offensive in 2008, Nkunda signed a peace agreement that involved a cease-fire, the return of civilians to their homes, and amnesty; but he continued to insist on FDLR disarmament. In late October 2008, the CNDP renewed hostilities against the Congolese government by seizing a major military camp near the Virunga National Park, which it used as a staging area for a southward advance toward Goma. Congolese and UN soldiers withdrew, leaving Mai Mai militia and FDLR to resist, and 100,000 people were displaced. In January 2009, the CNDP split with General Bosco "the Terminator" Ntaganda, a Congolese Tutsi who had fought with the RPF in the early 1990s, heading a faction that agreed to integrate into the Congolese military and transform their group into a political party. Unable to defeat the CNDP militarily, the Kabila administration made a deal with Rwanda to allow its forces to cross the border to engage the FDLR if they removed Nkunda. Later that month, Nkunda and his remaining three battalions were defeated by a combined Congolese Army–RDF operation that cleared rebels from the border area, and the fugitive general was arrested when he fled into Rwanda. He was never seen again. The FDLR regrouped, attacked villages, and clashed with the Congolese army in South Kivu.

In April 2012, Ntaganda and several hundred former CNDP fighters mutinied from the Congolese army after rumors spread that they were to be transferred away from their North Kivu home and that their leader was to face war crimes charges at the ICC. Calling themselves the March 23 Movement, or M23, in memory of the day in 2009 when they joined the political process, the mutineers rallied under the military leadership of Colonel Sultani Makenga in the Virunga National Park and then seized several towns near Goma. In November 2012, M23 fighters temporarily occupied Goma, which was suddenly abandoned by Congolese and UN troops, where they captured heavy weapons and ammunition. Although the Rwandan government denied international accusations that it was supplying M23, that claim soured its relations with the UN and the United States. In March 2013, Ntaganda, facing dissent within his movement and loss of support from Rwanda, surrendered himself to the U.S. embassy in Kigali and was eventually transported to The Hague. In November 2013, a UN special-intervention brigade consisting of South African, Tanzanian, and Malawian units together with Congolese forces embarked on an offensive that crushed the M23 movement, with many of its fighters fleeing into Uganda.[40]

The FDLR continued to function in parts of eastern Congo, where they became involved in illegal mineral extraction and smuggling facilitated by members of the Congolese military. By the late 2000s, the rank and file of the FDLR were mostly displaced and impoverished youth who had not been involved in the 1994 genocide in Rwanda. However, FDLR military commander General Sylvestre Mudacumura had been deputy commander of the Rwandan presidential guard during the 1994 genocide and in 2012 became the subject of an international arrest warrant for war crimes committed in eastern DRC. Some of the FDLR's European-based political leaders have been prosecuted for crimes committed in the DRC. In 2009 FDLR political leaders Ignace Murwanashyaka and Straton Musoni were arrested in Germany, where they were eventually convicted of crimes against humanity and war crimes and sentenced to 13 and 8 years imprisonment, respectively. In 2011 Callixte Mbarushimana, FDLR secretary, was arrested in France and sent to the ICC in The Hague, where he faced similar charges, but those were dropped because of insufficient evidence, and he was released in December 2012. In late February 2015, after the expiry of a demand by regional leaders for the FDLR to disarm, the Congolese military launched an offensive against the Hutu group, though UN support was withheld given the alleged involvement of several Congolese commanders in previous atrocities. While the Tanzanian and South African governments—which provided troops to the UN intervention brigade—expressed concern over the potential for heavy civilian casualties given the integration of the FDLR with local communities, the Rwandan government criticized the slowness of the UN to act against this group, which it continues to portray as a security threat.[41]

CONCLUSION

The modern history of the DRC is replete with accusations and counteraccusations of genocide. However, almost all of the accusations fail to meet international legal standards and may even fail to correspond with some of the alterative and broader definitions of genocide. The reign of terror imposed by Leopold II's Congo Free State in the late 19th century, though terrible, does not qualify as a retroactive genocide because there was no intent to exterminate. The allegation that Patrice Lumumba, independent Congo's first prime minister who so troubled the Americans and Belgians, perpetrated genocide against the Luba of Kasai in 1960 was an obvious contrivance to justify his overthrow and murder. Such demonizing language was not only employed by Katanga separatist leader Moise Tshombe but by the highest UN official. The deaths of hundreds of thousands or perhaps millions of Congolese during Africa's World War from 1998 to 2002 also fails to satisfy the legal definition of genocide; the domestic and foreign leaders involved were predatory, negligent, and greedy but not intentionally genocidal. In this they were reminiscent of Leopold II. While many rival groups in Ituri and the Kivus invoked the language of genocide after 2003, the violence that plagued those areas did not result in genocide, though terrible violence did take place. Accusations and fears of genocide became excuses for rebel and militia groups to retain their weapons so they could continue to control their fiefdoms and extract wealth. The only example of mass violence in Congo's history that seems to approach the legal standard required to prove an accusation of genocide occurred in 1996 and 1997 when the Rwandan military and its Congolese rebel allies attacked Rwandan Hutu refugees and pursued them for more than 1,000 kilometers across Central Africa. The concerted transcontinental chase would seem to indicate intent to destroy, and the target group was identified on the basis of national and ethnic identity. Of course, the counterargument is that the Rwandan and Congolese forces were in pursuit of dangerous Hutu Power fighters who had perpetrated genocide in Rwanda and were using civilian refugees as human shields, which led to unfortunate collateral damage. Ironically, the fight against genocide can potentially become an alibi for genocide.

CHAPTER 5

Sudan and South Sudan

Sudan's President Omar al-Bashir is the world's first sitting head of state to be indicted by the International Criminal Court (ICC) for genocide, crimes against humanity, and war crimes. Despite the existence of an international arrest warrant for him, al-Bashir frequently travels to countries in Africa, Asia, and the Middle East, where he has become something of a celebrity for defying what is often perceived as Western neocolonialism. Al-Bashir's foreign visits have sometimes resulted in controversy and embarrassment: for example, during a 2015 trip to South Africa, his aircraft was allowed to depart despite the issuing of a court order that he should remain in the country while a legal process determined whether to deliver him to the ICC. He is supported by the Arab League and the African Union (AU), and his presidential aircraft has sometimes been escorted by Sudanese jet fighters to prevent its interception in international airspace by powers that might want to enforce the warrant. Many see his indictment as evidence of double standards and neocolonialism in international justice, as African leaders seem to be the only ones prosecuted while their Western counterparts are free to commit horrendous atrocities. The indictment is also seen as an obstacle to lasting peace in Sudan, as a leader facing international criminal charges has little incentive to compromise when doing so may result in his incarceration. Others, including human rights activists, claim that allowing impunity for those responsible for mass violence will only encourage similar actions in the future. Although the al-Bashir indictment stems specifically from allegations of state-sponsored genocide and other crimes against communities in Darfur in western Sudan, there were other instances related to Sudan's long North-South Civil War, in which credible accusations of genocide were leveled against the Khartoum government. More recently, concerns of possible genocide have emerged within the context of newly independent South Sudan's own civil war.

The history of modern Sudan has been influenced by a particularly dangerous combination of racial, religious, ethnic, and regional identities and tensions that have been superimposed over competition for resources such as grazing land and oil. Since independence in 1956, Sudan has experienced long periods of violence and warfare, including two major North-South civil wars that eventually led to the 2011 separation of South Sudan, which has itself become the scene of conflict, and ongoing insurgencies in Sudan's western regions of Darfur and Kordofan. All of those conflicts produced genocide allegations. Although it is often confusing for outsiders, modern Sudanese have come to perceive themselves as belonging to different racial categories that are complex and fluid but can broadly be defined as Arab and African. Looking to the Middle East as a cultural and religious home, those subscribing to the Arab identity often speak Arabic as a first language, practice an orthodox form of Islam, sometimes (but not always) have a light skin color or specific types of names, and in some areas are associated with historically nomadic and pastoral communities. People from marginalized regions such as the south and the west who are not included or who have resisted inclusion in the Arab identity are usually categorized as African, or black. Those understood as African can be Muslim, Christian, or traditionalist, usually speak local African languages, may or may not have darker skin, and in some areas are associated with settled farming communities. The historically dominant Arabs see themselves as superior to the blacks, who are perceived as uncivilized, descendants of slaves, and a natural servant class. Furthermore, black Sudanese are often seen as migrant workers from an impoverished periphery and are frequently the brunt of racial jokes and negative stereotypes. The marginalized and resistant Africans seek external sympathy and support by portraying themselves as indigenous people who have been unjustly conquered and exploited by the supposedly foreign Arabs. In turn, the Sudanese Arabs insist that they are also Africans.[1]

THE SULTANATE OF DARFUR

The Fur people live in the western Nile River Basin around the mountains of Jebel Marra. Their area is called Darfur, meaning "land of the Fur." Speaking a Nilo-Saharan language called Fur, they have been cultivators and herders for a long time and have a history of trade with camel-raising nomads to the north and cattle-raising nomads to the south. While the Sultanate of Darfur may have originated in the 1400s, the founding warrior-leader Sulayman Solongdungu established its ruling Keira dynasty in the late 1600s and expanded his authority over a number of other farming communities such as the Masalit to the west and the Zaghawa to the north. Over time, Darfur became a multiethnic kingdom with the Fur at its center. It is likely that Sulayman wanted to increase his state's access to slaves, which were traded north to Egypt and east to the Nile for weapons, armor, war horses, and luxury cloth, with which to reward subordinate rulers. Slaves also served as soldiers in the Darfur sultan's army. Although Sulayman is popularly credited with introducing Islam to Darfur, the conversion process was a long one, undertaken by a series of wandering holy men associated with subsequent rulers. Nevertheless, Islam in Darfur became syncretic as many aspects of traditional local religion continued to be practiced, particularly among women.

From around 1700 to 1780, Darfur attempted to expand west through a frontier of hills and rivers and engaged in a long series of wars against the neighboring Sultanate of Wadai, located in what is now Chad. Since Wadai proved too strong to conquer and maintained control of the central trans-Saharan trade route from Fezzan to Tripoli on the North African coast, Darfur turned its attentions eastward to the open savannah of Kordofan that led to the Nile and its Arab cultural and religious influences. The shift in Darfur's regional focus created a lasting cultural and linguistic division between non-Arabic languages to the west and Arabic language to the east. In the 1780s, Darfur's Sultan Muhammad Tayrab initiated the conquest of Kordofan, which was completed by his successor, Abd al-Rahman, who established the first permanent capital at Al Fasher to the east of the Jebel Marra in 1792. The conquest of Kordofan increased Darfur's trade and communication with Egypt, including during the latter's brief period of French occupation at the turn of the 18th and 19th centuries.

In 1820 and 1821, Muhammad Ali, the modernizing ruler of Egypt, organized an invasion of what is now Sudan in an attempt to acquire gold and slaves for his new army. The Egyptians established the administrative center of Khartoum at the confluence of the Blue and White Nile; occupied Sennar, which had been the capital of the declining Funj state; and pushed into Kordofan. In August 1821, at the Battle of Bara, a 3,000-strong army from Egypt invaded Kordofan and used its firearms and cannon to defeat a Darfur army of 8,000 infantry and 1,200 cavalry. Egyptian plans to invade Darfur were abandoned when the invading army had to return to the Nile to suppress resistance there. Although the Egyptian conquest of Kordofan initially disrupted Darfur's trade with Egypt, business was reestablished and expanded in the 1840s and 1850s. That prompted Darfur to mount campaigns south into the Bahr el Ghazal region in search of more slaves and ivory for export. As such, Darfur came into conflict with decentralized groups of cattle-raising and Arabic-speaking Baqqara nomads on its southern frontier.[2]

Between 1856 and 1865, Khartoum warlord Al-Zubayr Rahma Mansur established a private army in Bahr el Ghazal that used firearms and river boats to dominate the region, from where he sent ivory and slaves to the Nile and then on to Egypt. In the 1860s, Egyptian antislavery policies deprived Al-Zubayr of the Nile trade route, which made him enter into an agreement with the Rizayqat Baqqara nomads, so that he could send his caravans north along an overland route through their territory. As a result,

Darfur was denied the resources of the Bahr el Ghazal frontier and control of the trade routes leading in and out of it. Conflict developed between Darfur and Al-Zubayr when, in 1873, the former reasserted its influence over some Rizayqat Baqqara groups, who began to attack the latter's caravans. That same year Al-Zubayr—whose forces had just defeated the army of newly arrived Khartoum adventurer Muhammad al-Bulalawi—accepted the position of Egyptian governor of Bahr el Ghazal. In 1874 Al-Zubayr's army, eventually supplemented by Egyptian forces, invaded and conquered Darfur, which became part of Egyptian-ruled Sudan. Militarily, the invaders enjoyed an enormous advantage in terms of firepower. Darfur's Sultan Ibrahim Qarad was killed in the last battle of the war and his family exiled to Egypt. Over the next few years, Darfur became the scene of a number of rebellions against Egyptian rule. In 1881 Charles Gordon, the British officer whom the Egyptians had made governor general of Sudan, appointed the young Austrian adventurer Rudolf Carl von Slatin as governor of Darfur. Slatin led campaigns that wore down rebels associated with the overthrown Keira dynasty.

In June 1881, the increasingly popular religious Sudanese leader Muhammad Ahmad proclaimed himself the Mahdi, a savior chosen by God to restore Islam to its pure form, and organized an army for holy war against the Egyptian occupation of Sudan. The movement had little support among the Fur, Masalit, and other farming people of the Darfur region who did not speak much Arabic and whose religion combined elements of Islam and traditional beliefs. However, the nomadic Arabic-speaking Baqqara of Darfur—who had also been influenced by traveling Fulani holy men who told them about the early-19th-century jihad that had established the Sokoto Caliphate in what is now northern Nigeria—joined the Mahdi's cause and rebelled against the Egyptian regime in the early 1880s. That added a strong religious element to the socioeconomic division between Fur and Baqqara. In January 1884, Slatin, who had led fierce resistance to the Mahdi's rebellion but lost heart after the annihilation of a British-led Egyptian relief force at Shaykan, surrendered to the Mahdists and was imprisoned in Khartoum. Darfur now fell under the Mahdists, who captured Khartoum and killed Gordon a year later. Although the Mahdi died in 1885 and was succeeded by Abdallahi ibn Mohammed, known as Khalifa (successor or steward), who originated from southwest Darfur, this had little impact on the people of that region who resented what they saw as another type of foreign rule. The Mahdist policy of conscripting young men for military service in Khartoum led to rebellion by the Baqqara, which was suppressed by Mahdist governor Yusuf Ibrahim, who was a Fur and son of the dead sultan. Subsequently, two rebellions broke out in Darfur against the Mahdists: one led by Yusuf, who was killed by an expedition from Khartoum, and another by a mysterious holy man called Abu Jummayza, who led Masalit, Fur, and Zaghawa rebels until his death in 1889. In 1891 Ali Dinar, a member of the Keira royal family who had succeeded Yusuf, and a few remaining rebels surrendered to the Mahdist governor at Al Fasher and were exiled to Khartoum.

In 1898 Anglo-Egyptian forces, advancing south from Egypt, defeated the Mahdists at the Battle of Omdurman near Khartoum and reconquered the Sudan. Around the time of the battle, Ali Dinar and his retainers escaped from Khartoum and returned to Al Fasher, where they seized control. Darfur recovered its autonomy as the British, who did not want to administer an area they considered unimportant, recognized Ali Dinar as sultan in return for an annual payment. Over the next few years, Ali Dinar suppressed the Mahdist remnants in Darfur and dispatched forces south to push back the Baqqara cattle-nomads. However, he had to accept the existence of a new Masalit Sultanate to the west that had emerged during the chaos of the Mahdist occupation, and the Rizayqat Baqqara became autonomous through support from the British in neighboring Kordofan. An important impact of the Mahdist era in Darfur was that the region's peoples became more sharply divided between devotees of purist Islam, who tended to be Arabic-speaking nomads, and those who practiced a local and broadly Sudanic version of Islam, who tended to belong to Fur or other farming communities.

In 1910 fighting broke out when French colonial forces from Chad pushed east into Darfur. Consequently, the French government requested that the British occupy the sultanate. In 1915 Sir Reginald Wingate, British commander of the Egyptian Army who had wanted to occupy Darfur after the Battle of Omdurman, pressured London to approve a British offensive against Darfur. He falsely claimed that German/Ottoman agents, within the context of the ongoing world war, were encouraging the sultan of Darfur to attack the British in neighboring Sudan. Wingate also realized that the French wanted to expand east from Chad into Darfur, and, with the occupation of German Cameroon, they would soon have the forces to do so. With permission from his old colleague in Sudan, Lord Kitchener, who was now London's secretary of state for war, Wingate organized the 2,000-strong Western Frontier Force (WFF), which was British led but composed entirely of Egyptian army units, some of which were made up of Sudanese soldiers. In late May 1916, the WFF decisively defeated the Fur army and sacked the capital of Al Fasher. After Sultan Ali Dinar was found and killed by a WFF patrol, Darfur was incorporated into the Anglo-Egyptian Sudan.

During Sudan's colonial era, the Nile River and Khartoum became the territory's economic and administrative center, with an emerging Western-educated northern Sudanese elite. On the other hand, Darfur became marginalized and was divided into a patchwork of ethnically defined tribal authorities administered by a network of local notables supervised by a few British officials. This system of indirect rule—the practice of governing through seemingly age-old local institutions—became the standard administrative practice of British colonial Africa because it was cheap and reduced resistance by creating the illusion that colonialism had not changed anything. Over the long term, it created intense regionalism and disparity, which resulted in problems for the future of many African countries. In Darfur, the colonial definition of tribal groups and the imposition of tribal administrations and ethnic homelands (called dars) created a view of the region's history as one of long conflict between indigenous Africans and settler Arabs, who were viewed as members of different and naturally antagonistic races. As they did in southern Sudan, which will be discussed below, the British limited outsider access to Darfur and allowed only the sons of tribal chiefs to pursue Western education. Many men left impoverished Darfur and became migrant workers on colonial agricultural projects around the Nile. A 1921 rebellion, largely caused by taxation, was suppressed and blamed on a brief resurgence of Mahdism.[3]

THE COLD WAR ERA: SUDAN, LIBYA, CHAD, AND DARFUR (1956–1990)

At the time of Sudan's independence in 1956, the marginalized western region of Darfur had become home to people with two rival identities: Arab pastoralists who considered themselves purist Muslims and non-Arab cultivators who practiced a localized form of Islam. Since the new Sudanese government inherited and accepted the British colonial view of a racialized country, Arab and non-Arab (African or black) identities began to crystallize. Officials from northern Sudan took over from British ones, and in 1971, in the name of modernization, Darfur's system of traditional government was abolished without an effective replacement. By the 1980s, population growth and desertification had led to intense competition over land between herders and farmers who subscribed to rival identities.

From the late 1960s, tensions between Darfur's racialized communities were enflamed by the impact of several interconnected conflicts involving Chad, Libya, and Sudan. Gaining independence from France in 1960, Chad struggled with regionalism: it had a relatively poor and arid north with a predominantly Muslim population and a comparatively prosperous south with Christian-traditionalist inhabitants. That led to a series of Chadian civil wars on which was superimposed global Cold War tensions and the personal ambitions of Libyan dictator Muammar Gaddafi. Seizing power in a 1969 coup, Gaddafi pursued grandiose dreams of establishing his own Islamic State of the Sahel, which would consist of Libya, Chad, and Sudan and facilitate the broad Arab cultural domination of the region. Under Gaddafi, who ironically also claimed to be a champion of Pan-Africanism, Libyans perceived to be of African descent, including the Toubou, were victimized. To create his great Sahelian state, Gaddafi established an Islamic Legion made up of Tuaregs from Mali and Niger and Pakistanis and Bangladeshis who had come to Libya as migrant workers but eventually found themselves fighting in Chad and other countries. From the 1960s to 1980s, France, and sometimes the United States, backed a succession of southern-based Chadian governments, and neighboring Libya and the Soviet Union sponsored northern insurgents. In the 1970s, Libya sent troops into Chad to seize the supposedly uranium-rich Aouzou Strip and directly support northern rebels. This foreign intervention prompted a split within northern Chad's insurgent movement between the anti-Libyan Armed Forces of the North (FAN) under Hissene Habre and the pro-Libyan People's Armed Forces (FAP) under Goukouni Oueddei. Oueddei established a pro-Libyan regime in Chad from 1979 to 1982 but was overthrown by Habre's FAN, which was renamed Chadian National Armed Forces (FANT). During much of the 1980s, Chad became divided between a south ruled by Habre, who was directly supported by French troops on the ground and indirectly by the United States, and a north occupied by Oueddei's rebel alliance, backed by Libyan forces. Oueddei eventually fell out with the erratic Gaddafi, who favored another Arab and Islamist Chadian rebel group called the Volcan Army, which was hostile to other groups perceived as predominantly black. In 1987's Toyota War, Habre and Oueddei formed an alliance that drove the Libyans out of most of northern Chad and into Darfur.[4]

As a marginalized frontier area, Darfur served as a staging area and sanctuary for a succession of rebel movements from Chad. Darfur's ability to provide sanctuary was facilitated by the lack of an effective border between Chad and Sudan, and the fact that a number of ethnic groups such as the Zaghawa lived in both countries. In the late 1960s, the first northern Chadian rebel group, the National Liberation Front of Chad (FROLINAT), was based in Darfur and was supported by Sudan's Islamist prime minister Sadiq al-Mahdi. In 1971, when violence between Chadian rebel factions resulted in dozens of deaths in Darfur, Sudan's military government of Colonel Jaafar Muhammad Numayri expelled FROLINAT. In the early 1970s, Gaddafi proposed to Numayri that they merge Libya and Sudan, but the latter rejected the proposal. As such, Gaddafi conspired to take Darfur from Khartoum and make the region part of his Islamic State of the Sahel. Endeavouring to install a friendly regime in Khartoum, Gaddafi supplied weapons and training camps in southern Libya to the exiled Sadiq al-Mahdi's 2,000 Sudanese Baqqara fighters, who were supported by Libya's Islamic Legion. Around the same time, a Sahelian drought prompted many northern Chadians, denied food aid by their southern-controlled government, to flee to Darfur, where they were seen as invading Arabs. With the failure of Sadiq's 1976 invasion and coup attempt in Sudan, Gaddafi and Numayri became implacable enemies. Gaddafi began to develop a Libyan military presence in Darfur, and Numayri began to back Habre's anti-Libyan FAN in Chad. After their 1980 defeat by Oueddei's Libyan-backed government in Chad, Habre's 10,000-strong FAN withdrew into western Darfur, where they gained control of the area and received support from Sudan, Egypt, and the United States. Two years later, Habre's forces used Darfur as a jumping-off point for a successful offensive into Chad that resulted in their seizure of the capital. In 1981 5,000 fighters from Libya's Islamic Legion occupied northern Darfur, and the United States supplied Numayri's Sudanese government with arms to confront them. Darfur became the site of a proxy war. Furthering the already serious racialization of Darfur, Gaddafi's propaganda portrayed the "Arabs" as revolutionary and progressive and the "Africans" as conservative and reactionary. To make matters worse, another regional drought in the early 1980s meant that Darfur's nomadic Arab pastoralists and settled African farmers competed more intensely for a constantly decreasing amount of useful land. The drought and famine also led to protests and a sudden change of government in Khartoum.

The military regime that overthrew Sudan's Numayri in April 1985 reestablished friendly relations with Gaddafi and allowed Libyan agents to work in Khartoum, but it did not permit the Islamic Legion to dominate Darfur. Given this new relationship with Sudan, Gaddafi ended his support for the Sudanese People's Liberation Movement (SPLM) in the south and provided Khartoum with weapons, light vehicles, and air support for its counterinsurgency campaign. Elected as president of Sudan in April 1986, Sadiq maintained good relations with his former Libyan patron but ultimately rejected the idea of Darfur joining Libya to form a Sahelian state. Using Darfur as a staging area for continuing operations in Chad, the Libyans built a road from Kufra in southeastern Libya to Kutum in northern Darfur, which brought in more Libyan regular troops and Islamic Legionaries who recruited and armed local Baqqara Arabs. During 1986, Habre, now in power in Chad, dispatched his FANT fighters to expel the Islamic Legion from northern Chad and drive them back into northern Darfur. Subsequently, Gaddafi reequipped the Islamic Legion and northern Chad's Arab Volcan Army rebels based at the Sudanese border town of Geneina, from where they dominated all of western and northern Darfur, and, in November 1987, both forces moved across the border into Chad.

Around the same time in the late 1980s, Gaddafi began supporting an emerging Arab supremacist organization in Darfur called the Arab Gathering, which was armed and trained in Kufra. In Sudan's Kordofan and Darfur regions, the Arab Gathering was also assisted by Baqqara militia, who were mobilized by Khartoum's extremist opposition movement, the National Islamic Front (NIF). Arab Gathering publications and audio recordings claimed that, while Arabs constituted the majority in Darfur, they had little political authority. Calling for the change of the name Darfur (land of the Fur) to Dar al-Arab (land of the Arabs), Arab Gathering statements at first hinted at and then urged Arabs to exterminate Darfur's non-Arab inhabitants. For political scientist Noah Bassil, the racism of northern Sudanese Arabs toward southern Africans was based mostly on culture, with the former trying to assimilate and civilize the latter. Nevertheless, as Bassil explains, "The Arabism of the Arab Gathering, as espoused by Gaddafi, was absolutist, however, and based on inflexible racial distinctions. The aim of the Gathering was not to assimilate non-Arabs to Arabism but to remove them from Darfur."[5] In the 1980s, within this context of growing hatred, Gaddafi supplied small arms to the Arabs of central and southern Darfur, and the non-Arab Fur people sought to defend themselves by creating the Federal Army of Darfur, with 6,000 fighters armed by Habre's government in Chad. In 1988, during what became known as the War of the Tribes, the Federal Army of Darfur was devastated by Rizayqat Baqqara Arabs sponsored by Tripoli and Khartoum. Fur survivors were massacred in what a Bahraini newspaper called genocide. Given that Gaddafi rejected Sadiq's demands for a Libyan and Chadian withdrawal from Darfur, Khartoum lost what little control it had in most of the region.

In April 1989, Idriss Deby, a FANT military commander, failed to overthrow Habre in Chad and fled to Darfur with his followers. Financed and directed by Gaddafi, Deby brought together a force of FANT defectors, Libyan Islamic Legion, and Chadian and Darfuri Arab mercenaries known as the Patriotic Salvation Movement (MPS), based in Darfur. Beginning in May 1989, Arab militias, including the Islamic Legion in Darfur, used their superior firepower to massacre the Fur, including 3,000 at the town of Nyala and 1,500 near Jebel Marra. Violence spread southwest to the border with Chad, where Chadian refugees used Libyan-supplied arms to attack the Fur. After Baqqara Arab leaders boycotted a traditional peace conference, fighting continued with several hundred killed on both sides, and 50,000 Fur sought protection at Nyala. The violence escalated when, in late June, Habre's FANT raided 160 kilometers inside Darfur in pursuit of MPS and then withdrew.

Sudan's pro-NIF regime of Brigadier Omar al-Bashir that overthrew Sadiq in late June 1989 gave Gaddafi and his Islamic Legion a free hand in Darfur. In mid-October 1989, Habre's Chadian forces staged "Operation Rezzou," in which they penetrated almost 200 kilometers into Darfur and engaged the MPS and Islamic Legion in a weeklong battle around Kutum in which hundreds of villages were destroyed and many civilians killed or wounded. The Islamic Legion suffered heavy casualties and withdrew to Libya. Needing Libyan oil and weapons to fight insurgents in southern Sudan, al-Bashir signed an agreement with Gaddafi that promised to turn Sudan's Darfur and Libya's Kufra into an integrated region. Around the same time, March 1990, Deby's MPS launched an invasion of Chad from Darfur that overwhelmed FANT positions on the border and took 1,000 prisoners. In early April, Habre's FANT embarked on a counteroffensive, but Deby's rebels retreated into Darfur, followed by Chadian soldiers who again burned villages and displaced civilians before pulling back across the border. With the excuse of quelling violence between Arabs and Fur during the Chadian April invasion, al-Bashir ordered the detention of non-Arab dissident leaders, including 130 Fur, and Sudanese soldiers began assisting Baqqara militia against the Fur. In November 1990, Deby's MPS again crossed into Chad and seized the capital from Habre, who had lost his French support because of human rights abuses.[6]

DARFUR CONFLICTS IN THE POST–COLD WAR ERA (1990–2010s)

During the 1990s, Sudan's al-Bashir Islamist government undertook an Arabization process in Darfur. At the start of that decade, Khartoum regained control of Darfur, given the departure of Deby's MPS and its Libyan allies for Chad. Consequently, al-Bashir's regime forcibly disarmed the Fur, and, in 1994 Darfur was reorganized into a number of new states in such a way that the Fur represented a minority in each. In 1998, in western Darfur, conflict erupted between Arab Bani Husayn herders and non-Arab Masalit farmers whose traditional leaders Khartoum had recently stripped of authority. Several hundred Masalit were killed, over 100 villages destroyed, and 5,000 Masalit fled to the border town of Geneina or into Chad. When fighting resumed in January 1999, despite a peace agreement and compensation, Khartoum declared that the Masalit were collaborating with the SPLA rebels in southern Sudan. With state resources stretched because of the war in the south, Khartoum extended a cheap counterinsurgency practice used in other parts of the country and armed and organized an Arab militia that included fighters from Chad and Kordofan. Those fighters were pitted against the Masalit. The pro-government Arab militia killed over 2,000 people, burned granaries, stole livestock, and drove 40,000 refugees into Chad, where many were killed in cross-border raids. The government avoided responsibility for the violence by having the Sudanese military disarm Masalit communities. These communities would be "coincidently" attacked a few days later by mounted Arab militias, who locals called Janjaweed (evil horsemen). In a short time, the Janjaweed militia and its tactics would be expanded into other parts of Darfur. In 2000 the mostly non-Arab police in Darfur were disarmed by the government, and their weapons given to Darfur Arab leader Musa Hilal, also an important member of the Arab Gathering, who recruited 2,000 Chadian Arabs and Sudanese Baqqara into the Janjaweed.

During the early 2000s, rebellion spread throughout Darfur. In July 2001, Fur and Zaghawa activists gathered in the Jebel Marra area, where they swore on the Koran to oppose the government's Arabization program. In November, funded by Darfuri residents of Khartoum, the rebels opened military training camps and made contact with Masalit leaders who had a similar agenda. Those guerrillas conducted their first operation in late February 2002 by attacking a military garrison in the remote mountains. In February 2003, approximately 300 rebels, now calling themselves the Darfur Liberation Front (DLF), temporarily captured Gulu, the capital of Jebel Marra Province in western Darfur, and attacked other security force outposts. In mid-March, the DLF, retitled the Sudan Liberation Movement/Army (SLM/A), again briefly took Gulu in an engagement that claimed the lives of 195 Sudanese soldiers. A second Darfur rebel group, the Justice and Equality Movement (JEM), was formed in the Netherlands in August 2001 by Darfuris who had lived in Khartoum. JEM retained a commitment to Islamic law, as opposed to the secular SLM/A, and fought for a utopian Sudan in which all people and regions would be equal. After the SLA's second attack on Gulu, government agents arranged a cease-fire, but it was violated within days by Arab militia, who murdered a Masalit leader, and Sudanese attack helicopters that devastated the town of Karnoi. In late March 2003, the SLA took the important Masalit town of Tine on the border with Chad and embarked on operations that illustrated the inadequacy of the few thousand Sudanese soldiers in Darfur. In late April, a combined force of SLA/JEM with 33 trucks mounted with heavy weapons raided the Al Fasher airport, where they destroyed helicopters and bombers and captured an air force major general, and another SLA contingent outside Kutum captured four tanks and apprehended the head of intelligence for north Darfur. A month later, north of Kutum, the SLA overwhelmed a Sudanese army unit, killing 500 and taking 300 prisoners. In mid-July, the SLA attacked Tine again and, a few weeks later, temporarily occupied Kutum, seizing arms and ammunition. The war in Darfur was going badly for the government.

Khartoum's counterinsurgency campaign in Darfur continued to rely on state-sponsored Arab militias. That was related to a paucity of state military resources in Darfur, given the long and increasingly expensive war in the south and the fact that the government considered the many army units made up of Darfuri soldiers to be unreliable for service in their home region. Janjaweed militia members were recruited from among bandits, demobilized soldiers, members of Arab communities engaged in land disputes with non-Arab neighbors, criminals released from prison, Arab Gathering fanatics, and unemployed youth. They received government salaries that were relatively good for the impoverished region, were issued army uniforms with special insignia, and cooperated with the military. In October 2002, Khartoum sent some 5,000 Janjaweed, trained and armed by the Sudanese army in camps in northern Darfur, to southern Darfur to drive the Fur from their ancestral home. A typical Janjaweed group consisted of around 100 horsemen, with perhaps a few vehicles. The group would attack a Fur community just before dawn, kill and mutilate the men, rape the women, kill or capture the children, destroy homes and infrastructure, burn fields, and steal livestock. The attackers often shouted racial insults at their victims, referred to them as "blacks" and "slaves," and told them that the land now belonged to the Arabs. By the start of 2003, hundreds of Fur had been killed, thousands injured, and tens of thousands displaced. During 2003, the Janjaweed, supported by government attack helicopters and transport aircraft pressed into service as bombers, slaughtered more Fur, Zaghawa, and Masalit. While many displaced people made it across the border to refugee camps in Chad, nearly 800,000 took shelter in squalid camps within Darfur, to which the government delayed the delivery of international humanitarian assistance until May 2004, by which time local agriculture had disappeared and many people had starved. Janjaweed leader Musa Hilal encouraged his men to continue what he called a jihad (holy war) and instructed them to "change the demography of Darfur and empty it of African tribes."[7]

In late August 2003, the Sudanese army inflicted heavy losses on the rebel SLA, which lost two senior commanders, north of Kutum. In turn, the SLA attempted to gain time to rebuild by signing a cease-fire agreement in September, but fighting quickly resumed. In late December 2003 and January 2004, JEM fighters thwarted two Janjaweed attempts to retake Tine and inflicted heavy casualties on the militias. In mid-February, three days after al-Bashir declared the rebellion suppressed, the insurgents shot down two army helicopters, and, in the subsequent weeks, they raided near Al Fasher and blocked the road from Khartoum to Nyala, the capital of South Darfur. At that stage, SLA and JEM consisted of around 27,000 fighters. With a purge of 25,000 Darfuri personnel from the regular Sudanese army in February and their replacement by conscripts from the paramilitary Popular Defense Forces (PDF), the Janjaweed accelerated their persecution of the non-Arab population, who were pursued into Chad. By that time, at least 30,000 people had been killed, 200,000 had fled to Chad, 1 million had been driven from their land, and 350,000 were expected to perish within a year from hunger and disease. International aid agencies were outraged when Khartoum denied them access to Darfur. In April 2004, Chad's Idriss Deby—who sympathized with the rebels as some of them shared his Zaghawa ethnic affiliation—facilitated a cease-fire offer, but it was rejected by SLM/A and JEM. The next month, Sudan's government refused a UN demand to disarm the Janjaweed as long as the insurgents had weapons.

The African Union Mission in Sudan (AMIS) was launched in July 2004 as a modest effort to monitor an ultimately abortive cease-fire and to facilitate humanitarian assistance in Darfur. Initially, AMIS consisted of several hundred troops from Rwanda and Nigeria airlifted to Darfur by the United States. A UN demand that Khartoum permit the arrival of more international peacekeepers or face sanctions on its important oil industry resulted in the growth of AMIS to 7,000 personnel by April 2005. However, the force was still too small and not properly equipped to protect civilians and humanitarian workers, who were harried by Janjaweed and bandits.

In the United States and Europe, there was mounting public outcry against what was first called the ethnic cleansing of Darfur, which increasingly began to be seen as a genocide sponsored by the Sudanese state. Several groups were established in the United States in 2004 to advocate for intervention to end atrocities in Darfur. The movement emerged in the context of the tenth anniversary of the genocide in Rwanda, during which a series of documentaries and films sparked popular interest in antigenocide activism. In July 2004, the Save Darfur Coalition was founded in the United States through the activities of the U.S. Holocaust Memorial Museum and the American Jewish World Service, which were interested in genocide education and prevention. The Save Darfur Coalition eventually established a permanent headquarters in Washington, D.C. Similarly, in October 2004, American university students formed the Genocide Intervention Network to raise funds to support the African Union mission in Darfur. The Save Darfur movement eventually enlisted such American celebrities as Mia Farrow and George Clooney as advocates. However, the U.S. government was reluctant to act with reference to Sudan, as it was embroiled in its own wars in Afghanistan and Iraq; and Britain and France were hesitant to alienate Islamist-ruled Sudan. Indeed, Sudan had expelled Islamist terrorist leader Osama bin Laden in 1996 and became an ally in the U.S. War on Terror after September 2001.

During 2004, governments and international organizations began to argue over whether the violence in Darfur amounted to genocide. The UN Security Council had demanded that Khartoum halt military operations and disarm the Janjaweed, and, at the end of August 2004, Secretary-General Kofi Anan reported that Sudan had failed to stop attacks on civilians. In September, the U.S. Bush administration, which had sent an investigative team to Chad's border with Sudan, declared that the government of Sudan and the Janjaweed were conducting genocide in Darfur but avoided committing its military by referring the matter to the UN to satisfy the international legal requirement to act against genocide.[8] Testifying before the U.S. Senate's Foreign Affairs Committee, Secretary of State Colin Powell maintained that "genocide has been committed in Darfur, and that the government of Sudan and the Janjaweed bear responsibility and genocide may still be occurring."[9] Around the same time, the European Parliament voted to urge the Sudanese government to end crimes against humanity taking place in Darfur "which can be construed as tantamount to genocide."[10] However, the AU heads of state, the Arab League, the Organization of Islamic Cooperation, and Sudan's government maintained that there was no genocide in Darfur.[11]

Given the referral by the United States, the UN Security Council appointed a committee to investigate alleged violations of international humanitarian and human rights law in Darfur, and specifically to determine whether genocide had occurred. Released in January 2005, the committee's report stated that "the Government of Sudan has not pursued a policy of genocide." While it concluded that killings had taken place and specific groups had been targeted, there was no evidence of genocidal intent, but rather a campaign to drive people from their homes as part of a brutal counterinsurgency program. Despite this, the report also raised the possibility that certain individuals, including government officials, might have harbored genocidal intent in ordering specific attacks and other actions. Emphasizing the dire nature of the situation, the report stated that "the crimes against humanity and war crimes that have been committed in Darfur may be no less serious and heinous than genocide."[12] The commission forwarded a confidential list of suspects to the UN Security Council and recommended their prosecution by the ICC. Since Khartoum was not a signatory to the Rome Treaty that had established the ICC, the UN Security Council specifically granted the ICC a mandate to look into the Darfur situation. The eventual results are discussed below.

Some scholars of international law criticized the UN commission's findings by noting, for instance, that the alleged genocidal intent of individuals had not been placed within a larger context that could have represented a corporate and genocidal project. In short, how many genocidal individuals and individual acts does it take to make a genocide? Furthermore, the commission, in finding that the Sudanese government had not enacted a "policy of genocide," seemed to ignore the important legal decision made in 2001 by the Appeals Court of the International Criminal Tribunal for the Former Yugoslavia that "the existence of a plan or policy is not a legal ingredient of the crime" of genocide. In technical legal terms, the UN Security Council had directed the commission to determine whether genocide had taken place—not whether there had been a specific government policy of genocide.[13]

In early May 2006, with perhaps 200,000 people dead and 2.5 million displaced in Darfur, American pressure on negotiators at the drawn-out peace talks in Abuja, Nigeria, produced a Darfur Peace Agreement (DPA). It included plans for the disarmament of the Janjaweed militia and rebel groups, the delivery of humanitarian relief, and a proposed referendum on the political future of Darfur. That agreement was signed by Sudan's government and the larger SLM/A faction of Minni Arko Minnawi, but not the smaller SLM/A faction of Abdul Wahid al Nur and JEM. At the end of June, the two insurgent groups that had not signed the DPA, plus the Sudan Federal Democratic Alliance (SFDA) of Ahmad Ibrahim Diraig, an exiled former governor and Fur, founded the National Redemption Front (NRF) in Asmara, Eritrea, under Diraig's leadership. As al-Bashir delayed the reinvention of AMIS as a larger UN peacekeeping force, violence in Darfur escalated during 2006, and aid organizations began to withdraw. In

November, the Sudanese army and Janjaweed were twice defeated by the NRF and banditry and fighting between SLM/A factions increased. In late December, the Janjaweed clashed with the NRF and the new SLA/Group 19 at Al Fasher.[14]

Several multinational peacekeeping forces became involved in the Darfur conflict. Al-Bashir eventually succumbed to mounting demands from the UN, AU, and Western democracies, as well as China, which had been accused of facilitating genocide in Darfur by selling weapons to Sudan. As such, Khartoum accepted the establishment of a combined AU-UN peacekeeping force. In October 2007, the African Union–United Nations Hybrid Operation in Darfur (UNAMID) began to deploy 20,000 soldiers and 6,000 police, into which the 9,000 existing AMIS members were absorbed. Its mandate was to protect civilians, facilitate the delivery of humanitarian aid, and to mediate between the government and rebels. UNAMID was a mostly African force, with personnel from Nigeria, Rwanda, Senegal, Ethiopia, South Africa, Egypt, Burkina Faso, Tanzania, Sierra Leone, and Gambia. During the late 2000s and early 2010s, UNAMID's mission was periodically extended, as it continued to take casualties from rebel and bandit attacks. International efforts to protect refugees from Darfur overlapped with peacekeeping missions in neighboring countries. In February 2008, the European Union Force (EUFOR) deployed 3,700 troops, half of them French, to protect civilians and ensure humanitarian assistance in eastern Chad and northeastern Central African Republic (CAR), where 200,000 refugees from Darfur had sought refuge. During 2009 and 2010, EUFOR was absorbed into the short-lived UN Mission in the CAR and Chad (MINURCAT), which sought to protect civilians but lacked a political mandate.[15]

Besides capturing weapons and equipment from government forces, rebel groups in Darfur gained military support from external sources. In retaliation for Khartoum's support for Islamist rebels in Eritrea, Asmara armed and funded Darfuri insurgents until 2006, when an offer of cheap Sudanese oil prompted it to change sides. In early 2003, the SPLA began to arm and train Darfuri rebels as part of an anti-Khartoum rebel alliance, and, in early 2010, the government of South Sudan began sponsoring JEM in the context of its conflict with Sudan over disputed oil fields. Gaddafi, who had fallen out with al-Bashir in the early 1990s over Khartoum offering sanctuary to Islamist radicals, still wanted to make Darfur part of greater Libya and therefore supplied the Darfuri rebels through Chad. During the 2011 revolution in Libya, rebels from Darfur fought on the side of Gaddafi, while the government of Sudan and the North Atlantic Treaty Organization (NATO) found themselves on the same side by supporting anti-Gaddafi forces. With Gaddafi's death, the Darfuri rebels returned home from Libya with new weapons, including surface-to-air missiles that threatened Sudan's hitherto unchallenged control of the skies. Although

President Deby of Chad initially remained neutral in the Darfur conflict, as mentioned above, the slaughter of his fellow Zaghawa people across the border led him to arm the rebels and provide them with staging areas in Chad. When Khartoum took revenge by organizing and arming Chadian rebels who crossed the frontier and launched a bloody but unsuccessful attack on N'Djamena in 2008, Deby declared he would no longer help insurgents from Darfur. In January 2010, the governments of Chad and Sudan signed an agreement to stop backing rebels in each other's countries, and the border was reopened after seven years.

In July 2008, Sudan's al-Bashir became the first serving head of state to be indicted by the ICC, which charged him with crimes against humanity and war crimes. While the court initially found insufficient grounds to add genocide to the list of charges, that legal opinion changed, and a second indictment for genocide issued in 2010 claimed that al-Bashir had acted with intent to eliminate a portion of the Fur, Masalit, and Zaghawa communities in Darfur. The ICC indictments made al-Bashir more determined to cling to power and bolstered his anticolonial credentials, which enhanced his relationship with Arab and African governments, who refused to enforce the arrest warrant. It also emboldened Darfuri rebels, whose claims to be fighting a genocidal regime were strengthened, and they made increasingly unrealistic demands for financial compensation for displaced people.

Negotiations held in Sirte, Libya, in October 2007 failed because several rebel leaders refused to attend, while those held in Doha, Qatar, in 2008 and 2009 produced an agreement between Khartoum and JEM that neither side followed. A new round of talks in Doha in 2011 resulted in an agreement between the government and the Liberation and Justice Movement (LJM), a coalition of 10 rebel groups created the previous year that established a compensation fund for victims, brought Darfuri representatives into the central government, and established a Transitional Darfur Regional Authority to administer the area until a referendum to determine its status within Sudan. However, JEM and several SLM/A factions rejected the deal and vowed to continue the war, though a general reduction in fighting allowed many displaced people to return home. Into the 2010s, Darfur continued to be an unstable and dangerous place.[16]

As with the conflict in the Democratic Republic of Congo (DRC) between 1998 and 2002, there has been considerable disagreement over the number of war-related deaths in Darfur from 2003 to 2010. At the low end, the Khartoum regime claims that 20,000 people died as a result of the conflict, and, at the high end, American Darfur advocacy groups put the figure at 544,000. In 2009 ICC prosecutor Luis Moreno-Ocampo claimed that 5,000 people were being killed every month in Darfur, though he presented no evidence and UN forces on the ground had not reported anything close to that level of violence. In 2010 Belgian researchers estimated that around

298,000 people had perished, mostly from disease and hunger caused by displacement, perhaps around 60,000 of them had been killed in violence, mostly during 2004, and the death rate steadily declined from 2004 to 2008.[17]

THE QUESTION OF GENOCIDE IN DARFUR

The question of whether genocide took place in Darfur during the 2000s has been the subject of heated debate. Although the Sudanese government usually claims that the Darfur conflict represented spontaneous violence between nomadic herders and settled farmers over a diminishing amount of useable land, it is obvious that the state sponsored the Janjaweed militia and supplied them with air support. Some scholars describe the horrendous loss of life in Darfur as the result of a counterinsurgency campaign gone wrong.[18] While the Sudanese government certainly responded to rebellion in Darfur that began in the early 2000s, its counterinsurgency symbolized the escalation of a long quest for domination by one racially and culturally defined group over another that it considered inferior. Such a situation has the potential for extremely deadly violence and destruction that might be defined as genocide. Another view maintains that the Sudanese state forces and allied militias conducted ethnic cleansing in Darfur in that they did not want to kill the Fur, Masalit, and Zaghawa but drive them off their land. That was the view of the report written by the UN investigative committee in 2005. Of course, depriving agricultural communities of their land and livestock will destroy their ability to produce food, and, given Darfur's conditions of desertification and drought, driving them from their land resulted in hunger and starvation. Furthermore, depriving such displaced people of food aid, which the Sudanese government did in Darfur in 2004, will have a predictable result.

Many academics, human rights activists, and international lawyers describe the actions of Sudanese state forces and allied militias in Darfur as genocide. Some books on the subject include the term genocide in their titles and employ it liberally throughout their texts, sometimes without clearly defining it. South Sudanese historian Jok Madut Jok states that "destruction of assets so as to render people desperate, dependent on outside handouts, and starving to death, has been one of the measures to effect genocide in Darfur."[19] For Eric Reeves, an American English literature professor and outspoken Darfur activist:

> What Khartoum was unable to accomplish with the massive violence of 2003–04, entailing wholesale destruction of African villages, will be achieved through a "genocide of attrition." Civilians displaced into camps or surviving precariously in rural areas will face unprecedented shortfalls in humanitarian assistance, primarily food and potable water.[20]

Gerard Prunier, an accomplished scholar of war and genocide in Africa, describes the state campaign in Darfur as progressing from counterinsurgency to "quasi-genocide" to a "final solution." Prunier states that if he uses his personal definition of genocide as an attempt to completely exterminate a political, religious, or ethnic group, then the violence in Darfur does not meet the standard. However, he also admits that "if we use the December 1948 definition it is obvious that Darfur is a genocide."[21]

Other scholars strongly disagree with applying the genocide label to the Darfur conflict. Most controversially, Ugandan academic Mahmood Mamdani subscribes to the brutal counterinsurgency theory and claims that the number of fatalities in Darfur was exaggerated by activists. Additionally, he maintains that by invoking the rhetoric of genocide to mobilize public opinion and international action, the Save Darfur movement helped prolong the conflict by endowing the rebels with a type of moral superiority as compared to the Sudanese government, which is portrayed as evil, and by furthering the Arab-versus-African racialization of the war. For Mamdani, "Rwanda was the site of genocide. Darfur is not. It is, rather, the site where the language of genocide has been turned into an instrument. It is where genocide has become ideological."[22] Those claims led to a high-profile public debate in 2009 between Mamdani and Save Darfur advocate John Prendergast. While Prendergast surprisingly conceded that he "wouldn't fall on his sword" over describing what had happened in Darfur as genocide, others accused Mamdani of being a stooge for the Khartoum regime. Andrew Natsios, who applied the term genocide to Darfur while serving as an official of the Bush administration, came to agree with Mamdani and claims that the Sudanese government's violence in Darfur "amounted to ethnic cleansing of the three rebellious tribes from their villages, as part of an unlimited and unconstrained counter-insurgency campaign whose purpose was to deprive the rebels of a base of supply and operations." He also writes that

> Advocacy groups could have made their arguments and calls to action without distorting what was already bad enough. They chose instead to mischaracterize the situation in order to keep their followers motivated, a strategy that strengthened Khartoum's case that the West did not understand what was happening in Darfur and made it much more difficult to find a diplomatic solution.[23]

My view is that the state and militia violence, including the consequent displacement, that happened in Darfur during the early and middle 2000s very likely represented a genocide under the existing international legal definition, which is the only definition of genocide that truly matters. Natsios is wrong to claim that statements made by the Arab Gathering in the 1980s about exterminating the non-Arab people of the region are irrelevant because they were made so long ago and that, even though some members of the movement later joined the government in Khartoum, there is no evidence of genocidal intent on the part of the state.[24] An alternate way to look at those 1980s declarations is that they formed part of the historic development of an ideology of genocide that influenced subsequent events in Darfur, in that the people who made and were exposed to the hate propaganda were active participants in the violence of the 2000s. In addition, Natsios's focus on state policy ignores the international legal precedent that proving genocidal intent is not linked to the existence of official genocidal policies or plans. Genocidal intent can be unofficial. Since the perpetrators of the alleged genocide remain in power in Sudan, a thorough investigation has never been conducted in Darfur itself, and there has never been a full discussion of evidence before a competent court. However, it is doubtful that the continued limited violence in Darfur from the late 2000s onward corresponds with the international legal definition of genocide. In the short-term, the international campaign that mobilized the rhetoric of genocide against the Sudanese government pressured Khartoum to stop the worst atrocities, but, in the long term, as Mamdani and Natsios have maintained, it was not helpful in resolving the conflict, which now looks almost intractable.

NORTH VERSUS SOUTH CONFLICTS

Since ancient times, the area of modern Sudan and South Sudan served as a source of slaves for different powers in Egypt, the Middle East, Asia Minor, and southern Europe. During the 640s and 650s, the Arabs who had recently conquered Egypt launched several invasions of Nubia in what is now Sudan. Those conflicts ended with an agreement called the baqt, which endured for most of the subsequent seven centuries and involved the Nubians sending slaves north to Egypt every year in exchange for agricultural produce. During the 1500s, the Nubians and Arabs of Sudan were conquered by the Funj, originally nomadic horsemen, who converted to Islam and established a state centered on the town of Sennar on the Blue Nile. Funj armies conducted slave raids to the south, where they clashed with the Shilluk people on the White Nile during the early 1600s. Around 1630, the Funj and Shilluk allied to counter the expansion of the Dinka into what is now part of South Sudan. The decline of the Funj Sultanate during the 1700s, a result of internal conflict, provided an opportunity for the Shilluk, who then rose as a regional power. By the beginning of the 1800s, a fairly well-established slave trade existed in Sudan where thousands of slaves each year were sent down the Nile by caravan or boat to Egypt or to the Red Sea port of Suakin for shipment to Arabia or Egypt.[25]

As explained above, much of what is now Sudan was conquered by the Egyptians under Muhammad Ali during the 1820s. At the time, Egypt was an autonomous part of the Ottoman Empire. In 1820 and 1821, the multinational Egyptian army, with firearms and artillery, defeated the traditional cavalry of the Shaiqiya Arabs and their Nubian infantry levies around Kurti on the Nile. Egyptian soldiers had been promised a bounty for each pair of ears taken from dead enemy, which led to the mutilation and killing of many civilians. In May 1821, the Egyptians arrived at the confluence of the Blue and White Nile Rivers, where they established the administrative center of Khartoum. Under Egyptian rule, the Sudanese slave trade increased dramatically, with slave raids launched to the west and east, and particularly in the Nuba Mountains and among the Dinka pastoralists in the south. Male slaves were sent to Egypt to form a new army meant to help suppress rebellion against the Ottoman Empire in Greece, and women and children were sold in Arabia to raise money to equip the force. When the Egyptians failed to find expected sources of gold in Sudan, they engaged in the ivory trade. In 1822 Egyptian demands for slaves and money prompted a widespread rebellion by Arabs along the Nile that was ruthlessly crushed with the help of Shaiqiya Arabs and Darfuri mercenaries. For the Egyptians and Nile Arabs, southern Sudan became a favorite hunting ground for slaves and ivory. Although the Egyptian slave raiders had firearms, the Dinka and other southern groups used poisoned arrows and serrated spears to mount ferocious resistance. The Shilluk employed canoes to raid Muslim villages along the Nile, and in 1826 and 1830 they drove Egyptian expeditions out of their area. Shilluk resistance was finally overtaken in the early 1840s, when Egyptian expeditions up the Nile broke through the vast Sudd swamp.

By 1860 some 12,000 to 15,000 slaves were sent north annually from southern Sudan. The south became dominated by private slaving companies from Khartoum that operated networks of small forts called zaribas, which Arab gunmen and their African auxiliaries used as bases for slaving and elephant hunting and around which dependent African communities settled. Influenced by British antislavery policies, Egypt attempted to restrict the slave trade during the 1870s, but that led to resistance by the Arab slavers of Sudan and contributed to the Mahdi's rebellion. From the mid-1880s to 1898—the period of the Mahdist state in Sudan—slavery once again became legal and slave raiding in the south continued. In Mahdist Sudan, slaves labored in local agricultural production, and slave exports were limited, given hostility with Egypt. Although the return of Anglo-Egyptian rule to Sudan at the end of the 1890s meant the technical abolition of slavery and the slave trade, the weakness of the colonial state meant that the practice continued in different ways. By that time, Sudanese Arabs had long associated slave status with black African people of the south, including the Shilluk, Dinka, and Nuer. This history of slavery influenced the development of a racial hierarchy in modern Sudan, in which northern Arabs commonly insulted southern Africans by referring to them as "slaves."[26]

During the colonial period, the British ruled northern and southern Sudan as separate territories. In the north, the British encouraged orthodox Islam through the spread of Koranic schools, opposed messianic Islam such as Mahdism, permitted the use of sharia law in local courts, discouraged the growth of a secular Westernized elite, and governed through an indirect-rule system that increased the power of local ethnic-oriented traditional leaders. Although slavery was officially outlawed in colonial Sudan, local British officials usually tolerated it for the sake of stability. British colonial rule reached southern Sudan in 1904 as a result of operations to clear the Sudd for navigation, and, over the next few decades, colonial forces subjugated southern communities. Through what was called the "Southern Policy," the British closed off the south to Muslims from the north and facilitated the spread of missionary Christianity and the use of English as an administrative language. Indirect rule was also imposed on the south, but it was not effective, as the historically decentralized Dinka and Nuer did not have the type of leaders that the British could co-opt. Taxation was imposed, and seminomadic pastoral communities such as the Nuer were forced to live in permanent settlements. The British colonial military in Sudan reflected the north-south division. Founded in 1910, the separate colonial military of southern Sudan was called the Equatorial Corps, in which the officer element was entirely British, the rank and file entirely southern Sudanese, the language of command was English, and Christianity was encouraged and Islam forbidden. The northern Sudanese soldiers who had initially occupied the south were sent home, as it was feared they would spread Islam. The Equatorial Corps would become a central institution of southern Sudanese identity. In 1924 the Sudan Defense Force (SDF) was established, which furthered the regional and racial division of the military by its organization into separate regional and racial elements comprising the Equatorial Corps, Eastern Arab Corps, Western Arab Corps, and Camel Corps. British worries about emerging Egyptian nationalism and protest led to the expulsion of Egyptian officers and officials from the Anglo-Egyptian Sudan, which became dominated by Britain.

In the decolonization era of the late 1940s and early 1950s, northern Sudanese nationalists abandoned the old idea of uniting with Egypt and pursued a political campaign for an independent Sudan. In 1948 British officials, given the lack of options for impoverished and isolated southern Sudan, convinced the few southern Sudanese political leaders to agree to participate in a newly formed Sudanese legislative council. That meant that when Sudan became independent in 1956 the new sovereign state included both north and south—despite the fact that they had been ruled by the British as completely separate territories. The north became the dominant region. The capital of Khartoum was located in the north, and Muslim Arab northerners immediately took control of the new government, civil service, and military, which they inherited from the British.[27]

SUDAN'S FIRST AND SECOND CIVIL WARS

The First Sudanese Civil War began just before the country's independence. In 1955 soldiers of the Equatorial Corps in the town of Torit, located in the southernmost part of southern Sudan, mutinied over the imposition of northern Sudanese officers who were replacing the British and an anticipated transfer to other parts of the country. The rebellion was crushed, but fugitives took to the bush, from where they launched a limited insurgency. In 1958 Khartoum's new military government embarked on an aggressive campaign of Arabization and Islamization in the southern region. Fleeing repression, educated and Westernized southerners went to neighboring countries where they formed the Sudan African Nationalist Union (SANU), which advocated the separation of the south from Sudan. Inside southern Sudan, a number of rebel groups were formed, with the mutineers of 1955 serving as a nucleus. Collectively known as Anyanya (snake venom), each group focused on recruiting from specific ethnic communities. They did not synchronize operations and occasionally fought each other. In 1964 an Anyanya group attacked the capital of Bahr el Ghazal Province and intercepted weapons being sent by the Sudanese government to Simba rebels in eastern Congo. The next year, the state responded by having the military garrison of Juba massacre 1,400 civilians, driving the rural population of Equatoria Province into "peace villages," where many died of disease and hunger, and forming anti-rebel militias in Bahr el Ghazal and the Upper Nile. During the early to middle 1960s, the Anyanya groups alienated rural communities by stealing their cattle; they rejected the movement's exiled intellectual leadership; and support from Ethiopia and Uganda was sporadic, as those regimes were combating their own regional separatist movements and did not want to be seen encouraging such ambitions.

In 1967 the rebels attempted to unify by creating the Southern Sudan Provisional Government (SSPG) with a military wing called the Anyanya National Armed Force (ANAF). While the SSPG collapsed within a year because of internal divisions, the military arm survived and was renamed the South Sudan Liberation Movement (SSLM), which became the beneficiary of Israeli sponsorship, given that Khartoum had taken the Arab side in the Arab-Israel confrontation. At the end of the 1960s, Ethiopian support for SSLM expanded, since the government of Sudan was backing rebels in Eritrea. Under the leadership of Colonel Joseph Lagu, a deserter from the Sudanese military, the SSLM evolved into a network of ethnically distinct units such as the Bari Anyanya in central Equatoria, the Dinka Anyanya in Bahr el Ghazal, and the Nuer Anyanya in the Upper Nile. Supported by Egypt and the Soviet Union, Khartoum dispatched more military resources to the south, including helicopters and armored vehicles. The government counterinsurgency campaign led to accusations of genocide by southern

Sudanese opposition leaders and their supporters in the West. By 1971, the war in southern Sudan had expanded but also reached a stalemate as the insurgents controlled the rural areas yet could not evict state forces from the towns. This impasse prompted Sudan's Numayri regime, which had taken power in a 1969 coup, to negotiate with the SSLM. The SSLM abandoned the pursuit of complete independence for the south, given the defeat of similar movements in Nigeria and the Congo. The conflict ended with the 1972 Addis Ababa Agreement, which gave some autonomy to southern Sudan and committed the government to the incorporation of former insurgents into a new, representative national military. A few rebels rejected the compromise and continued sporadic fighting under the label Anyanya II.[28]

Under pressure from Islamist politicians in Khartoum, the Numayri government resumed the program of Arabization and Islamization in southern Sudan in the early 1980s. There was already tension within Sudan's military, as northern officers resented the inclusion of southern former rebels and the ex-Anyanya were frustrated with their lack of progression through the ranks. In late 1982, Numayri ordered the transfer of some predominantly southern military units to the west and north. That provoked a January 1983 rebellion by the garrisons at Bor and Pibor, with some soldiers fleeing into the bush or moving across the border into Ethiopia. In response, Numayri invoked Republican Order Number One, which abrogated the Addis Ababa Agreement, deposed the elected southern regional government, made Arabic the official language, and canceled regional representation within the military. More southern soldiers deserted to the now-growing rebel movement, and a second civil war broke out. At the end of July, the Sudan People's Liberation Movement/Army (SPLM/A), with Colonel John Garang as political and military leader, published its manifesto to overthrow Numayri and inaugurate a federal and secular Sudan. The goal of independence for the south was abandoned, as the SPLM/A's primary supporter was Ethiopia, which was fighting multiple separatist insurgencies. In 1984 the SPLA attacked elements of Sudan's most successful development projects: the emerging oil industry around Bentiu and the Jonglei Canal, which was under construction by a French company. By 1985, the SPLA had 10,000 fighters in southern Sudan and another 20,000 in Ethiopia. As in the previous civil war, state forces in the south became confined to towns, and the SPLA, unlike the old Anyanya, cultivated support from rural people. The SPLA's 1987 seizure of Kurmuk—a town on the Sudan-Ethiopian border 720 kilometers southeast of Khartoum and close to a hydroelectric project that supplied most of the capital's electricity—enflamed northern Arab hatred of southern black Africans and incited Libya, Iraq, Saudi Arabia, and Jordan to pledge military support for Sudan. The SPLA suffered several setbacks in 1991, as it lost Ethiopian backing with the fall of the Mengistu dictatorship and violence broke out within the SPLA between rival factions—a predominantly Dinka group that remained loyal to Garang and an Nuer segment led by Riek Machar that advocated independence for the south but was ironically sponsored by Khartoum as a way to destabilize the rebel movement. In November 1991, at the town of Bor, Nuer fighters slaughtered at least 2,000 Dinka civilians and drove away many more who would subsequently die of hunger. Throughout much of the 1990s, the SPLA would fight its own civil war, while also engaging state forces in the larger civil war.

GENOCIDE DURING THE SECOND CIVIL WAR

People from the Dinka ethnic group became the target of Sudanese state-sponsored massacres. In 1985 a transitional government in Khartoum began to arm Arab Baqqara militias, called the Murahiliin, in southern Kordofan and southern Darfur to fight the SPLA and attack Dinka civilians who had moved north because of drought. The decision to mobilize militias was related to the state's lack of resources and distrust of its own military and the unpopularity of conscription in the north. The drought also prompted the impoverished Baqqara to join the militia, in which they were initially unpaid but told to reward themselves by looting livestock, possessions, and slaves. Areas of insurgent activity were designated as "ethics-free zones," which meant that militia leaders did not have to report their actions and therefore operated with impunity. By the middle of 1986, some 17,000 Dinka had gathered at Ed Daein in southern Darfur, where National Islamic Front (NIF) militants began to incite local Baqqara to destroy their church/community center. In late March 1987, after the church was attacked, police locked Dinka people into a train that was meant to take them out of town, but a large Baqqara mob barricaded the tracks and burned the railway cars and then attacked Dinka in the town. Some 1,500 Dinka were killed. As 250,000 Dinka people fled south, they were pursued by the Murahiliin, who were then intercepted by an SPLA offensive and driven back to the north. In February 1987, the new Sadiq government appointed the Baqqara general Fadlallah Burma Nasr as minister of defense, who then armed the southern Baqqara youth and directed them to deprive the SPLA of support by slaughtering the Dinka inhabitants of Bahr el Ghazal. The Dinka around Wau, the capital of Bahr el Ghazal, were attacked by an ethnic Fartit militia led by Major General Abu Qurun, also known as "Our Hitler" among state forces. Beginning in March 1988, the pro-government Murahiliin attacked Dinka communities in Bahr el Ghazal killing men, raping women, enslaving children, stealing livestock, and burning homes, schools, and clinics. The delivery of humanitarian aid to displaced people in camps was blocked, and many starved to death. In one case, food relief from the European Union sat on a railway siding for two years while displaced Dinka starved in a camp just 200 meters away. Amnesty International workers began to describe the militia violence in Bahr el Ghazal as genocide. For historian Jok Madut Jok, the state sponsorship of Baqqara militia was meant to encourage the Baqqara to continue voting for the Sadiq government and "to weaken the SPLA and its support base among the Dinka through a policy of genocide by extermination of the rural Dinka population." The Murahiliin were eventually incorporated into the state's paramilitary PDF, which was formed at the start of the 1990s. Those militia attacks decreased in 1990, given SPLA offensives and a realization among the militia leaders that they were not gaining much from the war.[29]

Located in southern Kordofan, the Nuba Mountains became the scene of horrific violence during the Second Sudanese Civil War. Historically, the area is inhabited by Arab cattle pastoralists and diverse African farming communities, collectively known as Nuba, who moved into the mountains long ago to escape slave raids. Diverse religious practices developed among the Nuba. Living in a closed district during the colonial era, Nuba elites converted to mission Christianity, many ordinary rural people continued to practice traditional religions, and those who engaged in migrant labor in other parts of the country often turned to Islam. By the time of independence in 1956, the Nuba, much romanticized by Western ethnographers and filmmakers, had become a marginalized people whose fertile land was often stolen by commercial farmers from other parts of the country. The northern-dominated regimes in Khartoum came to see the supposedly primitive Nuba as an embarrassment for Sudan within the Muslim world and made them targets for an Arab-Islamist civilizing mission. When Sudan's second civil war broke out in 1983, Nuba activists and youth were attracted to the SPLM/A objective of establishing a federal and secular Sudan in which the various marginalized groups in the south and west would come together and outnumber the hitherto dominant northern Arab minority. Although the Nuba elected their own parliamentary representatives during the 1986 Sudanese election, some of them were arrested, and military intelligence tortured and murdered suspected Nuba rebel sympathizers. In 1987 an SPLA brigade led by Yousif Kuwa Mekki, a Nuba teacher turned revolutionary, advanced into the Nuba Mountains, where it overcame army and militia garrisons and threatened the rest of southern Kordofan. The state, cash-strapped and distrustful of its own military, encouraged former army officers to found militias among the Arab communities of Kordofan that would fight the SPLA by attacking Nuba villages and seizing livestock. Displaced Nuba fled into the hills, and agriculture collapsed.

In 1989 Sudan's new Islamist government, particularly the Arab and Islamic Bureau under NIF leader Hassan al Turabi, initiated a program to create a national Islamist Sudanese identity that would be imposed on the Nuba through the declaration of jihad. The vice president, General Zubeir Mohamed Saleh, was put in charge of a campaign to resettle the Nuba population in a series of concentration camps euphemistically called "peace villages" in southern Kordofan to be forcibly Islamized—even those who were already Muslims, because they were considered to lack conformity with desired standards. International mujahidin, many veterans of the 1980s war against the Soviets in Afghanistan, were brought in to train local militias for the upcoming jihad, which went beyond the usual brutality of the state's counterinsurgency operations. In April 1992, President al-Bashir presided over a ceremony at El Obeid in which militia leaders were granted jihadist titles. Subsequently, six Kordofan Muslim clerics were directed to issue a fatwa (religious command) that sanctioned the killing of the rebels, who were portrayed as enemies of Islam as well as apostates and unbelievers. Educated Nuba were targeted by military intelligence death squads. In the camps, Nuba men and women were separated so they could not reproduce, and the Arab militia initiated a policy of rape against Nuba women with a view to eventually eliminate the Nuba identity. By late 1992, approximately 160,000 Nuba people had been resettled out of a total target population of 500,000. Many thousands died from disease and hunger. There was almost no international protest over the jihad in the Nuba Mountains, with the exception of a statement by the UN Department of Humanitarian Affairs in September 1992 and a motion of disapproval passed by the U.S. Congress in October. However, by the end of 1992, the obviously genocidal campaign had stalled for a number of reasons. First, and most importantly, Sudanese military operations against the SPLA failed, and state forces began to withdraw from the Nuba Mountains. Second, SPLA leader Yousif Kuwa cultivated support among the Nuba and orchestrated cultural revival, education, and religious tolerance to counter government terror. Third, although there was a government ban on news reports from the Nuba Mountains, rumors about the atrocities prompted disapproval among ordinary Sudanese in the north.

After 1992, state forces repeatedly launched offensives into the Nuba Mountains, but they failed to dislodge the SPLA. During the 1990s, the conflict in the Nuba Mountains increasingly became a Nuba civil war as the state expanded its militia beyond Arab fighters to include Nuba warlords and bandits and SPLA defectors. Beginning in 1995, a few international journalists and some humanitarian relief began to arrive in the Nuba area. While the last government offensive into the Nuba Mountains took place in May 2001, the terrorist attacks on the United States in September of that year encouraged Khartoum to engage in U.S.-sponsored talks that produced an internationally monitored cease-fire in that area in January 2002. That was the first cease-fire in the Second Sudanese Civil War.[30] Several academics point to the Nuba Mountains atrocities of the early 1990s as informing subsequent events in Darfur in the early 2000s. For Sudan scholar Alex de Waal, "The assault on the Nuba Mountains of Sudan in 1992, at the height of Sudan's civil war, represents the most clear-cut case of genocidal intent in modern Sudan . . . the Nuba war foreshadows many of the features of the Darfur conflict."[31] For Jok Madut Jok:

> The genocidal campaign in Darfur bears the same ideological appearance as the slave raiding in northern Bahr el-Ghazal from the mid-1980s to 2001, the 1992 Jihad against the Nuba, and the more recent oil related destruction in Upper Nile. Ideology is being used here to attract the fighters and imbue them with routine cruelty toward non-Arabs.[32]

INDEPENDENCE AND VIOLENCE IN SOUTH SUDAN

In 2002 Khartoum and the SPLA became more serious about negotiations. The al-Bashir government wanted to improve its relations with the United States, which was aggressively pursuing Islamist terrorists; the civil war was unpopular in the north, given casualties and conscription; and the beginning of oil production at the end of the 1990s provided revenue, but spending it on the military did not help the troubled economy. The U.S. Sudan Peace Act of October 2002 accused Khartoum of committing genocide during the civil war in the south, which put pressure on al-Bashir to negotiate, and American public funds were devoted to humanitarian assistance in rebel-held areas.[33] Although the SPLA had been strengthened by the end of its internal Nuer-Dinka struggle, Khartoum could use its oil revenues to continue the war, which the long-suffering southern civilians desperately wanted to end. During talks in Kenya, the al-Bashir regime agreed to a referendum in the south on self-determination, and the SPLA abandoned its pursuit of a secular Sudan by accepting Islamic law in the north. However, the Nuba Mountains and Blue Nile—where the SPLA controlled large areas and had recruited thousands of soldiers and where state forces had committed terrible atrocities—were not defined as being within South Sudan and would remain part of the Islamist-controlled north.

Delayed by the 2003 rebellion in Darfur, the Comprehensive Peace Agreement (CPA) was signed by the al-Bashir government and the SPLA in January 2005 and established an autonomous Government of South Sudan (GOSS). John Garang, SPLA leader, became a national vice president and GOSS president but was killed in a helicopter crash in July. The previous 20 years of civil war had claimed over 2 million lives and 4 to 6 million people had been internally displaced or had fled to refugee camps in neighboring countries. In January 2011, South Sudanese voted overwhelming for independence, and, in July of that year, South Sudan became a new state, with Juba as its capital and the SPLM's Salva Kiir Mayardit as president. As South Sudan became Africa's newest country, violence broke out in neighboring south Kordofan and Blue Nile between

Sudanese state forces and the local SPLA insurgents, who renamed themselves the Sudan People's Liberation Movement–North (SPLM-N). Fighting continued over the next few years, with several hundred thousand refugees crossing into South Sudan and Ethiopia. Some international activists point to a renewed genocide against the Nuba. At the same time, Sudan and South Sudan quickly began fighting over their oil-rich border area. In May 2011, the Sudanese army seized the oil-producing area of Abyei from the SPLA, and, in March 2012, the militaries of Sudan and South Sudan battled over the oil-producing towns of Heglig and Bentiu until a cease-fire was brokered by the African Union.

Further conflict between Khartoum and Juba was put on hold by the December 2013 outbreak of a horrific civil war in South Sudan between predominantly Dinka forces loyal to President Salva Kiir and the mostly Nuer faction supporting Vice President Riek Machar. Fighting began in Juba when the president accused his vice president of plotting a coup, and the former had Dinka soldiers attempt to disarm their Nuer colleagues, which also prompted the murder of Nuer civilians in the capital. In revenge, Nuer soldiers and militia killed Dinka people in other areas. There is some evidence that the government of Sudan, probably attempting to destabilize the new country, airdropped ammunition to Machar's Nuer forces, who styled themselves as the SPLA In Opposition (SPLA-IO).[34] Similarly, violence started between pro-government Dinka militia and Shilluk communities in Upper Nile state over access to river resources and the redefinition of internal political boundaries.

Genocide rhetoric was quickly mobilized with regard to the violence in South Sudan. In Canada, South Sudanese diasporic communities protested the "Nuer Genocide" and launched annual "Nuer Genocide" commemorations, seemingly modeled on those held by the Rwandan-Canadian community.[35] United Nations officials began to publically discuss the potential for genocide in South Sudan. At the start of May 2014, U.S. secretary of state John Kerry, while on an official visit to East Africa, warned that the continued ethnic violence in South Sudan "could really present a very serious challenge to the international community with respect to the question of genocide."[36] Around the same time, an African Union commission was conducting an investigation into the South Sudan conflict. The commission's membership included former Nigerian president Olusegun Obasanjo, who, as a prominent military commander during the Nigerian Civil War of 1967–1970, was well aware of the potential power of genocide accusations, and academic Mahmood Mamdani, who, as discussed above, had been strongly critical of the deployment of genocide accusations in the Darfur conflict. The commission's final report, the publication of which was delayed for a year, acknowledged that gross violations of human rights and war crimes, including "murder, rape and sexual violence, extermination, persecution, torture and other inhumane acts," had taken place in South Sudan and that they had been conducted in a "wide spread and systematic manner, and that evidence points to the existence of a state or organizational policy to launch attacks against civilians based on their ethnicity or political affiliation." Despite using terms like "extermination" and "organized policy," the commission also concluded that "there are no reasonable grounds to believe that the crime of genocide has occurred."[37] It seems likely that the genocide determination was avoided because it would undoubtedly make it more difficult to end the conflict, which dragged on through several rounds of negotiations, a tentative peace deal signed in August 2015, and the eventual return of Machar to South Sudan in April 2016. As part of a settlement between the Dinka and Nuer factions, the African Union announced that it would establish a special court in South Sudan to address crimes committed during the civil war. While it was unclear how such a court could prosecute leaders protected by armed factions, the point became moot when the peace deal broke down and fighting renewed in July 2016. Machar once again fled the country. While the UN Mission in South Sudan (UNMISS) was criticized for failing to protect civilians, the Kiir government questioned the need to deploy a more robust international protection force. At the end of 2016, UN officials and international activists renewed warnings of potential genocide in South Sudan comparable to what had happened in Rwanda in 1994 and accused South Sudan diasporic communities of encouraging ethnic hatred and violence.[38]

CONCLUSION

Sudan has the sad distinction of being Africa's most genocide-prone country. The emergence of intertwined, complex, and potent racial and religious identities that originated in the precolonial era and were then further exploited and enflamed by colonial and postcolonial regimes provided the context. There have been overlapping conflicts, which include but are not limited to Arab versus African, Muslim versus non-Muslim, purist Muslim versus syncretic Muslim, north versus south, center versus periphery, and herder versus farmer. In the postcolonial period, a northern-based, Arab and Islamist regime in Khartoum attempted to dominate the supposedly inferior inhabitants of marginalized regions in the west and south. As Straus points out, Sudan's Arab-Islamic elites saw other Sudanese as external to the state, and, when faced with resistance and given the vast size of the country, it used promises of material gain to pit marginalized, regional Arab groups against them.[39] Since the 1980s, there have been several examples of state-sponsored mass violence in Sudan that appear to correspond to the international legal definition of genocide. While academics and activists have debated the existence of genocidal intent, it seems obvious that the Sudanese government directly or indirectly targeted specific communities based on locally well-understood racial and ethnic identities with extermination or partial extermination as a goal. Those efforts included the late 1980s campaign against the Dinka in Bahr el Ghazal, the 1992 jihad against the Nuba in Kordofan, and the 2003–2004 attacks on the Fur, Masalit, and Zaghawa in Darfur. Although the massacres of Dinka and Nuba were relatively unknown in the wider world when they were happening and are still not well studied, the nature of the war in Darfur became the subject of an international controversy facilitated by new communications technology and inspired by global awareness of genocide, given what had happened in Rwanda a decade earlier. Unfortunately, and illustrative of the problem of genocide as a concept, the mobilization of genocide rhetoric against Khartoum by international activists and politicians during the 2000s might have reduced violence in Darfur, but it also stood in the way of achieving a lasting settlement. No one has ever been held accountable for those crimes, and the current government of Sudan, which has been in power since 1989, bears responsibility for many of them. Tragically, the new state of South Sudan, emerging from six decades of warfare, inherited a legacy of ethnic politics and ethnic violence that its leaders have not been able to overcome and that has prompted new international concerns about genocide, as well as more debate about the application and impact of the term.

CHAPTER 6

Nigeria

Nigeria is the leading economic and political power in West Africa and is among the continent's most prominent states. With over 180 million people, it is Africa's most populous country and the seventh most populous country in the world. Comprising over 570,000 square kilometers, Nigeria is a large country by West African standards and consists of several distinct geographic zones. On the coast of the Atlantic's Gulf of Guinea, southern Nigeria is heavily forested, and a riverine environment with mangrove swamps characterizes the Niger Delta. Above the coastal forest zone are the hills and plateaus of the Middle Belt. Moving north, the country becomes increasingly arid, turning from savannah to the semi-desert of the Sahel. Nigeria is divided by the Niger River, Africa's third-longest river, which runs for almost 1,200 kilometers from the west and empties into the Atlantic at the Niger Delta and has many tributaries, the most important of which is the Benue River in the east. Although Nigerians represent several hundred different ethnic groups, the three largest ethnic identities also correspond with religious identities, and each originates in a distinct region of the country. Broadly, southern Nigeria is inhabited mostly by Christians, with the Yoruba in the west and the Igbo in the east, while northern Nigeria is dominated by the Muslim Hausa.

From the 1970s, oil production and export, which is based in the Niger Delta, became the most important sector of Nigeria's economy, which vies with South Africa for the title of Africa's largest economy. Politically, postcolonial Nigeria has been plagued by regional, ethnic, and religious conflicts that led to it being ruled by a series of military regimes for most of the years between 1966 and 1999. The defining event of postcolonial Nigerian history was the Civil War of 1967 to 1970, one of postcolonial Africa's deadliest conflicts, in which the federal military government defeated the secessionist state of Biafra in the east, associated mostly with the Igbo ethnic group. In the lead-up to the conflict and during the fighting, the Biafran regime mobilized the language of genocide to justify its separation from Nigeria and to garner international diplomatic, military, and humanitarian support. Debates about whether the mass violence of the 1966 to 1970 period can be accurately characterized as genocide continue to this day and reflect persistent tensions over ethnicity and regionalism within the context of an economy based heavily on oil export from the formerly separatist area.

THE PRECOLONIAL PERIOD

By the 15th century, the Hausa city states in what is now northern Nigeria were heavily involved in the Trans-Sahara trade, exporting such commodities as gold, cloth, hides, kola nuts, and slaves. As in other parts of Sahelian West Africa, Islam had spread south into the area via the Sahara trade routes, and an Arabic script had been adapted to Hausa language. By around 1700, the nominally Muslim Hausa rulers were illegally enslaving fellow Muslims and oppressively taxing their subjects. During the 18th century, leaders from the pastoral Fulani community were at the forefront of a series of jihads across Sahelian West Africa that sought to revitalize and purify Islam and establish new states. In the late 1700s, Fulani Muslim scholar Usman dan Fodio traveled throughout Hausa territory and built a network of supporters and allies who were dissatisfied with the Hausa states. In 1804 dan Fodio's followers rebelled and declared jihad against the Hausa state of Gobir, which had been weakened by wars with its Hausa neighbors. By the end of 1808, the jihad had subdued all the major Hausa states, including those to the east that had been dominated by Borno. In 1809 dan Fodio established a new capital at Sokoto that became the center of a new Islamic caliphate. Within a few years, the old Hausa rulers had been replaced by Fulani emirs who owed allegiance to the caliph at Sokoto. While the jihadist army had initially been composed of infantry forces, it evolved into a predominantly cavalry force, like those that had been common on the Sahel for centuries. The army did not readily adopt firearms, which were beginning to come north from the coast where European seafarers exchanged them for slaves. With the death of dan Fodio in 1817, his son Muhammad Bello ruled the Sokoto Caliphate for the next 20 years—a time in which Islam was strengthened and expanded among the elite, inter-Hausa wars became less frequent, and the use of slave labor on plantations increased. The largest African empire of its day, Sokoto stretched from modern Burkina Faso in the west, across northern Nigeria, to what is now Cameroon in the east.[1]

Inhabiting what is now western Nigeria, stretching from the Sahel below the lower Niger River south to the coastal forest, Yoruba farmers produced a food surplus and began to form a series of city-states around 1,000 years ago. By the early 1500s, Oyo had used cavalry acquired from the north to expand west into the forest gap and became a major intermediary in the trade between coastal groups in the south and the Hausa in the north. During the 1700s, Oyo attempted to expand south but was blocked by Dahomey, which had acquired firearms through the coastal slave trade with Europeans. Oyo collapsed in 1833 when it was cut off from access to the coastal slave trade by a resurgent Dahomey and deprived of a supply of war horses from the hostile Sokoto Caliphate to the north, which had taken over the Yoruba states of Nupe and Ilorin. During the 1820s and 1830s, refugees from Oyo moved south into the forest zone, where some recreated their state at New Oyo and others founded new states such as Ibadan and Ijaye which built militaries based on firearms rather than horses. Those Yoruba states fought a series of 19th-century wars to fill the vacuum created by the fall of Oyo. In 1840, at the Battle of Osogbo, the military meritocracy of Ibadan halted the southward expansion of the Fulani jihad and then pushed associated Ilorin's forces further north. Subsequently, during the 1850s and 1860s, Ibadan became an expansionist power and fought a series of conflicts with a competing alliance of Yoruba states headed by Ijaye, particularly over control of coastal trade. Since those Yoruba wars produced a large number of slaves for export and they were fought in the final stages of the Trans-Atlantic slave trade, the Yoruba were some of the last West African slaves taken to the Americas, which meant that they sometimes retained a distinct identity such as in Brazil.[2]

Located in the forest east of the Yoruba states and west of the Niger River, the farmers and artisans of the Kingdom of Benin engaged in the Trans-Sahara trade at least 1,000 years ago. During the 1400s and 1500s, Benin expanded and became a successful military empire in what is now southwestern Nigeria and participated in the developing coastal slave trade. A civil war in the late 1600s and early 1700s contributed to the decline of Benin, which spent much of the 18th century suppressing rebellions and trying to reassert claims over the Lagos Lagoon to the west. The forested Niger River Delta in what is now southeastern Nigeria was (and is) inhabited by the Igbo people in the interior and the Ijo closer to the coast. The organizational structure of those communities varied from small centralized states to independent villages governed by councils of elders. During the 1700s, this area experienced an intensification of slaving and became the source for most slaves taken from West Africa, which led to a militarization of delta communities; warfare became more widespread and destructive. On the eastern delta, the basic unit of social organization shifted from traditional houses based on kinship to the "canoe house," which was a small trading and fighting group that operated and maintained a canoe. As the primary instrument of capturing and exporting slaves, successful canoe houses could spawn networks of satellites. By the 1800s, eastern delta trading towns like Bonny and Calabar consisted of a dozen or more canoe houses with the head of the senior house also serving as head of the town and commander of its canoe fleet. Delta towns became fortified and decentralized groups banded together in federations for mutual defense. When the oceanic slave trade was curbed by the British in the early to mid-1800s, the same canoe houses that had been responsible for slaving easily switched to the export of palm oil, which was valued by industrializing Western Europe.[3]

THE COLONIAL ERA

In 1861 the British, as part of their effort to combat the West African slave trade, seized the coastal trading center of Lagos, which later served as a base for further colonial expansion into what is now western Nigeria. Concerned about French and German competition in the area and disruption of coastal trade, the British intervened to end wars between Yoruba states in 1886, and most Yoruba rulers agreed to call on the Lagos governor to solve future disputes. With the 1892 British conquest of Ijebu, which had refused to discuss trade terms, most Yoruba rulers signed away their sovereignty to the British the following year. In 1894 the British bombarded New Oyo, which became the last Yoruba state to come under British control. In the 1850s, the British consul in the Bight of Biafra, who had gained considerable power by negotiating disputes between local rulers and British traders, imposed treaties that promoted British free trade, suppression of the slave trade, and assisted missionaries. In 1885 Britain—having gained rights to control the foreign affairs of local states such as Calabar and intervene to promote free trade—declared the Oil Rivers Protectorate (renamed the Niger Coast Protectorate in 1893). In 1887 Jaja, a former slave who as the powerful ruler of Opobo had denied British traders free access, was lured into negotiations, arrested, and exiled to the Caribbean. The Kingdom of Benin, which had rejected several British treaty offers and executed a British diplomatic mission, was invaded and conquered by the British Benin Punitive Expedition in 1897. In 1886 George Goldie's National African Company, an amalgamation of the three largest British trading firms on the Niger River, was granted a charter by the British government to gain control of the Niger and Benue rivers by making treaties with local rulers and suppressing the slave trade. While the British protectorate had secured the coast and Niger Delta, Goldie's renamed Royal Niger Company (RNC) was meant to forestall French and German penetration of the navigable rivers of the Nigerian hinterland. The RNC signed a succession of treaties, though it is unclear if the signatories understood they were signing away their sovereignty, and created a monopoly by imposing high import duties that drove out other European and African merchants. The Brass people of the Niger Delta, who could no longer afford to import food because of the new trade regulations, resisted the RNC until their main town was bombarded by British forces from the coast. In 1897 the RNC, worried about French intrusion, used superior firepower to seize the Yoruba kingdoms of Nupe and Ilorin from the Sokoto Caliphate. The next year, the British government bought the RNC from Goldie, and British officer Frederick Lugard arrived to form the West African Frontier Force (WAFF), which conquered Borgu and convinced the French to withdraw into what became colonial Dahomey (later the Republic of Benin). In 1900 the RNC territory south of the Niger and Benue rivers was joined to the Niger Coast Protectorate to form the Protectorate of Southern Nigeria. Former RNC territory in the north and Ilorin on the south side of the Niger became the Protectorate of Northern Nigeria, with Lugard as its first commissioner. Subsequently, Lugard embarked on the conquest of the Sokoto Caliphate, which had rejected a British resident and seemed likely to serve as an avenue for French encroachment from the north. Since the caliphate was decentralized, each major town was conquered separately between 1900 and 1903. The British justified those actions based on suppressing slavery. In 1904, east of Sokoto, the British annexed Borno, which had been greatly weakened by recent conquest by Sudanese slavers who were in turn defeated by the French around Lake Chad.[4]

In 1914 the British combined the protectorates of Southern and Northern Nigeria into the single colonial territory of Nigeria, with Lugard as the first governor. However, for the next five decades, the British ruled this vast and populous territory as three separate regions. Each region was associated with a major ethnic group: the Igbo in the east, the Yoruba in the west, and the Hausa-Fulani in the north. Located close to the southern coast, the East and West regions became relatively prosperous as the scene of coastal trade, predominantly Christian given the activities of missionaries and with a significant Western-educated elite, who were products of mission schools. On the other hand, the North was predominantly Muslim and controlled by conservative local rulers (emirs) who governed on behalf of the British. Afraid of the mobilizing potential of Islam, the British limited access to the north by missionaries, which meant fewer opportunities for Western education, and the region became comparatively impoverished and marginalized. Indeed, northern Nigeria became one of the classic examples of the British colonial administrative system of indirect rule, which was meant to promote a cheap form of colonialism by relying on low-paid local traditional rulers and discouraging resistance by making it seem as if change was minimal. Since the British saw the Hausa as inherently martial and the colonial army represented one of the few employment opportunities for northern men, the rank and file of the colonial military in Nigeria became dominated by poorly educated northerners. The institutionalization of those regional divisions led to the rise of colonial ethnic stereotypes, which became popular within Nigerian society. In this view, the northern Hausa-Fulani were disciplined people and proud members of a broader Islamic civilization, the western Yoruba were lazy and duplicitous, as well as the most culturally unique, and the eastern Igbo were ambitious and highly educated in the Western context but the most prone to ethnocentrism.

During the 1950s, the decolonization process in Nigeria was characterized by negotiation between outgoing British officials and emerging African political leaders from each of the three regions over what form the future independent state would take. In 1944 American-educated Nigerian journalist and nationalist Nnamdi Azikiwe formed the National Congress of Nigeria and the Cameroons (NCNC), which was an umbrella organization for many smaller groups that supported the idea of a broad Nigerian identity and self-government for the entire country. During the negotiations of the 1950s, NCNC advocated for a strong central government that would promote national unity rather than strong regional governments. Based in the south, one of its largest NCNC-aligned groups was the Igbo State Union, for which Azikiwe, an Igbo himself, was president. In 1951 Obafemi Awolowo, a Yoruba nationalist who had studied law in Britain, formed the Action Group to prevent the NCNC from gaining control in the west and to promote Nigerian self-government. Formed in 1949, the Northern People's Congress (NPC) was a conservative Muslim movement that sought to encourage northern unity and uphold the regional autonomy of the north against southern Christian influences. It was led by Sir Ahmadu Bello, a Western-educated descendant of Usman dan Fodio, who was awarded with the title Sardauna (Warlord) of Sokoto. In 1954, with the adoption of a constitution that made Nigeria into a federation of three regions, Azikiwe became premier of the Eastern Region, Awolowo became premier of the Western Region, and Bello became premier of the Northern Region. The constitution tried to balance the powers of the regional and central governments, and in 1957 Abubakar Tafawa Balewa, the NPC's vice president, but who was not from the northern Fulani elite, became the first prime minister of Nigeria. In October 1960, Nigeria became independent and, based on the previous year's election, the central government was controlled by an NPC-NCNC coalition with Balewa as prime minister and Azikiwe as ceremonial governor general. Awolowo's Action Group formed the official opposition. In 1963, when Nigeria became a republic, Balewa continued as prime minister, and Azikiwe became ceremonial president.[5]

INDEPENDENCE, COUPS, AND MASSACRES (1960–1966)

During the first years of Nigeria's independence, Balewa's coalition government was increasingly dominated by northerners from the NPC who gave out official appointments to northerners at the expense of more qualified southerners. The rapid Africanization of the military's officer corps in the late 1950s meant that the rank and file remained mostly northern, but the officers were mostly southerners—indeed mostly Igbo, given their greater access to education. To address the issue, the Balewa government extended the new national recruiting quotas to the officer corps, which meant that half could come from the north and a quarter from each of the west and east. As such, northerners would control the military. Furthermore, state funds were used to develop the north, which had lagged behind in colonial times, but this alienated people in the south. Since oil had been discovered in the Niger Delta in 1958 and oil revenues became increasingly important to the Nigerian government and its development projects, easterners began to think that their wealth was being stolen for the benefit of other regions. Southern anger was also enflamed by the 1963 census, which was widely believed to have fraudulently inflated the northern population to national majority status so that the Northern Region could have greater control over the federal government and its resources. Lastly, the federal election of December 1964 and the Western regional election of October 1965, which saw a continuation of the political status quo, were conducted so poorly as to cause many Nigerians to lose faith in their democratic process.

In January 1966, a group of mostly Igbo army officers, popularly called the Five Majors, led by Major Kaduna Nzeogwu, staged a coup that ousted the civilian politicians from the north who were accused of electoral fraud and corruption. Yoruba and Hausa-Fulani leaders were killed, including Western Region premier S. L. Akintola and prominent northerners Prime Minister Balewa and Northern Region premier Bello. Eventually, given that the Five Majors lacked a clear plan on how to govern Nigeria, Major General Johnson Aguiyi-Ironsi, another Igbo and commander of the Nigerian Army, took power. With similar goals as the Five Majors, Ironsi outlawed political parties and appointed military governors in each region. When Ironsi abolished the federal system in May, it seemed to northerners as part of a conspiracy to place them under the domination of southern, and particularly Igbo, civil servants and military officers. That prompted a late July countercoup by northern military officers and noncommissioned officers, led by Lieutenant Colonel Murtala Mohammed, in which Ironsi and several hundred Igbo officers and soldiers were killed. Appointed as head of state and commander of the armed forces by the coup makers, northerner Lieutenant Colonel Yakubu Gowon immediately reinstated the federal system.[6]

In the north, resentment toward southerners had been brewing long before 1966. Igbo merchants from the south had moved north before independence and dominated commerce in the historically marginalized region, where local people felt they did not have a chance to compete economically. Furthermore, extremist northern Muslims resented what they saw as southern Christian intrusion. Those factors led to violent incidents. The expansion of Igbo economic opportunities in the northern tin mining town of Jos during the Second World War led to two days of rioting between Hausa and Igbo in 1945 that left two people dead. The colonial army was brought in to restore order. In 1953, given southern political desires for self-government in 1956, which was opposed by northern leaders who felt they would not be ready, the arrival of a southern political delegation in Kano prompted rioting that targeted the city's "strangers' quarter," in which 36 southerners, including 21 Igbo, were killed.[7] During the second half of the 1950s, southerners were excluded from the Africanization of the northern civil service, and northern businessmen began to lobby the NPC regional government for preferential access to government contracts.

It is telling that the 1966 massacres of Igbo living in the north did not start in January when the Five Majors staged what was widely seen as an Igbo coup. In late May 1966, students at Ahmadu Bello University in the northern town of Zaria protested Ironsi's decree that turned Nigeria into a unitary state and appeared to confirm their fears of southern domination. That led to a week of rioting in northern towns, including Kaduna, Kano, Jos, Katsina, and Sokoto in which mobs killed perhaps 3,000 southerners, particularly those identified as Igbo, and destroyed their property. The July countercoup, as stated above, also involved the killing of Igbo soldiers. In the north, massacres continued in September and October, with mobs now joined by northern soldiers who mutinied, killed their northern officers, who tried to stop them, and seized weapons from military armories. False reports of northerners being killed in eastern Nigeria originally broadcast by Radio Cotonou in Dahomey and then repeated by a Nigerian government radio station in Kaduna in late September contributed to the violence. In Kano, at the start of October, thugs and mutinous soldiers went to the airport and railway station, where they murdered Igbos trying to leave the region. Police and army officers were too fearful to intervene. The Kano violence stopped when Lieutenant Colonel Hassan Katsina, governor of the Northern Region, and the emir of Kano drove around the city in a jeep and shamed the mobs, looters, and mutineers into returning to their homes or barracks. The Fifth Battalion, the unit involved in the mutiny, was disbanded over the incident. Trains heading out of the north were stoned by mobs and sometimes stopped so that Igbo could be disembarked and killed. There was often confusion over how to identify an Igbo—with certain stereotypical names, accents, knowledge of English, and Western dress marking victims for death. In a few isolated incidents, northern army officers saved the lives of their Igbo colleagues or subordinates. Estimates of the number of fatalities resulting from the 1966 massacres vary considerably from 30,000 to 50,000. Around 1.5 million refugees left the north and flooded into the Eastern Region.[8] At the end of 1966, the Eastern Region's Ministry of Information published a booklet entitled *Nigerian Pogrom* that accused the Muslim elites and politicians of the north of plotting the extermination of easterners in their area. Calling the massacres a genocide, it compared them to the Ottoman killing of Armenians and the Nazi killing of Jews.[9] Although historians who wish to claim that the 1966 massacres represented a genocide point to the seeming coordination of the violence in a number of cities and the absence of central government intervention as indicating the existence of an intentional plan to exterminate the Igbo living in the north, no direct evidence of that assertion has been presented. As Gowon stated, the new military government was simply unprepared, overwhelmed, and unable to act against mutinous soldiers and angry mobs.[10]

THE CIVIL WAR (1967–1970)

After the July 1966 military coup, Eastern regional military governor Lieutenant Colonel Chukwuemeka Odumegwu Ojukwu refused to attend meetings of Nigeria's Supreme Military Council (SMC) or to recognize Gowon as head of state and blamed the Gowon regime for the massacres of Igbos in the north. Almost immediately, the Biafran government transferred all oil revenues to its own accounts. At the beginning of January 1967, Gowon, Ojukwu, the other regional military governors, and other members of the Nigerian SMC attended a conference at Aburi in Ghana hosted by Lieutenant General Joseph Ankrah, who had recently come to power in his own military coup. On Ojukwu's suggestion, they agreed to resolve the crisis without violence. During the negotiations, the historic political aims of Nigeria's regional leaders were reversed: the northern-dominated federal government of Gowon advocated for a strong central government that they controlled, whereas the Eastern Region's Ojukwu desired a federal system with strong regional governments. However, the articulate and clever Ojukwu dominated the talks, and the subsequent Aburi Agreement favored his agenda. Regions would gain confederal status without a boundary change, all members of the SMC would have veto power, all regions would have to agree on major decisions, salaries would be paid to displaced people, and the federal head of state would be recognized as commander of the armed forces. Nevertheless, by mid-March, it was clear that the Aburi Agreement would not be implemented, as Gowon's federal government realized that it would deprive it of control of the Eastern Region's oil revenues, which were needed to develop other parts of the country.[11]

On May 30, 1967, Ojukwu, authorized by the Eastern Region Consultative Assembly and Advisory Committee of Chiefs and Elders, declared the secession of the east as the independent Republic of Biafra, which was named after the geographic Bight of Biafra. Its capital would be Enugu. Around the same time, Gowon declared emergency powers, including press censorship and a ban on political activity, and reorganized the 4 large regions into 12 smaller states. When Biafra declared independence, the federal government began mass military mobilization and acquisition of weapons. The federal government received military assistance from Britain, which was committed to maintaining its former colony as a single country and was heavily invested in the Nigerian oil industry. The Soviet Union also supported Gowon's regime, given that the need for oil overshadowed Cold War rivalries. The United States, embroiled in the Vietnam War, deferred to Britain on the Biafra issue and banned the sale of weapons to the breakaway state. While no country provided official military assistance to Biafra, several powers provided covert support such as France, which wanted to take over British oil interests in the separatist state, and the increasingly marginalized Portugal, Rhodesia, and South Africa, which wanted oil and were desperate for a black-ruled African ally. Cote d'Ivoire, Gabon, Zambia, and Tanzania were the only African countries to recognize Biafra.

On July 6, 1967, in what was initially called a police action, Nigerian federal forces launched an offensive to suppress the Biafran secession. Based in the north, the First Infantry Division advanced south into Biafra in two columns. In mid-July, the left column (on the east side) captured Garkem-Ogoja, and the right column (on the west side) took Nsukka. Biafran forces put up stiff resistance at Nsukka but lacked ammunition. In response, during July and August, Biafran forces invaded the Mid-Western Region west of the Niger River to threaten the federal capital of Lagos to distract federal forces in the north. Biafran troops advanced through Benin City and eventually halted at Ore, 160 kilometers east of Lagos, with limited federal forces opposing them. While the Biafrans had believed that the mixed Yoruba and Igbo population of the mid-west would support them, this plan backfired, as the invasion and subsequent looting discredited Biafra's claims of fighting in self-defense. It was hoped that the Yoruba identity of Brigadier Victor Banjo, commander of the Biafran invasion force, would appeal to mid-westerners, but he was executed when discovered to be conspiring against Ojukwu. By late September, the federal Second Infantry Division under Brigadier Murtala Mohammed had advanced east and driven the Biafrans out of Benin City to the Niger River's east bank. Between October and December, in a sequence of poorly planned and executed operations, the federal forces failed to cross the river. Around the same time, the Third Marine Commando Division, originating from Lagos, landed on the coast of the Niger Delta and captured the cities of Bonny and Okrika in late July and Calabar in mid-October. This federal amphibious campaign was facilitated by Biafra's lack of a significant navy. Bonny was a vital oil industry terminal, and its capture blocked supply ships from access to Biafran-controlled Port Harcourt, where the local airport became Biafra's only link to the outside world. With the First Infantry Division's seizure of Enugu in early October, Biafran forces were surrounded in the Igbo heartland, which was packed with refugees. From the beginning of 1968, the war became a stalemate, with the gradually shrinking and overcrowded Biafra blockaded by federal forces. In early 1968, Mohammed's Second Infantry Division abandoned attempts to cross the Niger River and took Onitsha by moving via the Enugu-Onitsha road. Given Biafran harassment of its supply lines, the division engaged in looting and abuse of civilians. A Nigerian offensive from April to June 1968 again reduced Biafran territory. At the end of April, the Third Marine Division traversed the Cross River from Calabar to Port Harcourt, which was taken a few weeks later in May and continued its advance to seize Aba in August and Owerri in September. To the north, the federal First Division advanced cautiously, capturing Abakaliki and Afikpo. By the end of 1968, the Biafrans clung to a small territory but were bolstered by international humanitarian airlifts that delivered aid and sometimes weapons and the arrival of some foreign mercenaries. Arguably, the relief operations that sustained the doomed Biafra prolonged the war and thus contributed to more suffering and loss of life. The federal forces then focused on maintaining a blockade to starve secessionist Biafra into submission, which, as discussed below, would lead to accusations of genocide.

In April and May 1969, the Nigerian First Division embarked on an offensive that captured the new Biafran capital of Umuahia. In June, Biafra launched a desperate offensive meant to knock the federals off balance and used mercenary piloted light aircraft to raid federal oil facilities and airfields. In December 1969, federal commanders initiated a final offensive to end the war. In January 1970, the Third Marine Commando Division, now under future president Colonel Olusegun Obasanjo, pushed up from the coast with armored vehicles penetrating Biafran lines. On January 9, federal troops once again captured Owerri and on January 13 took Amichi, which was the last Biafran-held town. Ojukwu flew to exile in Cote d'Ivoire, leaving General Phillip Effiong, Biafra's army commander, to surrender formally. Biafran forces had been massively outnumbered. The federal military had expanded from 8,000 troops in 1967 to 250,000 in 1970, while Biafra began the war with 3,000 and ended with 30,000. The estimates of total combat casualties range from 90,000 to 120,000. However, estimates of civilian fatalities vary from 0.5 million to 3 million, and it is clear that the overwhelming majority were from the Eastern Region and died from starvation or disease related to the federal blockade.[12]

BIAFRA AND THE WIDER WORLD

From early in the conflict, the Biafran regime mobilized the rhetoric of genocide in an effort to motivate its own people for the fight and enlist international sympathy and support. When South African–based mercenary leader Mike Hoare visited Biafra in May 1967 to assess the potential for external intervention in the emerging conflict, Ojukwu explained the independence movement to him by stating that "genocide stares us in the face. We want nothing more to do with a people that seek to destroy us."[13] In November 1967, Nnamdi Azikiwe, the Igbo former president of Nigeria who was hiding out in the Biafran enclave at Onitsha, wrote to a British newspaper calling on the world to "recognize the natural and inalienable right of the Ibo and fellow easterners to self-determination" and that "to do otherwise, is to turn a blind eye to an unjustifiable pogrom and inexcusable genocide of eight-million Ibo-speaking peoples . . . contrary to the international convention on genocide and the internationally accepted standards of civilized life."[14] Explaining the secession from Nigeria as a response to genocide, Biafran propaganda portrayed the breakaway republic as a stronghold of Christian modernity in Africa that was under attack by backward Muslim forces from the north. The Igbo were cast in the role of the "Jews of Africa," who were threatened by a postcolonial African holocaust. Biafran propaganda was directed from a public relations ministry and distributed through local and international newsletters, which included written pieces and cartoons, and Radio Biafra, which broadcast in Nigerian and European languages and stayed on the air throughout the war. In late 1967, the Biafran government engaged Markpress, a Swiss-based public relations firm owned by an American, to facilitate its global media campaign. Markpress orchestrated the publication of thousands of pro-Biafra news pieces in various newspapers around the world and organized and funded visits by journalists to the separatist republic.[15] By early April 1968, through the diplomatic efforts of Azikiwe, who visited Paris, presidents Leopold Senghor of Senegal and Julius Nyerere of Tanzania had denounced the Nigerian campaign against Biafra as genocide.[16] Accusations that the Gowon regime was conducting genocide against the people of Biafra were used to try to pressure the British government to halt arms shipments to Nigeria. In early August 1968, Ojukwu addressed the OAU in Addis Ababa, Ethiopia, where he pointed to the 1966 massacres of Igbo in the north as genocide and claimed that Gowon was becoming the Hitler of Africa. Furthermore, Ojukwu played the neocolonial card by claiming that the current genocide against the Igbo was being financed and directed by non-African powers to further their economic aims. Although he did not mention Britain, it was obvious that London was the federal government's primary backer.

Those genocide assertions gained traction after the fall of Port Harcourt in May 1968, which completed the Nigerian blockade and caused starvation in Biafra. The international media published pictures of starving people and compared the situation to Nazi concentration camps of the Second World War. Within Britain, church leaders, petition writers, and protestors called for an end to arms sales to Nigeria, and there were fiery debates within parliament, with some members warning against possible extermination and genocide. Radio Biafra reported that Biafran protestors carried signs reading "Britain responsible for genocide against Biafra" and broadcast a statement from Biafran commissioner for information Dr. Ifegwu Eke that "Britain continues massive arms sales in aid of genocide."

To counter those accusations, the Nigerian government invited Canada, Sweden, Poland, Britain, the OAU, and the UN secretary-general to form a team of observers to be sent to the war zone, including occupied parts of Biafra, to investigate claims of "wanton destruction" and "charges of genocide." From September 1968 to January 1970, the observers visited prisoner camps, refugee camps, and communities occupied by federal forces and dispatched numerous reports claiming that "there is no evidence of genocide against the Ibo people." In November 1968, British foreign secretary Michael Stewart, eager to justify his government's continued support for the Nigerian federal government, told parliament that "the story about genocide has been proved beyond doubt to be completely false." On the other hand, the Biafran government, its supporters, and later scholars criticized the observer team for being in the pocket of the federal government, for not including any legal experts who could professionally investigate the allegations of genocide, and for not looking into the massacres of 1966.[17]

Cleverly playing on American religious and ideological sensibilities, Ojukwu called for direct intervention by the United States to end Muslim genocide against Christian Biafra and to counter the intrusion of Soviet Communism, which he claimed had been invited in by the federal Nigerian regime.[18] In the United States, a pro-Biafra lobby developed quickly and included Christian church groups and the American Jewish Committee, which released a statement that this was "the first time that the American Jewish Community as a whole organized for the support of sufferers who were not Jews." American television networks broadcast news and documentaries on Biafra; the Committee to Keep Biafra Alive published a full-page advertisement in American newspapers featuring a picture of Adolf Hitler with a caption reading "Welcome Back"; and a pro-Biafra lobby developed within the U.S. Congress. In addition, a number of state governors declared a Biafra Month, pressed for international action, described the federal military campaign as genocide, and compared what was happening to the Holocaust. During the 1968 presidential election in the United States, candidate Richard Nixon criticized the Lyndon Johnson administration for not acting against the "genocide" that was taking place in Biafra. However, once Nixon moved into the White House, his administration continued the existing American policy toward Biafra by not granting it diplomatic recognition and remaining neutral in the Nigerian Civil War. It appears that while Nixon wanted to shift toward a more sympathetic policy that would press for negotiations and facilitate the delivery of aid to Biafra, he was blocked by National Security Advisor Henry Kissinger and the U.S. State Department, which saw American interests as directly linked to supporting federal Nigeria.[19]

By the middle of 1968, pro-Biafran protest had increased dramatically in France, West Germany, and the Scandinavian countries, and to some extent in Ireland and Italy. In predominantly Catholic countries, reports from Catholic missionaries in Biafra were influential. A British government official speculated that "many Germans find a psychological compensation in protesting against allegations of genocide in Nigeria for their failure to make similar protests in Germany under Hitler."[20] In France, an opinion poll illustrated that Biafra had overtaken Vietnam as the greatest international concern among the population. Although France, Belgium, and the Netherlands had imposed an arms sales embargo on both sides of the Nigerian Civil War in June 1968, French President Charles de Gaulle quickly bowed to pressure from the French left, including students and workers' movements, and initiated covert shipments of weapons and ammunition to Biafra through the former French colonies of Gabon and Cote d'Ivoire in August. The humanitarian services of French doctors in Biafra, including Bernard Kouchner, who much later became France's foreign minister, and their criticism of Nigerian army violence against Biafran civilians led to the establishment of Medecins sans Frontier (Doctors without Borders). The Paris-based International Committee for the Study of the Crimes of Genocide, an informal group of lawyers from several countries, conducted an investigation and declared that genocide had been committed by Nigerian forces against Biafra, but this was ignored by most governments. The conclusion of this unofficial committee would later become the main piece of evidence mobilized by historians seeking to prove that the federal Nigerian war against Biafra constituted genocide.[21]

In Canada, the government of Pierre Trudeau, given its own problems with Quebec separatism, which had recently been enflamed by France's de Gaulle, refused to acknowledge the Biafran secession. However, Christian and Jewish groups formed the Nigeria/Biafra Relief Fund of Canada and pressed the government to supply aid to Biafra. This position gained popular support from July 1968, when pictures of starving Biafrans were broadcast on television. With Trudeau's refusal to act and Canada's participation in the much criticized observer team, the Relief Fund organized Canairelief, which joined the Red Cross air relief effort based on the island of Fernando Po and flew 670 flights into Biafra to deliver more than 11,000 tons of food and medical supplies between January 1969 and January 1970. A Canadian Air Force C-130 transport aircraft flew eight relief missions but was withdrawn after the Port Harcourt airport was overrun by federal Nigerian forces, and it is likely that Nigerian diplomatic pressure was also a factor in the suspension of those flights. Furthermore, two Canadian opposition members of parliament accompanied by a Canadian journalist visited Biafra in October 1968 and returned home claiming that the accusations of genocide were true and strongly recommending that Canada help to negotiate a cease-fire and provide relief to Biafra. Stephen Lewis, another left-wing opposition parliamentarian, who did not visit Biafra, wrote that "genocide is an ugly, impossible word. I don't know precisely how one defines it. But if it means, even in part, the deliberate, indiscriminate killing of a people or a tribe, then there is concrete evidence to be found in the terrible Nigerian-Biafran civil war." Such pressure resulted in the Trudeau government pledging money to support the Canairelief in early January 1970, but Biafra surrendered several days later, which meant the end of relief flights.[22]

To counter the work of Markpress on behalf of Biafra during the war, the Nigerian government hired the British advertising agency Galizine, Grant, and Russell, which arranged for the publication of pro-federal accounts in the international press. For example, in June 1968, a British newspaper reported that Tony Asika, an Igbo political scientist who supported the federal government and was visiting Britain, undermined the genocide claim by pointing out that thousands of Igbos worked for the federal army and civil service, and he asked if it was likely that Igbos like himself would be engaged in the extermination of their own people. A long pro-federal advertisement in a British newspaper accused Igbo Biafran soldiers of carrying out "acts of genocide" against the minorities of Biafra such as the Ibibio, who were not supportive of secession.[23] For British journalist John Young:

> Highly charged emotional overtones have been added to the argument by the misleading use of the word genocide. Possibly there are hints of this in the 1966 massacres of Ibos in the north in spite of the bravery of many northerners who came to their aid. But to suppose that the victims of a civil war, however savage, are necessarily to be compared with those of systematic slaughter, such as Hitler perpetrated against the Jews or the Spanish colonists against the Indians of South America, is sheer self-delusion.[24]

Biafran genocide claims were seriously undermined in 1969 when Azikiwe, the Igbo former president of Nigeria who had once supported the separatist state, reversed his position on genocide and declared that the federal government had no intention of committing genocide and that "that accusation of genocide is palpably false."[25] Even after he had fled Biafra, Ojukwu kept pressing the international community on the need to prevent genocide in eastern Nigeria. In January 1970, he wrote a press release that urged the dispatch of food aid and an international peacekeeping force to the former secessionist state "to prevent a genocide that would make 1939–45 Europe a mere child's play."[26] Despite the fact that no such force was created, Ojukwu's fears proved unfounded. There would be no postwar revenge massacres or genocide.

POST–CIVIL WAR NIGERIA

At the end of the war, Gowon famously declared that there was "no victor and no vanquished." As such, the Nigerian federal government embarked on a campaign of postwar national reconciliation, launched a reconstruction program in the east, and outlawed ethnically based political parties. Pardoned by the Nigerian government, Ojukwu returned home in 1982, and with the exception of a brief imprisonment during the military coup of 1984, he lived freely and participated in politics until his death in 2011. However, resentment among easterners lingered, because, during the war, many had lost their property in other regions, many did not get back previous government jobs, and minimal compensation was provided for worthless Biafran currency. Importantly, many easterners maintained that they were not receiving their fair share of oil revenue generated in their region and that the money had been squandered by Nigeria's subsequent military regimes, which were seen as corrupt and wasteful.

The end of the Cold War and the rise of democratic ambitions across Africa at the start of the 1990s affected southeastern Nigeria. While the Niger Delta territory of the Ogoni minority generated about half of Nigeria's oil wealth, their fishing economy was spoiled by oil pollution, and they derived little benefit from the petroleum industry. In the early 1990s, the Movement for the Survival of the Ogoni People (MOSOP) presented the Nigerian military government with demands for greater political representation, a share of oil revenues, and protection for their environment. When this was rejected, MOSOP and its supporters resorted to riots and limited violence that resulted in the death of four conservative chiefs. Consequently, in 1994, the military regime of General Sani Abacha arrested nine MOSOP leaders, including celebrated author Ken Saro-Wiwa, and convicted them in a farcical and internationally condemned trial, and they were hanged. Saro-Wiwa had written a series of newspaper pieces compiled into a book that accused the federal government and multinational oil companies (particularly Shell) of perpetrating genocide against the Ogoni and called on the international community for assistance.[27] The killing of Saro-Wiwa led to international sanctions against Nigeria's military regime and contributed to pressures that led to democratization. Although Shell Oil Company paid the Ogoni community $15.5 million (U.S.) in 2009 to settle an international legal action, the persistence of environmental problems and violence in Ogoniland prompted continued accusations of genocide.

The sudden death of military regime leader Sani Abacha and the transition to civilian rule in the late 1990s led to the rise of separatist movements in parts of Nigeria. Launched in the late 1990s, the Oodua People's Congress demanded an independent state for the Yoruba of the southwest. In 1999 the Movement for the Actualization of the Sovereign State of Biafra

(MASSOB) was established with the aim of achieving independence for the Igbo of southeastern Nigeria. It engaged in peaceful protest, including mass rallies, displays of the Biafra flag, distribution of an unofficial Biafran currency, and the opening of a "Biafra embassy" in Washington, D.C. MASSOB also encouraged Igbos living in the north to defend themselves from violence by northerners. The Nigerian state of President Olusegun Obasanjo responded with force, and MASSOB leader Ralph Uwazuruike, an Indian-trained lawyer inspired by the nonviolent approach of Gandhi, was charged with treason in 2005; federal forces also arrested other key members. Central to MASSOB's separatist ideology is that the federal military government engaged in genocide against the Igbo during the Nigerian Civil War of 1967–1970 and from the late 2000s a number of Igbo scholars, perhaps partly inspired by the rise of global antigenocide campaigns such as related to Darfur, wrote articles and books in support of that view. While MASSOB maintained a nonviolent approach, armed groups emerged in southeastern Nigeria using the concept of self-determination as an excuse for piracy. Around 2005, armed groups—the most prominent of which was the Movement for the Emancipation of the Niger Delta (MEND)—began using small and fast boats to raid oil industry facilities and kidnap expatriate oil workers in the Delta area around Port Harcourt, with ransom money from the oil companies used to buy more weapons. Oil companies hired private security contractors, and the oil-dependent Nigerian government launched a major offensive in the Delta during 2009 and then offered insurgents amnesty.[28]

Violence in Nigeria's southeast was overshadowed by the start of Islamist insurgency in the north. In 2009 a radical Islamist group called Boko Haram, Hausa language for "Western education is sinful," emerged in Nigeria's northeast within the context of poverty, unemployment, state corruption, and existing tensions between Muslims and Christians. It sought to impose a "pure" Muslim society and establish an Islamic state. Boko Haram launched a campaign of bombing, assassination, and kidnapping, which provoked a brutal security force response that some say exacerbated the problem and caused the declaration of a state of emergency in the north by the federal government. The U.S. government, concerned about Boko Haram's links to the global jihadist movement, began to assist Nigerian security forces, though this was limited given the Nigerian military's poor human rights record. Declaring allegiance to the Islamic State fighting in Iraq, Syria, and Libya, Boko Haram eventually spread into the neighboring countries of Cameroon and Niger.[29]

CONCLUSION

There is little reason to believe that the horrific mass violence that took place in Nigeria from 1966 to 1970 corresponds with the international legal definition of genocide. Those who argue the case for an Igbo genocide or a Biafra genocide claim to present incriminating evidence but then fail in the attempt, and in some instances employ self-referential citations and quote fictional novels. There is no evidence that the federal or Northern regional governments directed the terrible 1966 massacres of Igbo in the north. The soldiers who took part in the killings were mutineers. Similarly, if the federal siege of Biafra from 1968 to 1970 is seen as a program to intentionally exterminate part of all of the Igbo or Biafran people, then other military blockades such as the federal North imposed on the confederate South during the American Civil War or the Allies enforced against Nazi Germany during the Second World War must be seen in the same light, which would be ridiculous. Sieges and blockades have been an ugly but common feature of warfare since ancient times. As part of what Carl von Clausewitz called "policy by other means," they target the inhabitants of specific fortifications, cities, regions, or countries in an effort to impose some political or economic agenda. In the Nigerian case, the federal intention in blockading Biafra was to eliminate the secessionist state, not to exterminate the population. Sieges and blockades could be genocidal if they form part of a campaign of intentional extermination, but most historical examples do not fall into this category. Ironically, genocide accusations by the Biafra regime and its international supporters, which played a major role in mobilizing support for the militarily weak secessionist state, likely caused the Nigerian Civil War to be longer and deadlier than it would have otherwise been. In this situation, the rhetoric of genocide caused many preventable civilian deaths within Biafra. The resurgence of genocide accusations related to southeastern Nigeria in the post–Cold War era is a product of regional marginalization and dissatisfaction, and such language is meant to mobilize people in pursuit of political agendas.

Conclusion

Aside from the cases discussed in the previous chapters, many horrific instances of mass violence that occurred in colonial and postcolonial Africa have been labeled as genocide. Most of those accusations do not measure up to the international legal definition, and a few have never been thoroughly investigated. They often involved authoritarian regimes, both colonial European and postcolonial African, responding to political opposition and/or regional secessionist movements. Many of the genocide allegations were retrospective in that they were made during the 1990s and 2000s within the context of heightened awareness of genocide issues but related to large-scale violence that had taken place decades, or even centuries, before. Frequently, those genocide charges were sensationalist, meant to vilify political opponents and enhance claims of victimhood among the accusers as a way of achieving separatist or other political aspirations.

CAMEROON AND KENYA: LATE COLONIAL CONFLICTS AND POSTCOLONIAL POLITICS

In 1948 African intellectuals and labor leaders in Cameroon formed the Union of the Peoples of Cameroon (UPC), led by Ruben Um Nyobe, which criticized the French government for failing to prepare the former German colony and UN mandate for independence. The UPC demanded independence from France and reunification with Southern Cameroons, a small section of the former German colony of Cameroon that had been administered by the British since the end of the First World War. Nyobe's movement gained popular support in Cameroon's south and west, sympathized with the liberation struggles being fought against the French in Indochina and Algeria, and was backed by the French Communist Party. The French administration responded by encouraging conservative pro-French Cameroonian groups and having security forces harass UPC activists. As a result, in May 1955, violence broke out in the southwest, including the city of Douala, where UPC activists destroyed the property of regime supporters and military units were brought in from neighboring French territories to restore order. After its banning by French authorities in July 1955, UPC leaders fled to British-ruled Southern Cameroons and organized an armed wing called the National Organization Committee (CNO) that tried to use sabotage to undermine the first territorial elections. In December 1956, moderate nationalists who were willing to work with the French took over Cameroon's territorial administration, and French paratroopers seized control of the southwestern town of Eseka. The UPC rebellion continued in the west and southwestern areas among the Bassa and Bamileke peoples. In 1957 the UPC was banned in British Southern Cameroons and subsequently moved to Sudan, Egypt, Ghana, and Guinea and received assistance from China. Within southwestern Cameroon, UPC insurgents targeted the economy by sabotaging the railway and created a liberated zone that was meant to serve as a staging area for expanded operations against the French in the rest of the country. French efforts to isolate the UPC by securing roads, railways, and towns failed, and insurgent attacks increased. In December 1957, at the request of Cameroonian prime minister Andre-Marie Mbida, the French military brought in additional troops from Chad and launched an aggressive counterinsurgency campaign that involved relocating the rural population of Sanaga-Maritime region into fortified villages along roads and dispatching patrols to hunt down guerrillas. In September 1958, Nyobe was killed by French forces, which ended the Bassa element of the insurrection, and, during that year, some 2,000 rebels surrendered in Sanaga-Maritime.

In 1958, with a dramatic change in French policy that moved toward granting rapid independence to its Sub-Saharan African territories, including Cameroon, UPC aims became redundant, and the group split. One faction joined the legal political process and gained seats in Cameroon's assembly, while another continued the insurgency as the Cameroonian Army of National Liberation (ALNK), led by Felix-Roland Moumie, which fought in the predominantly Bamileke West region around the town of Bafoussam. In January 1960, Cameroon gained independence, and its president, Ahmadou Ahidjo, invited the French military to eliminate the rebels. Five French battalions, supported by ground attack aircraft and armored vehicles, initiated an offensive that crushed the insurgency after eight months. The French, who lost 30 soldiers, claimed to have killed 3,000 insurgents, but it is likely that thousands more displaced people died in the forest from disease and hunger. In November 1960, French intelligence poisoned Moumie in Switzerland. Limited ALNK resistance in western Cameroon continued until 1971, when the group's leader, Ernest Ouandie, was captured and executed. Given the results of a referendum, British Southern Cameroons was reincorporated into Cameroon in October 1961.

As with other former French territories in Africa, Cameroon became an authoritarian one-party state, supported by the former colonial power.[1]

The French military campaign in decolonization-era Cameroon was hardly mentioned by the international media of the time. Accusations that France had carried out genocide against the Bamileke began in the 1960s, perhaps partly inspired by similar accusations during neighboring Nigeria's Civil War, and escalated over the next few decades given the rise of a Southern Cameroons independence movement within the former British-administered area. With Cameroon's abandonment of a federal system in 1972, the former Southern Cameroons lost its partial autonomy, which meant that the area's Anglophone population began to see themselves as unfairly dominated by the country's Francophone majority. Like other African countries, Cameroon engaged in political liberalization in the early 1990s, which, although the long-time authoritarian and French-sponsored regime of Paul Biya survived, meant that a space was opened for more public discussion of Southern Cameroons secession. The 1988 publication of a memoir by Max Bardet, a French helicopter pilot who served in Cameroon during the earlier counterinsurgency campaign, strengthened the claims of genocide. He wrote that "in two years, the regular army destroyed Bamileke country in the South. They massacred between 300,000 and 400,000 people. A veritable genocide! The race was practically exterminated. Spears against automatic weapons, the Bamileke had no chance of surviving. Villages were erased, much like Attila."[2] Most authors making the case for a French genocide against the Bamileke would employ this quote. Eventually, separatists argued that the Cameroonian state, supported by French neocolonialism, had a long history of perpetrating genocide that, they claimed, had begun with the Bamileke ethnic group of the West region and then applied to the entire people of Southern Cameroons. Within this context of genocide accusation, some Southern Cameroons separatists claimed that France and the Cameroonian government had employed a chemical weapon to kill 1,700 Southern Cameroonians in 1986 and then covered up the incident by portraying it as a natural disaster involving poisonous gas erupting from Lake Nyos. Some have called this the Lake Nyos Genocide. Another conspiracy theory involved rumors that a state vaccination program represented a surreptitious effort to sterilize the young women of Southern Cameroons.[3] During the 2000s, with the emergence of a global antigenocide movement and revelations that France had facilitated the 1994 genocide in Rwanda, many more Cameroonians and others, including veterans of the 1950s rebellion, called on the government of France to acknowledge its role in perpetrating a genocide against the Bamileke during the decolonization era, to open long-sealed official records related to the war, and to provide reparations to survivors in Cameroon. That overlapped with and supported broader southern Cameroon separatists' continued accusations that the

Cameroonian state was conducting an ongoing genocide against the people of their region. In 2015, after years of denial by French officials, French president Francois Hollande visited Cameroon and publically acknowledged his country's role in "tragic events" there during the late 1950s and early 1960s but stopped short of making an apology or describing the campaign as genocidal.[4]

During the 1950s, the Kenya Land and Freedom Army, called Mau Mau by the British, fought an insurgency against British colonial rule in Kenya. The rebellion mostly involved the Kikuyu people of the White Highlands near Nairobi who, compared to other indigenous groups in Kenya, had been disproportionally affected by white settlement. Imposing a state of emergency between 1952 and 1960, the British government dispatched large military forces to Kenya, mobilized a loyalist Kikuyu Home Guard, detained and tortured thousands of suspected insurgents, and forcibly resettled 1 million Kikuyu into 800 "protected villages" surrounded by barbed wire and watchtowers. While the British employed overwhelming military force to crush the Mau Mau movement, the changing international context led to the granting of independence and majority rule to Kenya in 1963. Although a massive literature developed on aspects of the Mau Mau war, the term "genocide" was not applied to the British counterinsurgency campaign until the 2000s. Several factors may have contributed to this lack of genocide narrative, including the marginalization of Mau Mau insurgent veterans in the first few decades of Kenya's postcolonial history, the lack of a secessionist movement among the Kikuyu, who represent one of Kenya's largest and most prominent ethnic communities, and the propagation of a myth that such post–Second War British counterinsurgency campaigns as took place in Kenya and Malaya had been conducted with minimal force. The British security forces suffered 600 dead and claimed to have killed 10,500 Mau Mau. That view changed in the mid-2000s, when historian Caroline Elkins estimated the total number of deaths during the Mau Mau conflict at between 130,000 and 300,000, which she presented as a British-perpetrated genocide against the Kikuyu. Elkins's fatality count was challenged by demographer John Blacker, who put the figure at around 50,000, half of whom were children, and other scholars such as David Anderson and Huw Bennett, who acknowledged the shocking violence of the campaign but maintain that there was no evidence that British officials had intended to exterminate all or part of the Kikuyu. Indeed, the British military in Kenya possessed the means to kill even more Kikuyu than it did and often rejected white settlers' demands for more severe action. Around the same time that this academic debate unfolded in the 2000s, political change in Kenya led to greater official recognition for elderly Mau Mau veterans and survivors of the detention camps, and some Kenyans took the British government to court in pursuit of damages. In 2011 a British court ruled that some 12,000 Kenyan claimants had the right to make legal claims against the British government, which, two years later, agreed to pay them compensation. That led to another legal case against the British government by 40,000 Kenyans. While those legal claims did not include formal accusations of genocide, the debate over the appropriateness of the term certainly heightened international awareness of British atrocities committed in Kenya during the 1950s. The idea that the British army had liberated concentration camps in 1940s Germany only to build their own in 1950s Kenya seemed extremely contradictory[5]

The rhetoric of genocide worsened the violence that followed Kenya's 2007 elections, which involved politicized ethnic mobs of Kikuyu, Luo, and Kalenjin killing members of each other's ethnic groups and destroying property. Kenyan political leaders, aware of international guilt over the failure to intervene in Rwanda during 1994 and the newly instituted UN doctrine of "responsibility to protect," attempted to garner Western sympathy and mobilize their followers by accusing each other of genocide and ethnic cleansing. For example, members of President Mwai Kibaki's ruling and mostly Kikuyu Party of National Unity (PNU) spread rumors that Raila Odinga's Orange Democratic Movement (ODM), a predominantly Luo party, was in league with former colonial power Britain, which wanted to reverse the recent rehabilitation of Mau Mau veterans, in a conspiracy to conduct genocide against the Kikuyu so as to permanently reduce their population by 1 million and therefore cancel their advantage in electoral politics. As such, many Kikuyu greatly feared becoming genocide victims if the ODM came to power.[6] The international media also played a role in fueling the violence as its broadcasts were "stuck in the pornography of mayhem and genocide long after the national media had shifted to more balanced reporting."[7] In 2008 the Kenya National Commission on Human Rights investigated the specific accusation of genocide and found unequivocally that it had not occurred during the disturbances, as there had been no intent to destroy ethnic communities. It did, however, conclude that ethnic cleansing had taken place, in that people from certain ethnic groups had been evicted from specific areas. Although Kenyan politicians reached a settlement and formed a new government, the ICC demanded justice, though this did not involve genocide charges. In 2011 the ICC indicted Kenyan cabinet minister Uhuru Kenyatta, son of the country's first president, who had been jailed by the British during Mau Mau for crimes against humanity, in that he allegedly directed and funded armed Kikuyu groups that massacred Kenyans from other communities. In 2014 Kenyatta became the first serving head of state (he was elected president the previous year) to appear before the ICC, which later withdrew its charges given lack of evidence; ICC lawyers claimed the evidence was withheld by the Kenyan government. Similar charges were also dropped against other Kenyan politicians, including Deputy President

William Ruto, who had entered into a political alliance with Kenyatta in 2013 and who had allegedly directed ethnic Kalenjin mobs against Kikuyu victims during the violence of 2007–2008. Given the continued ethnic orientation of Kenya's political parties, some observers warn of the dangers of genocide during the country's next election. The ICC indictment of Kenyan leaders contributed to further complaints that the international judicial body was a racist and hypocritical Western institution that was only interested in pursuing Africans.[8]

ETHIOPIA: POLITICAL GENOCIDE

Ethiopia has a long history of regional secessionist insurgencies. The independence of the neighboring Republic of Somalia, a combination of the former British Somaliland and Italian Somaliland, in 1960 provided the context for ethnic Somali separatist movements in Ethiopia's Ogaden region, including the Ogaden Liberation Front (OLF), which was formed in 1963 and crushed by Ethiopian forces the following year, and the Western Somali Liberation Front (WSLF), which was launched at the end of the 1960s and fought a guerrilla war until the end of the 1980s. In the early 1950s, the United Nations federated Eritrea, a former Italian colony on the Red Sea coast that had been occupied by the British during the Second World War, to neighboring Ethiopia. Consequently, at the start of the 1960s, the Eritrea Liberation Front (ELF), supported by Muslim Arab countries in the Middle East, initiated a guerrilla struggle against Ethiopian occupation forces, which responded with a brutal counterinsurgency campaign that alienated most Eritreans. In 1973 Christian and secular elements within the ELF broke away to form the revolutionary socialist Eritrean People's Liberation Front (EPLF), which began to fight a conventional war to expel the Ethiopian military.

In 1974 the pro-Western Ethiopian emperor Haile Selassie was overthrown by a military coup that eventually brought a Soviet-backed military regime called the Derg, led by Colonel Mengistu Haile Mariam, to power. In 1977 the Mengistu regime launched the Red Terror campaign, which involved the detention, torture, and murder of political opponents such as intellectuals and university students, with estimates of the death toll ranging from 30,000 to 100,000 and much higher. Although Mengistu's Ethiopia, with the help of Soviet weapons and Cuban troops, repelled a Somali invasion during the Ogaden War of 1977–1978, the brutal military regime stimulated further regional secessionism. From 1978 to 1983, the Mengistu regime launched at least seven separate offensives against Eritrean independence fighters that pushed them into Eritrea's mountainous north, destroyed the ELF, and resulted in the death of around 30,000 Eritreans and 50,000 Ethiopians. The most ambitious government offensive in Eritrea was the Red Star campaign, which began in 1982 and involved almost 180,000 Ethiopian troops, mostly conscripts, but completed failed to dislodge the EPLF, which ultimately counterattacked to regain lost territory. During the late 1970s, rebellion broke out in Ethiopia's northern Tigray Province, where, by the early 1980s, feuding rebel groups had combined into the Tigray People's Liberation Front (TPLF), which fought a guerrilla war for the self-determination of all Ethiopia's peoples. In Tigray, the Mengistu regime alienated civilians by imposing unpopular land reform, forcibly resettling peasants away from insurgent areas, terrorizing urban elites, and persecuting the Ethiopian Church. While Mengistu's counterinsurgency program in Tigray involved destroying crops and depriving people of international food aid, which created a catastrophic famine in the early 1980s, the TPLF gained international legitimacy by coordinating humanitarian assistance from Sudan. Around the same time, the EPLF and TPLF formed a sometimes shaky anti-Mengistu alliance.

The reduction in hitherto massive Soviet military assistance in the late 1980s fatally weakened the Ethiopian state. In December 1986, the EPLF embarked on an offensive in Eritrea that ultimately led to their decisive victory at the Battle of Afabet in March 1988. Subsequently, the TPLF broke the existing military stalemate in Tigray by embarking on its own offensive. The TPLF offensive prompted a massive August 1988 counterattack from the Mengistu regime, which recaptured Tigrayan towns and massacred civilians. In early 1989, EPLF forces advanced into Tigray and helped the TPLF, which was transforming into a conventional military, to expel Ethiopian state forces from the province. Shortly thereafter, the Soviet Union halted military aid to Ethiopia, and the TPLF and other rebel groups such as the Oromo People's Democratic Organization (OPDO), which consisted mostly of captured government troops, formed a broad anti-Mengistu coalition known as the Ethiopian People's Revolutionary Democratic Front (EPRDF). During the first half of 1991, the EPRDF and EPLF drove Mengistu's forces out of the provinces of Gondar, Gojjam, and Wollo, and the EPLF continued to gain control of Eritrea. In May 1991, Mengistu fled to Zimbabwe, and, later in the month, the EPLF took Asmara, capital of Eritrea, and EPRDF and EPLF forces captured the national capital of Addis Ababa. The EPRDF and Oromo Liberation Front (OLF) formed a transitional government under TPLF chairman Meles Zenawi, who, under a new constitution that created a multiparty democracy, was elected prime minister in 1995 and 2005. The OLF quickly withdrew from the government and resumed its regional insurgency, while the Zenawi administration was criticized for increasing authoritarianism. In Eritrea, where the EPLF formed a provisional government in May 1991, a UN-supervised referendum was held in April 1993 that resulted almost immediately in independence. The EPLF renamed itself the People's Front for Democracy and Justice (PFDJ) and quickly imposed a single-party state under former rebel leader Isaias Afewerki.[9]

In 1992 the Ethiopian transitional government established a special prosecutor's office to address serious crimes committed by the ousted Mengistu regime. The Zimbabwean government of Robert Mugabe refused demands to return Mengistu to Ethiopia, citing the lack of an extradition agreement between the two countries and the former ruler's contribution to Zimbabwe's struggle for majority rule and independence during the late 1970s. From 1994 to 2006, officials of the former Ethiopian government were put on trial, and 55 of them were convicted of genocide and crimes against humanity. Of those convicted, 25 had been tried in absentia, including Mengistu, who was initially sentenced to life imprisonment but on appeal was changed to death. Central to those convictions was the fact that Ethiopia, in 1957, became one of the few countries to extend its legal definition of genocide beyond the international norm to include the extermination of political groups and to add "population transfer or dispersion" to the list of illegal genocidal methods. At the beginning of the Mengistu trial, the court addressed the difference between international and domestic law by deciding that the international definition of genocide provided a minimal level of protection, which Ethiopia, as a sovereign state, was free to expand. In a dissenting opinion, one of the three judges maintained that Mengistu was guilty of homicide and not genocide, as his regime had repealed the part of Ethiopia's genocide law that afforded political groups protection through its decrees in the late 1970s.[10] If the international legal definition of genocide had been applied in this case, then Mengistu would likely never have been convicted: the charges focused on the death of some 2,000 political opponents (real or imagined) during the Red Terror of 1977–1978, which did not target national, ethnic, racial, or religious groups.

Ironically, at the same time that Mengistu and others were convicted of genocide, Ethiopia's Zenawi administration was itself accused of conducting genocide against the Anuak people of Gambella Province in the western part of the country. The marginalized Anuak had long been victimized by successive regimes in Addis Ababa. In the 1980s, violence broke out in Gambella between Anuak communities and people from other parts of Ethiopia, called highlanders, who had been moved there by the Mengistu regime and between Anuak people and ethnic Nuer, many of whom had moved into Ethiopian from adjacent southern Sudan to escape civil war. Indeed, in the mid-1980s, the U.S.-based indigenous rights organization Cultural Survival accused the Mengistu regime of committing genocide against the Anuak. In 1985 the predominantly Anuak Gambella People's Liberation Movement (GPLM) began a guerrilla war against the Mengistu state and eventually joined the anti-Mengistu coalition that overthrew the dictatorship in 1991. However, in December 2003, the Ethiopian military and state-sponsored militias began a series of massacres of Anuak communities that eventually claimed several thousand lives. This was prompted by continued violence between Anuak, highlanders, and Nuer and discoveries of gold and oil in Gambella. In 2005 members of the Anuak diaspora in North America formed the Anuak Justice Council (AJC) to pursue nonviolent solutions to the problems of the Anuak people, which involved presenting complaints against the Ethiopian government to the UN, the ICC, and various Western governments such as the United States and Canada. Tragically, the outbreak of civil war in newly independent South Sudan in 2013 resulted in many South Sudanese Nuer fleeing across the border into Gambella, where they were allegedly armed by the Ethiopian military and encouraged to attack Anuak people in early 2016. The GPLM called this a "Second Genocide of the Anuak."[11]

In recent years, there have been other accusations against the Ethiopian state, dominated by Tigrayans from the north, for perpetrating genocide against marginalized ethnic groups. In 2015 a protest movement among the Oromo emerged to challenge their historic discrimination that has occurred despite the fact that they represent the country's largest ethnic community. Given the violent government response, there is now talk of an "Oromo genocide." Some claim that Western governments have been hesitant to criticise genocide allegedly carried out by the Ethiopian state given its support for the U.S. "Global War on Terror" and, in particular, military operations against Islamist extremists in Somalia.[12]

ZIMBABWE: PARANOIA AND OVERREACTION

In 1965 the white minority government of Southern Rhodesia (now Zimbabwe), led by Prime Minister Ian Smith, unilaterally declared independence from Britain to avoid engaging in political reforms that would grant equal rights to the black majority. Consequently, the African nationalists of the Zimbabwe liberation movement embarked on an armed struggle in pursuit of majority rule and independence. However, in 1964 a disagreement over strategy resulted in the division of the exiled movement, with Joshua Nkomo leading the Zimbabwe African People's Union (ZAPU) and Ndabaningi Sithole leading the Zimbabwe African National Union (ZANU). Those groups developed military wings, with ZAPU forming the Zimbabwe People's Revolutionary Army (ZIPRA), and ZANU forming the Zimbabwe African National Liberation Army (ZANLA). By the 1970s, those organizations had developed differing ethnic orientations, revolutionary ideologies, and external alliances. Based in Zambia, ZAPU-ZIPRA derived its support from the Ndebele minority of Rhodesia's southwestern Matabeleland region and, given its Soviet support, adopted a Leninist strategy that favored forming a conventional army that would invade Rhodesia and seize power at a key moment that would never take place. Based in Mozambique, ZANU-ZANLA recruited mostly from Rhodesia's Shona majority in the eastern half of the country, and Chinese sponsorship meant that they focused on peasant mobilization and guerrilla warfare. Several OAU-backed attempts to unify the Zimbabwe liberation movement failed. At the end of the 1970s, with Rhodesian forces unable to control the countryside and the end of the war in sight, ZIPRA and ZANLA insurgents fought over the country's southwestern region. In 1979 the British-sponsored Lancaster House Talks produced an agreement that ended the war and resulted in universal suffrage and independence for Zimbabwe the following year. Under this agreement, insurgents would report to assembly areas for either demobilization or incorporation into a new Zimbabwean security force structure that would also include former Rhodesian state forces. An election resulted in ZANU-PF (ZANU-Patriotic Front) forming the first independent government under Prime Minister Robert Mugabe in April 1980. Still led by Joshua Nkomo, ZAPU became an opposition party.[13]

Problems related to the integration of the new Zimbabwe Defense Force (ZDF) led to violence in the early 1980s. In 1981 ZIPRA veterans at Entumbane in Bulawayo rebelled over delays in the integration process, poor living conditions in their camp, and favoritism toward former ZANLA fighters affiliated with the ZANU-PF administration. There were also disturbing rumors that former ZIPRA insurgents were disappearing once they were integrated into the ZDF. The mutiny was crushed by former Rhodesian police and military units. With the discovery of arms caches in southwestern Matabeleland in early 1982, ZAPU-ZIPRA leaders were arrested and charged with treason or fled the country. Some ZIPRA veterans deserted the ZDF or their integration camps and took to the bush as dissidents who targeted state officials. Attempts by apartheid South Africa to destabilize independent Zimbabwe produced paranoia within Mugabe's fledgling government. In 1982 South African agents blew up aircraft at a Zimbabwean Air Force base in Gweru, and South Africa attempted to form a counterrevolutionary group called Super-ZAPU in Matabeleland that failed to attract much support. In addition, Zimbabwean troops were becoming involved in fighting the South African–backed Mozambique National Resistance (RENAMO) that was destabilizing Mozambique. As such, the Mugabe administration overreacted to events in Matabeleland by dispatching a special ZDF unit called 5 Brigade to suppress a relatively small number of dissidents. Trained by a detachment of North Korean instructors, the 3,500-strong 5 Brigade was composed almost entirely of former ZANLA fighters who were Shona people from eastern Zimbabwe. Commanded by Colonel Perence Shiri, 5 Brigade's motto was the Shona phrase "Gukurahundi," meaning "the rain that washes away the rubbish," and it was likely that the rural Ndebele people came to think this referred to them. Between 1983 and 1987, 5 Brigade imposed a reign of terror on rural Matabeleland and parts of Midlands Province. Local Ndebele and Kalanga people were forced to participate in all-night "pungwes," in which they sung Shona songs praising ZANU-PF, their crops and houses were destroyed, they were subjected to curfew and collective punishment, and they became victims of public beatings and summary executions. Corpses were disposed of in mass graves or thrown down abandoned mine shafts. It has been estimated that some 20,000 people were killed. In April 1984, Catholic priest John Gough gave a sermon in Harare that accused the Zimbabwe state of conducting genocide in Matabeleland, which government officials strongly denied. The violence ended with the December 1987 Unity Accord, in which ZAPU leaders such as Nkomo agreed to the absorption of their organization into ZANU-PF, and they were rewarded with senior government positions under Mugabe, who became an executive president. In 1988 Mugabe granted amnesty to dissidents—the actual number of whom appears to have been just over 120—and security force members for crimes committed during the period of violence in the 1980s that Zimbabweans have come to call "Gukurahundi." As a result, there were no official investigations of the violence, and no one was ever charged with any crime related to this episode. While foreign governments knew about the massacres in Matabeleland, including the British, who were selling arms to Zimbabwe at the time, those events were not widely reported in international media. In fact, the media generally portrayed Mugabe in a positive light, given his policy of reconciliation with the white minority.

In 1997 the Catholic Commission for Justice and Peace in Zimbabwe, a human rights organization that had been critical of the Smith regime during the 1970s, published the results of an intensive investigation into the violence in Matabeleland and the Midlands during the 1980s. While the report did "not seek to apportion blame" and sought only to "break the silence surrounding this phase of the nation's history," it revealed that at least 3,000 people (and perhaps double that number or more) had been killed, 7,000 people tortured, and at least 680 homes destroyed. The report did not label those events as genocide.[14] At the funeral of Vice President Nkomo in 1999, Mugabe broke his usual silence over the Gukurahundi massacres by regretfully calling it a "moment of madness." Rumors circulated that one reason the elderly Mugabe refused to relinquish power was that doing so would make him and his supporters vulnerable to possible international indictments related to mass violence in the 1980s. Accusations that the Mugabe regime conducted genocide against the Ndebele in the 1980s gained momentum at the start of the 2000s with the emergence of the Movement for Democratic Change (MDC), Zimbabwe's first serious political opposition party, and the state-sanctioned occupation of white-owned commercial farms, which crippled the economy and created the worst hyperinflation in recorded history. MDC leaders such as Morgan Tsvangirai and Tendai Biti repeatedly referred to the Gukurahundi massacres as genocide, and the opposition media frequently compared Mugabe to Hitler. Of course, in making those statements, MDC politicians were rallying support within their electoral stronghold of Matabeleland, where bitter memories of Gukurahundi remained strong. Some Ndebele extremists began to talk of the possible secession of Matabeleland from Zimbabwe as a reaction to the attempted extermination of the region's inhabitants. As Mugabe became an international pariah—around the same time as a rise in international awareness of what had happened in Rwanda a decade before—accusations that he and his regime had committed genocide were taken up outside Zimbabwe. In 2003 and 2004, some Canadian members of parliament and a legal team that included an exiled Zimbabwean lawyer requested that Canada's minister of justice employ relatively new legislation to indict Mugabe for genocide, though that did not happen. In 2010 Genocide Watch, an American-based group dedicated to preventing genocide, urged the prosecution of Mugabe for genocide related to events in the 1980s and recommended that since the ICC could not address the issue because it had happened before the court's founding, a special UN-Zimbabwean tribunal could be established, modeled on one in Cambodia that prosecuted members of the former Khmer Rouge regime. Obviously, any potential prosecution of Mugabe for genocide during the 1980s—which is highly unlikely to ever happen—would struggle with the argument that the excessive violence of 5 Brigade was aimed at suppressing ZAPU dissidents as a political group and did not specifically target the Ndebele people on the basis on their ethnicity. Going beyond Gukurahundi, some have suggested that the economic collapse and subsequent sharp decline in living standards caused by Mugabe's bungled land grab of the 2000s as well as his regime's political oppression should be considered genocide against all Zimbabweans.[15]

THE TUAREGS: TRANSNATIONAL MARGINALIZATION AND RADICALIZATION

In precolonial times, the nomadic Tuareg people of Sahelian West Africa used their camels to ferry trade goods north and south across the Sahara desert. They often resisted control by the region's powerful empires, such as Mali and Songhai. Although French colonial rulers suppressed a number of Tuareg rebellions during the late 19th and early 20th century, they ultimately encouraged and racialized the historic feeling of superiority of the light-skinned Tuaregs over black people who lived further south and whom the Tuareg had enslaved in the past. Upon decolonization in the early 1960s, the Tuareg population of the Sahel and Sahara was split between the new states of Niger, Mali, and Algeria, with small groups also living in Burkina Faso, Libya, and Nigeria. They had never been consulted on this division. In Mali and Niger, the Tuaregs became an impoverished and marginalized minority living in the remote north with little influence in governments based in the relatively more developed south and dominated by the larger southern black population. In 1962 small and poorly armed groups of Tuaregs in northern Mali launched a rebellion with the aim of establishing their own state, to be called Azawad in parts of Mali, Niger, and Algeria. The Soviet-backed Malian government of Modibo Keita crushed the insurgency over the next two years but subjected the Tuareg population to such extreme brutality that many fled to neighboring countries and began to think seriously about secession. In 1968, given economic problems, a military coup replaced Keita with Moussa Traore, who turned Mali toward the West.

A major drought in the 1970s and early 1980s devastated Tuareg communities in Mali and Niger and encouraged many Tuareg men to move north to Libya to work in the oil industry or enlist in Libyan dictator Muammar Gaddafi's Islamic Legion, which fought in Palestine, Lebanon, Afghanistan, and other parts of Africa. At the end of the 1980s, given the conclusion of the war in Afghanistan and the disbanding of Gaddafi's legion, many radicalized and militarily experienced Tuareg men returned to Mali and Niger. As a result, Tuareg rebellions broke out in both Mali and Niger in 1990. While Mali's Traore regime initially embarked on another brutal counterinsurgency campaign, the lack of an external sponsor meant that those operations could not be sustained while the rebels were armed and given sanctuary by Libya. This compelled Traore to negotiate with the rebels, and, in the Algerian-mediated Tamanrasset Accords of January 1991, they agreed to a cease-fire and prisoner exchange, withdrawal of combatants from certain areas, the integration of insurgents into the state military, and the creation of semiautonomous regions in the north. Although the corrupt and oppressive Traore was overthrown by yet another coup in March 1991, some Tuareg rebels who had rejected the accords joined the peace process, which continued. However, violence in northern Mali continued into the mid-1990s as non-Tuareg communities formed an armed group called the Malian Patriotic Movement, also known as Ganda Koi, which attacked Tuaregs. In Niger, the Tuareg rebellion was ended by the April 1995 Ouagadougou Accords, in which the government promised to absorb the rebels into the military and assist others in returning to civilian life.

Delays in implementing the peace agreements led to another series of Tuareg rebellions in the 2000s. Supported by Algeria, Tuareg rebels in Mali attacked towns in 2006 but then quickly entered into another agreement with the government to continue the military integration and to launch development projects in the north. In Niger, Tuareg militias formed the Nigeriens' Movement for Justice (MNJ), which demanded a greater share of the area's uranium mining and better representation in the government and military. In February 2007, the MNJ attacked military posts and mining facilities and kidnapped foreign nuclear engineers. In August, the Nigerien government of Mamadou Tandja declared a state of emergency in the

Agadez Region, which limited press freedom and personal liberties and restricted access by international humanitarian organizations. Fear of state-sponsored genocide spread throughout Tuareg communities in northern Niger. International human rights activists denounced Niger's military—trained by the United States in the context of its post-2001 Global War on Terror—for committing atrocities. There were reports that black Nigerien troops were separating civilians based on their skin color and killing those with light skin. In March 2008, British anthropologist and Tuareg advocate Jeremy Keenan, on behalf of Tuareg communities that had been attacked by the Nigerien military, sent a letter to Jan Egeland, special advisor on conflict to the UN secretary-general, reporting that the policy of President Tandja and the Nigerien military constituted genocide under the 1948 convention. He did not receive a response. In June 2008 Niger's military launched a ground and air offensive against MNJ positions in the Air Mountains that led to intense fighting and accusations of ethnic cleansing against the state. Inspired by events in Niger, Tuareg rebels renewed their struggle in northern Mali in 2007 and besieged the town of Tinzaouaten on the Algerian border, where they fired on an American transport aircraft delivering supplies to the Malian army. In early 2009, a Malian government offensive pushed some Tuareg rebels into Algeria while convincing others to accept the previous year's peace offer by moving into assembly areas and awaiting integration into state forces. Although prospects for peace looked bleak in Niger, the Malian settlement along with new lucrative mining contracts and diplomatic pressure brought about by the kidnapping of two Canadians and four Europeans led to a negotiated cease-fire in June 2009.

The 2011 collapse of Gaddafi's regime in Libya meant that many Tuareg members of the Libyan military returned home to northern Mali with heavy weapons. Late that year, they formed the National Movement for the Liberation of Azawad (MNLA), which attracted veterans of the 1990–1995 and 2006–2008 rebellions, as well as disgruntled Fula and Arabs, and deserters from state forces. From January to March 2012, the MNLA captured all major towns in the north as the Malian military, despite resupply by American air drops, was compelled to retreat. Simultaneously, Ansar Dine (Defenders of the Faith), an Islamist group seeking to establish sharia law in the region, took control of northeast Mali. In the capital of Bamako, news of rebel victories in the north incited revenge attacks on Tuaregs, and popular anger toward the administration of Amadou Toumani Toure led to a military coup in March and the formation of a new civilian government that promised to continue the war against the rebels. In early April, MNLA declared the independence of Azawad, though no other country recognized it. Widespread international condemnation occurred when Islamists from the Movement for Oneness and Jihad in West Africa (MOJWA), which clashed with the secular MNLA, captured the famous historic center of Timbuktu, where they vandalized tombs and shrines, which they considered heretical. Intervention by the Economic Community of West African States (ECOWAS) and the UN was delayed, and it appeared that Bamako would fall to the advancing northern rebels. In turn, in January 2013, France, responding to a plea from the Malian government, launched Operation Serval, in which French military units were flown to Mali with the assistance of the United States and Britain. French air power based in Chad devastated rebel forces operating in the open terrain, and that allowed mechanized French forces to quickly recapture northern towns, including Timbuktu, where they were cheered by crowds who were tired of living under sharia law. Revenge attacks on Tuaregs and Arabs, and sometimes on anyone with light skin, by Malian soldiers and civilians prompted concerns over a possible genocide in northern Mali. In February, the UN special advisor on the prevention of genocide, Adama Dieng, issued a warning about the danger of reprisals and urged the Malian military to protect all Malian citizens. Continued insurgency and counterinsurgency in northern Mali, where UN peacekeepers and French troops remain, have not allayed those concerns. Many Tuaregs have now left Mali and Niger for North Africa. Genocide-prevention activist Web sites routinely list the Tuareg minority of Mali and Niger as in danger of extermination, while Tuareg rights activists claim that the Tuareg have been the target of genocidal polices from French colonial times until today. There are also claims that French nuclear tests in the Sahel during the 1960s and more recently the environmental effects of uranium mining, which caused cancer and birth defects, contributed to this process.[16] With a more optimistic view, Scott Strauss attributes the Malian political traditions of democracy, pluralism, and national unity with discouraging leaders from engaging in mass violence against Tuareg civilians during those periodic rebellions. Unfortunately, he says little about Niger.[17]

CENTRAL AFRICAN REPUBLIC (CAR): CIVIL WAR, STATE COLLAPSE, AND GENOCIDE WARNINGS

Granted independence from France in 1960, the Central African Republic (CAR) was initially dominated by leaders from the southern riverine region, whereas communities in the northern savannah, including a Muslim minority in the northeast, were marginalized. From 1965 to 1979, the CAR was ruled by megalomaniacal military dictator Jean Bedel Bokassa. After the oppressive Bokassa had himself crowned emperor in 1977 and began warming to Gaddafi, he was overthrown by the French military, which restored the country's original president, David Dacko, to power. In 1981, following a disputed election, General Andre Kolingba formed a military regime backed by France that used the CAR as a staging area for military operations across Francophone Africa during the 1980s and

1990s. By the early 1990s, Kolingba had manipulated the composition of the CAR military so that 70 percent of it was composed of soldiers from his own southern Yakoma ethnic group, which constituted only 5 percent of the population. The military became politicized and ethnicized. Given post–Cold War political reforms that France pressured Kolingba to enact, Ange-Felix Patasse was elected in 1993 and became the CAR's first head of state from the northern region. In turn, Patasse replaced Yakoma members of the military with people from his own northern Sara-Kaba ethnic group. In the late 1990s, the politicized military was riven by a series of violent antigovernment mutinies that were suppressed by French troops. Patasse expanded his presidential guard and recruited militias from the north. In 1998 French forces in the CAR were absorbed into the UN Mission for the Central African Republic (MINURCA), which provided security for elections that Patasse won the next year. Following the withdrawal of MINURCA in 2000, the CAR was rocked by general strikes and attempted coups.

The Second Congo War of 1998–2002 strongly influenced events in the neighboring CAR. In 2002 exiled general Francois Bozize launched an armed insurgency in the CAR, backed by Chad and the Kabila regime in the DRC. Patasse's brutal counterinsurgency campaign was supported by Gaddafi's Libya and rebels from the DRC led by Jean-Pierre Bemba, who were implicated in massive human rights abuses. In March 2003, Bozize's mostly Chadian force seized the capital of Bangui, and Bozize declared himself president. Abandoned by the French, Patasse fled the country. When Bozize won elections in 2005, rebellions broke out in the north, including among supporters of the ousted Patasse. The state military responded with extreme violence toward the northern population. With French military intervention on behalf of Bozize's government, a number of northern rebel groups signed a peace agreement in 2008 and began a long and troubled demobilization process. The UN again briefly deployed peacekeepers from 2008 to 2010, and, in January 2011, Bozize won elections that gave him a second presidential term.

In December 2012, an alliance of northern rebel groups that eventually called itself Seleka (union), frustrated with Bozize's failure to implement previous agreements, abruptly seized most northern towns, including the diamond-mining center of Bria, and advanced on Bangui. With France and the United States ignoring Bozize's calls for assistance, the Economic Community of Central African States (ECCAS) dispatched a multinational force that halted the rebels just 70 kilometers from the capital. In March 2013, a cease-fire broke down, and the rebels again took the offensive, seizing Bangui. Bozize fled the country, and rebel leader Michel Djotodia declared himself president and became the first Muslim to hold the position. Forces loyal to Bozize continued to resist Seleka, and southern Christian civilians formed the anti-balaka (a reference to a traditional protection charm) militia and embarked on massacres of the CAR's Muslim minority, who began to flee the country. Mosques were destroyed, and many Muslims were forced to convert to Christianity. At the end of 2013, the UN warned that the CAR was at risk of "spiraling into genocide," and the French foreign minister declared that it was "on the verge of genocide." Such concerns, widely reported in international media, prompted the UN to authorize the deployment of the International Support Mission to the CAR (MISCA), which would be made up mostly of troops from African countries, supplemented by French forces. The next year, MISCA was absorbed into the UN Multidimensional Integrated Stabilization Mission in the Central African Republic (MINUSCA), which was specifically tasked to protect civilians. Furthermore, in January 2014 Djotodia resigned and was replaced by the nonpartisan Catherine Samba-Panza, formerly mayor of Bangui. Those developments reduced but did not completely end the violence. While at least 6,000 people were killed, around 800,000 were displaced, including 400,000 who became cross-border refugees, most of whom were Muslims. Some towns were completely cleared of Muslim inhabitants. Seleka rebel leaders began to call for the permanent partition of the CAR into a Muslim north and a Christian south.

Charged with investigating the previous two years of violence in the CAR, a UN commission reported in January 2015 that, while both sides had carried out terrible human rights violations and that the anti-balaka militia had committed crimes against humanity by ethnically cleansing Muslims from many areas, there was no indication that genocide had taken place. That led to the transitional government's creation of a special court composed of international judges reporting to the ICC that would conduct trials related to those atrocities. In July 2014, negotiations held in Brazzaville, Republic of Congo, produced a shaky ceasefire, and, in May the next year, perhaps buoyed by the result of the UN report that took the genocide issue off the table, a conference in Bangui produced a peace pact accepted by most rebel groups. In February 2016, Faustin-Archange Touadera, an academic and previous prime minster under the Bozize regime, became president through a mostly peaceful election. A new government was formed and continued the uncertain peace process.[18] In this case, the international warnings of genocide may have prompted the deployment of an intervention force that reduced the violence while the withdrawal of such rhetoric then opened space for local negotiations.

THE SAN OF SOUTHERN AFRICA: GENOCIDE OF INDIGENOUS PEOPLE

Since the 1990s, a view has developed that southern Africa's hunter-gatherer San societies, particularly those in what is now the Cape region of South Africa where such communities virtually disappeared, had fallen victim to a long history of genocide by European settlers. This view was informed by earlier and similar claims made about settler colonialism and indigenous people in North America and Australia and political change in modern South Africa that raised the possibility of compensation for past human rights abuses. As explained by scholars like Mohamed Adhikari, throughout the 1700s, the expanding Dutch settlers of the Cape Colony conducted repeated armed extermination campaigns against the area's Khoi herders and San hunter-gatherers. In 1777 the Dutch East India Company that administered the colony adopted an official policy of extermination of the San. Armed settler groups known as commandos killed San men on sight, enslaved San women and children, and drove San people from water sources. While the British occupation of the Cape Colony at the start of the 19th century saw the official colonial policy toward the San shift to cultural assimilation within the broader and subordinate Cape Coloured (or mixed race) society, armed settlers in the region continued to hunt and kill San up until the 1890s. Large agricultural African groups also despised and exploited the San and furthered their extermination. Consequently, most surviving San people were forced into the inhospitable Kalahari Desert within the region's interior. By the early 21st century, the total number of San people in southern Africa, a region with a population of many millions, was barely 100,000, with only 7,500 in South Africa and 52,000 in Botswana. While some critics argue that this process took place over much too long a period to be considered genocide, there is little doubt that various colonial regimes and societies in southern Africa intended to eliminate the San whether through killing or acculturation.[19]

Accusations of contemporary genocide against the San became highly controversial in post–Cold War Botswana. In the 1990s, Basarwa, the local name for San or Bushmen hunter-gatherers, from Botswana's Central Kalahari Game Reserve (CKGR) formed an association called First People of the Kalahari (FPK) that sought to address their historic marginalization and recover land from which the government had recently evicted them. They were assisted by a UK-based global indigenous-rights advocacy group called Survival International that provided funding, legal expertise, and international media exposure. Basarwa activists and their supporters claimed that the Botswana government—dominated by the majority Tswana ethnic group, who had long victimized the Basarwa—had pushed the Basarwa off their land to make way for industrial diamond mining. With a paternalist approach, the government responded that the resettlement had been undertaken to preserve wildlife hunted by the Basarwa and to provide better basic services such as education to the Basarwa community. Basarwa activists and their international allies, including such high-profile personalities as Gloria Steinem, who protested that Botswana's diamonds were really blood diamonds—akin to those smuggled out of conflict zones such as Sierra Leone or the DRC—that should be boycotted by ethnical Western buyers, and that the eviction of the Basarwa from CKGR represented the latest step in a government-perpetrated genocide against them. Those accusations were particularly galling to the Botswana government because they seemed to jeopardize the country's economic success, which was built on diamond exports and its reputation as one of Africa's most peaceful and stable states. In 2006 the FPK won an historic court case in Botswana and were allowed to return to their land, though the state refused to provide them with such infrastructure as running water. For anthropologist Jacqueline Solway, the genocide allegation was irresponsible as it endangered the livelihood of all Botswana's people and served to further alienate Basarwa from their fellow Botswana citizens and "is not only absurd, but makes a mockery of events such as the 1994 Rwanda genocide."[20]

Appendix: Maps

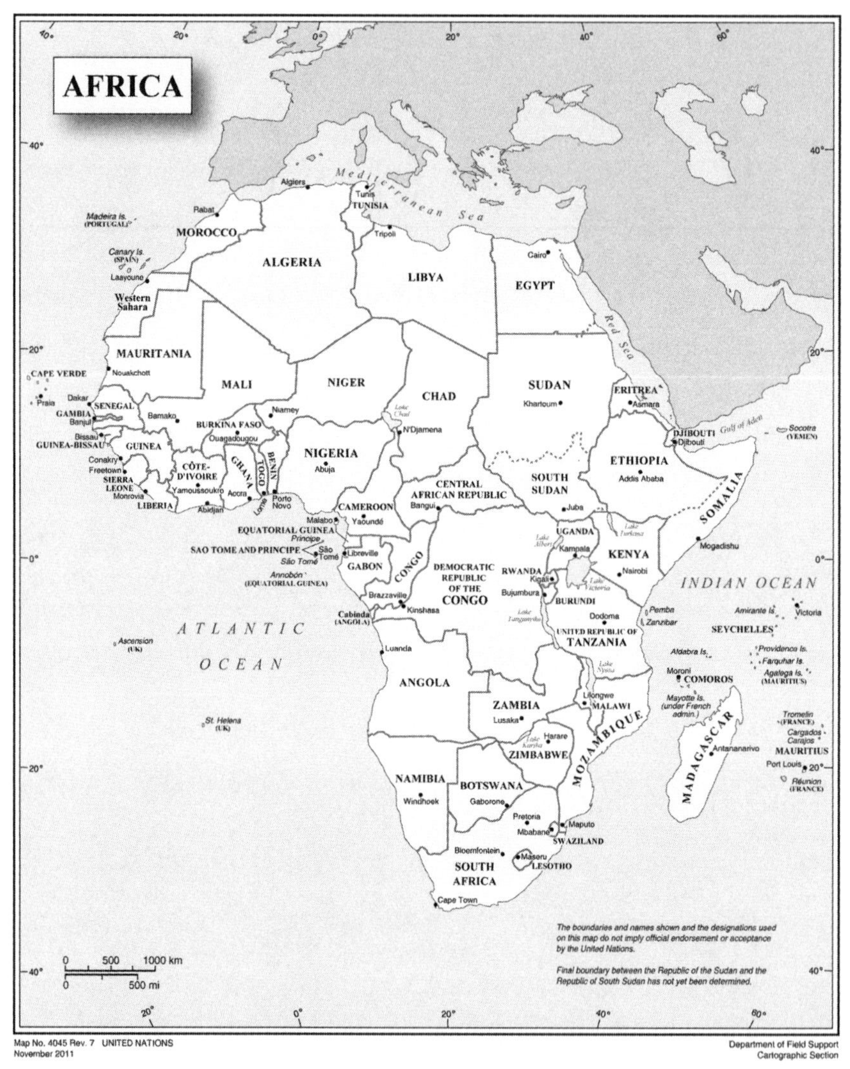

(Africa, Map No. 4045 Rev. 7, November 2011, UNITED NATIONS. Used by permission of the United Nations.)

(Democratic Republic of the Congo, Map No. 4007 Rev. 11, May 2016, UNITED NATIONS. Used by permission of the United Nations.)

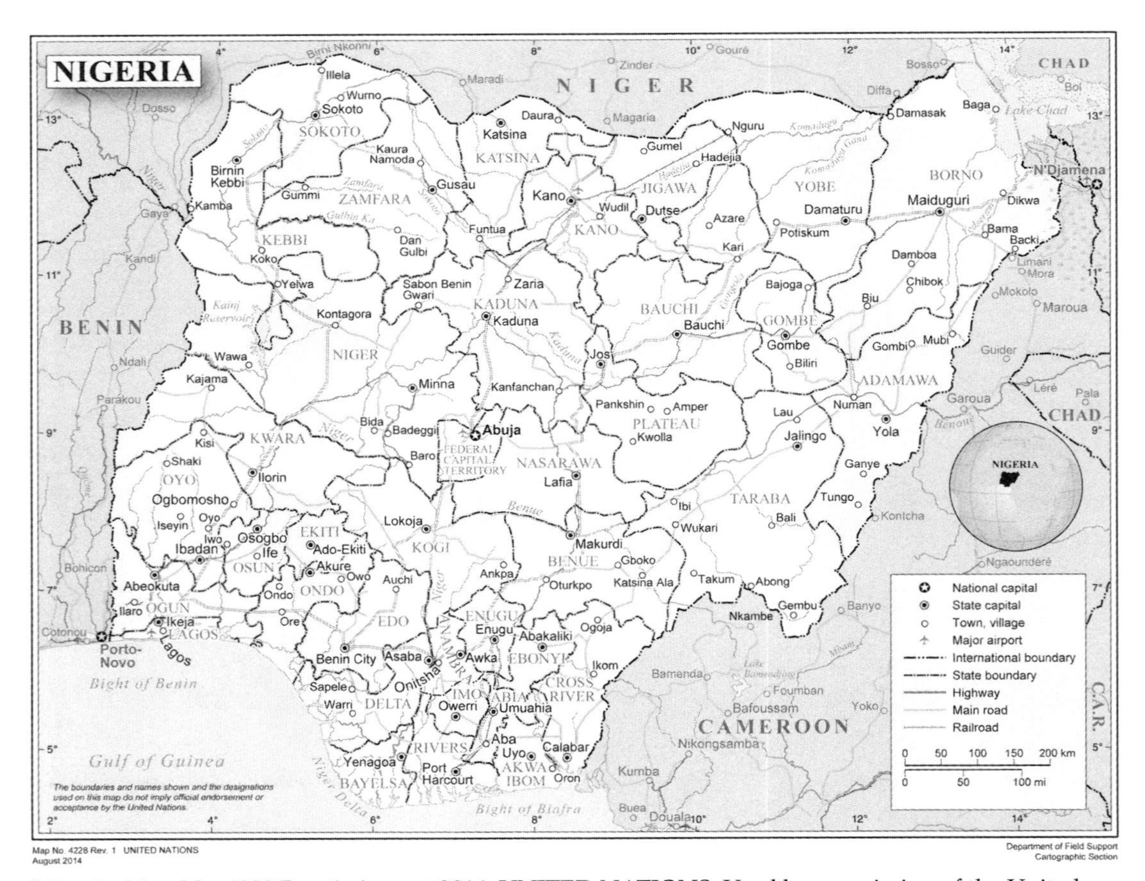

(Nigeria, Map No. 4228 Rev. 1, August 2014, UNITED NATIONS. Used by permission of the United Nations.)

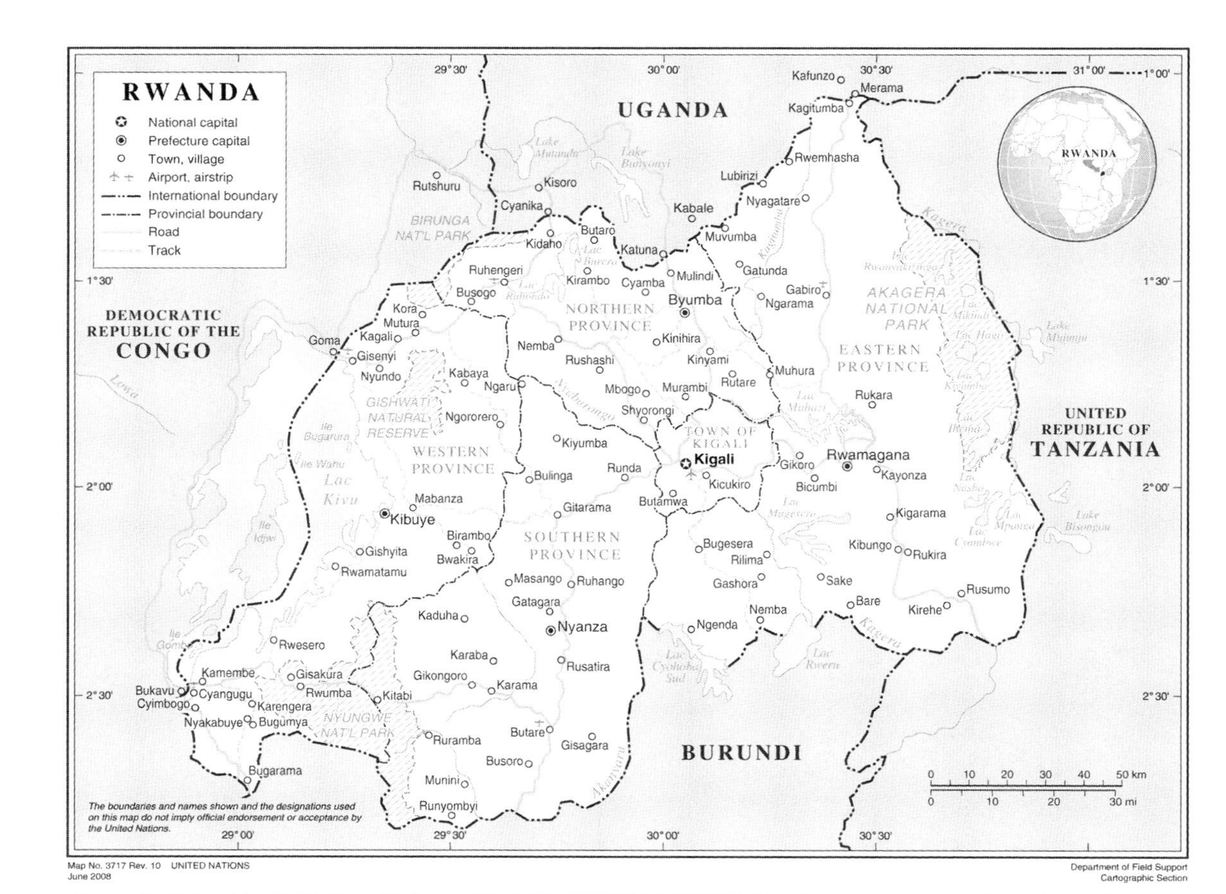

(Rwanda, Map No. 3717 Rev. 10, June 2006, UNITED NATIONS. Used by permission of the United Nations.)

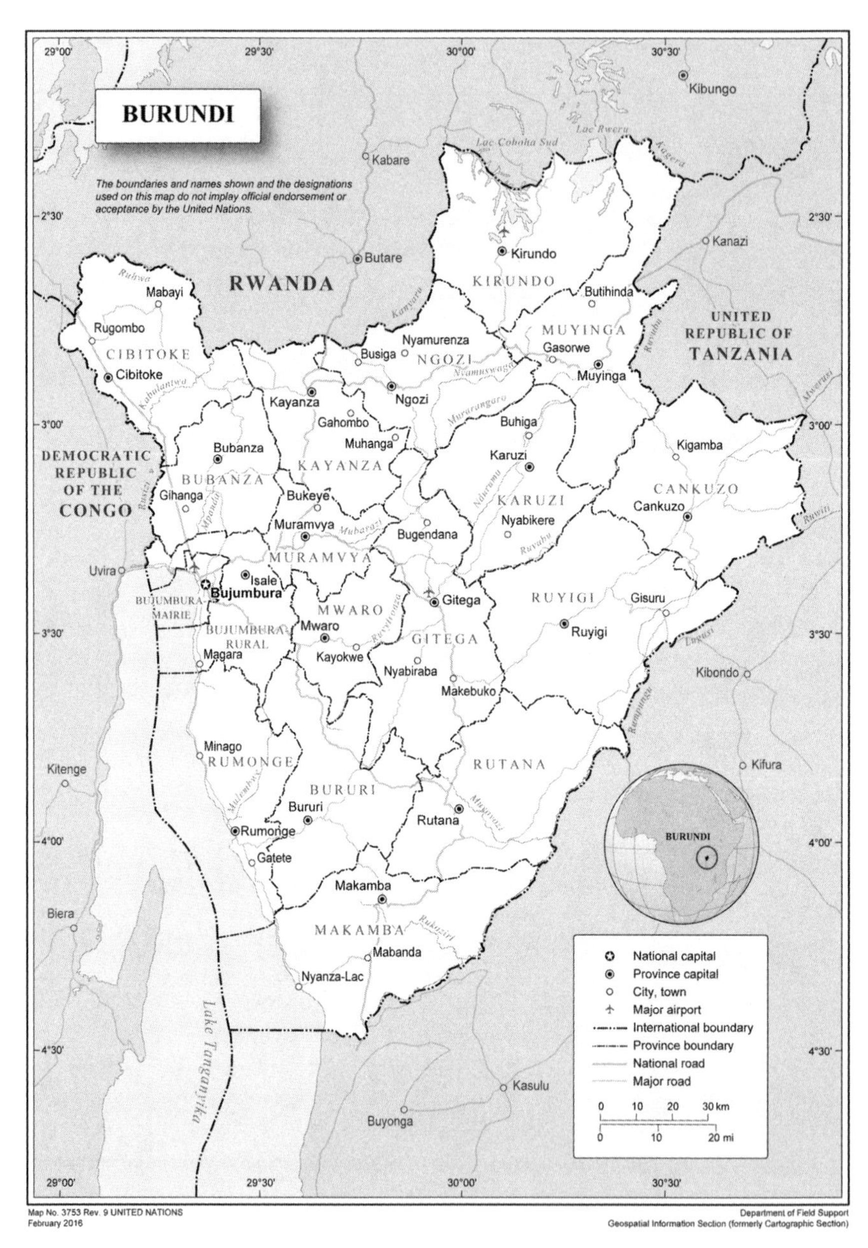

(Burundi, Map No. 3753 Rev. 9, February 2016, UNITED NATIONS. Used by permission of the United Nations.)

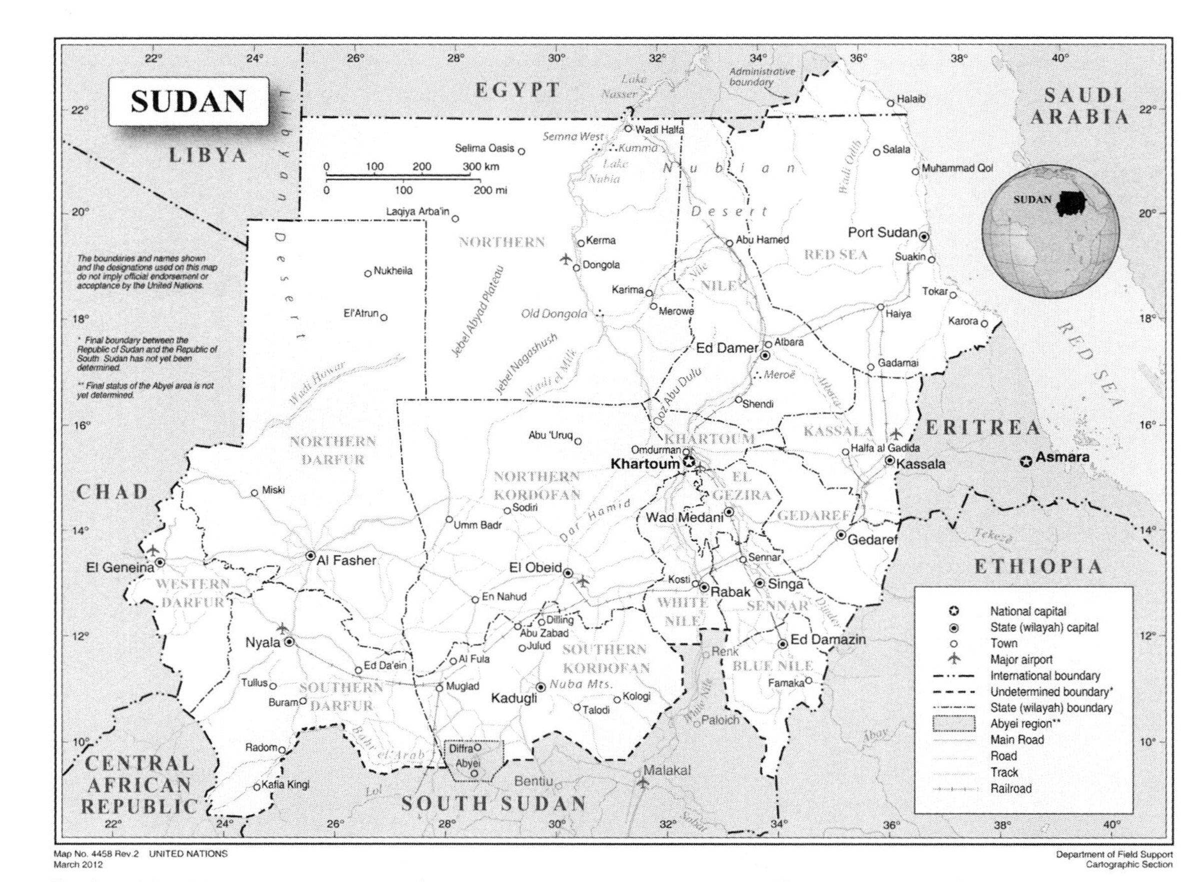

(Sudan, Map No. 4458 Rev. 2, March 2012, UNITED NATIONS. Used by permission of the United Nations.)

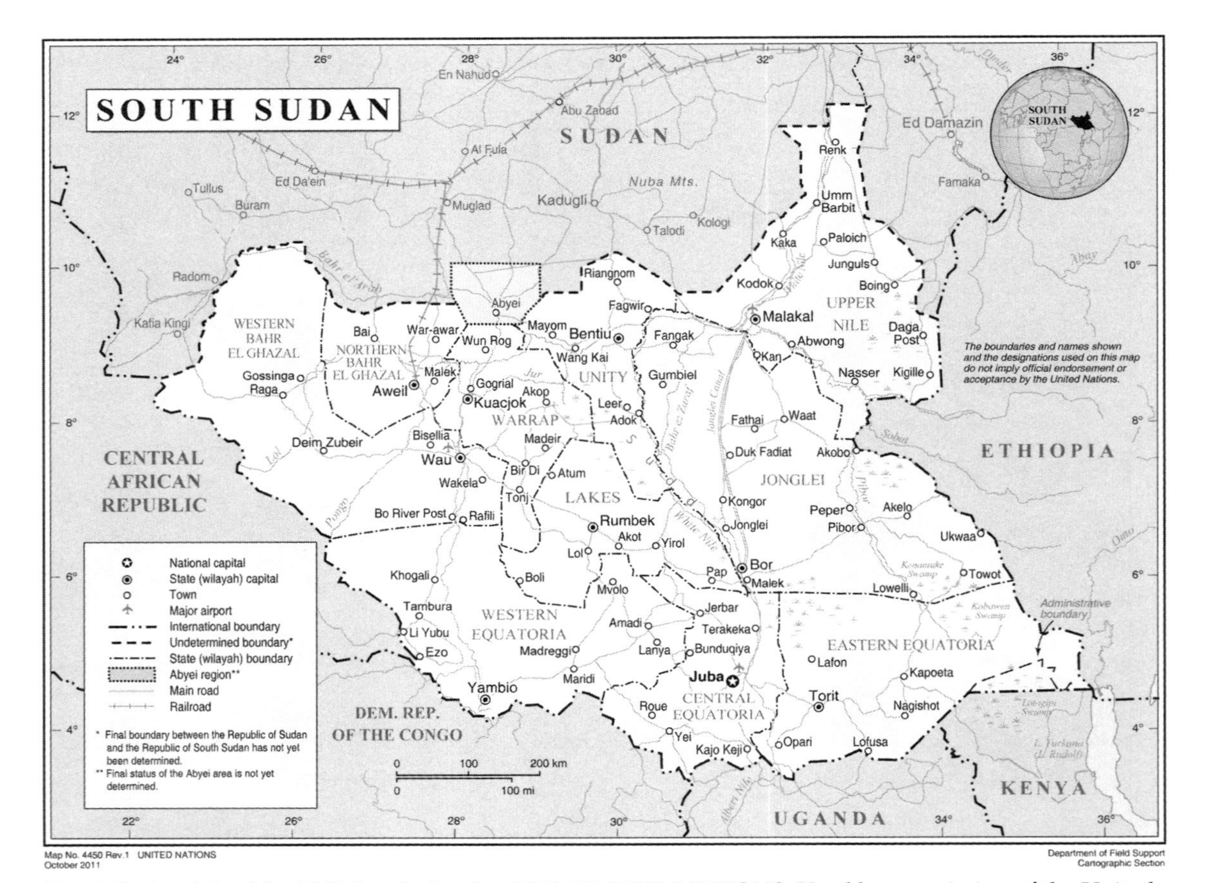

(South Sudan, Map No. 4460 Rev. 1, October 2011, UNITED NATIONS. Used by permission of the United Nations.)

Timeline

1600s	Establishment of the Sultanate of Darfur
c.1700–1780	Wars between Darfur and Wadai
1777	Dutch East India Company in the Cape adopts extermination policy toward San hunter-gatherers
1780s–1790s	Darfur conquests Kordofan
1804–1809	Establishment of Sokoto Caliphate in Northern Nigeria
1820–1821	Egyptian invasion of Sudan; establishment of Khartoum
1821	Egyptian invasion of Kordofan
1830s–1840s	Expansion of Egyptian and Arab slave raiding into southern Sudan
1850s–1860s	Expansion of slaving in Bahr el Ghazal
1861	British occupation of Lagos, Nigeria
1874	Egyptian conquest of Darfur
1880s–1890s	Conflict between Nama and Herero in Namibia
1881–1898	Mahdist state in Sudan
1881	Rwanda invades Burundi, War of Rito
1881	Henry Morton Stanley begins establishment of the Congo Free State on behalf of Leopold II

1884	Mahdist conquest of Darfur
1884	Germany declares a protectorate over South-West Africa (Namibia)
1884–1885	Berlin Conference
1885	British establish Oil Rivers Protectorate in eastern Nigeria
1886	British government grants charter to George Goldie's Royal Niger Company
1890	Germans establish fort at Windhoek, Namibia
1891	Katanga is incorporated into the Congo Free State
1892	British conquest of Ijebu, western Nigeria
1893–1894	Arab War; Congo Free State expands east
1893–1894	German-Nama War in Namibia
1894	First German colonial expedition arrives in Rwanda
1895	Death of Rwanda's King Rwabugiri
1896	Germans intervene in Herero leadership conflict
1896	Germans establish post at Bujumbura on Lake Tanganyika
1896	Coup at Rucunshu in Rwanda
1897	British conquer Kingdom of Benin in what is now Nigeria
1896–1897	Rinderpest epizootic across Southern and East Africa
1897	Rwandan ruler Musinga accepts a German protectorate and begins to extend his state north
1898	Reestablishment of independent Darfur Sultanate
1899–1902	Second Anglo-Boer War (South African War)
1900	Missionaries of the White Fathers arrive in Rwanda
1900	British establish protectorates of Southern Nigeria and Northern Nigeria
1900–1903	British conquest of the Sokoto Caliphate in Northern Nigeria
1902	German punitive expedition against Burundi
January 1904	Herero rebel against German rule
August 1904	Germans defeat Herero at Battle of Waterberg, Namibia

October 1904	In Namibia, German General Lothar von Trotha issues extermination order for the Herero; Nama rebellion begins; genocide of the Herero and Nama begins
1904	Formation of Congo Reform Association; Roger Casement submits report on the Congo Free State to the British government
1904	British colonial rule established in southern Sudan; beginning of Southern Policy
March 1905	Germans open prison camp on Shark Island, Luderitz Bay, Namibia
October 1905	Death of Nama leader Hendrik Witbooi in Namibia
1905	Germans put down rebellion in Burundi
1906	Germans employ prisoners as slave labor to construct railway in Namibia; Nama prisoners sent to Shark Island camp, where some are the subject of forced medical experimentation
March 1907	Germans end military operations in South-West Africa; end of Herero and Nama rebellion
April 1907	Germans in Namibia close Shark Island camp
1908	Congo Free State becomes the Belgian Congo
1908	Death of Burundi's ruler Mwezi Gisabo
1900s–1912	Resistance to the expansion of Musinga's rule over northern Rwanda; German colonial forces suppress rebellions
1910	British creation of Equatorial Corps in southern Sudan
1914	British combine Southern and Northern Nigeria into a single territory
1914–1918	First World War
1915	Mwambutsa becomes king of Burundi
1915	South African invasion of German South-West Africa
1916	Anglo-Egyptian invasion of Darfur
1916	Belgian forces occupy Rwanda and Burundi
1918	British government publishes Blue Book describing German atrocities in South West Africa from 1904 to 1907

1919	German government publishes White Book describing atrocities by other colonial powers in Africa
1920s	Rebellion in eastern Burundi
1924	British creation of Sudan Defense Force (SDF)
1924	Belgium gains League of Nations mandate for Rwanda-Burundi
1926	Belgians impose new and more authoritarian administrative system in Rwanda
1926	All-white legislature in South-West Africa votes to destroy copies of the 1918 Blue Book on German atrocities
1929	Belgians impose new administrative system in Burundi that eliminated Hutu chiefs
1928	Rebellion in northern Rwanda; attacks on Tutsi
1931	Belgians depose traditionalist Musinga as king of Rwanda and replace him with Catholic convert Mutara Rudahigwa; taxation and forced labor intensified
1933–1934	Belgians conduct official census on Rwanda and classify all inhabitants as either Tutsi, Hutu, or Twa; identity card system imposed
1934	Rebellion in predominantly Hutu area of northwest Burundi
1939–1945	Second World War
1944	Formation of National Congress of Nigeria and the Cameroons (NCNC)
1945	Attacks on Igbo in mining town of Jos in northern Nigeria
1948	Formation of the Union of the Peoples of Cameroon (UPC)
1949	Formation of Northern People's Congress (NPC) in Nigeria
1950	United Nations federates Eritrea to Ethiopia
1951	Formation of Action Group in western Nigeria
1952	British declare emergency in Kenya; Mau Mau war begins
1953	Attacks on southeasterners (mostly Igbo) in Kano, northern Nigeria
1950s	Rise of Hutu Power movement in Rwanda
1955	Violence breaks out in the French-administered territory of Cameroon

1955	Mutiny of Equatorial Corps in southern Sudan; start of Sudan's first civil war
1956	Independence of Sudan
1957	Nigeria gains self-government
1957	Bahutu Manifesto published; formation of Muhutu Social Movement (MSM) by Gregoire Kayibanda and Association for the Promotion of the Hutu Masses (APROSOMA) by Joseph Gitera
1957	French bring in additional troops to combat insurgency in Cameroon
1958	Sudan government policy of Islamization and Arabization in the south
1958	Oil discovered in southeastern Nigeria
1959	Belgians announce plans for a territorial government election in Rwanda at the end of the year
September 1959	Formation of the Rwandan National Union (UNAR), which is mostly supported by Tutsi elites and the monarchy
October 1959	In Rwanda, MSM is renamed Party for the Emancipation of the Hutu (PARMEHUTU)
November 1959	Social revolution in Rwanda; takeover by Hutu Power leaders
January 1960	Independence of Cameroon
February 1960	French forces begin expanded counterinsurgency operations in western Cameroon
June 1960	PARMEHUTU wins local government elections in Rwanda
June 1960	Belgian Congo becomes independent; Congolese army mutinies; Katanga and South Kasai secede from Congo
July 1960	UN Operation in the Congo (ONUC) deploys
July 1960	Establishment of Eritrea Liberation Front (ELF)
September 1960	Katanga leader Moise Tshombe accuses Congo's Prime Minister Patrice Lumumba of committing genocide
October 1960	Lumumba overthrown by Congolese military led by Joseph Mobutu

October 1960	Nigeria becomes independent
January 1961	Lumumba executed in Katanga
September 1961	Union for National Progress (UPRONA) wins legislative elections in Burundi
September 1961	Death of UN secretary-general Dag Hammarskjold in mysterious air crash in Northern Rhodesia
October 1961	UPRONA leader Crown Prince Louis Rwagasore assassinated in Burundi
1961	Exiled Rwandan Tutsi begin to form armed groups in neighboring countries
March 1962	Rwandan states forces massacre 1,000 to 2,000 Tutsi in Byumba
July 1962	Rwanda becomes independent, with Gregoire Kayibanda as president
July 1962	Burundi becomes independent as a constitutional monarchy under King Mwambutsa
September 1962	South Kasai succession ended
1962–1964	Tuareg rebellion in northern Mali
1963	Founding of Sudan African National Union (SANU) in exile
January 1963	UN forces crush Katanga secession in Congo; ONUC withdraws
December 1963	A poorly planned invasion of Rwanda by Tutsi exiles is defeated
December 1963	Independence of Kenya
December 1963–March 1964	Around 20,000 Tutsi massacred in Rwanda; observers compare it to the Holocaust
1963–1964	Ogaden Liberation Front (OLF) fights insurgency against Ethiopian state
1964–1965	Rebellion in eastern Congo; Belgian and U.S. intervention
January 1965	Assassination of Burundi's first Hutu prime minister, Pierre Ngendandumwe
October 1965	Coup in Burundi by Tutsi military officers led by Michel Micombero

November 1965	Mobutu established American-sponsored dictatorship in Congo (later renamed Zaire)
November 1965	Rhodesia unilaterally declares independence from Britain
January 1966	Five Majors coup in Nigeria
May 1966	Military regime abolishes Nigerian federal system; massacres of easterners in northern Nigeria
July 1966	Coup in Nigeria brings Yakubu Gowon to power
September/ October 1966	Massacres of Igbo in northern Nigeria
November 1966	Micombero's military regime declares Burundi a republic
January 1967	Aburi Conference in Ghana
May 1967	Biafra declares independence from Nigeria; start of Nigerian civil war
Late 1967	Biafran government engages Swiss-based PR firm Markpress
August 1968	Biafran leader Ojukwu addresses OAU and accuses Nigerian federal government of genocide; France begins covert military assistance to Biafra
September 1968	International observers begin visit to federal Nigerian forces and conclude no genocide being committed
September 1969	Muammar Gaddafi comes to power in Libya
1969	Burundian Hutu exiles launch armed struggle from Tanzania
1969	Creation of Southern Sudan Liberation Movement (SSLM)
1969	Jaafar Muhammad Numayri comes to power in Sudan
January 1970	End of Biafran secession from Nigeria and end of Nigerian Civil War
1971	Execution of Cameroonian insurgent leader Ernest Ouandie
April 1972	Incursion of Hutu rebels in the south of Burundi and subsequent genocide against the Hutu

1972	Addis Ababa Agreement ends Sudan's first civil war
July 1973	Coup in Rwanda brings Juvenal Habyarimana to power
1973	Founding of Eritrean People's Liberation Front (EPLF)
September 1974	Ethiopian military deposes Emperor Haile Selassie
1975	Founding of Tigray People's Liberation Front (TPLF)
1976	Failed coup attempt in Sudan by Sadiq al-Mahdi
1976	Military coup in Burundi brings Colonel Jean-Baptiste Bagaza to power; Burundi is one-party state under UPRONA
1977–1978	Ogaden War between Ethiopia and Somalia; Western Somali Liberation Front (WSLF) continues insurgency in Ogaden part of Ethiopia
1977–1978	Red Terror in Ethiopia
1978	Rwandan military regime transformed into one-party state under the National Revolutionary Movement for Development (MRND)
1979	Rwandan exiles in Uganda form the Rwandese Refugee Welfare Association (RRWA)
April 1980	Independence of Zimbabwe
1980	RRWA changes its name to Rwandese Alliance for National Unity (RANU)
1980	Party for the Liberation of the Hutu People (PALIPEHUTU) formed by Burundian refugees in Tanzania; PALIPEHUTU eventually forms armed wing called National Forces of Liberation (FNL)
1981	RANU moves from Uganda to Kenya
February 1981	Battle of Entumbane in Zimbabwe; beginning of dissident issue in Matabeleland
1981–1986	Rwandan exiles join the National Resistance Army (NRA) and fight in the insurgency in southern Uganda
1982	Hissene Habre's Armed Forces of the North (FAN) use Darfur as a jumping-off point for taking power in Chad
1982	Exiled former Biafran separatist leader Ojukwu returns to Nigeria

1983–1987	Zimbabwe's 5 Brigade conducts reign of terror in rural Matabeleland and Midlands
January 1983	Rebellion by Sudan military garrisons in the south
June 1983	Sudan government issues Republican Order Number One; start of Sudan's second civil war
July 1983	Formation of Sudan People's Liberation Movement/Army (SPLM/A)
1983–1985	Famine in Ethiopia; military government blocks food aid to rebel areas
1983–2005	Second Sudan Civil War
April 1984	Catholic priest accuses Zimbabwe government of genocide
April 1985	Numayri regime overthrown in Sudan
1985	Burundian regime imposes restrictions on Catholic Church
1985	Sudan transitional government arms Arab Baqqara militia called Murahiliin in southern Kordofan and southern Darfur to attack Dinka moving north
1985	UN Whitaker Report describes German massacres of Herero and Nama from 1904 to 1907 as genocide
1986	Sadiq al-Mahdi becomes prime minister of Sudan
1986	Lake Nyos disaster in Cameroon; some claim it was actually a chemical weapon
March 1987	Massacre of Dinka at Ed Daein in southern Darfur
1987	Military coup in Burundi brings Pierre Buyoya to power
1987	RANU returns to Uganda and changes its name to the Rwandese Patriotic Front (RPF)
1987	Toyota War in Chad
1987	Arab Gathering statements about potential extermination of Africans in Darfur
1987	SPLA moves into Nuba Mountains (southern Kordofan)
December 1987	Unity Accord in Zimbabwe; end of violence in southwest
March 1988	Battle of Afabet in Ethiopia

1988	War of the Tribes in Darfur; Arab militias slaughter Fur civilians
1988	Violence in northern Burundi; state massacre of Hutu
1988–1989	Government militia (Murahiliin) attacks on Dinka in Bahr el Ghazal
1989	South West Africa becomes independent Namibia
April 1989	Idriss Deby forms Chadian Patriotic Salvation Movement (MPS) in Darfur
May 1989	Chadians, Libyan Islamic Legion, and Sudan militias attack Fur people in Darfur
June 1989	Coup in Sudan brings Omar al-Bashir and the National Islamic Front (NIF) to power
October 1989	Habre's Chadian forces enter Darfur in pursuit of MPS
1990	Deby's MPS leaves Darfur and invades Chad, where it seizes power
September 1990	The RPF invades Rwanda from Uganda; French intervene on behalf of the Habyarimana regime
December 1990	Publication of "Hutu Ten Commandments" in Rwanda
1990–1995	Tuareg rebellions in Mali and Niger
1991	National unity government in Burundi
January 1991	RPF launch guerrilla campaign based out of the Virunga Mountains in Rwanda
May 1991	Mengistu Haile Mariam flees Ethiopia
August 1991	Beginning of internal conflict within the SPLA
November 1991	SPLA Nuer faction massacres Dinka at the town of Bor in southern Sudan
April 1992	Habyarimana regime in Rwanda introduces multiparty democracy
1992	Formation of Hutu Power militias in Rwanda
1992	Sudan government jihad against the Nuba of the Nuba Mountains
February 1993	RPF offensive comes to within 23 kilometers of Kigali; cease-fire declared
April 1993	Independence of Eritrea

June 1993	Predominantly Hutu and moderate Front for Democracy in Burundi (FRODEBU) wins election in Burundi
July 1993	Founding of Thousand Hills Radio-Television (RTML) in Rwanda that begins broadcasting anti-Tutsi hate propaganda
August 1993	Signing of Arusha Accords between Rwandan government and RPF
October 1993	Launch of United Nations Assistance Mission in Rwanda (UNAMIR)
October 1993	Assassination of Burundi's first Hutu president, Melchior Ndadaye, by Tutsi soldiers; massacre of Tutsi in rural areas; Burundian Hutus flee to Rwanda
January 1994	UNAMIR commander General Romeo Dallaire reports plot to eliminate the Tutsi population; request for reinforcements rejected
April 1994	Assassination of Rwanda's President Juvenal Habyarimana and Burundi's President Cyprien Ntaryamira; beginning of the genocide against the Tutsi in Rwanda; war between the state and RPF is renewed; French and Belgians evacuate their citizens
May 1994	UN reverses previous decision and authorizes the reinforcement of UNAMIR, but it is too late
June 1994	Burundian Hutu leaders form National Council for the Defense of Democracy (CNDD) and armed wing Forces for the Defense of Democracy (FDD)
June–July 1994	French military conducts Operation Turquoise in southwest Rwanda
July 1994	RPF take control of Rwanda; genocide ends; refugees flee Rwanda and move into Zaire and Tanzania
August 1994	Ibuka (remember) organization formed in Belgium
November 1994	UN establishes the International Criminal Tribunal for Rwanda (ICTR) based in Arusha, Tanzania
1994	Political reorganization of Darfur
1995	Beginning of Burundian Civil War; Hutu rebels of CNDD-FDD and PALIPEHUTU-FNL fight Tutsi military
April 1995	RPF conduct Kibeho Massacre in Rwanda

November 1995	Ibuka organization launched in Rwanda
November 1995	Execution of Nigerian activist Ken Saro-Wiwa
July 1996	Coup by the Tutsi military returns Pierre Buyoya to power in Burundi
October 1996	Rwanda and Uganda invade Zaire and sponsor rebellion by Laurent Kabila's Alliance of Democratic Forces for the Liberation of Congo (AFDL); Rwandan army attacks refugee camps in eastern Zaire; start of First Congo War
1996	Sudan government expels Osama bin Laden
New Year's Eve 1997	Burundian FDD rebels attack Bujumbura airport
1997	Publication of Catholic Commission for Justice and Peace in Zimbabwe's report on 1980s violence in Matabeleland and Midlands
May 1997	Laurent Kabila, supported by Rwanda and Uganda, takes power in Zaire and changes name of country to Democratic Republic of Congo; end of First Congo War
May 1997	Rwandan soldiers and Zairean allies massacre Rwandan Hutu refugees around Mbandaka in Zaire
September 1997	Rwandan army officially withdraws from the DRC
December 1997	Rwandan and Burundian soldiers enter eastern DRC
1997–1998	Exiled Rwandan Hutu fighters organize the Army for the Liberation of Rwanda (ALIR) and mount attacks into Rwanda
July 1998	Kabila government in the DRC expels Rwandan troops
August 1998	Rwanda and Uganda invade eastern DRC in support of rebellion by Rally for Congolese Democracy (RCD) and Movement for the Liberation of Congo (MLC); Zimbabwe, Angola, and Namibia intervene on behalf of Kabila regime; start of Second Congo War, or Africa's World War
1998	Beginning of oil production and export in Sudan
1998	Public execution of alleged genocide perpetrators in Rwanda
1998	UN report alleges possible genocide by Rwandan army against Rwandan Hutu refugees in the DRC

1998	Jean-Paul Akayesu is convicted by the ICTR, which represents the first instance in which a court enforces the 1948 UN Convention on the Prevention and Punishment of the Crime of Genocide
1998	Herero leaders in Namibia demand compensation for genocide from German government
September 1998	Burundian military destroys rebel FDD bases and Burundian refugee camps in South Kivu, DRC
1998–1999	State-sponsored militia attacks on Masalit communities in western Darfur
1999	Formation of Movement for the Actualization of the Sovereign State of Biafra (MASSOB)
July 1999	Lusaka Agreement leads to abortive cease-fire in the DRC; creation of UN Mission in the Democratic Republic of Congo (MONUC)
1999	Ugandan military creates Ituri Province in northeast DRC
2000	RPF leader Paul Kagame becomes president of Rwanda
May–June 2000	Rwandan and Ugandan forces and respective Congolese rebel allies clash in Kisangani
August 2000	Burundian peace agreement negotiated in Tanzania rejected by rebel groups
September 2000	Rwandan Hutu exiles form Democratic Forces for the Liberation of Rwanda (FDLR) in eastern DRC
January 2001	Assassination of Laurent Kabila
2001	Appeals court of the International Criminal Tribunal for the Former Yugoslavia decides that the existence of a plan or policy is not an ingredient in the crime of genocide
2001	A Belgian court convicts two Rwandan nuns for murder and war crimes that took place in Rwanda in 1994
2001	Beginning of Gacaca court system in Rwanda
2001	Herero community in Namibia files lawsuit in the United States against the German government and a German bank for using slave labor during the 1904–1907 rebellion

July–August 2001	Darfur rebel groups formed; Justice and Equality Movement (JEM) and Darfur Liberation Front (DLF), which eventually becomes Sudan Liberation Movement (SLM)
September 2001	Terrorist attacks on the United States
January 2002	Cease-fire in the Nuba Mountains
January 2002	End of Dinka-Nuer conflict within SPLA
February 2002	First attacks by Darfur rebels on government garrisons
April 2002	Agreement between the DRC Kabila regime and MLC rebels signed in Sun City, South Africa
July 2002	Pretoria Accord between the DRC Kabila regime and Rwandan government
September 2002	Luanda Agreement between the DRC and Uganda governments
October 2002	Most foreign forces have pulled out of the DRC; MONUC peacekeeping force expanded
October 2002	Beginning of state-sponsored Janjaweed militia attack on Fur, Masalit, and Zaghawa in Darfur
October 2002	U.S. government passes Sudan Peace Act, which accuses Sudan government of genocide in southern Sudan
December 2002	FDD leader Pierre Nkurunziza agrees to cease-fire in Burundian Civil War
December 2002	The DRC government and major rebel groups sign Global and Inclusive Accord (AGI); end of Second Congo War, though violence continues in eastern DRC
2002	Violence and fears of genocide in Ituri Province, DRC
March 2003	Rebel forces of Francois Bozize seize power in Central African Republic
April 2003	African Union Mission in Burundi (AMIB) deploys
May 2003	FRODEBU's Domitien Ndayizeye assumes power in Burundi
May 2003	Laurent Nkunda leads mutinous Banyamulenge (Congolese Tutsi) troops in eastern DRC

June 2003	Ugandan forces withdraw from the DRC
June–September 2003	Operation Artemis; European Union dispatches Interim Emergency Multinational Force (IEMF) to Bunia in Ituri Province, DRC
August 2003	UN envoy declares that genocide may have been committed in Ituri Province, DRC
September 2003	MONUC's Ituri Brigade replaces IEMF
October 2003	Burundi peace agreement signed in Pretoria, South Africa, but war continues as PALIPEHUTU-FNL refuse to sign
December 2003	Violence against Anuak people in western Ethiopia
2003	Expansion of insurgency in Darfur
2003	Negotiations continue in Kenya between Sudan government and SPLM/A
2003–2004	Politicians and lawyers request that Canadian government indict Robert Mugabe for genocide conducted in the 1980s
April 2004	SLM and JEM rebels in Darfur reject cease-fire proposed by Chad's Idriss Deby
May 2004	Sudan government allows delivery of humanitarian aid to displaced people in Darfur
June 2004	AMIB absorbed into new United Nations Operation in Burundi (ONUB)
July 2004	Save Darfur Coalition established in the United States
July 2004	African Union Mission to Sudan (AMISS) launched to monitor abortive cease-fire
August 2004	Kofi Anan reports that Sudan government has failed to adhere to United Nations demand to halt military operations and disarm Janjaweed militia
2004	National genocide memorial opened in Kigali, Rwanda
2004	Film *Hotel Rwanda* released
2004	German government minister apologizes for genocide in Namibia but rejects claims for compensation
October 2004	Genocide Intervention Fund established in the United States

September 2004	U.S. government declares that genocide had been committed in Darfur
September 2005	United Nations commission reports that the Sudan government had not pursued a policy of genocide in Darfur but that crimes against humanity and war crimes had taken place
2005	Two films, *Shooting Dogs* and *Sometimes in April,* released about the genocide in Rwanda
2005	Bozize wins elections in Central African Republic, and rebellions break out in the north
March 2005	Thomas Lubanga of the Union of Congolese Patriots (UPC) becomes first person detained on an ICC arrest warrant
August 2005	Pierre Nkurunziza of CNDD-FDD becomes president of Burundi after winning election
2005	MONUC operations take place against Ituri militias in the DRC
2005	Cameroonian insurgent veterans demand compensation from France
2005	Publication of book that accuses Britain of conducting genocide in Kenya in the 1950s
2005	Formation of Anuak Justice Council (AJC)
2005	Comprehensive Peace Agreement for southern Sudan; autonomous Government of South Sudan created
2005–2006	MONUC and DRC forces conduct operations against FDLR in eastern DRC
2006	Banyamulenge rebels in eastern DRC form National Congress for the Defense of the People (CNDP)
2006	PALIPEHUTU-FNL agree to cease-fire in Burundi
May 2006	Darfur Peace Agreement (DPA) signed in Abuja, Nigeria, between Sudan government and SLM faction that is rejected by JEM and other SLM factions
2006	A French judge issues international arrest warrants for RPF leaders, including Paul Kagame for the shooting down of President Habyarimana's aircraft in April 1994; Rwanda's RPF government severs diplomatic links with France

2006	San (Basarwa) group wins court case in Botswana, preceded by accusations of genocide against Botswana government
2006	Fighting continues in Darfur
2006	Namibian national assembly votes to support genocide compensation claims against Germany
2006–2009	Tuareg rebellions in Mali and Niger; accusations of genocide against government of Niger
December 2006	Former Ethiopian leader Mengistu convicted in absentia of genocide
February 2007	Nationalist and Integrationist Front (FNI) is the last militia group in Ituri, DRC to begin disarmament and demobilization
October 2007	Deployment of African Union; United Nations Hybrid Operation in Darfur (UNAMID)
2007–2008	Postelection violence in Kenya; leaders accuse each other of practicing genocide
April 2008	Battle between Burundian army and FNL rebels
2008	Rebels in northern CAR begin long and ultimately unsuccessful peace process
2008–2009	Demobilization of FNL rebels in Burundi
2009	Beginning of Boko Haram insurgency in northeastern Nigeria
July 2008	Sudan's President Omar al-Bashir indicted by the International Criminal Court (ICC) for crimes against humanity and war crimes committed in Darfur
October 2008	CNDP offensive in eastern DRC
2008	RPF government in Rwanda created National Commission for the Fight against Genocide
January 2009	Laurent Nkunda arrested by Rwandan military
March 2009	CNDP makes agreement with DRC government
April 2009	Darfur debate at Columbia University in the United States
May 2009	A Canadian court convicts Desire Munyaneza for genocide, war crimes, and crimes against humanity relating to events that took place in Rwanda in 1994

2010	Genocide Watch urges prosecution of Mugabe for genocide in 1980s Zimbabwe
July 2010	Second ICC indictment of al-Bashir adds genocide to the list of his crimes in Darfur
August 2010	Pierre Nkurunziza begins second term as Burundi's president
2010	Belgian researchers conclude that around 298,000 people died because of violence and displacement in Darfur between 2004 and 2008
2010	Rwandan investigation concludes that President Habyarimana's aircraft had been shot down in April 1994 by Hutu Power elements within the Rwandan military
2010	Rwanda and France reestablish diplomatic links
July 2010	MONUC renamed United Nations Organization Stabilization Mission in the Democratic Republic of Congo (MONUSCO)
January 2011	South Sudan votes overwhelmingly for independence
July 2011	Another Darfur Peace Agreement signed in Doha, Qatar, between Sudan's government and a coalition of 10 small rebel groups from Darfur known as the Liberation and Justice Movement (LJM); JEM and SLM factions reject deal
July 2011	South Sudan becomes an independent state; fighting continues between Sudanese government forces and Sudan People's Liberation Movement–North (SPLM-N) rebels in southern Kordofan and Blue Nile (which are not included in South Sudan)
2011	Rebels from Darfur fight alongside pro-Gaddafi forces in Libyan civil war
2011	British court rules that Kenyans can sue the British government for human rights abuses suffered in the 1950s
2011	ICC indicts Kenyan politicians, including Uhuru Kenyatta, for crimes against humanity related to the postelection violence of 2007–2008
January 2012	After a long legal struggle, Canada deports Leon Mugesera to Rwanda to face charges related to inciting the 1994 genocide

January 2012	Start of Tuareg and Islamist rebellion in Mali
March 2012	ICC finds Thomas Lubanga guilty of conscripting child soldiers in Ituri, DRC
March 2012	German parliament vote down a motion by left-wing opposition members to recognize German colonial crimes in South West Africa as genocide; removal of German colonial monuments in Namibia
April 2012	CNDP renames itself M23 and mounts a rebellion in North Kivu, eastern DRC; they came to protect local Tutsi from potential genocide by the Hutu FDLR
December 2012	An alliance of northern rebel groups called Seleka relaunches war against the Bozize government in the CAR
2012	A French investigation into the downing of Rwandan president Habyarimana's aircraft in April 1994 reports that it could not have been shot down by the RPF unit that was present in Kigali
2012	Gacaca courts conclude in Rwanda
January 2013	Start of French intervention in Mali: Operation Serval
February 2013	UN advisor on prevention of genocide warns Malian military to prevent revenge attacks on Tuaregs and others
March 2013	CNDP/M23 leader Bosco "the Terminator" Ntaganda surrenders himself to the U.S. embassy in Rwanda and is transported to The Hague to face ICC charges of war crimes
March 2013	Seleka rebels capture capital of the CAR; Bozize flees country; Christian anti-balaka militias begin revenge killings of Muslims
November 2013	UN intervention brigade launches campaign that defeats M23 rebels in eastern DRC
December 2013	Start of South Sudanese Civil War between Dinka and Nuer factions of the SPLA; continuing violence between Dinka and Shilluk militias over land and resources
December 2013	UN and French officials warn of possible genocide in the CAR; International Support Mission to the CAR (MISCA) deployed

2013	British government agrees to pay damages to survivors of human rights abuses in 1950s Kenya
February 2014	A court in Germany convicts Onesphore Rwabukombe of aiding and abetting genocide in Rwanda in 1994
April 2014	Deployment of UN Multidimensional Integrated Stabilization Mission in the Central African Republic (MINUSCA)
March 2014	A court in France convicts Pascal Simbikangwa of genocide and complicity in crimes against humanity related to events in Rwanda in 1994
May 2014	U.S. secretary of state John Kerry warns of possible genocide in South Sudan
July 2014	Negotiations occur between the CAR transitional government and rebels in Brazzaville, Republic of Congo
October 2014	African Union Commission reports that atrocities have been committed in South Sudan but no evidence of genocide (report released to public in 2015)
October 2014	Uhuru Kenyatta becomes first serving head of state to appear before the ICC but charges soon dropped
2015–16	Accusations of Ethiopian state genocide against Oromo
January 2015	UN report concludes no genocide in the CAR, though considerable human rights abuses
February 2015	DRC forces launch offensive against FDLR rebels
April 2015	Violence erupts in Burundi over Nkurunziza's plan to seek a third presidential term
May 2015	Peace talks occur in the CAR
May 2015	Failed coup attempt in Burundi
August 2015	Tentative peace deal reached for South Sudan
August 2015	Nkurunziza begins third term as Burundi's president
February 2016	Election of Faustin-Archange Touadera as the CAR president in a mostly peaceful election
April 2016	Return of Riek Machar to South Sudan indicates beginning of peace process
July 2016	Fighting resumes in South Sudan
December 2016	New international warnings of potential genocide in South Sudan

Glossary

Abdul Wahid al Nur: Leader of the Sudan Liberation Movement (SLM) faction that rejected the 2006 Darfur Peace Agreement (DPA).

Abu Qurun: Leader of a state-sponsored ethnic Fartit militia that attacked Dinka communities in Sudan's Bahr el Ghazal region in the late 1980s. Among Sudanese state forces, he was known as "Our Hitler."

Aburi Conference: Negotiations held in Aburi, Ghana, in January 1967 between the Nigerian federal military government and the military government of Nigeria's Eastern Region. The failure of both sides to implement an agreement reached at these talks led to the secession of Biafra from Nigeria and the Civil War of 1967 to 1970.

Addis Ababa Agreement (1972): An agreement signed in Addis Ababa, Ethiopia in 1972 between the government of Sudan and the Southern Sudan Liberation Movement (SSLM) that ended the country's first civil war.

African Union (AU): An international governmental organization of African states formerly known as the Organization of African Unity (OAU).

African Union Mission in Burundi (AMIB): The first peacekeeping mission launched by the African Union, which monitored the peace process in Burundi and protected political leaders during 2003 and 2004. It was absorbed into the United Nations Operation in Burundi (ONUB).

African Union Mission to Sudan (AMIS): An African Union peacekeeping operation mounted in Darfur from July 2004 until December 2007, when it was absorbed by the new African Union–United Nations Hybrid Operation in Darfur (UNAMID).

African Union–United Nations Hybrid Operation in Darfur (UNAMID): An international peacekeeping mission in Darfur that began to deploy in October 2007 and absorbed the existing African Union Mission to Sudan (AMIS).

Aguiyi-Ironsi, Johnson: A Nigerian army general of Igbo ethnicity who became Nigerian head of state following the Five Majors coup of January 1966.

Ahmad Ibrahim Diraig: An exiled former governor of Darfur who formed the Sudan Federal Democratic Alliance (SFDA) in 1994 to advocate for a more-inclusive political system. In 2006, he became leader of the new National Redemption Front (NRF) that was formed in Eritrea among the rebel groups that had rejected the Darfur Peace Agreement (DPA).

Al-Bashir, Omar: A Sudanese military officer who took power in a 1989 military coup and created an Islamist regime. As the current president of Sudan, he is the first serving head of state to be indicted by the International Criminal Court (ICC) for crimes against humanity, war crimes, and genocide.

Anti-balaka militia: Referring to a traditional protection charm, these armed groups took revenge on the Central African Republic's Muslim minority after the Seleka rebel alliance seized power in the capital in 2013. These killings prompted UN and French officials to warn of potential genocide in the country.

Anuak: An ethnic group in Ethiopia's Gambella province that has been victimized by a succession of states in what some call genocide.

Anyanya: A rebel movement formed in southern Sudan in the late 1950s that fought Sudan's first civil war. "Anyanya" means snake venom.

Anyanya National Armed Force (ANAF): A coalition of Anyanya groups formed in the late 1960s during Sudan's first civil war. It was renamed Southern Sudan Liberation Movement (SSLM).

Arab Gathering: An Arab supremacist movement formed in Darfur in the 1980s that was supported by Gaddafi's Libya and made public statements threatening to exterminate the region's African population.

Army for the Liberation of Rwanda (ALIR): An exiled group of Rwandan Hutu extremists based in eastern Zaire (DRC) during the late 1990s that conducted raids into Rwanda.

Arusha Accords: A 1993 power-sharing agreement between the Rwandan government of Juvenal Habyarimana and the Rwandan Patriotic Front (RPF) that was negotiated in Arusha, Tanzania.

Association for the Promotion of the Hutu Masses (APROSOMA): Formed in late 1957 in southern Rwanda by the anti-Tutsi leader Joseph Gitera, this organization advocated for improved conditions for the Hutu majority.

Bagaza, Jean-Baptiste: A Burundian military officer of Tutsi-Hima identity from Bururi Province. He came to power in a coup in 1976 and ruled the country until he was deposed by Pierre Buyoya, another Tutsi-Hima officer, in 1987.

Bagosora, Theoneste: A Rwandan Hutu former military officer and ministry of defense official in the early 1990s who was involved with a conspiracy to assassinate President Juvenal Habyarimana and exterminate the country's Tutsi minority to avoid sharing power with the Rwandan Patriotic Front (RPF). After the 1994 genocide against the Tutsi, he fled to Zaire and then Cameroon, where he was arrested in 1997. In 2008, the International Criminal Tribunal for Rwanda (ICTR) convicted him of genocide, crimes against humanity, and war crimes and eventually sentenced him to 35 years imprisonment.

Bahutu Manifesto: Published in 1957 by Gregoire Kayibanda and Archbishop Andre Perraudin, this document explained the problems of Rwanda in terms of the racial division between Hutu and Tutsi and called for the emancipation of the Hutu and the implementation of racial quotas in education and employment that would favor the majority.

Bamileke: An ethnic group in western Cameroon who were victimized by French counterinsurgency during the 1950s and early 1960s. Some claim that this victimization amounted to genocide.

Banyamulenge: Rwandan Tutsi who moved into the eastern part of the DRC during the 19th century. The term literally means "the people of Mulenge."

Baqqara (Baggara): A term used to refer to nomadic cattle pastoralists in parts of Sudan, Chad, and other neighboring countries who speak a version of Arabic as a first language. There are different groups of Baqqara, including the Rizayqat of western Sudan.

Bemba, Jean-Pierre: Leader of the rebel Movement for the Liberation of Congo (MLC) during the Second Congo War of 1998–2002. He served as vice president in the DRC's transitional government from 2003 to 2006 when he was defeated in the presidential election by Joseph Kabila. In 2008, he was arrested in Belgium and transferred to the International Criminal Court (ICC), where, in 2016, he was convicted of crimes against humanity and war crimes for the atrocities committed by MLC in the Central African Republic. His was the first ICC conviction to include crimes related to sexual violence.

Biafra: The southeastern region of Nigeria in which a separatist government declared independence in 1967. After a federal military campaign that some called genocidal, it was reincorporated into Nigeria in 1970.

Bizimungu, Pasteur: During the 1980s, he was a Hutu official in the Rwandan government of Juvenal Habyarimana. In the early 1990s, he joined the Rwandan Patriotic Front (RPF) and served as president of Rwanda from immediately after the 1994 genocide until his resignation in 2000. He was widely seen as a puppet of Deputy President Paul Kagame. Subsequently, Bizimungu formed an opposition party that was quickly banned, and, from 2002 to 2007, he was imprisoned for corruption and inciting violence.

Bruguiere, Jean-Louis: A French judge who, in 2006, issued arrest warrants for a number of Rwandan Patriotic Front (RPF) leaders on suspicion of involvement in the downing of Rwanda's presidential aircraft in April 1994.

Bururi Province: A southern province of Burundi that was home to many of the Tutsi-Hima military officers who dominated the country from 1965 to 2005.

Buyoya, Pierre: A Burundian military officer of Tutsi-Hima identity who originated from Bururi Province. He came to power in a military coup in 1987 and initiated reforms that led to the rise of an elected civilian government in 1993. In the 1993 election, Buyoya ran for president but was defeated by Melchior Ndadaye, who became Burundi's first Hutu president. Buyoya again came to power in a military coup in 1996, led the state during the Burundian Civil War, and relinquished the presidency in 2003 as part of a negotiated peace process.

Chadian National Armed Forces (FANT): A new name for Hissene Habre's Armed Forces of the North (FAN) after it took power in Chad in 1982. In the middle 1980s, it drove the Libyan Islamic Legion out of Chad and into neighboring Darfur.

Christian Democratic Party (PDC): A political party founded in Burundi in the late 1950s that was dominated by a faction of the traditional royal family, who feared losing power to the Hutu majority. It was supported by the Belgian colonial administration that wanted to install a friendly government in postcolonial Burundi.

Classe, Leon-Paul: A long-serving and influential French missionary to Rwanda during the first half of the twentieth century who was an ardent supporter of the idea of Tutsi racial superiority.

Coalition for the Defense of the Republic (CDR): A Hutu extremist political party formed in Rwanda in 1992.

Comprehensive Peace Agreement (CPA): An agreement signed between the government of Sudan and the Sudan People's Liberation Movement/Army (SPLM/A) in Kenya in January 2005 that ended the Second Sudanese Civil War. The SPLM/A abandoned the ideal of a secular Sudan by accepting Islamic Law in the north, and the government agreed to the establishment of an autonomous Government of South Sudan and an eventual referendum on full independence in the south.

Congo Free State: The colonial state established over the Congo Basin by Leopold II and the International African Association during the late 19th century. Given international condemnation of its brutality, the Congo Free State was sold to Belgium in 1908 and became the Belgian Congo.

Congo Reform Association: An international humanitarian group formed in 1904 to campaign against atrocities committed by the Congo Free State.

Dallaire, Romeo: The Canadian general who commanded the United Nations Assistance Mission to Rwanda (UNAMIR) during 1994. He warned his UN superiors in New York, including Kofi Anan, head of peacekeeping, of an impending genocide in Rwanda but was ignored.

Darfur: Land of the Fur people. The name can refer to the precolonial Sultanate of Darfur or the marginalized western region of modern Sudan.

Darfur Liberation Front (DLF): A rebel group formed by Fur, Masalit, and Zaghawa people in Darfur during the early 2000s to oppose the Sudanese government's program of Arabization. It changed its name to Sudan Liberation Movement/Army (SLM/A). It included plans for the disarmament of the Janjaweed militia and rebel groups, the delivery of humanitarian relief, and a proposed referendum on the political future of Darfur.

Darfur Peace Agreement (2006): A 2006 agreement signed in Abuja, Nigeria, between the government of Sudan and the Sudan Liberation Movement (SLM) of Minni Arko Minnawi but did not include several other SLM factions or the Justice and Equality Movement (JEM).

Darfur Peace Agreement (2011): A 2011 agreement signed in Doha, Qatar, between the Sudanese government and a coalition of 10 small Darfur rebel groups called the Liberation and Justice Movement (LJM). It was rejected by the Justice and Equality Movement (JEM) and several factions of the Sudan Liberation Movement.

Deby, Idriss: A Chadian National Armed Forces (FANT) commander who failed to overthrow Hissene Habre in 1989 and fled to Darfur, where he formed the Patriotic Salvation Movement (MPS). In November 1990, Deby's MPS crossed into Chad and overthrew Habre. Deby became president of Chad and remains in that position today.

Democratic Forces for the Liberation of Rwanda (FDLR): An exiled group of Rwandan Hutu extremists based in South and North Kivu provinces in eastern DRC. It was formed in 2000 from remnants of the ALIR and other former members of the FAR and Interahamwe, as well as other Rwandan refugees.

Dinka: The largest ethnic group in South Sudan; speakers of a Nilotic language.

Fadlallah Burma Nasr: Sudan's minister of defense who, during the late 1980s, armed Arab militia in Bahr el Ghazal and directed them to attack Dinka people.

Federal Army of Darfur: An armed group formed in Darfur during the late 1980s to protect Fur people from massacre by Libyan and Sudanese government-sponsored Arab militias.

First People of the Kalahari (FPK): Formed in the 1990s, this advocacy group protested the Botswana government's eviction of a San (or Basarwa) community from the Central Kalahari Game Reserve (CKGR) and tried to mobilize international support by describing the action as genocide.

Forces for the Defense of Democracy (FDD): The armed wing of Burundi's National Council for the Defense of Democracy (CNDD).

Front for Democracy in Burundi (FRODEBU): A moderate and mainly Hutu political party founded in Burundi in 1993.

Front for National Salvation (FRONASA): A group of Ugandan exiles based in Tanzania during the 1970s and opposed to the brutal dictatorship of Idi Amin.

Fur: A people who inhabit an area of western Sudan known as Darfur. They speak a Nilo-Saharan language called Fur and historically lived in settled communities that engaged in cultivation and herding. In precolonial times, they formed the core population of the Sultanate of Darfur, but, as part of modern Sudan, their area became impoverished and marginalized.

Gacaca: A system of local community courts used in Rwanda to expedite the trials of people accused of crimes connected to the 1994 genocide.

Gaddafi, Muammar: The dictator of Libya who took power in a 1969 military coup and held it until he was killed in an uprising in 2011. Sponsored by the Soviet Union during the Cold War, he pursued a dream of establishing an "Islamic State of the Sahel" that would have involved merging Libya with parts of neighboring Chad and Sudan.

Gahutu, Remy: An outspoken Burundian Hutu exile leader who was involved in the formation of Tabara in 1978 and the Party for the Liberation of the Hutu People (PALIPEHUTU) in 1980. He died in Tanzania in 1990, having possibly been murdered by agents of the Burundian Tutsi military regime.

Ganwa: Members of the extended royal family of Burundi. Although popularly associated with the Tutsi identity, Ganwa often claim that they represent a distinct group.

Garang, John: Leader of the Sudan People's Liberation Movement/Army (SPLM/A) from its creation in 1983 to his death in a helicopter crash in 2005.

Genocide Intervention Network: Formed by university students in the United States in 2004, it encouraged international intervention in Darfur and raised funds to support the African Union peacekeeping mission in Darfur.

Gizenga, Antoine: Deputy prime minister of the Democratic Republic of Congo in 1960 who, after the overthrow of Prime Minister Patrice Lumumba, led a rebellion in the eastern part of the country during the early 1960s. Later, he served as prime minister during 2007 and 2008.

Gowon, Yakubu: A colonel in the Nigerian army who became the Nigerian head of state following the military coup of July 1966. He led the Nigeria federal government during the Civil War of 1967 to 1970.

Gukurahundi: A Shona saying that means "the rain that washes away the rubbish." It was the slogan of 5 Brigade, a unit of the Zimbabwean Defense Force, which victimized the people of rural Matabeleland from 1982 to 1987 in the name of pursuing alleged dissidents. Today, Zimbabweans often refer to this episode as "Gukurahundi," and some claim that it represented a genocide against the Ndebele people.

Habre, Hissene: Leader of the Chadian rebel group Armed Forces of the North (FAN) that was formed in 1976 and used Darfur as a staging area during the early 1980s. Habre seized power in Chad in 1982 and was supported by France and the United States in a war against Libyan forces and allied Chadian rebels. Overthrown in 1990, he fled to Senegal, where in 2015 he was brought before an African Union–appointed court to face charges of crimes against humanity and torture related to his time in power in Chad. He was convicted in 2016 and sentenced to imprisonment for life.

Habyarimana, Agathe: The wife of Rwanda's President Juvenal Habyarimana. She was a central figure in the planning of the genocide against the Tutsi in 1994 and was evacuated to France by the French military.

Habyarimana, Juvenal: In the early 1960s, he became the first Rwandan commander of the Rwandan military. In 1973 he overthrew President Gregoire Kayibanda in a military coup and ruled the country until his death in April 1994. Under his regime, Hutu from the north of the country gained control of the government.

Hamitic Theory: A colonial racial theory that postulated that a mysterious group of people known as "Hamites" had moved into Africa in the distant past and influenced the creation of African states. European colonizers saw the Tutsi as the Hamites of Rwanda and Burundi.

Hammarskjold, Dag: Secretary-general of the United Nations during the beginning of the Congo Crisis of the early 1960s. He died when his aircraft crashed, under what are now seen as mysterious circumstances, in Northern Rhodesia (Zambia) in 1961.

Harroy, Jean-Paul: The last Belgian governor-general of Rwanda and Burundi who served from 1955 to independence in 1962. In Rwanda, he advocated a switch from Tutsi to Hutu dominance, which influenced the social revolution. In Burundi, he supported the Christian Democratic Party (PDC), led by a pro-Belgian section of the royal family that was pitted against Crown Prince Louis Rwagasore's Union for National Progress (UPRONA).

Hassan al-Turabi: A prominent Islamist leader in postcolonial Sudan. He was secretary-general of Sudan's National Islamic Front (NIF) from the 1960s to 1999 and its successor, the National Congress Party, from 1999 until his death in 2016. During the late 1980s and 1990s, his movement was centrally involved in atrocities in Darfur and southern Sudan.

Hema: A historically pastoral community in Ituri Province of the Democratic Republic of Congo (DRC).

Hutu: An identity that is associated with the majority of people in Rwanda and Burundi and is associated with a historic way of life centered on cultivation. European colonizers saw them as an essentially inferior race that had been subjugated by the pastoral Tutsi during precolonial times. Under colonial rule, they became the main producers of such cash crops as tea and coffee and had limited opportunities for advancement.

Hutu Power: Developed in the 1950s by Hutu elites, this political concept puts forth the notion that the Hutu represent the indigenous inhabitants of Rwanda and Burundi who were unjustly dispossessed by foreign Tutsi invaders. As such, it advocates the idea that the Hutu majority should dominate the government of these countries.

Ibuka: A Kinyarwanda word meaning "remember." Founded in Belgium in 1994 but now based in Kigali, it is an umbrella organization for various associations made up of survivors of the genocide against the Tutsi in Rwanda.

Igbo: The largest ethnic group of southeastern Nigeria.

Igbo Pogroms: Massacres of Igbo people in northern Nigeria that took place in May, September, and October 1966.

Impuzamugambi: A Kinyarwanda term meaning "those with a common purpose." It was a militia organized by Rwanda's Hutu extremist Coalition for the Defense of the Republic (CDR) party in the early 1990s.

Inkotanya: A Kinyarwanda term meaning "those who struggle together" and used to refer to Rwandan Patriotic Front (RPF) rebels during the early 1990s.

Intagoheka: A Kirundi term for "those who do not sleep." It was a Hutu militia in Burundi during the 1990s.

Interahamwe: A Kinyarwanda term meaning "those who work together." It was a militia organized by Rwanda's ruling National Revolutionary Movement for Development (MRND) party during the early 1990s.

Interim Emergency Multinational Force (IEMF): A United Nations–approved European Union military intervention in Ituri Province of the DRC conducted primarily by French troops from June to September 2003. It represented the European Union's first autonomous military operation outside Europe and was relieved by a newly formed MONUC Ituri Brigade.

International African Association: A supposedly humanitarian group formed by Belgian King Leopold II in the late-19th century to arrange the colonial conquest of the Congo River Basin.

International Criminal Court (ICC): Created by an 1998 international treaty known as the Rome Statute and based in The Hague in the Netherlands, the ICC began functioning in 2002 with the aim of conducting trials related to accusations of genocide, crimes against humanity, war crimes, and crimes of aggression. It is meant to judge cases that national courts are unable or unwilling to deal with and is empowered to act with reference to offenses committed within the more than 120 states that signed and ratified the treaty, or when empowered by the United Nations Security Council. The ICC has been criticized for focusing exclusively on African issues and ignoring accusations against such major powers as the United States, which has not ratified the Rome Statute.

International Criminal Tribunal for Rwanda (ICTR): A United Nations–backed international court established in Arusha, Tanzania, in 1995 to conduct trials of people accused of leading roles in the 1994 genocide in Rwanda.

Islamic Legion: An international military force created by Libyan dictator Muammar Gaddafi. It was involved in violence in Darfur and Chad during the 1970s and 1980s.

Ituri Province: A northeastern province of the DRC created by Ugandan occupation forces in 1999. It was formerly part of Orientale Province.

Janjaweed: A Sudanese government-sponsored Arab militia first formed in the late 1990s to attack Masalit communities in western Darfur, but then was expanded over the whole Darfur region in the early 2000s as a cheap way to mount a counterinsurgency campaign.

Justice and Equality Movement (JEM): A rebel group formed in Darfur in the early 2000s that opposed the Sudanese government's Arabization of the region but that supported the continuation of Islamic law. Its main goal was and is the equality of all people and regions in Sudan.

Kabila, Joseph: The son of Laurent Kabila who seized the leadership of the DRC when his father was assassinated in 2000.

Kabila, Laurent: A Congolese revolutionary during the 1960s, he led the Rwandan- and Ugandan-backed Alliance of Democratic Forces for the Liberation of Congo (AFDL) that overthrew Mobutu Sese Seko during the First Congo War of 1996–1997.

Kagame, Paul: A Rwandan Tutsi exile who became an early member of the Ugandan National Resistance Movement/Army (NRM/NRA) in the 1980s. In 1990, after the death of Fred Rwigyema, he took command of the Rwandan Patriotic Front (RPF), which had just invaded Rwanda. Following the 1994 genocide against the Tutsi in Rwanda and the RPF military occupation of the country, he became Rwanda's deputy president and minister of defense. He became president of Rwanda in 2000.

Kalonji, Albert: Separatist leader of South Kasai during the Congo Crisis of the early 1960s.

Kanguka: Kinyarwanda for "wake up." Launched in 1987, this Rwandan newspaper criticized the Habyarimana government and sympathized with the Rwandan Patriotic Front (RPF).

Kangura: Kinyarwanda for "wake others up." Launched in 1990, this Rwandan newspaper was funded by the Habyarimana government and spread anti-Tutsi hate propaganda.

Kanyarengwe, Alexis: A Rwandan Hutu military officer who fled the country after a failed coup attempt in 1980. In the early 1990s, he served as chairman of the RPF that had invaded Rwanda.

Kasavubu, Joseph: First president of the Democratic Republic of Congo from 1960 to 1965. He was the leader of the Bakongo Alliance (ABAKO), which was a political party based in the western part of the country.

Katanga: The most southerly province of the Democratic Republic of Congo. From 1971 to 1997, it was called Shaba Province.

Katanga, Germain: Leader of a militia group called Patriotic Resistance Force in Ituri (FRPI) that was active in the northeastern DRC during the 2000s. He was handed over to the ICC in 2007 and convicted of crimes against humanity and war crimes in 2014.

Kayibanda, Gregoire: Founding leader of the Party for the Emancipation of the Hutu (PARMEHUTU). He served as the first elected president of independent Rwanda from 1962 until his overthrow by the military in 1973.

Kenyatta, Uhuru: Elected president of Kenya in 2013, he became the first serving head of state to appear before the ICC to answer charges related to crimes against humanity allegedly committed in the wake of Kenya's troubled 2007 election. The ICC later dropped the charges due to lack of evidence.

Kibeho massacre: In 1995 Rwandan Patriotic Front (RPF) soldiers fired on refugees in a camp in southern Rwanda, killing perhaps 5,000 people.

Kiga (plural = Bakiga): A generic name for the people who inhabit the mountainous north of Rwanda that was conquered by the royal court of Musinga and the Germans in the early 1900s.

Kinyamateka: A Kinyarwanda term meaning "about history." It was a newspaper in 1950s Rwanda managed by Gregoire Kayibanda.

Kordofan: A region located in central/western Sudan.

Lendu: A historically agricultural group in Ituri Province of the DRC.

Leopold II: The constitutional monarch of Belgium who formed the International African Association that orchestrated the private colonial conquest of the Congo River Basin.

Liberation and Justice Movement (LJM): A coalition of 10 small Darfur rebel groups formed in 2010 that engaged in negotiations with the government of Sudan in Doha, Qatar, and signed a second Darfur Peace Agreement in 2011.

Logiest, Guy: A Belgian military officer who commanded Congolese troops during an intervention in Rwanda in 1959 that facilitated a Hutu seizure of power.

Lubanga, Thomas: Founding leader of the rebel Union of Congolese Patriots (UPC) in Ituri Province of the DRC in 2001. In 2005, he became the first person ever arrested on an ICC warrant and transferred to The Hague where, in 2012, he was convicted of conscripting child soldiers, for which he was sentenced to 14 years in prison. He was also the first person ever convicted by the ICC.

Lumumba, Patrice: The first prime minister of the DRC elected on independence in 1960. He was overthrown in October 1960, flown to the separatist region of Katanga, and murdered in January 1961.

Machar, Riek: Led an ethnic Nuer faction that split from the Sudan People's Liberation Army (SPLA) in 1991 and fought the predominantly Dinka SPLA of John Garang throughout the 1990s. He later rejoined the SPLM/A and became vice president of independent South Sudan in 2011. Dismissed from office in 2013 for allegedly plotting a coup, he led a Nuer faction called the SPLA-In Opposition (SPLA-IO) in South Sudan's civil war.

Mai Mai militia: Local self-defense groups formed in the eastern DRC provinces of South Kivu and North Kivu during the late 1990s.

Makenga, Sultani: Leader of the M23 rebel group in eastern DRC who, along with many of his fellow rebels, fled to Uganda in 2013.

March 23 Movement (M23): A Congolese Tutsi rebel group formerly known as the National Congress for Defense of the People (CNDP). In 2012, it renewed its rebellion against the DRC government in North Kivu and in 2013 was suppressed by a UN special intervention brigade.

Markpress: A Swiss-based public relations firm hired by the secessionist state of Biafra during the Nigerian Civil War (1967–1970).

Masalit: A people who inhabit part of western Sudan and eastern Chad. Historically, they spoke a Nilo-Saharan language and practiced cultivation and herding.

Mayardit, Salva Kiir: A veteran of the Anyanya movement during the First Sudanese Civil War, he eventually became head of the Sudan People's Liberation Army (the military wing of the Sudan People's Liberation Movement: SPLM) during the Second Sudanese Civil War. After the death of SPLM leader John Garang in 2005, he became president of the autonomous government of South Sudan and president of independent South Sudan in 2011.

Mbarushimana, Callixte: An FDLR political leader based in France who was arrested in 2011 and sent to the ICC but later released, given insufficient evidence of war crimes and crimes against humanity.

Mengistu, Haile Mariam: Between 1977 and 1991, Mengistu led Ethiopia's military regime that tortured and murdered political opponents and conducted brutal counterinsurgency campaigns against several regional separatist groups. In 2006, an Ethiopian court convicted an exiled Mengistu of genocide and crimes against humanity.

Micombero, Michel: A Burundian army officer of Tutsi-Hima identity from the south of the country who seized power in a military coup in 1965. His regime orchestrated the 1972 genocide of educated Hutu and Hutu students. In 1976, he was overthrown by a military coup led by his cousin, Jean-Baptiste Bagaza.

Minni Arko Minnawi: A leader of the Sudan Liberation Movement (SLM) in Darfur. His faction accepted the 2006 Darfur Peace Agreement (DPA), which was rejected by other factions. He withdrew from the DPA in 2010, and his part of the SLM joined other rebel groups to form the Sudan Revolutionary Front.

Mobutu Sese Seko: The American- and French-backed dictator of Zaire (now DRC) from the 1960s until 1997, when he was overthrown by a rebellion backed by forces from Rwanda and Uganda.

Movement for the Actualization of the Sovereign State of Biafra (MASSOB): Formed in 1999, this organization aspires to use peaceful protest to reestablish the secessionist state of Biafra in southeast Nigeria.

Movement for the Emancipation of the Niger Delta (MEND): Formed in the mid-2000s, this armed rebel group raids oil-production facilities and kidnaps oil workers in Nigeria's Niger Delta.

Movement for the Liberation of Congo (MLC): A rebel group formed in the DRC in 1998 and led by Jean-Pierre Bemba. It derived most of its support from the north of the country, was active in the Central African Republic (CAR), and was backed by Uganda.

Movement for the Survival of the Ogoni People (MOSOP): Formed in 1990, this movement of the Ogoni people of Nigeria's Niger Delta advocates for greater political representation, a share of oil revenues generated in their region, and protection for their environment.

Movement of Progressive Students of Burundi (MEPROBA): A group of Burundian Hutu student exiles formed in Belgium during the 1970s.

Mudacumura, Sylvestre: Deputy commander of the Rwandan presidential guard during the 1994 genocide, he eventually became military leader of the FDLR in eastern DRC. In 2012, the ICC issued an arrest warrant against him on charges of war crimes committed in DRC.

Mugabe, Robert: The first prime minister of independent Zimbabwe from 1980 to 1987 and then president of Zimbabwe from 1987 onward. He led an increasingly authoritarian regime that imposed a reign of terror on the people of rural Matabeleland in the 1980s.

Mugesera, Leon: A Rwandan government official who, in 1992, told supporters that the country's Tutsi minority should be exterminated. While he was not in Rwanda during the 1994 genocide, he was deported from Canada to Rwanda in 2012 to face criminal charges related to inciting genocide.

Mugunga camp: A massive concentration of Rwandan refugees in eastern Zaire (DRC) that was forcefully dismantled by the Rwandan Patriotic Army (RPA) in late 1996.

Muhutu Social Movement (MSM): An organization formed by Gregoire Kayibanda in 1957 that advocated for the general improvement of conditions for the Hutu majority in Rwanda.

Munyaneza, Desire: A Rwandan shopkeeper in Butare in 1994 who participated in the genocide against the Tutsi and subsequently fled to Canada where, in 2009, he was convicted of genocide and crimes against humanity and sentenced to life imprisonment.

Murahiliin: A Sudanese government-sponsored Baqqara militia that massacred Dinka people in Bahr el Ghazal during the late 1980s and were then deployed to other parts of the country.

Murwanashyaka, Ignace: An FDLR political leader based in Germany who was arrested by German authorities in 2009 and eventually convicted by a German court of war crimes and crimes against humanity.

Musa Hilal: A traditional leader among Sudan's Rizayqat Baqqara Arabs and leader of the Janjaweed militia in Darfur from 2003. In 2008, he became chief advisor to Sudan's Ministry of Federal Affairs.

Museveni, Yoweri: Leader of Ugandan exile movements based in Tanzania, including Front for National Salvation (FRONASA) in the 1970s and National Resistance Movement/National Resistance Army (NRM/NRA) in the 1980s. He led a successful insurgency in southern Uganda during the first half of the 1980s that led to the NRM/NRA's seizure of power there in 1986. He has remained the president of Uganda since that time.

Musinga: King of Rwanda from 1896 to 1931. In the early 1900s, he used an alliance with the Germans to extend his dominance over the north of Rwanda, but then eventually chaffed under more intrusive Belgian administration after the First World War. Belgian authorities banished him to the Congo and replaced him with his son, Mutara Rudahigwa.

Musoni, Straton: An FDLR political leader based in Germany who was arrested by German authorities in 2009 and eventually convicted by a German court of war crimes and crimes against humanity.

Mutara Rudahigwa: He became king of Rwanda after the Belgian deposition of his father, Musinga, in 1931 and reigned up until his death in 1959 during the Hutu seizure of power. He was the first Christian king of Rwanda and was popularly called "the King of the Whites."

Mwambutsa: As a child, he became the king of Burundi during the First World War when the Belgians occupied the territory. With the independence of Burundi in 1962, he became a constitutional monarch until fleeing the country during a military coup in 1965.

Mwezi Gisabo: Ruler of the Kingdom of Burundi during the late 19th and very early 20th century. He initially resisted German colonial intrusion but then cooperated with it to extend his territorial authority.

National Army of the Congo (ANC): The independent Congo's new army formed after the 1960 mutiny of the Force Publique.

National Commission for the Fight against Genocide: A branch of the Rwandan government created in 2008 to coordinate genocide commemoration activities, develop strategies for fighting genocide and "genocide ideology," counter genocide denial and trivialization, and assist genocide survivors.

National Congress for the Defense of the People (CNDP): Formed in 2006 in North Kivu Province of the DRC, this was a Congolese Tutsi militia group led by Laurent Nkunda, who was then replaced by Bosco Ntaganda. It claimed to protect Congolese Tutsi from the exiled Rwandan Hutu extremists of the FDLR. In 2009, Ntaganda agreed to reintegrate into the Congolese military and to turn the CNDP into a political party. It rebelled again in 2012, taking the name March 23 or M23.

National Council for the Defense of Democracy (CNDD): A group that split from the moderate Front for Democracy in Burundi (FRODEBU) in 1994 to fight for democracy in Burundi.

National Forces of Liberation (FNL): Formed in 1985 in Tanzania, this was the armed wing of the Party for the Liberation of the Hutu People (PALIPEHUTU).

National Islamic Front (NIF): An extremist Islamist political party in Sudan that was formed in 1976 and led by Hassan al-Turabi. Coming to power with the 1989 military coup, the NIF regime of the 1990s was committed to maintaining Islamic law throughout the country and was involved in atrocities in Darfur and southern Sudan. Renamed the National Congress Party in the late 1990s, it began to distance itself from radical Islamists after the 2001 terrorist attacks on the United States.

National Liberation Council (CNL): A coalition of leftist rebel groups lead by Pierre Mulele and Gaston Soumialot in the DRC during the 1960s. They briefly established the People's Republic of Congo, which was recognized by the Soviet Union, Cuba, and Communist China.

National Liberation Front of Chad (FROLINAT): The first rebel group formed in northern Chad in the 1960s and based in neighboring Darfur.

National Redemption Front (NRF): A coalition of Darfur rebel groups, including the Justice and Equality Movement (JEM) and factions of the Sudan Liberation Movement (SLM) that had not signed the Darfur Peace Agreement of 2006, and the exiled Sudan Federal Democratic Alliance (SFDA) of Ahmad Ibrahim Diraig.

National Resistance Movement/National Resistance Army (NRM/NRA): Led by Yoweri Museveni, this movement fought an insurgent campaign in southern Uganda against the northern-dominated regime of Milton Obote. Seizing power in 1986, it remains the government of Uganda. During the 1980s, the NRM/NRA contained many Rwandan exiles, including Fred Rwigyema and Paul Kagame.

National Revolutionary Movement for Development (MRND): Led by Juvenal Habyarimana, this was the ruling and only legal political party in Rwanda from the late 1970s to the early 1990s.

Nationalist and Integrationist Front (FNI): An ethnic Lendu militia group based in the DRC's Ituri Province during the mid- to late 2000s.

Ndadaye, Melchior: A leader of the Front for Democracy in Burundi (FRODEBU), who became Burundi's first Hutu president in June 1993 but was assassinated by the Tutsi-controlled army in October of that year. His death outraged Hutu civilians, who massacred Tutsi, which, in turn, prompted the Tutsi military to slaughter Hutus.

Ndayizeye, Domitien: A leader of the Front for Democracy in Burundi (FRODEBU) who served as president of the country from 2003 to 2005.

Neutral Military Observer Group (NMOG): Mandated by the Organization of African Unity (OAU), this group of military observers from Senegal, Nigeria, Zimbabwe, and Mali monitored a cease-fire in Rwanda in 1992 and 1993.

Ngendandumwe, Pierre: The first Hutu prime minister of Burundi who was assassinated by a Rwandan Tutsi refugee in January 1965.

Ngudjolo Chui, Mathieu: A leader within the Lendu militia called the Nationalist and Integrationist Front (FNI) that was active in Ituri Province of the DRC during the 2000s. He was handed over to the ICC in 2008 to face charges of war crimes and crimes against humanity but was released in 2012 given insufficient evidence.

Niyitegeka, Felicitas: A Rwandan Hutu nun who hid Tutsi students from killers during the 1994 genocide and was killed when they were discovered.

Nkore: A precolonial African kingdom in what is now Uganda. Historically, Nkore's pastoralist Hima minority dominated the agriculturalist Iru majority.

Nkunda, Laurent: Leader of the Congolese Tutsi militia known as the National Congress for Defense of the People (CNDP) formed in the eastern DRC in 2006. Although his group was initially supported by Rwanda, international pressure prompted the Rwandan government to detain him in 2009.

Nkurunziza, Pierre: A Hutu leader of the National Council for the Defense of Democracy (CNDD) and Forces for the Defense of Democracy (FDD) during Burundi's Civil War in the late 1990s and early 2000s. He was elected president of Burundi in 2005 and remains in power.

North Kivu: A province in eastern DRC that borders Rwanda and Uganda.

Ntaganda, Bosco: A Congolese Tutsi militia leader involved in violence in the DRC's Ituri Province in the early 2000s, who then took over the leadership of the National Congress for the Defense of the People (CNDP) in North Kivu in 2009. In 2012, he led a rebellion by the M23 group in North Kivu, but, given infighting, he surrendered himself to the U.S. embassy in Kigali the next year and was transferred to the ICC to face charges of war crimes related to his time in Ituri.

Ntare V (Charles Ndizeye): He became king of Burundi in 1966 and was deposed by the military later the same year. He returned from exile in 1972 and was killed by the military on the same day that Hutu rebels invaded the country.

Ntaryamira, Cyprien: The second Hutu president of Burundi who died in the same aircraft as Rwanda's President Juvenal Habyarimana in April 1994.

Ntibantunganya, Sylvestre: The civilian president of Burundi and a member of the Front for Democracy in Burundi (FRODEBU), who was overthrown by a military coup in 1996 and replaced by Pierre Buyoya.

Nuba Mountains: A mountainous area located in the southeast of Sudan's Kordofan region.

Nuba People: A collection of diverse communities that inhabit the Nuba Mountains of Sudan who were targeted for extermination by the Sudanese government during the 1990s.

Nuer: A major ethnic group in South Sudan who speak a Nilotic language.

Numayri, Jaafar Muhammad: A Sudanese military officer who took power in 1969 and was overthrown by another military coup in 1985. His government ended the First Sudanese Civil War through the Addis Ababa Agreement of 1972 and started the Second Sudanese Civil War by imposing Islamic law in 1983.

Nzeugwu, Kaduna: Leader of the Five Majors coup in Nigeria in January 1966.

Ojukwu, Chukwuemeka Odumegwu: A Nigerian military officer and ethnic Igbo who became military governor of the eastern region in 1966. From May 1967 to January 1970, he led the breakaway Republic of Biafra against the federal military government of Nigeria during the Nigerian Civil War. He returned from exile in 1982 and died in 2011.

Operation Amaryllis: The French military intervention in Rwanda in April 1994 that evacuated European civilians and Agathe Habyarimana, widow of the assassinated president.

Operation Artemis: A 2003 European Union military intervention in Ituri Province of the DRC.

Operation Noroit (North Wind): A French military intervention in Rwanda in the early 1990s that prevented the RPF from defeating the Armed Forces of Rwanda (FAR) and seizing control of the country.

Operation Silverback: The Belgian and Italian military intervention in Rwanda in 1994 that evacuated European civilians.

Operation Turquoise: A French military operation that created a supposedly safe zone for refugees in southwestern Rwanda in 1994. In some instances, French soldiers facilitated the genocide against the Tutsi in that area, and the zone of occupation provided an avenue whereby defeated Rwandan state forces and perpetrators of genocide escaped into neighboring Zaire.

Organization of African Unity (OAU): An international governmental organization of African states founded in 1963. Its name was changed to African Union (AU) in 2002.

Oueddei, Goukouni: A northern Chadian rebel leader who headed the People's Armed Forces (FAP) that held power from 1979 to 1982 and was supported by Gaddafi's Libya. While he fought against Hissene Habre's French-backed regime during the early and middle 1980s, Oueddei eventually joined with the government to expel the Libyans from northern Chad in the 1987 Toyota War.

Party for the Emancipation of the Hutu (PARMEHUTU): In Rwanda, in late 1959, Hutu leader Gregoire Kayibanda transformed his Muhutu Social Movement (MSM) into a political party that called for the end of Tutsi colonialism and feudalism and remained close to Belgium.

Party for the Liberation of the Hutu People (PALIPEHUTU): Formed in 1980, in a Tanzanian refugee camp for Burundian exiles, this group planned to overthrow the Tutsi military regime in Burundi and establish a majority rule government.

Party of the People (PP): Inspired by the recent Hutu revolution in Rwanda, it was a Burundian political party formed in the late 1950s that was blatantly pro-Hutu and supported by some Belgian officials and settlers.

Patriotic Resistance Force in Ituri (FRPI): An ethnic Ngiti militia group based in Ituri Province of the DRC from 2002 to 2006. It was allied to the Lendu FNI militia.

Patriotic Salvation Movement (MPS): A Chadian rebel movement formed in Darfur by Idriss Deby in 1989. Backed by Gaddafi's Libya, it invaded Chad in late 1990 and seized power.

People's Armed Forces (FAP): A Libyan-backed rebel group based in northern Chad that took power in Chad from 1979 to 1982. Led by Goukouni Oueddei, it fought against Hissene Habre's regime in the mid-1980s but then allied with it in 1987 to expel Libyans from northern Chad.

Perraudin, Andre: A Swiss Catholic missionary in Rwanda for most of the late 20th century who became an archbishop in 1959. He sympathized with the aspirations of the Hutu majority and coauthored the "Bahutu Manifesto" with Gregoire Kayibanda.

Popular Defense Force (PDF): A paramilitary organization formed by the Sudanese government at the start of the 1990s. Many state-sponsored militias were eventually incorporated into the PDF.

Radio Muhabura: Meaning "lead the way" in Kinyarwanda, this was a RPF radio station based in Uganda that broadcast antigovernment propaganda into Rwanda during the early 1990s.

Rally for Congolese Democracy (RCD): A rebel group formed in eastern DRC in 1998 and backed by Rwanda.

Rally for Congolese Democracy–Goma (RCD-G): A rebel group that split from the original RCD in 1999 but was based mostly around the city of Goma and backed by Rwanda.

Rally for Congolese Democracy–Kisangani (RCD-K): A rebel group resulting from the division of the original RCD in 1999, based around the city of Kisangani, and supported by Uganda.

Rally for Congolese Democracy–Liberation Movement (RCD-ML): A splinter group from RCD-K formed after 2000 when the group moved to Ituri Province.

Red Terror: A campaign of torture and murder conducted by Ethiopia's military regime against its political opponents during the late 1970s.

Republican Democratic Movement (MDR): An opposition political party in Rwanda during the 1990s that was initially involved in a coalition government with the RPF after the 1994 genocide.

Republican Order Number One: A 1983 decree by the government of Sudan that abrogated the Addis Ababa Agreement and prompted the start of the Second Sudanese Civil War.

Rucunshu coup: In 1896, Kanjogera, a widow of the late King Rwabugiri, staged a violent seizure of power in Rwanda that brought her son, Musinga, to power.

Rwabugiri: King of the precolonial state of Rwanda from 1865 to 1895. He initiated numerous wars against neighboring groups and further centralized the state, which polarized the existing Tutsi and Hutu identities.

Rwagasore, Louis: The son of King Mwambutsa and crown prince of Burundi who led the Union for National Progress (UPRONA) in the late 1950s and the early 1960s. In 1961, he was assassinated shortly after his election as Burundi's first prime minister.

Rwagasore Youth Revolutionaries (JJR): The youth wing of the ruling UPRONA that conducted massacres of Hutu intellectuals and students in 1972.

Rwanda Armed Forces (FAR): The Rwandan state military under the Habyarimana administration of 1972 to 1994.

Rwanda Defense Force (RDF): The name of the Rwandan state military, formerly the Rwandan Patriotic Army (RPA), from 2002 to today.

Rwandan Democratic Rally (RADER): This short-lived political party was formed in Rwanda in 1959 by moderate Tutsi who wanted to cooperate with the Belgian colonial administration and Hutu political leaders.

Rwandan National Guard (GNR): The Belgian-led military of Rwanda after independence in 1962.

Rwandan National Union (UNAR): A primarily Tutsi Rwandan political party formed in 1959 that demanded the immediate granting of independence to the country as a constitutional monarchy.

Rwandan Patriotic Army (RPA): The name of the armed wing of the Rwandan Patriotic Front (RPF) from 1990 to 2002, when it was renamed the Rwanda Defense Force (RDF).

Rwandan Patriotic Front (RPF): A new name for the Rwandan Alliance for National Unity (RANU) adopted in 1987. The RPF invaded Rwanda in 1990 and seized power during the 1994 genocide. Led by Paul Kagame, the RPF remains the government of Rwanda.

Rwandese Alliance for National Unity (RANU): Originally called the Rwandese Refugee Welfare Association (RRWA), this new name was adopted in 1980 to reflect a more militant political stance among Rwandan exiles, including the desire to eventually return to Rwanda. It was based in Kenya from 1981 to 1986.

Rwandese Refugee Welfare Association (RRWA): A self-help group formed by Rwandan refugees in Uganda in 1979.

Rwasa, Agathon: A Hutu extremist leader of the National Forces of Liberation (FNL) during Burundi's civil war in the late 1990s and 2000s. Although he agreed to a cease-fire in 2006, his forces were still fighting in 2008 but then embarked on a demobilization process. He became a political opposition leader in Burundi and went into hiding during the controversial election of 2010.

Rwigyema, Fred: A Rwandan Tutsi exile who became an important leader within the Ugandan National Resistance Movement/Army (NRM/NRA) and eventually led the RPF's invasion of Rwanda in 1990. He was killed by several RPF colleagues after a dispute over military strategy.

Sadiq al-Mahdi: The great grandson of Sudan's late-19th-century Mahdi and leader of the moderate Islamist Umma Party, he served as prime minister of Sudan from 1966 to 1967 and from 1986 to 1989. During his second term in power, he was supported by Gaddafi's Libya and initiated Sudanese state sponsorship of Arab militias that were pitted against African communities in Darfur and southern Sudan.

San: Also called Basarwa and Bushmen, these historic hunter-gatherer communities of Southern Africa were targeted for extermination by European settlers during the 1700s and 1800s. They became a marginalized minority, inhabiting such interior deserts as the Kalahari. In modern Botswana, state attempts to resettle a San group was called genocide by local and international activists.

Saro-Wiwa, Ken: A Nigerian writer and activist who led MOSOP. He accused multinational oil companies, including Shell, and the Nigerian federal government of committing genocide against the Ogoni people of the Niger Delta. In 1994, he was arrested by the Nigerian military and executed the next year.

Save Darfur Coalition: An organization formed in New York City in July 2004 by the U.S. Holocaust Memorial Museum and the American Jewish World Service. It established a head office in Washington, D.C. and engaged in raising public awareness of atrocities being committed in Darfur and advocated for international intervention. In 2011, it merged with the Genocide Intervention Network to form a new organization called United to End Genocide.

Seleka: Meaning "union" in the Sanga language of the Central African Republic, this alliance of northern-based rebel groups seized power in March 2013, which prompted revenge killings of Muslims by the Christian anti-balaka militia.

Sendashonga, Seth: A Hutu member of the RPF and minister in Rwanda's post-genocide government of the mid-1990s who began to ask questions about his organization's involvement in massacres and assassinations. He fled to Kenya, where he tried to form a Rwandan opposition group, but was assassinated in 1998.

Seromba, Athanese: A Catholic priest in western Rwanda during the 1994 genocide who encouraged his Tutsi parishioners to hide in his church but then called Hutu militia who burned the structure. After the genocide, he worked as a priest in Italy but surrendered himself to the ICTR where, in 2006, he was found guilty of genocide and crimes against humanity and eventually sentenced to life imprisonment.

Simba: Kiswahili word for "lion" and a term used to describe rebels active in eastern Democratic Republic of Congo during the 1960s.

Simbananiye, Arthemon: A senior Burundian civil servant and former minister of foreign affairs who directed the genocide of educated Hutu and Hutu students in 1972.

Simbikangwa, Pascal: An intelligence head in Rwanda's Habyarimana government who, after the 1994 genocide, fled to France where he was eventually convicted of genocide and complicity in crimes against humanity and sentenced to 25 years imprisonment in 2014.

Social Darwinism: A pseudoscientific theory that emerged during the late 19th century and claimed that humanity can be divided into a hierarchy of races.

Social revolution: The violent overthrow of Tutsi officials by Hutu leaders in Rwanda during 1959.

South Kivu: A province in eastern DRC that borders Rwanda and Burundi.

Southern Policy: The British colonial policy used to administer southern Sudan during the first half of the 20th century that encouraged Christianization and the English language.

Southern Sudan Liberation Movement (SSLM): A combination of rebel groups in southern Sudan formed in 1969 that fought the country's first civil war.

Sudan African Nationalist Union (SANU): Formed in 1963 during the First Sudanese Civil War, this exiled movement advocated the separation of southern Sudan from Sudan.

Sudan Defense Force (SDF): The British colonial military established in Sudan in 1924. It was divided into regional elements including the Equatorial Corps, Eastern Arab Corps, Western Arab Corps, and Camel Corps.

Sudan Federal Democratic Alliance (SFDA): A group formed by exiled Sudanese in 1994 to advocate for a more-inclusive political system in Sudan.

Sudan Liberation Movement/Army (SLM/A): Formed in Darfur during the early 2000s, this secular rebel group consisted of Fur, Masalit, and Zaghawa fighters who opposed the Sudan government's program of Arabization in the region. It was initially called the Darfur Liberation Front (DLF). With the signing of the Darfur Peace Agreement in 2006, the movement split into different factions, some of which supported and others which opposed the deal.

Sudan Peace Act: A law passed in the United States in October 2002 that accused the Sudanese government of committing genocide during the civil war in the south.

Sudan People's Liberation Movement/Army (SPLM/A): Formed in 1983 and led by John Garang, this southern Sudanese rebel movement advocated a federal and secular Sudan. It fought the Second Sudanese Civil War, and, with the Comprehensive Peace Agreement of 2005, it formed the autonomous government of South Sudan and the government of independent South Sudan in 2011.

Sudan People's Liberation Movement–North (SPLM-N): When South Sudan became independent in 2011, members of the SPLM/A active in Kordofan and

Blue Nile, which remained part of Sudan, renamed themselves SPLM-North and continued their struggle against the Khartoum government.

Survival International: A British-based global indigenous rights organization that helped the First People of the Kalahari (FPK), a minority rights group in Botswana, to pressure the government of Botswana by portraying it as committing genocide against the San (or Basarwa).

Tabara: The first overtly political group founded by Burundian Hutu exiles in 1978.

Territorial Guard of Ruanda-Urundi (GTRU): Established by the Belgians in 1960, this was the first colonial military recruited in Rwanda and Burundi.

Thousand Hills Radio-Television (RTML): Established in 1993, this radio station in Rwanda broadcast anti-Tutsi hate propaganda and actively encouraged and directed killing during the 1994 genocide.

Toyota War: A 1987 conflict in which French- and United States-backed Chadian forces drove Gaddafi's Libyans out of northern Chad.

Tshombe, Moise: Leader of separatist Katanga during the Congo Crisis of the early 1960s and prime minister of the DRC in 1964–1965.

Tuareg: The historically nomadic people of the Sahara and Sahel of West Africa who were split between Niger, Mali, and Algeria upon the independence of those states from France in the early 1960s. Counterinsurgency campaigns in Mali and Niger against Tuareg separatist rebellions have been alleged as genocide.

Tutsi: An identity that is associated with the historic pastoral minority in Rwanda and Burundi. It is probable that the ancestors of the Tutsi, during precolonial times, moved into the Great Lakes Area from further north in what is now South Sudan and Ethiopia. European colonizers, given their racial theories, saw the Tutsi as members of a biologically superior race that had conquered the supposedly inferior Hutu. Under colonial rule, the Tutsi became a favored group, gained preferential access to Western education, and occupied administrative positions within the colonial state.

Twa: A small and historically marginalized community in Central Africa, including Rwanda and Burundi. Called pygmies in colonial times, they were historic forest hunter-gatherers and specialized in making pots to trade.

Twagiramungu, Faustin: A Hutu member of the Republican Democratic Movement (MDR), he became the first postgenocide prime minister of Rwanda in 1994. Tensions stemming from violence carried out by the RPF including the Kibeho massacre, prompted him to resign from the unity government. In 2003, Twagiramungu, his party banned, ran for president but lost to RPF incumbent Paul Kagame, who won with a remarkable 95 percent of the vote.

Ugandan People's Defense Force (UPDF): The current state military of Uganda. It originates from the National Resistance Army (NRA) that took power in 1986 and was then renamed in 1995.

Union for National Progress (UPRONA): Led by Crown Prince Louis Rwagasore, this Burundian political party of the late 1950s and early 1960s demanded immediate independence from Belgium.

Union of Congolese Patriots (UPC): A pro-Hema rebel group formed in Ituri Province of the DRC in 2001 and supported initially by Uganda and then by Rwanda. Its fighters were demobilized in the mid-2000s, and it became a political party.

United Nations Assistance Mission for Rwanda (UNAMIR): A United Nations peacekeeping mission in Rwanda meant to supervise the implementation of the Arusha Accords in 1993 and 1994. Commanded by Canadian general Romeo Dallaire, it was ill-prepared to deal with the genocide that began in April 1994.

United Nations Mission in the Democratic Republic of Congo (MONUC): Initially created to supervise the stalled peace process for the DRC in 1999, this international peacekeeping force reached substantial numbers with the creation of a transitional government and the withdrawal of foreign forces in 2002 and 2003. In 2010, it represented the UN's largest peacekeeping force, with over 20,000 personnel, and its name was changed to UN Organization Stabilization Mission in the DRC (MONUSCO) to reflect that it was now supporting an elected government.

United Nations Multidimensional Integrated Stabilization Mission in the Central African Republic (MINUSCA): Created to augment an existing international peacekeeping mission in the CAR in 2014, this force was mandated to protect civilians, given concerns about the possibility of genocide in the country.

United Nations Observer Mission to Uganda-Rwanda (UNOMUR): A United Nations military mission formed in 1993 that tried to ensure that the Ugandan government was not supplying RPF rebels in Rwanda.

United Nations Operation in Burundi (ONUB): An international military force that supervised the peace process in Burundi from 2004 to 2007. It took over from the African Union Mission in Burundi (AMIB).

United Nations Organization Stabilization Mission in the Democratic Republic of Congo (MONUSCO): The new name of MONUC from 2010.

Uwilingiyimana, Agathe: The interim prime minister of Rwanda who, along with the 10 Belgian soldiers who were guarding her, was murdered in early April 1994 at the start of the genocide against the Tutsi.

Volcan Army: An Arab rebel group formed in northern Chad in the 1970s and sponsored by Gaddafi's Libya.

War of the Tribes: A 1988 conflict between Libyan and Sudanese government-sponsored Arab militias and the Federal Army of Darfur, which sought to defend Fur people from massacres that a Bahraini newspaper called genocide.

Yousif Kuwa Mekki: A Nuba former teacher who led SPLA forces in the Nuba Mountains in the 1990s and opposed the Sudan state genocide against the Nuba people.

Yusuf Ibrahim: A member of the royal family of the Sultanate of Darfur who led a rebellion against Mahdist rule in the late 1880s.

Zaghawa: Speaking a Nilo-Saharan language, the Zaghawa people inhabit western Sudan and eastern Chad.

Zero Network: A secret network of Hutu extremists formed within the Rwandan state and military during 1992.

Zubeir Mohamed Saleh: The vice president of Sudan who was put in charge of a program to eliminate the Nuba population of the Nuba Mountains at the start of the 1990s.

Notes

INTRODUCTION

1. Howard Ball, *Genocide: A Reference Handbook* (Santa Barbara, CA: ABC-CLIO, 2011), 10.

2. Hirad Abtahi and Philippa Webb, *The Genocide Convention: The Traveau Preparatoires*, Vol. One (Leiden: Martinus Nijhoff, 2008), 35.

3. Ibid., 36.

4. Ball, *Genocid*e, 12.

5. Ball, *Genocide*, 10–14; Colin Tatz and Winton Higgins, *The Magnitude of Genocide* (Santa Barbara, CA: Praeger Security International, 2016), 17–25; Augustine Brannigan, *Beyond the Banality of Evil: Criminology and Genocide* (Oxford University Press, 2013), 49–54.

6. William Schabas, *Genocide in International Law: The Crime of Crimes* (Cambridge University Press, 2009); Hannibal Travis, *Genocide, Ethnonationalism and the United Nations: Exploring the Causes of Mass Killing Since 1945* (New York: Routledge, 2013), 21–23.

7. Frank Chalk and Kurt Jonassohn, *The History and Sociology of Genocide: Analyses and Case Studies* (New Haven, CT: Yale University Press, 1990), 35.

8. Firew Kebede Tiba, "The Mengistu Genocide Trial in Ethiopia," *Journal of International Criminal Justice*, 5 (2007), 513–528; John Quigley, *The Genocide Convention: An International Law Analysis* (New York: Routledge, 2016), 41–44; http://www.preventgenocide.org/lt/LRBK99.htm

9. John Quigley, *The Genocide Convention*, 41–44.

10. Caroline Fournet, "Reflection on the Separation of Powers: The Law of Genocide and the Symptomatic French Paradox," in Ralph Henham and Paul Behrens (eds.), *The Criminal Law of Genocide: International, Comparative and Contextual Contexts* (Aldershot, UK: Ashgate, 2007), 212.

11. Domink J. Schaller, "Raphael Lemkin's View of European Colonial Rule in Africa: Between Condemnation and Admiration," *Journal of Genocide Research* 7, no. 4 (2005), 535; Horst Drechler, *"Let Us Die Fighting": The Struggle of the Herero and Nama against German Imperialism, 1884–1915* (London: Zed Press, 1980, originally published in German in 1966), 155.

12. Samantha Power, *A Problem from Hell: America and the Age of Genocide* (New York: New Republic, 2002).

13. Gareth Evans, *Responsibility to Protect: Ending Mass Atrocity Crimes Once and for All* (Washington, D.C.: Brookings Institute, 2008); Julia Hoffman and Andre Nollkaemper (eds.), *Responsibility to Protect: From Principle to Practice* (Amsterdam: Pallas Publications, 2012); W. Andy Knight and Frazer Egerton (eds.), *The Routledge Handbook of the Responsibility to Protect* (London: Routledge, 2012).

14. Catherine and David Newbury, "The Genocide in Rwanda and the Holocaust in Germany: Parallels and Pitfalls," *Journal of Genocide Research* 5, no. 1 (2003), 135–145.

15. Scott Straus, *Making and Unmaking Nations: War, Leadership and Genocide in Modern Africa* (Ithaca, NY: Cornell University Press, 2015), 89.

16. Samuel Totten and Paul R. Bartrop, *Encyclopedia of Genocide*, Vol. 2 (Westport, CT: Greenwood Press, 2008), 280; Alex Alvarez, *Governments, Citizens and Genocide: A Comparative and Interdisciplinary Approach* (Bloomington: Indiana University Press, 2001), 29; Michael R. Mahoney, "The Zulu Kingdom as a Genocidal and Post-Genocidal Society, c.1810 to the Present" *Journal of Genocide Research* 5, no. 2 (2003), 251–268; for serious scholarship on the Zulu Kingdom, see C. Hamilton (ed.), *Mfecane Aftermath: Reconstructive Debates in Southern African History* (Johannesburg: Witwatersrand University Press, 1995); John Laband, *Rope of Sand: The Rise and Fall of the Zulu Kingdom in the Nineteenth Century* (Johannesburg: Jonathan Ball Publishers, 1995); and Dan Wylie, *Myth of Iron: Shaka in History* (Pietermaritzburg: University of KwaZulu-Natal Press, 2006).

17. For the genocide claim, see Michael Lieven, "'Butchering the Brutes All Over the Place': Total War and Massacre in Zululand, 1879," *History* 84, no. 276 (October 1999), 614–632; for a repetition of Lieven, see Dominik J. Schaller, "Genocide and Mass Violence in the 'Heart of Darkness': Africa and the Colonial Period," in D. Bloxham and D. A. Moses (eds.), *The Oxford Handbook of Genocide Studies* (Oxford: Oxford University Press, 2010), 345–364; for a critique by a noted historian of the Zulu Kingdom, see John Laband, "Zulu Civilians during the Rise and Fall of the Zulu Kingdom, c.1817–1879," in J. Laband (ed.), *Daily Lives of Civilians in Wartime Africa: From Slavery Days to Rwandan Genocide* (Westport, CT: Greenwood, 2007), 51–84.

CHAPTER 1

1. John Hobson, *Imperialism: A Study* (London: George Allen and Unwin, 1902); V. I. Lenin, *Imperialism: The Highest Stage of Capitalism* (New York: International Publishers, 1969, originally published 1916); Ronald Robinson and John Gallagher, *Africa and the Victorians: The Official Mind of Imperialism* (London: MacMillan, 1961); A. G. Hopkins, *An Economic History of West Africa* (London: Longman, 1973).

2. For more on the Scramble, see Thomas Pakenham, *The Scramble for Africa: White Man's Conquest of the Dark Continent, 1876–1912* (New York: Harper

Collins, 1991) and Bruce Vandervort, *Wars of Imperial Conquest in Africa 1830–1914* (Bloomington: Indiana University Press, 1998).

3. For an overview of the region's history of settler colonization, see Martin Meredith, *Diamonds, Gold and War: The British, the Boers and the Making of South Africa* (New York: Public Affairs, 2007).

4. Helmut Bley, *South West Africa under German Rule, 1894–1914* (Evanston, IL.: Northwestern University Press, 1971), 67; Horst Drechsler, *"Let Us Die Fighting": The Struggle of the Herero and Nama against German Imperialism, 1884–1915* (London: Zed Press, 1980); Jan-Bart Gewald, *Herero Heroes: A Socio-Political History of the Herero of Namibia, 1890–1923* (Oxford: James Currey, 1999).

5. Jon M. Bridgman, *The Revolt of the Hereros* (Berkeley: University of California Press, 1981); Jeremy Sarkin, *Germany's Genocide of the Herero: Kaiser Wilhelm II, His General, His Settlers, His Soldiers* (Cape Town: University of Cape Town Press, 2010), 142–149.

6. Isabell V. Hull, *Absolute Destruction: Military Culture and the Practises of War in Imperial Germany* (Ithaca, NY: Cornell University Press, 2005), 56. Hulls places the German suppression of the rebellion within the context of imperial German military culture, which, free of civilian oversight, developed a propensity toward extreme violence.

7. Bridgman, *Revolt of the Hereros*, 128.

8. Bley, *South West Africa under German Rule*, 162.

9. Gewald, *Herero Heroes*, 169.

10. Casper Erichsen, *"The Angel of Death Has Descended Violently among Them": Concentration Camps and Prisoners-of-War in Namibia, 1904–1908* (Leiden: African Studies Centre, 2005).

11. Drechler, *"Let Us Die Fighting,"* 214; Bley, *South West Africa under German Rule*, 150; Sarkin, *Germany's Genocide of the Herero*, 137–141.

12. Jeremy Silvester and Jan-Bart Gewald, *"Words Cannot Be Found": German Colonial Rule in Namibia: An Annotated Reprint of the 1918 Blue Book* (Leiden: Brill, 2003).

13. Heinrich Schnee, *German Colonization Past and Future: The Truth about the German Colonies* (New York: Alfred A. Knopf, 1926), 117

14. Kurt Jonassohn (with Karin Solveig Bjornson), *Genocide and Gross Violations of Human Rights in Comparative Perspective* (New Brunswick, NJ: Transaction Publishers, 1999), 72–82. Lau died in a car accident in Namibia in 1996.

15. Tilman Dedering, "The German-Herero War of 1904: Revisionism of Genocide or Imaginary Historiography," *Journal of Southern African Studies* 19, no. 1 (March 1993), 80–88.

16. Sarkin, *Germany's Genocide of the Herero*; Jeremy Sarkin, *Colonial Genocide and Reparations Claims in the 21st Century: The Socio-Legal Context of Claims under International Law by the Herero against Germany for Genocide in Namibia, 1904–1908* (Westport, CT: Praeger Security International, 2009).

17. David Olusoga and Casper W. Erichsen, *The Kaiser's Holocaust: Germany's Forgotten Genocide and the Colonial Roots of Nazism* (London: Faber and Faber, 2010); Benjamin Madley, "From Africa to Auschwitz: How German South West Africa Incubated Ideas and Methods Adopted and Developed by the Nazis in Eastern Europe," *European Historical Quarterly* 35, no. 3 (2005), 429–464.

18. Thomas Weber, *Hitler's First War: Adolph Hitler, the Men of the List Regiment, and the First World War* (Oxford: Oxford University Press, 2011), 337.

19. Eric Van Grasdorff, Nicolai Roeschert, and Firoze Manji, "Germany's Genocide in Namibia: Unbearable Silence or How Not to Deal with Your Colonial Past," *Pambazuka News*, issue 577, March 20, 2012, http://www.pambazuka.org/en/category/features/80911; Johanna Schmeller, "Germany Refuses to Acknowledge Herero Massacres as Genocide," *Deutsche Welle*, March 23, 2012, http://www.dw.de/germany-refuses-to-acknowledge-herero-massacres-as-genocide/a-15830118.

20. "Reiterdenkmal Gallops Again on Christmas," *The Namibian*, December 26, 2013; Justin Huggler, "Germany to Recognize Herero Genocide and Apologize to Namibia," *The Telegraph*, July 14, 2016, http://www.telegraph.co.uk/news/2016/07/14/germany-to-recognise-herero-genocide-and-apologise-to-namibia/

CHAPTER 2

1. For a discussion of the psychological aspect, see Helen Hintjens, "Explaining the 1994 Genocide in Rwanda," *Journal of Modern African Studies* 37, no. 2 (June 1999), 241–286; for an emphasis on overpopulation, see Jared Diamond, *Collapse: How Societies Choose to Fail or Succeed* (New York: Penguin, 2005), 311–328.

2. Mahmood Mamdani, *When Victims Become Killers: Colonialism, Nativism and the Genocide in Rwanda* (Princeton University Press, 2001), 18.

3. Jan Vansina, *Antecedents to Modern Rwanda: The Nyiginya Kingdom* (Madison: University of Wisconsin Press, 2004), 38.

4. Ibid., 75.

5. Walter Rodney, *How Europe Underdeveloped Africa* (Dar es Salaam: Tanzania Publishing House, 1972), 125–126.

6. Frank Rusagara, *Resilience of a Nation: A History of the Military in Rwanda* (Kigali: Fountain Publishers, 2009), 44 and 50.

7. Mamdani, *When Victims*, 55.

8. Vansina, *Antecedents*, 61.

9. John Iliffe, *Honour in African History* (Cambridge University Press, 2005), 164–165.

10. Vansina, *Antecedents*, 140–195.

11. Alison Liebhafsky Des Forges, *Defeat Is the Only Bad News: Rwanda under Musinga, 1896–1931* (Madison: University of Wisconsin Press, 2011), chapters 1 to 5; Vansina, *Antecedents*, 164–195 and for the quote see 126; R. Murindwa, *Nyabingi Movement: People's Colonial Struggles in Kigezi 1910–1930* (Kampala: Centre for Basic Research, 1991).

12. Musinga and Queen Mother Kanjogera were exiled to the south end of Lake Kivu, where the latter died in 1933, and, during the Second World War, the former king was sent to eastern Congo, where he passed away.

13. Des Forges, *Defeat Is the Only Bad News*, chapters 6 to 9, the labor camp quote is on p. 246.

14. Mamdani, *When Victims*, 76–102.

15. J. J. Carney, *Rwanda before the Genocide: Catholic Politics and Ethnic Discourse in the Late Colonial Era* (Oxford University Press, 2014), 51–84; for the first Hutu priests, see Mamdani, *When Victims*, 89.

16. Carney, *Rwanda before the Genocide*, 109.

17. Rene Lemarchand, *Rwanda and Burundi* (New York: Praeger Publishers, 1970), 225.

18. For the 1963–1964 genocide, see Gerard Prunier, *The Rwanda Crisis: History of a Genocide* (New York: Columbia University Press, 1995), 54–57; Lemarchand, *Rwanda and Burundi*, 72, 197–227, 280–283, 356–357; Mamdani, *When Victims*, 125–131.

19. "Genocide Charge in Rwanda," *The Times*, January 29, 1964.

20. "Rwanda Policy of Genocide Alleged," *The Times*, February 2, 1964.

21. Marcel Kabanda, "Kangura: The Triumph of Propaganda Refined," in Allan Thompson (ed.), *The Media and the Rwanda Genocide* (London: Pluto Press, 2007), 69.

22. Colin M. Waugh, *Paul Kagame and Rwanda: Power, Genocide and the Rwandan Patriotic Front* (London: MacFarland, 2004), 28.

23. "Witnesses Confirm Massacre of about 35 000 Tutsis," *The Times*, February 10, 1964.

24. Margery Perham, "Man's Cruelty to Man," *The Times*, February 17, 1964.

25. Deborah Mayersen, "Deep Cleavages That Divide: The Origins and Development of Ethnic Violence in Rwanda," *Critical Race and Whiteness Studies*, 8 (2), 2012, 12.

26. National Archives (UK) FO 371, S. Falle, "Rwanda Refugees in Burundi—Minutes," February 4, 1964.

27. "Rwanda Killings 'Political,'" *The Times*, February 6, 1964.

28. Prunier, *Rwanda Crisis*, 57–61; Mamdani, *When Victims*, 132–136.

29. Prunier, *Rwanda Crisis*, 74–98; Mamdani, *When Victims*, 137–149.

30. Prunier, *Rwanda Crisis*, 61–67.

31. E. D. Mushemza, *Banyarwanda Refugees in Uganda 1959–2001* (Kampala: Fountain Publishers, 2007), 58–70.

32. Prunier, *Rwanda Crisis*, 67–74; Mamdani, *When Victims*, 159–184.

33. Prunier, *Rwanda Crisis*, 93–126; Andrew Wallis, *Silent Accomplice: The Untold Story of France's Role in the Rwandan Genocide* (London: I. B. Tauris, 2006) 14–36; Genevieve Maser, "The Pursuit of Hutu Power: The Forces Armees Rwandaises, 1960–94," MA Thesis, Dalhousie University, 2010.

34. Prunier, *Rwanda Crisis*, 172.

35. Prunier, *Rwanda Crisis*, 114–186; Mamdani, *When Victims*, 185–189.

36. For the quote, see "Broadcasting Genocide: Censorship, Propaganda and State-Sponsored Violence in Rwanda, 1990–94," 26–27, www.article19.org; Allan Thompson (ed.), *The Media and the Rwanda Genocide* (London: Pluto Press, 2007).

37. Prunier, *Rwanda Crisis*, 186–212. For the message, see Romeo Dallaire, *Shake Hands with the Devil: The Failure of Humanity in Rwanda* (Toronto: Random House, 2003), 145–147.

38. Linda Melvern, "Rwanda: At Last We Know the Truth," *The Guardian*, January 10, 2012, http://www.theguardian.com/commentisfree/2012/jan/10/rwanda-at-last-we-know-truth

39. For the transitional government, see Andre Guichaoua, *From War to Genocide: Criminal Politics in Rwanda* (Madison: University of Wisconsin Press, 2015); for the number of participants, see Scott Straus, *The Order of Genocide: Race, Power, and War in Rwanda* (Ithaca: Cornell University Press, 2007); for overviews of the genocide, see Philip Gourevitch, *We Wish to Inform You That Tomorrow We Will Be Killed with Our Families: Stories from Rwanda* (New York: Farrar, Straus and Giroux, 1999); Alison Des Forbes, *Leave None to Tell the Story: Genocide in Rwanda* (Human Rights Watch, 1999); Linda Melvern, *Conspiracy to Murder: The Rwanda Genocide*

(London: Verso, 2006); for personal accounts from killers and survivors, see Jean Hatzfeld, *Machete Season: The Killers in Rwanda Speak* (New York: Farrar, Straus and Giroux, 2005); Jean Hatzfeld, *Life Laid Bare: The Survivors in Rwanda Speak* (New York: Other Press, 2006); and Jean Hatzfeld, *The Antelope's Strategies: Living in Rwanda after the Genocide* (New York: Farrar, Straus and Giroux, 2009); for published accounts by survivors, see Yolande Mukagasana, *La mort ne veut pas de moi* (Paris: Fixot, 1997); Immaculée Ilibagiza, *Left to Tell: Discovering God amidst the Rwandan Holocaust* (Carlsbad, CA: Hayhouse, 2006); and Berthe Kayitesi, *Demain ma vie: Enfants Chief de famille dan le Rwanda d'apres* (Paris: Teper, 2009).

40. Timothy Longman, *Christianity and Genocide in Rwanda* (Cambridge University Press, 2010); Jacques Pauw, *Dances with Devils: A Journalist's Search for the Truth* (Cape Town: Zebra Press, 2006), 107–108; Jean d'Amour Dusengumuremyi, *No Greater Love: Testimonies on the Life and Death of Felicitas Niyitegeka* (Germany: Dignity Press, 2015).

41. For UNAMIR, see Dallaire, *Shake Hands;* Henry Kwami Anyidoho, *Guns over Kigali: The Rwandese Civil War, 1994* (Accra: Woeli Publishing, 1997).

42. Wallace, *Silent Accomplice*, 82–84; Lieutenant Colonel Uwe F. Jansohn, "Operation Amaryllis: French Evacuation Operation in Rwanda 1994—Lessons Learned for Future German Noncombat Evacuation Operations," Master of Military Art and Science Thesis, Fort Leavenworth, Kansas, U.S. Army Command and General Staff College, 2000.

43. Rory Carroll, "US Chose to Ignore Rwandan Genocide," *The Guardian*, March 31, 2004, http://www.theguardian.com/world/2004/mar/31/usa.rwanda; Jared Cohen, *One Hundred Days of Silence: America and the Rwanda Genocide* (Lanham, MD: Rowman and Littlefield, 2007), 190.

44. Prunier, *Rwanda Crisis*, 268–273; for RPF revenge massacres, see Jacque Pauw, *Rat Roads of Africa: One Man's Incredible Journal* (Cape Town: Zebra Press, 2012).

45. Wallace, *Silent Accomplice*, 122–145; for more on the role of France in the genocide, see Vénuste Kayimahe, *France-Rwanda: Les coulisses d un genocide. Témoignage d un rescapé* (Paris: Dagorno, 2002).

46. Gerard Prunier, *Africa's World War: Congo, the Rwanda Genocide and the Making of a Continental Catastrophe* (Oxford University Press, 2009), 6–24, 37–46, 294–295.

47. Phil Clark, *The Gacaca Courts: Post-Genocide Justice and Reconciliation in Rwanda* (Cambridge University Press, 2010); Paul Christoph Bornkamm, *Rwanda's Gacaca Courts: Between Retribution and Reparation* (Oxford University Press, 2012); "Justice Compromised: The Legacy of Rwanda's Community-Based Gacaca Courts," *Human Rights Watch,* May 31, 2011, https://www.hrw.org/report/2011/05/31/justice-compromised/legacy-rwandas-community-based-gacaca-courts; "Rwanda: Justice after Genocide—20 Years On," *Human Rights Watch,* March 28, 2014, https://www.hrw.org/news/2014/03/28/rwanda-justice-after-genocide-20-years

48. Thiery Cruvellier, *Court of Remorse: Inside the International Criminal Tribunal for Rwanda* (Madison: University of Wisconsin Press, 2010); Judge Vagn Joensen to UN Security Council, "Report on the Completion Strategy of the International Criminal Tribunal for Rwanda as of 5 May 2015," May 15, 2015, http://www.unictr.org/sites/unictr.org/files/legal-library/150515-completion-strategy-en.pdf

49. Gerald Gahima, *Transitional Justice in Rwanda: Accountability for Atrocity* (London: Routledge, 2013); "Rwanda: Justice after Genocide—20 years on," https://www.hrw.org/news/2014/03/28/rwanda-justice-after-genocide-20-years; Max L.

Rettig, "Transnational Trials as Transitional Justice: Lessons from the Trials of Two Rwandan Nuns in Belgium," *Washington University Global Studies Law Review* 11, no. 2 (2012), 365–414, http://openscholarship.wustl.edu/cgi/viewcontent.cgi?article=1311&context=law_globalstudies

50. Peter Hohenhaus, "Commemorating and Commodifying the Rwandan Genocide: Memorial Sites in a Politically Difficult Context," in Leanne White and Elspeth Frew (eds.), *Dark Tourism and Place Identity: Managing and Interpreting Dark Places* (London: Routledge, 2013), 142–155; Jens Meierhenrich, "Topographies of Forgetting and Remembering: The Transformation of Lieux de Memoire in Rwanda," in Scott Strauss and Lars Waldorf (eds.), *Remaking Rwanda: State Building and Human Rights after Mass Violence* (Madison: University of Wisconsin Press, 2011), 283–297; Lars Waldorf, "Goats and Graves: Reparations in Rwanda's Community Courts," in Carla Ferstman, Mariana Goetz, and Alan Stephens (eds.), *Reparations for Victims of Genocide, War Crimes and Crimes Against Humanity* (Leiden: Martinus Nijhoff, 2009), 515–539.

51. Heidy Rombouts, *Victim Organization and the Politics of Reparations: A Case Study on Rwanda* (Cambridge: Intersentia, 2004); Rachel Ibreck, "The Politics of Mourning: Survivor Contributions to Memorials in Post-Genocide Rwanda," *Memory Studies,* 3, 4 (2010), 330–343; Berthe Kayitesi, "Building Resilience through Associations: The Case of the Survivors of the Genocide against the Tutsi of Rwanda," Africa Conference, University of Texas at Austin, March 29–31, 2013.

52. Eduoard Kayihura and Kerry Zukus, *Inside the Hotel Rwanda: The Surprising True Story and Why It Matters Today* (Dallas: BenBella Books, 2014); Alexandre Dauge-Roth, *Writing and Filming the Genocide of the Tutsis in Rwanda: Dismembering and Remembering Traumatic History* (Lanham, MD: Lexington Books, 2010).

53. Edward Hernan and David Peterson, *The Politics of Genocide* (New York: Monthly Review Press, 2010); Abdul Joshua Ruzibiza, *Rwanda: L-histoire secrete* (Paris: Editions du Panama, 2005); Pierre Pean, *Noires Fureurs, Blancs Menteurs* (Paris: Mille et Une Nuit, 2006); Alan Kuperman, "Provoking Genocide: A Revised History of the Rwandan Patriotic Front," *Journal of Genocide Research* 6, no. 1 (2004), 61–84; Christian Davenport and Allan C. Stam, "What Really Happened in Rwanda?" *Pacific Standard,* October 6, 2009; Rene Lemarchand, "Rwanda: The State of Research," *Online Encyclopedia of Mass Violence,* May 27, 2013, 14–15, http://www.massviolence.org/rwanda-the-state-of-research,742

CHAPTER 3

1. Rene Lemarchand made this statement as one of the few scholars to focus on the history of genocide in Burundi. However, it is technically incorrect, as the 1963–1964 massacres of Tutsi in Rwanda likely represented the first incident of violence in postcolonial Africa that corresponded to the international legal definition of genocide. However, the mass murder of Hutu in Burundi in 1972 was the first genocide in postcolonial Africa to approach the scale of a mass event involving hundreds of thousands of victims. Rene Lemarchand, "Burundi 1972: Genocide Denied, Revised and Remembered," in Rene Lemarchand (ed.), *Forgotten Genocides: Oblivion, Denial and Memory* (Philadelphia: University of Pennsylvania Press, 2011), 37.

2. Wm. Roger Louis, *Ruanda-Urundi 1884–1919* (Oxford: Clarendon Press, 1963) 114–121; Jean-Pierre Chretien, *The Great Lakes of Africa: Two Thousand Years of History* (New York: Zone Books, 2003) 249–251; Nigel Watt, *Burundi: The Biography of a Small African Country* (London: Hurst, 2008), 23–32; Michele Wagner, "Burundi to c.1800" and "Burundi: Nineteenth Century: Pre-colonial," in Kevin Shillington (ed.), *Encyclopedia of African History*, vol. 1 (New York: Fitzroy Dearborn, 2005), 185–188.

3. Rene Lemarchand, *Burundi: Ethnic Conflict and Genocide* (Cambridge University Press, 1994), 22, 44–47; Michele Wagner, "Burundi: Colonial Period: German and Belgian," in Kevin Shillington (ed.), *Encyclopedia of African History*, vol. 1 (New York: Fitzroy Dearborn, 2005), 188–190.

4. Lemarchand, *Burundi: Ethnic Conflict and Genocide*, 51–63; Rene Lemarchand, *Rwanda and Burundi* (London: Pall Mall, 1970).

5. Lemarchand, *Burundi: Ethnic Conflict and Genocide*, 61–75.

6. For accounts of the 1972 genocide, see Lemarchand, "Burundi 1972," 37–50; Lemarchand, *Burundi: Ethnic Conflict and Genocide*, 76–105; Rene Lemarchand, *The Dynamics of Violence in Central Africa* (Philadelphia: University of Pennsylvania Press, 2009), 129–140; Watt, *Burundi*, 33–38; Warren Weinstein and Robert A. Schrire, *Political Conflict and Ethnic Strategies: A Case Study of Burundi* (Syracuse, NY: Syracuse University, 1976); Aidan Russell, "Rebel and Rule in Burundi, 1972," *International Journal of African Historical Studies* 48, no. 1 (2015), 73–97.

7. Lemarchand, "Burundi 1972," 43; Amadou Diallo, *La Mort de Diallo Telli* (Paris: Karthala, 1983).

8. Jean-Pierre Chretien and Jean-Francois Dupaquier, *Burundi 1972: Au Bord du Genocides* (Paris: Karthala, 2007).

9. Chretien, *The Great Lakes*, 316.

10. David K. Leonard and Scott Straus, *Africa's Stalled Development: International Causes and Cures* (London: Lynne Rienner, 2003), 73.

11. For Burundian refugees in Tanzania, see Liisa Malkki, *Purity and Exile: Violence, Memory and National Cosmology among Hutu Refugees in Tanzania* (University of Chicago Press, 1995); Marc Sommers, *Fear in Bongoland: Burundian Refugees in Urban Tanzania* (New York: Berghahn Books, 2001); Simon Turner, *Politics of Innocence: Hutu Identity, Conflict and Camp Life* (New York: Berghahn Books, 2010); see also Lemarchand, *Burundi: Ethnic Conflict and Genocide*, 144–145 and Watt, *Burundi*, 85–91.

12. Lemarchand, *Burundi: Ethnic Conflict and Genocide*, 106–130; Watt, *Burundi*, 39–46.

13. Lemarchand, *Dynamics*, 141–157; Watt, *Burundi*, 47–98; Godfrey Mwakikagile, *Burundi: The Hutu and the Tutsi: Cauldron of Conflict and Quest for Dynamic Compromise* (Dar es Salaam: New Africa Press, 2012), 75–77; Patricia Daley, *Gender and Genocide in Burundi: The Search for Spaces of Peace in the Great Lakes Region* (Bloomington: Indiana University Press, 2008); Josiah Marineau, "Securing Peace in Burundi: External Interventions to End the Civil War, 1993–2006," in Toyin Falola and Charles Thomas (eds.), *Securing Africa: Local Crises and Foreign Interventions* (New York: Routledge, 2014), 229–248.

14. "International Commission of Inquiry for Burundi," United Nations Security Council, S/1996/682, point 496.

15. Watt, *Burundi*, 47–97. Filip Reyntjens, *The Great African War: Congo and Regional Geopolitics, 1996–2006* (Cambridge University Press, 2009), 170–178; Gerard Prunier, *Africa's World War: Congo, the Rwanda Genocide and the Making of a Continental Catastrophe* (Oxford University Press, 2009) 59–67, 288–289; Annemarie Peen Rodt, "The African Mission in Burundi: The Successful Management of Violent Ethno-Political Conflict," *Ethnopolitics Papers*, no. 10, May 2011, 1–31.

16. "Repression and Genocidal Dynamics in Burundi," International Federation for Human Rights, November 2016, http://www.responsibilitytoprotect.org/burundi%20report%20fidh.pdf

CHAPTER 4

1. There is a relatively large body of literature on the precolonial history of what is now the Democratic Republic of Congo (DRC). Classic works include David Birmingham, *Central Africa to 1870* (London: Cambridge University Press, 1981); Thomas Q. Reefe, *The Rainbow and the Kings: A History of the Luba Empire to 1891* (Los Angeles: University of California Press, 1981); John Thornton, *The Kingdom of Kongo: Civil War and Transition, 1641–1718* (Madison: University of Wisconsin Press, 1983); John C. Yoder, *The Kanyok of Zaire: An Institutional and Ideological History to 1895* (Cambridge University Press, 1992).

2. Neal Ascherson, *The King Incorporated: Leopold the Second and the Congo* (London: Granta Books, 1999); Adam Hochschild, *King Leopold's Ghost: A Story of Greed, Terror and Heroism in Colonial Africa* (New York: Mariner Books, 1999); Sydney Langford Hinde, *The Fall of the Congo Arabs* (New York: Negro Universities Press, 1969).

3. Domink J. Schaller, "Raphael Lemkin's View of European Colonial Rule in Africa: Between Condemnation and Admiration," *Journal of Genocide Research* 7, no. 4 (2005), 535.

4. Hochschild, *King Leopold's Ghost*, 225.

5. Georges Nzongola-Ntalaja, *The Congo: From Leopold to Kabila: A People's History* (London: Zed Books, 2007), 22.

6. Thomas W. Simon, *The Laws of Genocide: Prescriptions for a Just World* (Westport, CT: Praeger Security International, 2007), 76–77.

7. Rhoda E. Howard-Hassmann, "Genocide and State-Induced Famine: Global Ethics and Western Responsibility for Mass Atrocities in Africa," *Perspectives on Global Development and Technology* 4, no. 3–4 (2005), 492.

8. Robert G. Weisbord, "The King, the Cardinal and the Pope: Leopold II's Genocide in the Congo and the Vatican," *Journal of Genocide Research* 5, no. 1 (2003), 35.

9. Jeanne M. Haskin, *The Tragic State of the Congo: From Decolonization to Dictatorship* (New York: Algora Publishing, 2005), 2.

10. David Renton, David Seddon, and Leo Zeilig, *The Congo; Plunder and Resistance* (London: Zed Press, 2007), 51.

11. Yaa-Lengi M. Ngemi, *Genocide in the Congo (Zaire): In the Name of Bill Clinton, and of the Paris Club, and of the Mining Conglomerates, So It Is!* (New York: Writers' Club Press, 200), 14.

12. Guy Vanthemsche, *Belgium and the Congo, 1885–1980* (Cambridge University Press, 2012), 24–25.

13. David Van Reybrouck, *Congo: The Epic History of a People* (New York: Harper Collins, 2014), 95.

14. For the Congo Crisis of the 1960s, see Georges Nzongola-Ntalaja, *The Congo from Leopold to Kabila: A People's History* (London: Zed Books, 2007); David Van Reybrouck, *Congo.*

15. Larry Devlin, *Chief of Station, Congo: A Memoir of 1960–67* (New York: Public Affairs, 2007), 95.

16. Georges Nzongola-Ntalaja, *The Congo*, 101–106; Haskin, *Congo*, 26.

17. Emmanuel Gerard and Bruce Kuklick, *Death in the Congo: Killing Patrice Lumumba* (Cambridge, MA: Harvard University Press, 2015), 90.

18. Daniel J. Crowley, "Politics and Tribalism in the Katanga," *The Western Political Quarterly* 16, no. 1 (March 1963), 71 and 74.

19. "Annual Report of the Secretary General on the Work of the Organization, June 16, 1960–June 15, 1961," United Nations, New York 1961, Supplement 1 (A/4800), 33.

20. "Katanga State of Civil War Recognized," *The Times,* February 2, 1961, 10.

21. "Pro-Lumumba Forces Built up to Meet Mobutu Threat," *The Times,* February 13, 1961, 9.

22. Georges Nzongola-Ntalaja, *The Congo*, 106.

23. Susan Williams, *Who Killed Dag Hammarskjold? The UN, the Cold War and White Supremacy in Africa* (New York: Columbia University Press, 2011); Christopher Othen, *Katanga, 1960–63: Mercenaries, Spires and the African Nation That Waged War on the World* (Stroud, UK: The History Press, 2015).

24. Frank Villafana, *Cold War in the Congo: The Confrontation of Cuban Military Forces, 1960–67* (New Brunswick, New Jersey: Transaction Publishers, 2012); Mike Hoare, *Congo Mercenary* (Boulder, Colorado: Paladin Press, 2008, originally published 1967); Major Thomas P. Odom, "Dragon Operations: Hostage Rescues in the Congo, 1964–65" (Fort Leavenworth, Kansas: Combat Studies Institute, 1988).

25. Lieutenant Colonel Thomas P. Odom, "Shaba II: The French and Belgian Intervention in Zaire in 1978" (Fort Leavenworth, Kansas: U.S. Army Command and General Staff College, Combat Studies Institute, 1993); Edward George, *The Cuban Intervention in Angola, 1965–1991: From Che Guevara to Cuito Cuanavale* (London: Frank Cass, 2005) 125–126, 133, 236; Emizet Francois Kisangani and F. Scott Bobb, *Historical Dictionary of the Democratic Republic of the Congo* (Lanham, Maryland: Scarecrow Press, 2010); Michael Schatzberg, *The Dialectics of Oppression in Zaire* (Bloomington: Indiana University Press, 1988).

26. Rene Lemarchand, *The Dynamics of Violence in Central Africa* (Philadelphia: University of Pennsylvania Press, 2008) 10–15; "Zaire: Lawlessness and Insecurity in North and South Kivu," *Amnesty International*, November 1996; Filip Reyntjens, *The Great African War: Congo and Regional Geopolitics, 1996–2006* (Cambridge University Press, 2009), 10–23.

27. For the quotes, see Alexander de Waal, *Famine Crimes: Politics and the Disaster Relief Industry in Africa* (Oxford: James Currey, 1997), 207.

28. Filip Reyntjens, *Great African War*, 45–143; Gerard Prunier, *Africa's World War: Congo, the Rwanda Genocide and the Making of a Continental Catastrophe* (Oxford University Press, 2009) 67–148.

29. United Nations, "Report of the Secretary General's Investigative Team Charged with Investigating Serious Violations of Human Rights and

International Humanitarian Law in the Democratic Republic of Congo," S1998/581, 7. For accounts by Rwandan refugees in Zaire, see Marie Beatrice Umutesi, *Surviving the Slaughter: The Ordeal of a Rwandan Refugee in Zaire* (Madison: University of Wisconsin Press, 2004) and Pierre-Claver Ndacyayisenga, *Dying to Live: A Rwandan Family's Five-Year Flight across the Congo* (Montreal: Baraka Books, 2013).

30. Kisangani Ezimet, "The Massacre of Refugees in Congo: A Case of UN Peacekeeping Failure and International Law," *The Journal of Modern African Studies* 38, no. 2 (2000), 181.

31. Gerard Prunier, *Africa's World War*, 181–283; Filip Reyntjens, *Great African War*, 195–261; Phillip Roessler and John Prendergast, "Democratic Republic of Congo," in William J. Durch (ed.), *Twenty-First Century Peace Operations* (Washington, D.C.: United States Institute of Peace, 2006), 229–318.

32. Thomas Turner, *The Congo Wars: Conflict, Myth and Reality* (New York: Zed Books, 2007), 3.

33. Yaa-Lengi M. Ngemi, *Genocide in the Congo*, 5.

34. "Human Security Report, 2009: The Shrinking Costs of War," Human Security Report Project, Simon Fraser University, January 2010.

35. "Ituri: Covered in Blood; Ethnically Targeted Violence in Northeastern DR Congo," *Human Rights Watch* 15, no. 11 (A), (July 2003).

36. "DR Congo Pygmies Appeal to UN," BBC News, May 23, 2003, http://news.bbc.co.uk/2/hi/africa/2933524.stm

37. "DRC: Indications of Genocide in Ituri Exist, Rights Envoy Says," IRIN News, September 1, 2003, http://www.irinnews.org/report/45864/drc-indications-of-genocide-in-ituri-exist-rights-envoy-says

38. Filip Reyntjens, *Great African War*, 215–221; "Operation Artemis: The Lessons of the Interim Emergency Multinational Force," United Nations, Peacekeeping Best Practises Unit, Military Division, October 2004; Phillip Roessler and John Prendergast, "Democratic Republic of Congo," 279–288; "DRC: More Rebels Hand in Arms in Ituri," IRIN News, May 11, 2007, www.irinnews.org.

39. Filip Reyntjens, *Great African War*, 207–215; Phillip Roessler and John Prendergast, "Democratic Republic of Congo," 288–295.

40. "U.N. Gunships Battle Rebels in East Congo," CNN, October 27, 2008, www.cnn.com; "DRC: Civilians at Risk of Further Fighting after Nkunda Arrest," IRIN News, January 26, 2009, www.irinnews.org; Albert Kampale, "DR Congo Rebel Chief Pledges to Withdraw from Captured Towns," Associated Foreign Press, July 8, 2012; "DR Congo's M23 Rebel Chief Sultani Mukenga Surrenders," BBC News, November 7, 2013, http://www.bbc.com/news/world-africa-24849814; Kurt Mills, *International Responses to Mass Atrocities in Africa: Responsibility to Protect, Prosecute and Palliate* (Philadelphia: University of Pennsylvania Press, 2015), 104–106.

41. "Kinshasa Government Attacks FDLR Rebels without the UN," Institute for Security Studies (ISS) Peace and Security Council Report, March 3, 2015, https://www.issafrica.org/pscreport/situation-analysis/kinshasa-government-attacks-fdlr-rebels-without-the-un; "Rwandan Rebel Leaders Jailed in Germany for Crimes," *The Guardian*, September 28, 2015, http://www.theguardian.com/global-development/2015/sep/28/rwandan-rebel-leaders-jailed-in-germany-for-war-crimes

CHAPTER 5

1. For a discussion of identity in Sudan, see Jok Madut Jok, *Sudan: Race, Religion and Violence* (London: Oneworld Publications, 2016), 1–35.

2. R. S. O'Fahey, *The Darfur Sultanate: A History* (New York: Columbia University Press, 2008), 41–85; Gerard Prunier, *Darfur: The Ambiguous Genocide* (Ithaca, NY: Cornell University Press, 2005), 8–16; M. W. Daly, *Darfur's Sorrow: A History of Destruction and Genocide* (Cambridge University Press, 2007), 16–39.

3. O'Fahey, *Darfur Sultanate*, 261–304; Andrew McGregor, *A Military History of Modern Egypt: From the Ottoman Conquest to the Ramadan War* (Westport, CT: Praeger Security International, 2006), 209–213; Daly, *Darfur's Sorrow*, 61–144; Prunier, *Darfur*, 16–36.

4. Mario J. Azevedo, *Roots of Violence: A History of War in Chad* (New York: Routledge, 1998); Kenneth M. Pollock, *Arabs at War: Military Effectiveness, 1948–1991* (Lincoln: University of Nebraska Press, 2002), 375–423; Sam Nolutshungu, *The Limits of Anarchy: Intervention and State Formation in Chad* (University of Virginia Press, 1995).

5. Noah R. Bassil, *The Post-Colonial State and Civil War in Sudan: The Origins of Conflict in Darfur* (London: I.B. Tauris, 2013), 154.

6. Prunier, *Darfur*, 36–80; Daly, *Darfur's Sorrow*, 178–269; Julie Flint and Alex de Waal, *Darfur: A Short History of a Long War* (London: Zed Books, 2005), 17–65; Robert O. Collins, *A History of Modern Sudan* (Cambridge University Press, 2010), 178–179, 272–286.

7. Lydia Polgreen, "Over Tea, Sheik Denies Stirring Darfur's Torment," *New York Times*, June 6, 2006, http://www.nytimes.com/2006/06/12/world/africa/12darfur.html?pagewanted=print&_r=0

8. Prunier, *Darfur*, 81–123; Flint and de Waal, *Darfur*, 66–117; Collins, *Sudan*, 287–299; Daly, *Darfur's Sorrow*, 270–316.

9. "Powell Declares Genocide in Sudan," BBC, September 9, 2004, http://news.bbc.co.uk/2/hi/3641820.stm

10. Karen E. Smith, *Genocide and the Europeans* (Cambridge University Press, 2010), 223.

11. Collins, *Sudan*, 292–293.

12. Report of the International Commission of Inquiry on Darfur to the United Nations Secretary General, Pursuant to Security Council Resolution 1564 of September 18, 2004, Geneva, January 25, 2005.

13. William A. Schabas, "Has Genocide Been Committed in Darfur? The State Plan or Policy Element in the Crime of Genocide," in Ralph Henham and Paul Behrens (eds.), *The Criminal Law of Genocide: International, Comparative and Contextual Aspects* (Aldershot, UK: Ashgate, 2007), 39–47; Claus Kress, "The Darfur Report and Genocidal Intent," *Journal of International Criminal Justice* 3 (2005), 562–578.

14. Collins, *Modern Sudan*, 296–299.

15. Joachin A. Koops, Norrie MacQueen, Theirry Tardy, and Paul D. Williams (eds.), *The Oxford Handbook of United Nations Peacekeeping Operations* (Oxford University Press, 2015).

16. Andrew S. Natsios, *Sudan, South Sudan and Darfur: What Everyone Needs to Know* (Oxford University Press, 2012), 144–162, 186–193.

17. Natsios, *Sudan*, 150–155; Olivier Degomme and Debarati Guhu-Sapir, "Pattern of Mortality Rates in Darfur Conflict," *The Lancet* 375, no. 9711, January 2010, 294–300.

18. Alex de Waal, "Counter-Insurgency on the Cheap," *London Review of Books* 26, no. 15 (August 5, 2004), 25–27; Rob Crilly, *Saving Darfur: Everyone's Favourite African War* (London: Reportage, 2010).

19. Jok, *Sudan*, 143.

20. Eric Reeves, "Genocide by Attrition in Sudan," *Washington Post*, April 6, 2008, http://www.washingtonpost.com/wp-dyn/content/article/2008/04/04/AR2008040403087.html; see also Eric Reeves, *A Long Day's Dying: Critical Moments in the Darfur Genocide* (Toronto: Key Publishing, 2007).

21. Prunier, *Darfur*, 156.

22. Mahmood Mamdani, *Survivors and Saviors: Darfur, Politics and the War on Terror* (New York: Double Day, 2009), 8.

23. Natsios, *Sudan*, 154–155.

24. Natsios, *Sudan*, 154.

25. B. A. Ogot (ed.), *UNESCO General History of Africa: Africa from the Sixteenth to Eighteenth Century* (Oxford: James Currey, 1999), 91–103; Kevin Shillington, *History of Africa*, 163–166.

26. McGregor, *Military History of Egypt*, 67–84; Collins, *Modern Sudan*, 16; Ronald Lamothe, *Slaves of Fortune: Sudanese Soldiers and the River War 1896–98* (Woodbridge, UK: James Currey, 2011), 11–19.

27. Collins, *Modern Sudan*, 33–68; Robert O. Collins, *Civil Wars and Revolution in the Sudan: Essays on the Sudan, Southern Sudan and Darfur, 1902–2004* (Hollywood, CA: Tsehai Publishers, 2005), 171–202, 271; M. W. Daly, *Empire on the Nile: The Anglo-Egyptian Sudan, 1898–1934* (Cambridge University Press, 1986).

28. Collins, *Modern Sudan*, 69–115; for genocide accusations, see *The Times*, May 7, August 20, and August 28, 1969.

29. Collins, *Modern Sudan*, 133–271; Natsios, *Sudan*, 57–143, 163–185; Alexander de Waal, *Famine Crimes: Politics and the Disaster Relief Industry in Africa* (Oxford: James Currey, 1997), 94–95; Jok Madut Jok, *War and Slavery in Sudan* (Philadelphia: University of Pennsylvania Press), 201. For the militia, see 23–24, and for the quote see 80.

30. Alex de Waal, "The Nuba Mountains, Sudan," in Samuel Totten and William Parsons (eds.), *Centuries of Genocide: Essays and Eye-witness Accounts* (New York: Routledge, 2013), 421–445; Samuel Totten, *Genocide by Attrition: The Nuba Mountains of Sudan* (London: Transaction Publishers, 2015).

31. De Waal, "Nuba Mountains," 421.

32. Jok, *Sudan*, 145.

33. "Sudan Peace Act," Public Law 107–245, October 21, 2002, Washington, D.C.

34. "Weapons and Ammunition Airdropped to SPLA-IO Forces in South Sudan," Conflict Armament Research, June 2015, http://www.conflictarm.com/wp-content/uploads/2015/06/Weapons_and_ammunition_airdropped_to_SPLA-iO_forces_in_South_Sudan.pdf

35. "Calgary Marked the First Annual Juba Nuer Genocide Memorial Service," *The Upper Nile Times*, December 21, 2014, http://uppernile times.net/news/calgary-marked-the-first-annual-juba-nuer-genocide-memorial-service/

36. "John Kerry Warns of South Sudan Genocide," BBC News, May 1, 2014, http://www.bbc.com/news/world-africa-27245641

37. "Final Report on the African Union Commission of Inquiry on South Sudan," Addis Ababa, October 15, 2014, 298; "Rape and Cannibalism in South Sudan, African Union Says," BBC News, October 29, 2015, http://www.bbc.com/news/world-africa-34657418

38. "African Union Announces South Sudan War Crimes Court," BBC News, September 29, 2015, http://www.bbc.com/news/world-africa-34393329; "Only Swift Action Can Avert South Sudan Genocide, says UN Human Rights Chief," *The Guardian*, December 14, 2016, https://www.theguardian.com/global-development/2016/dec/14/south-sudan-swift-action-genocide-un-human-rights-chief

39. Straus, *Making and Unmaking the State*, 236.

CHAPTER 6

1. Murray Last, *The Sokoto Caliphate* (London: Longmans, 1967); Joseph Smaldone, *Warfare in the Sokoto Caliphate: Historical and Sociological Perspectives* (London: Cambridge University Press, 1977).

2. Samuel Johnson, *History of the Yorubas* (London: Routledge and Kegan Paul, 1921); J. F. Ade Ajayi and R. S. Smith, *Yoruba Warfare in the Nineteenth Century* (Cambridge University Press, 1964); S. A. Akintoye, *Revolution and Power Politics in Yorubaland, 1840–1893* (New York: Humanities Press, 1971); Toyin Falola, *Ibadan: Foundation, Growth and Change, 1830–1960* (Ibadan: Bookcraft, 2012).

3. Jacob Egharevba, *A Short History of Benin* (Ibaban University Press, 1968, originally published 1934); Alan Ryder, *Benin and the Europeans, 1485–1897* (London: Longmans, 1969); Elizabeth Isichei, *The Ibo People and the Europeans: The Genesis of a Relationship—to 1906* (New York: St. Martin's Press, 1973); Elizabeth Isichei, *A History of the Igbo People* (London: MacMillan, 1976).

4. John E. Flint, *Sir George Goldie and the Making of Nigeria* (London: Oxford University Press, 1960); Bruce Vandervort, *Wars of Imperial Conquest in Africa 1830–1914* (Bloomington: Indiana University Press, 1998); Toyin Falola and Matthew M. Heaton, *A History of Nigeria* (Cambridge University Press, 2008) 85–109.

5. Falola and Heaton, *History of Nigeria*, 110–157.

6. N. J. Miners, *The Nigerian Army 1956–66* (London: Methuen, 1971); Jimi Peters, *The Nigerian Military and the State* (London: I. B. Tauris, 1997).

7. Leonard Plotnicov, "An Early Nigerian Civil Disturbance: The 1945 Hausa-Ibo Riots in Jos," *The Journal of Modern African Studies* 9, no. 2 (August 1971), 297–305; Victor A. O. Adetula, "Environmental Degradation, Land Shortage and Identity Conflicts on the Jos Plateau in Nigeria," in Sam Moyo, Dzodzi Tsikata, and Yakham Diop (eds.), *Land in the Struggles for Citizenship in Africa* (Dakar: CODESRIA, 2015), 47; Larry Jay Diamond, *Class, Ethnicity and Democracy in Nigeria: The Failure of the First Republic* (Syracuse University Press, 1988), 49–52.

8. Toyin Falola and Adebayo O. Oyebade, *Hot Spot Sub-Saharan Africa* (Santa Barbara, CA: Greenwood Press, 2010), 73–74; Grace O. Okoye, *Proclivity to Genocide: Northern Nigeria Ethno-Religious Conflict, 1966 to Present* (Lanham, MD: Lexington Books, 2014), 115–118; Max Siollun, *Oil, Politics and Violence: Nigeria's Military Coup Culture, 1966–76* (New York: Algora Publishing, 2009), 133–136.

9. Douglas Anthony, "'Ours Is a War of Survival': Biafra, Nigeria and Arguments about Genocide, 1966–70," *Journal of Genocide Research* 16, no. 2–3, 205–225.

10. For an unconvincing genocide argument about 1966, see G. N. Uzoigwe, *Visions of Nationhood: Prelude to the Nigerian Civil War, 1960–67* (Trenton, NJ: Africa World Press, 2011), 93–114; *Nigerian Pogrom: The Organized Massacres of Eastern Nigerians* (Enugu: Ministry of Information, 1966).

11. Solliun, *Oil, Politics and Violence*, 151–157.

12. Falola and Heaton, *History of Nigeria*, 158–180; John de St. Jorre, *The Brothers' War: Biafra and Nigeria* (London: Faber and Faber, 2012 originally published 1972); John Stremlau, *The International Politics of the Nigerian Civil War, 1967–70* (Princeton University Press, 1977).

13. Mike Hoare, "Mercenaries Must Keep out of Nigeria's Conflict," *The Times*, December 1, 1967, 11.

14. Nnamdi Azikiwe, "Nigeria's Future," *The Times*, November 16, 1967, 11.

15. Roy Doron, "Marketing Genocide: Biafran Propaganda Strategies during the Nigerian Civil War, 1967–70," *Journal of Genocide Research* 16, no. 2–3 (2014), 227–246; for comparisons to Jews, see William Norris, "Strong Hopes Now for Peace in Nigeria," *The Times*, April 29, 1968, 9.

16. "Pressure on Lagos to Accept Ceasefire," *The Times*, April 10, 1968, 7.

17. Karen Smith, "The UK and 'Genocide' in Biafra," *Journal of Genocide Research* 16, no. 2–3 (2014), 247–262; Karen Smith, *Genocide and the Europeans* (Cambridge University Press, 2010), 69; For radio reports, see "Defiant Exercise Book Newspapers of Biafra," *The Times*, May 8, 1968, 7 and "Biafran Arms Supply Plane Seized," *The Times*, June 18, 1968, 6; for the observers, see Michael Wolfers, "Security Zone Plan by Observers in Nigeria," *The Times*, October 16, 1968.

18. "Biafra Calls for Action by US," *The Times*, February 1, 1968, 6.

19. Daniel J. Sargent, *A Superpower Transformed: The Remaking of American Foreign Relations in the 1970s* (Oxford University Press, 2015), 70–80.

20. Smith, *Genocide and the European*, 70, note 12.

21. Smith, *Genocide and the Europeans*, 69–71; Francis Terry McNamara, *France in Black Africa* (Washington, D.C.: National Defense University, 1989), 179–180.

22. Stephanie Bangarth, "The Politics of African Intervention: Canada and Biafra, 1967–70," in Michael K. Carroll and Greg Donaghy (eds.), *From Kinshasa to Kandahar: Canada and Fragile States in Comparative Perspective* (University of Calgary Press, 2016), 53–72; Peter Bush, "Biafra and the Canadian Churches, 1966–70," *Historical Papers 2003: Canadian Society of Church History*, 129–147; "Biafra Investigation," *The Times*, October 9, 1968.

23. Doron, "Marketing Genocide," 241; "A Pro-Federal Igbo," *The Times*, June 22, 1968, 8; "Advertisement," *The Times*, July 5, 1968, 9.

24. John Young, "How Can the War in Nigeria Be Stopped," *The Times*, December 3, 1968.

25. Doron, "Marketing Genocide," 242; "Dr. Azikiwe Offers Safety to Ibos," *The Times*, October 9. 1969.

26. "'Food for My People': Call by Ojukwu," *The Times*, January 16, 1970.

27. Ken Saro-Wiwa, *Genocide in Nigeria: The Ogoni Tragedy* (Port Harcourt, Nigeria: Saros International Publishers, 1992).

28. April Gordon, *Nigeria's Diverse Peoples: A Reference Sourcebook* (Santa Barbara, CA: ABC-Clio, 2003), 210–213; Cyril Obi and Siri Aas Rustad (eds.), *Oil and Insurgency in the Niger Delta: Managing the Complex Politics of Petro-Violence* (London: Zed

Books, 2011); Omalade Adunbi, *Oil Wealth and Insurgency in Nigeria* (Bloomington: Indiana University Press, 2015); for works on the Biafra or Igbo genocide, see Carol Ijeoma Njoku, "A Paradox of International Criminal Justice: The Biafra Genocide," *Journal of Asian and African Studies* 48, no. 6 (2013), 710–726; Chima Korieh, "Biafra and the Discourse on the Igbo Genocide," *Journal of Asian and African Studies* 48, no. 6 (2013), 727–740.

29. Mike Smith, *Boko Haram: Inside Nigeria's Unholy War* (London: I. B. Tauris, 2015); Virginia Comolli, *Boko Haram: Nigeria's Islamist Insurgency* (London: Hurst and Company, 2015).

CONCLUSION

1. Richard A. Joseph, "Ruben Um Nyobe and the 'Kamerun' Rebellion," *African Affairs* 73, no. 293 (October 1974), 428–448; Martin R. Atangana, "French Capitalism and Nationalism in Cameroon," *African Studies Review* 40, no. 1 (April 1997), 83–111; Martin Atangana, *The End of French Rule in Cameroon* (Lanham, MD: University Press of America, 2010).

2. Max Bardet and Nina Thellier, *O.K. Cargo: La saga africaine d'un pilot d'helicoptere* (Paris: Grasset, 1988).

3. Albert Mukong, *The Case for Southern Cameroons* (CAMFECO, 1990), 123; Godfrey B. Tangwa, *I Spit on Their Graves: Testimony Relevant in the Democratization Struggle in Cameroon* (Bamenda, Cameroon: Langaa Publishing, 2010, originally published 1996), 11.

4. Martin Ayong Ayim, *Former British Southern Cameroons Journey towards Complete Decolonization, Independence and Sovereignty* (Bloomington, IN: Author House, 2010); Christina Okello, "Hollande Acknowledges Colonial Era Cameroon Massacres but Critics Want Apology," July 7, 2015, http://en.rfi.fr/africa/20150705-hollande-acknowledges-colonial-era-cameroon-massacres-critics-want-apology

5. Caroline Elkins, *Imperial Reckoning: The Untold Story of Britain's Gulag in Kenya* (New York: Henry Holt, 2005); John Blacker, "The Demography of Mau Mau: Fertility and Mortality in Kenya in the 1950s: A Demographer's Viewpoint," *African Affairs*, 106 (2007), 205–227; David Anderson, *Histories of the Hanged: The Dirty War in Kenya and the End of Empire* (London: Weidenfeld and Nicolson, 2005); Huw Bennett, *Fighting the Mau Mau: The British Army and Counter-Insurgency in the Kenya Emergency* (Cambridge University Press, 2013); Katie Engelhart, "40,000 Kenyans Accuse UK of Abuse in Second Mau Mau Case," *The Guardian*, October 29, 2014, https://www.theguardian.com/world/2014/oct/29/kenya-mau-mau-abuse-case

6. Jerome Lafargue and Musambayi Katumanga, "Kenya in Turmoil: Post-Election Violence and Precarious Pacification," in Jerome Lafargue (ed.), *The General Elections in Kenya, 2007* (Dar es Salaam: Mkuki na Nyota Publishers, 2009), 18; P. Kagwanja, "Courting Genocide: Populism, Ethno-nationalism and the Informalization of Violence in Kenya's 2008 Post-Election Crisis," in P. Kagwanja and R. Southall (eds.), *Kenya's Uncertain Democracy: The Electoral Crisis of 2008* (New York: Routledge, 2010), 116.

7. Kimani Njogu (ed.), *Healing the Wound: Personal Narratives about the 2007 Post-Election Violence in Kenya* (Nairobi: Twaweza Communications, 2009), 157.

8. Sosteness Francis Materu, *The Post-Election Violence in Kenya: Domestic and International Legal Responses* (The Hague: Asser Press, 2015), 59–60.

9. Bahru Zewde, *A History of Modern Ethiopia, 1855–1991* (Oxford: James Currey, 2009); Gebru Tareke, *The Ethiopian Revolution: War in the Horn of Africa* (New Haven: Yale University Press, 2009); Richard Reid, *Frontiers of Violence in North-East Africa: Genealogies of Conflict Since 1800* (Oxford University Press, 2011).

10. Firew Kebede Tiba, "The Mengistu Genocide Trial in Ethiopia," *Journal of International Criminal Justice*, 5 (2007), 513–528.

11. "Ethiopia's Policy of Genocide against the Anuak of Gambella," Cultural Survival, 10, 3 (Fall 1986), https://www.culturalsurvival.org/ourpublications/csq/article/ethiopias-policy-genocide-against-anuak-gambella; "Genocide Watch: The Anuak of Ethiopia," January 2004, http://www.genocidewatch.org/images/Ethiopia_23_Jan_04_The_Anuak_of_Ethiopia.pdf; http://www.anuakjustice.org/index.htm; "Targeting the Anuak: Human Rights Violations and Crimes against Humanity in Ethiopia's Gambella Region," *Human Rights Watch,* March 2005, 17, no. 3(a); "Ethiopia: Second Genocide Being Committed against Anuaks in Gambella," http://www.geeskaafrika.com/14944/ethiopia-second-genocide-being-committed-against-anuaks-in-gambella/

12. For example see Asafa Jalata, "The Genocidal Massacres of Oromos at the Irreecha Festival: The Lies of the Tigre-led Ethiopian Government," *Ayyaantuu News,* October 4, 2016, http://www.ayyaantuu.net/the-genocidal-massacres-of-oromos-at-the-irreechaa-fesival-the-lies-of-the-tigre-led-ethiopian-government/

13. D. Martin and P. Johnson, *The Struggle for Zimbabwe* (New York: Monthly Review, 1981); P. Moorcroft and P. McLaughlin, *The Rhodesian War: A Military History* (London: Pen and Sword, 2008); E. Sibanda, *The Zimbabwe African People's Union, 1961–1987* (Trenton: Africa World Press, 2005).

14. "Report on the 1980s Disturbances in Matabeleland and the Midlands," Catholic Commission for Justice and Peace in Zimbabwe, March 1997, http://www.rhodesia.nl/Matabeleland%20Report.pdf; Glenn Frankel, "Where Is the Genocide? Atrocity Tales Disproven, Zimbabwean Officials Say," *Washington Post,* May 12, 1984, https://www.washingtonpost.com/archive/politics/1984/05/12/where-is-the-genocideatrocity-tales-disproven-zimbabwean-officials-say/d29f4fa9-fe15-429d-a99a-69014688fa10/

15. Blessing Miles Tendi, *Making History in Mugabe's Zimbabwe: Politics, Intellectuals and the Media* (Berlin: Peter Lang, 2010), 219; Sabelo J. Ndlovu-Gatsheni (ed.), *Mugabeism? History, Politics and Power in Zimbabwe* (New York: Palgrave-MacMillan, 2015); "Ottawa Asked to Back Indictment of Mugabe," *The Globe and Mail,* October 8, 2003, http://www.theglobeandmail.com/news/national/ottawa-asked-to-back-indictment-of-mugabe/article1167849/; Gift Phiri, "Lawyers Appeal to Canada over Mugabe's 'Genocide," *Zimbabwe Independent,* April 7, 2006, http://www.theindependent.co.zw/2006/04/07/lawyers-appeal-to-canada-over-mugabes-genocide/; "Genocide Watch Calls for Prosecution of Zimbabwe's Robert Mugabe for Genocide," *Genocide Watch,* September 16, 2010, http://www.genocidewatch.org/zimbabwe.html; James Kirchick, "The New African Genocide," CBS News, March 8, 2007, http://www.cbsnews.com/news/the-new-african-genocide/

16. Stewart Tristan Webb, "Mali's Rebels: Making Sense of the National Movement for the Liberation of Azawad Insurgency," in S. N. Romaniuk and S. T. Webb

(eds.), *Insurgency and Counter-insurgency in Modern War* (London: CRC Press, 2016), 135–144; Jeremy Keenan, *The Dying Sahara: US Imperialism and Terror in Africa* (London: Pluto Press, 2013), 74–76; "Mali: UN Genocide Advisor Warns of Reprisals against Tuareg and Arab Populations," February 1, 2013, http://www.un.org/apps/news/story.asp?NewsID=44058#.V5-btTVA7E8

17. Straus, *Making and Unmaking Nations*, 172.

18. Brian Titley, *Dark Age: The Political Odyssey of Emperor Bokassa* (Montreal: McGill-Queen's, 1997); Richard Bradshaw and Juan Fandos-Rius, *Historical Dictionary of the Central African Republic* (Lanham, MD: Rowman and Littlefield, 2016); "Ethnic Cleansing in Central African Republic, No Genocide: UN Inquiry," January 8, 2015, http://www.reuters.com/article/us-centralafrica-inquiry-idUSKBN0KH2BM20150108

19. Mohamed Adhikari, *Anatomy of a South African Genocide: The Extermination of the Cape San Peoples* (Athens: Ohio University Press, 2011); Robert K. Hitchcock and Wayne A. Babchuk, "Genocide of Khoekhoe and San Peoples of Southern Africa," in S. Totten and R. Hitchock (eds.), *Genocide of Indigenous Peoples: A Critical Bibliographic Review*, vol. 8 (London: Transaction Publishers, 2011), 143–172; A. Dirk Moses (ed.), *Genocide and Settler Society: Frontier Violence and Stolen Indigenous Children in Australian History* (New York: Berghahn Books, 2004).

20. Jacqueline Solway, "Human Rights and NGO 'Wrongs': Conflict Diamonds, Culture Wars and the 'Bushman Question,'" *Africa: The Journal of the International African Institute* 79, no. 3 (2009), 321–346.

Bibliography

BOOKS

Abtahi, Hirad and Webb, Philippa. *The Genocide Convention: The Traveau Preparatoires*, Vol. 1. Leiden: Martinus Nijhoff, 2008.
Ade Ajayi, J. F. and Smith, R. S. *Yoruba Warfare in the Nineteenth Century*. Cambridge University Press, 1964.
Adhikari, Mohamed. *Anatomy of a South African Genocide: The Extermination of the Cape San Peoples*. Athens: Ohio University Press, 2011.
Adunbi, Omalade. *Oil Wealth and Insurgency in Nigeria*. Bloomington: Indiana University Press, 2015.
Akintoye, S. A. *Revolution and Power Politics in Yorubaland, 1840–1893*. New York: Humanities Press, 1971.
Alvarez, Alex. *Governments, Citizens and Genocide: A Comparative and Interdisciplinary Approach*. Bloomington: Indiana University Press, 2001.
Anderson, David. *Histories of the Hanged: The Dirty War in Kenya and the End of Empire*. London: Weidenfeld and Nicolson, 2005.
Anyidoho, Henry Kwami. *Guns over Kigali: The Rwandese Civil War, 1994*. Accra: Woeli Publishing, 1997.
Ascherson, Neal. *The King Incorporated: Leopold the Second and the Congo*. London: Granta Books, 1999.
Atangana, Martin. *The End of French Rule in Cameroon*. Lanham, MD: University Press of America, 2010.
Ayong Ayim, Martin. *Former British Southern Cameroons Journey Towards Complete Decolonization, Independence and Sovereignty*. Bloomington, IN: Author House, 2010.
Azevedo, Mario J. *Roots of Violence: A History of War in Chad*. New York: Routledge, 1998.

Ball, Howard. *Genocide: A Reference Handbook*. Santa Barbara, CA: ABC-Clio, 2011.

Bardet, Max and Thellier, Nina. *O.K. Cargo: La saga africaine d'un pilot d'helicoptere* (Paris: Grasset, 1988).

Bassil, Noah R. *The Post-Colonial State and Civil War in Sudan: The Origins of Conflict in Darfur*. London: I. B. Tauris, 2013.

Bennett, Huw. *Fighting the Mau Mau: The British Army and Counter-Insurgency in the Kenya Emergency*. Cambridge University Press, 2013.

Birmingham, David. *Central Africa to 1870*. London: Cambridge University Press, 1981.

Bley, Helmut. *South West Africa under German Rule, 1894–1914*. Evanston, Ill.: Northwestern University Press, 1971.

Bornkamm, Paul Christoph. *Rwanda's Gacaca Courts: Between Retribution and Reparation*. Oxford University Press, 2012.

Bradshaw, Richard and Fandos-Rius, Juan. *Historical Dictionary of the Central African Republic*. Lanham, MD: Rowman and Littlefield, 2016.

Brannigan, Augustine. *Beyond the Banality of Evil: Criminology and Genocide*. Oxford University Press, 2013.

Carney, J. J. *Rwanda before the Genocide: Catholic Politics and Ethnic Discourse in the Late Colonial Era*. Oxford University Press, 2014.

Chalk, Frank and Jonassohn, Kurt. *The History and Sociology of Genocide: Analyses and Case Studies*. New Haven, CT: Yale University Press, 1990.

Chretien, Jean-Pierre. *The Great Lakes of Africa: Two Thousand Years of History*. New York: Zone Books, 2003.

Chretien, Jean-Pierre and Dupaquier, Jean-Francois. *Burundi 1972: Au Bord du Genocides*. Paris: Karthala, 2007.

Clark, John F., ed. *The African Stakes of the Congo War*. Basingstoke, UK: Palgrave, 2002.

Clark, Phil. *The Gacaca Courts: Post-Genocide Justice and Reconciliation in Rwanda*. Cambridge University Press, 2010.

Cohen, Jared. *One Hundred Days of Silence: America and the Rwanda Genocide*. Lanham, MD: Rowman and Littlefield, 2007.

Collins, Robert O. *A History of Modern Sudan*. Cambridge University Press, 2010.

Collins, Robert O. *Civil Wars and Revolution in the Sudan: Essays on the Sudan, Southern Sudan and Darfur, 1902–2004*. Hollywood, CA: Tsehai Publishers, 2005.

Comolli, Virginia. *Boko Haram: Nigeria's Islamist Insurgency*. London: Hurst and Company, 2015.

Crilly, Rob. *Saving Darfur: Everyone's Favourite African War*. London: Reportage, 2010.

Cruvellier, Thiery. *Court of Remorse: Inside the International Criminal Tribunal for Rwanda*. Madison: University of Wisconsin Press, 2010.

Daley, Patricia. *Gender and Genocide in Burundi: The Search for Spaces of Peace in the Great Lakes Region*. Bloomington: Indiana University Press, 2008.

Dallaire, Romeo. *Shake Hands with the Devil: The Failure of Humanity in Rwanda*. Toronto: Random House, 2003.

Daly, M. W. *Darfur's Sorrow: A History of Destruction and Genocide*. Cambridge University Press, 2007.

Daly, M. W. *Empire on the Nile: The Anglo-Egyptian Sudan, 1898–1934*. Cambridge University Press, 1986.

Dauge-Roth, Alexandre. *Writing and Filming the Genocide of the Tutsis in Rwanda: Dismembering and Remembering Traumatic History*. Lanham, MD: Lexington Books, 2010.
de St. Jorre, John. *The Brothers' War: Biafra and Nigeria*. London: Faber and Faber, 2012, originally published 1972.
de Waal, Alexander. *Famine Crimes: Politics and the Disaster Relief Industry in Africa*. Oxford: James Currey, 1997.
des Forges, Alison. *Leave None to Tell the Story: Genocide in Rwanda*. New York: Human Rights Watch, 1999.
des Forges, Alison Liebhafsky. *Defeat Is the Only Bad News: Rwanda under Musinga, 1896–1931*. Madison: University of Wisconsin Press, 2011.
Destexhe, A. *Rwanda and Genocide in the Twentieth Century*. New York University Press, 1995.
Devlin, Larry. *Chief of Station, Congo: A Memoir of 1960–67*. New York: Public Affairs, 2007.
Diamond, Jared. *Collapse: How Societies Choose to Fail or Succeed*. New York: Penguin, 2005.
Diamond, Larry Jay. *Class, Ethnicity and Democracy in Nigeria: The Failure of the First Republic*. Syracuse University Press, 1988.
Dusengumuremyi, Jean d'Amour. *No Greater Love: Testimonies on the Life and Death of Felicitas Niyitegeka*. Germany: Dignity Press, 2015.
Egharevba, Jacob. *A Short History of Benin*. Ibaban University Press, 1968, originally published 1934.
Elkins, Caroline. *Imperial Reckoning: The Untold Story of Britain's Gulag in Kenya*. New York: Henry Holt, 2005.
Erichsen, Casper. *"The Angel of Death Has Descended Violently among Them": Concentration Camps and Prisoners-of-War in Namibia, 1904–1908*. Leiden: African Studies Centre, 2005.
Evans, Gareth. *Responsibility to Protect: Ending Mass Atrocity Crimes Once and for All*. Washington, D.C.: Brookings Institute, 2008.
Falola, Toyin. *Ibadan: Foundation, Growth and Change, 1830–1960*. Ibadan: Bookcraft, 2012.
Falola, Toyin and Heaton, Matthew M. *A History of Nigeria*. Cambridge University Press, 2008.
Falola, Toyin and Oyebade, Adebayo O. *Hot Spot Sub-Saharan Africa*. Santa Barbara, CA: Greenwood Press, 2010.
Flint, John E. *Sir George Goldie and the Making of Nigeria*. London: Oxford University Press, 1960.
Flint, Julie and de Waal, Alex. *Darfur: A Short History of a Long War*. London: Zed Books, 2005.
Gahima, Gerald. *Transitional Justice in Rwanda: Accountability for Atrocity*. London: Routledge, 2013.
George, Edward. *The Cuban Intervention in Angola, 1965–1991: From Che Guevara to Cuito Cuanavale*. London: Frank Cass, 2005.
Gerard, Emmanuel and Kuklick, Bruce. *Death in the Congo: Killing Patrice Lumumba*. Harvard University Press, 2015.
Gewald, Jan-Bart. *Herero Heroes: A Socio-Political History of the Herero of Namibia, 1890–1923*. Oxford: James Currey, 1999.

Gordon, April. *Nigeria's Diverse Peoples: A Reference Sourcebook*. Santa Barbara, CA: ABC-Clio, 2003.

Gourevitch, Philip. *We Wish to Inform You That Tomorrow We Will Be Killed with Our Families: Stories from Rwanda*. New York: Farrar, Straus and Giroux, 1999.

Guichaoua, Andre. *From War to Genocide: Criminal Politics in Rwanda*. Madison: University of Wisconsin Press, 2015.

Haskin, Jeanne M. *The Tragic State of the Congo: From Decolonization to Dictatorship*. New York: Algora Publishing, 2005.

Hatzfeld, Jean. *The Antelope's Strategies: Living in Rwanda after the Genocide*. New York: Farrar, Straus and Giroux, 2009.

Hatzfeld, Jean. *Life Laid Bare: The Survivors in Rwanda Speak*. New York: Other Press, 2006.

Hatzfeld, Jean. *Machete Season: The Killers in Rwanda Speak*. New York: Farrar, Straus and Giroux, 2005.

Hernan, Edward and Peterson, David. *The Politics of Genocide*. New York: Monthly Review Press, 2010.

Hinde, Sydney Langford. *The Fall of the Congo Arabs*. New York: Negro Universities Press, 1969.

Hoare, Mike. *Congo Mercenary*. Boulder, Colorado: Paladin Press, 2008, originally published 1967.

Hobson, John. *Imperialism: A Study*. London: George Allen and Unwin, 1902.

Hochschild, Adam. *King Leopold's Ghost: A Story of Greed, Terror and Heroism in Colonial Africa*. New York: Mariner Books, 1999.

Hoffman, Julia and Nollkaemper, Andre, eds. *Responsibility to Protect: From Principle to Practice*. Amsterdam: Pallas Publications, 2012.

Hopkins, A. G. *An Economic History of West Africa*. London: Longman, 1973.

Hull, Isabel V. *Absolute Destruction: Military Culture and the Practices of War in Imperial Germany*. Ithaca, New York: Cornell University Press, 2005.

Ilibagiza, Immaculee. *Left to Tell: Discovering God amidst the Rwandan Holocaust*. Carlsbad, CA: Hayhouse, 2006.

Iliffe, John. *Honour in African History*. Cambridge University Press, 2005.

Isichei, Elizabeth. *A History of the Igbo People*. London: MacMillan, 1976.

Isichei, Elizabeth. *The Ibo People and the Europeans: The Genesis of a Relationship–to 1906*. New York: St. Martin's Press, 1973.

Johnson, Samuel. *History of the Yorubas*. London: Routledge and Kegan Paul, 1921.

Jok, Jok Modut. *War and Slavery in Sudan*. Philadelphia: University of Pennsylvania Press, 2001.

Jonassohn, Kurt with Karin Solveig Bjornson. *Genocide and Gross Violations of Human Rights in Comparative Perspective*. New Brunswick, NJ: Transaction Publishers, 1999.

Kayihura, Eduoard and Zukus, Kerry. *Inside the Hotel Rwanda: The Surprising True Story and Why It Matters Today*. Dallas: BenBella Books, 2014.

Kayimahe, Vénuste. *France-Rwanda: Les coulisses d un genocide. Témoignage d un rescapé*. Paris: Dagorno, 2002.

Kayitesi, Berthe. *Demain ma vie: Enfants Chief de famille dan le Rwanda d'apres*. Paris: Teper, 2009.

Keenan, Jeremy. *The Dying Sahara: US Imperialism and Terror in Africa*. London: Pluto Press, 2013.

Kisangani, Emizet Francois and Bobb, F. Scott. *Historical Dictionary of the Democratic Republic of the Congo*. Lanham, Maryland: Scarecrow Press, 2010.
Knight, W. Andy and Egerton, Frazer, eds. *The Routledge Handbook of the Responsibility to Protect*. London: Routledge, 2012.
Koops, Joachin A., MacQueen, Norry, Tardy, Theirry, and Williams, Paul D., eds. *The Oxford Handbook of United Nations Peacekeeping Operations*. Oxford University Press, 2015.
Lamothe, Ronald. *Slaves of Fortune: Sudanese Soldiers and the River War 1896–98*. Woodbridge, UK: James Currey, 2011.
Last, Murray. *The Sokoto Caliphate*. London: Longmans, 1967.
Lemarchand, Rene. *Burundi: Ethnic Conflict and Genocide*. Cambridge University Press, 1994.
Lemarchand, Rene. *The Dynamics of Violence in Central Africa*. Philadelphia: University of Pennsylvania Press, 2009.
Lemarchand, Rene. *Rwanda and Burundi*. London: Pall Mall, 1970.
Lenin, V. I. *Imperialism: The Highest Stage of Capitalism*. New York: International Publishers, 1969, originally published 1916.
Leonard, David K. and Straus, Scott. *Africa's Stalled Development: International Causes and Cures*. London: Lynne Rienner, 2003.
Longman, Timothy. *Christianity and Genocide in Rwanda*. Cambridge University Press, 2010.
Louis, William Roger. *Ruanda-Urundi 1884–1919*. Oxford: Clarendon Press, 1963.
Malkki, Liisa. *Purity and Exile: Violence, Memory and National Cosmology among Hutu Refugees in Tanzania*. University of Chicago Press, 1995.
Mamdani, Mahmood. *Citizen and Subject: Contemporary Africa and the Legacy of Late Colonialism*. Princeton University Press, 1996.
Mamdani, Mahmood. *Survivors and Saviors: Darfur, Politics and the War on Terror*. New York: Double Day, 2009.
Mamdani, Mahmood. *When Victims Become Killers: Colonialism, Nativism and the Genocide in Rwanda*. Princeton University Press, 2001.
Martin, D. and Johnson, P. *The Struggle for Zimbabwe*. New York: Monthly Review, 1981.
Materu, Sosteness Francis. *The Post-Election Violence in Kenya: Domestic and International Legal Responses*. The Hague: Asser Press, 2015.
McGregor, Andrew. *A Military History of Modern Egypt: From the Ottoman Conquest to the Ramadan War*. Westport, CT: Praeger Security International, 2006.
McNamara, Francis Terry. *France in Black Africa*. Washington, D.C.: National Defense University, 1989.
Melvern, Linda. *Conspiracy to Murder: The Rwanda Genocide*. London: Verso, 2006.
Melvern, Linda. *A People Betrayed: The Role of the West in Rwanda's Genocide*. London: Zed Books, 2005.
Meredith, Martin. *Diamonds, Gold and War: The British, the Boers and the Making of South Africa*. New York: Public Affairs, 2007.
Mills, Kurt. *International Responses to Mass Atrocities in Africa: Responsibility to Protect, Prosecute and Palliate*. Philadelphia: University of Pennsylvania Press, 2015.
Miners, N. J. *The Nigerian Army 1956–66*. London: Methuen, 1971.
Moorcroft, P. and McLaughlin, P. *The Rhodesian War: A Military History*. London: Pen and Sword, 2008.

Moses, Dirk A., ed. *Genocide and Settler Society: Frontier Violence and Stolen Indigenous Children in Australian History*. New York: Berghahn Books, 2004.
Mukagasana, Yolande. *La mort ne veut pas de moi*. Paris: Fixot, 1997.
Mukong, Albert. *The Case for Southern Cameroons*. Silver Spring, MD: CAMFECO, 1990.
Murindwa, R. *Nyabingi Movement: People's Colonial Struggles in Kigezi 1910–30*. Kampala: Centre for Basic Research, 1991.
Mushemza, E. D. *Banyarwanda Refugees in Uganda 1959–2001*. Kampala: Fountain Publishers, 2007.
Mwakikagile, Godfrey. *Burundi: The Hutu and the Tutsi: Cauldron of Conflict and Quest for Dynamic Compromise*. Dar es Salaam, Tanzania: New Africa Press, 2012.
Natsios, Andrew S. *Sudan, South Sudan and Darfur: What Everyone Needs to Know*. Oxford University Press, 2012.
Ndacyayisenga, Pierre-Claver. *Dying to Live: A Rwandan Family's Five-Year Flight across the Congo*. Montreal: Baraka Books, 2013.
Ndlovu-Gatsheni, Sabelo J., ed. *Mugabeism? History, Politics and Power in Zimbabwe*. New York: Palgrave-MacMillan, 2015.
Ngemi, Yaa-Lengi M. *Genocide in the Congo (Zaire): In the Name of Bill Clinton, and of the Paris Club, and of the Mining Conglomerates, So It Is!* New York: Writers' Club Press, 2000.
Nigerian Pogrom: The Organized Massacres of Eastern Nigerians. Enugu: Ministry of Information, 1966.
Njogu, Kimani, ed. *Healing the Wound: Personal Narratives about the 2007 Post-election Violence in Kenya*. Nairobi: Twaweza Communications, 2009.
Nolutshungu, Sam. *The Limits of Anarchy: Intervention and State Formation in Chad*. University of Virginia Press, 1995.
Nzongola-Ntalaja, Georges. *The Congo: From Leopold to Kabila: A People's History*. London: Zed Books, 2007.
Obi, Cyril and Rustad, Siri Aas, eds. *Oil and Insurgency in the Niger Delta: Managing the Complex Politics of Petro-Violence*. London: Zed Books, 2011.
O'Fahey, R. S. *The Darfur Sultanate: A History*. New York: Columbia University Press, 2008.
Ogot, B. A., ed. *UNESCO General History of Africa: Africa from the Sixteenth to Eighteenth Century*. Oxford: James Currey, 1999.
Okoye, Grace O. *Proclivity to Genocide: Northern Nigeria Ethno-Religious Conflict, 1966 to Present*. Lanham, MD: Lexington Books, 2014.
Olusoga, David and Erichsen, Casper W. *The Kaiser's Holocaust: Germany's Forgotten Genocide and the Colonial Roots of Nazism*. London: Faber and Faber, 2010.
Othen, Christopher. *Katanga, 1960–63: Mercenaries, Spires and the African Nation that Waged War on the World*. Stroud, UK: The History Press, 2015.
Pakenham, Thomas. *The Scramble for Africa: White Man's Conquest of the Dark Continent, 1876–1912*. New York: Harper Collins, 1991.
Pauw, Jacques. *Dances with Devils: A Journalist's Search for the Truth*. Cape Town: Zebra Press, 2006.
Pauw, Jacques. *Rat Roads of Africa: One Man's Incredible Journal*. Cape Town: Zebra Press, 2012.
Pean, Pierre. *Noires Fureurs, Blancs Menteurs*. Paris: Mille et Une Nuit, 2006.
Peters, Jimi. *The Nigerian Military and the State*. London: I. B. Tauris, 1997.

Pollock, Kenneth M. *Arabs at War: Military Effectiveness, 1948–1991*. Lincoln: University of Nebraska Press, 2002.

Power, Samantha. *A Problem from Hell: America and the Age of Genocide*. New York: New Republic, 2002.

Prunier, Gerard. *Africa's World War: Congo, the Rwanda Genocide and the Making of a Continental Catastrophe*. Oxford University Press, 2009.

Prunier, Gerard. *Darfur: The Ambiguous Genocide*. Ithaca, NY: Cornell University Press, 2005.

Prunier, Gerard. *The Rwanda Crisis: History of a Genocide*. New York: Columbia University Press, 1995.

Quigley, John. *The Genocide Convention: An International Law Analysis*. New York: Routledge, 2016.

Reefe, Thomas Q. *The Rainbow and the Kings: A History of the Luba Empire to 1891*. Los Angeles: University of California Press, 1981.

Reeves, Eric. *A Long Day's Dying: Critical Moments in the Darfur Genocide*. Toronto: Key Publishing, 2007.

Reid, Richard. *Frontiers of Violence in North-East Africa: Genealogies of Conflict since 1800*. Oxford University Press, 2011.

Renton, David. Seddon, David, and Zeilig, Leo, *The Congo: Plunder and Resistance*. London: Zed Press, 2007.

Reyntjens, Filip. *The Great African War: Congo and Regional Geopolitics, 1996–2006*. Cambridge University Press, 2009.

Robinson, Ronald and Gallagher, John. *Africa and the Victorians: The Official Mind of Imperialism*. London: MacMillan, 1961.

Rodney, Walter. *How Europe Underdeveloped Africa*. Dar es Salaam: Tanzania Publishing House, 1972.

Rombouts, Heidy. *Victim Organization and the Politics of Reparations: A Case Study on Rwanda*. Cambridge: Intersentia, 2004.

Rusagara, Frank. *Resilience of a Nation: A History of the Military in Rwanda*. Kigali: Fountain Publishers, 2009.

Ruzibiza, Abdul Joshua. *Rwanda: L-histoire secrete*. Paris: Editions du Panama, 2005.

Ryder, Alan. *Benin and the Europeans, 1485–1897*. London: Longmans, 1969.

Sargent, Daniel J. *A Superpower Transformed: The Remaking of American Foreign Relations in the 1970s*. Oxford University Press, 2015.

Sarkin, Jeremy. *Colonial Genocide and Reparations Claims in the 21st Century: The Socio-Legal Context of Claims under International Law by the Herero against Germany for Genocide in Namibia, 1904–1908*. Westport, CT: Praeger Security International, 2009.

Sarkin, Jeremy. *Germany's Genocide of the Herero: Kaiser Wilhelm II, His General, His Settlers, His Soldiers*. University of Cape Town Press, 2010.

Saro-Wiwa, Ken. *Genocide in Nigeria: The Ogoni Tragedy*. Port Harcourt, Nigeria: Saros International Publishers, 1992.

Schabas, William. *Genocide in International Law: The Crime of Crimes*. Cambridge University Press, 2009.

Schatzberg, Michael. *The Dialectics of Oppression in Zaire*. Bloomington: Indiana University Press, 1988.

Schnee, Heinrich. *German Colonization Past and Future: The Truth about the German Colonies*. New York: Alfred A. Knopf, 1926.

Sibanda, E. *The Zimbabwe African People's Union, 1961–1987*. Trenton: Africa World Press, 2005.

Silvester, Jeremy and Gewald, Jan-Bart. *"Words Cannot be Found": German Colonial Rule in Namibia: An Annotated Reprint of the 1918 Blue Book*. Leiden: Brill, 2003.

Simon, Thomas W. *The Laws of Genocide: Prescriptions for a Just World*. Westport, CT: Praeger Security International, 2007.

Siollun, Max. *Oil, Politics and Violence: Nigeria's Military Coup Culture, 1966–76*. New York: Algora Publishing, 2009.

Smaldone, Joseph. *Warfare in the Sokoto Caliphate: Historical and Sociological Perspectives*. London: Cambridge University Press, 1977.

Smith, Karen. *Genocide and the Europeans*. Cambridge University Press, 2010.

Smith, Mike. *Boko Haram: Inside Nigeria's Unholy War*. London: I. B. Tauris, 2015.

Sommers, Marc. *Fear in Bongoland: Burundian Refugees in Urban Tanzania*. New York: Berghahn Books, 2001.

Straus, Scott. *Making and Unmaking Nations: War, Leadership and Genocide in Modern Africa*. Ithaca, NY: Cornell University Press, 2015.

Straus, Scott. *The Order of Genocide: Race, Power, and War in Rwanda*. Ithaca: Cornell University Press, 2007.

Stremlau, John. *The International Politics of the Nigerian Civil War, 1967–70*. Princeton University Press, 1977.

Tangwa, Godfrey B. *I Spit on Their Graves: Testimony Relevant in the Democratization Struggle in Cameroon*. Bamenda, Cameroon: Langaa Publishing, 2010, originally published 1996.

Tareke, Gebru. *The Ethiopian Revolution: War in the Horn of Africa*. New Haven: Yale University Press, 2009.

Tatz, Colin and Higgins, Winton. *The Magnitude of Genocide*. Santa Barbara, CA: Praeger Security International, 2016.

Tendi, Blessing Miles. *Making History in Mugabe's Zimbabwe: Politics, Intellectuals and the Media*. Berlin: Peter Lang, 2010.

Thornton, John. *The Kingdom of Kongo: Civil War and Transition, 1641–1718*. Madison: University of Wisconsin Press, 1983.

Titley, Brian. *Dark Age: The Political Odyssey of Emperor Bokassa*. Montreal: McGill-Queen's, 1997.

Totten, Samuel and Bartrop, Paul R. *Encyclopedia of Genocide*, vol. 2. Westport, CT: Greenwood Press, 2008.

Totten, Samuel. *Genocide by Attrition: The Nuba Mountains of Sudan*. London: Transaction Publishers, 2015.

Travis, Hannibal. *Genocide, Ethnonationalism and the United Nations: Exploring the Causes of Mass Killing Since 1945*. New York: Routledge, 2013.

Turner, Simon. *Politics of Innocence: Hutu Identity, Conflict and Camp Life*. New York: Berghahn Books, 2010.

Turner, Thomas. *The Congo Wars: Conflict, Myth and Reality*. New York: Zed Books, 2007.

Umutesi, Marie Beatrice. *Surviving the Slaughter: The Ordeal of a Rwandan Refugee in Zaire*. Madison: University of Wisconsin Press, 2004.

Uzoigwe, G. N. *Visions of Nationhood: Prelude to the Nigerian Civil War, 1960–67*. Trenton, NJ: Africa World Press, 2011.

Van Reybrouck, David. *Congo: The Epic History of a People*. New York: Harper Collins, 2014.

Vansina, Jan. *Antecedents to Modern Rwanda: The Nyiginya Kingdom*. Madison: University of Wisconsin Press, 2004.

Vanthemsche, Guy. *Belgium and the Congo, 1885–1980*. Cambridge University Press, 2012.

Villafana, Frank. *Cold War in the Congo: The Confrontation of Cuban Military Forces, 1960–67*. New Brunswick, New Jersey: Transaction Publishers, 2012.

Wallis, Andrew. *Silent Accomplice: The Untold Story of France's Role in the Rwandan Genocide*. London: I. B. Tauris, 2006.

Watt, Nigel. *Burundi: The Biography of a Small African Country*. London: Hurst, 2008.

Waugh, Colin M. *Paul Kagame and Rwanda: Power, Genocide and the Rwandan Patriotic Front*. London: MacFarland, 2004.

Weber, Thomas. *Hitler's First War: Adolph Hitler, the Men of the List Regiment, and the First World War.* Oxford University Press, 2011.

Weinstein, Warren and Schrire, Robert A. *Political Conflict and Ethnic Strategies: A Case Study of Burundi*. Syracuse, NY: Syracuse University, 1976.

Williams, Susan. *Who Killed Dag Hammarskjold? The UN, the Cold War and White Supremacy in Africa*. New York: Columbia University Press, 2011.

Yoder, John C. *The Kanyok of Zaire: An Institutional and Ideological History to 1895*. Cambridge University Press, 1992.

Zewde, Bahru. *A History of Modern Ethiopia, 1855–1991*. Oxford: James Currey, 2009.

ARTICLES AND CHAPTERS

Adetula, Victor A. O. "Environmental Degradation, Land Shortage and Identity Conflicts on the Jos Plateau in Nigeria." In Sam Moyo, Dzodzi Tsikata, and Yakham Diop (eds.), *Land in the Struggles for Citizenship in Africa*. Dakar: CODESRIA, 2015, 37–68.

Anthony, Douglas. "'Ours Is a War of Survival': Biafra, Nigeria and Arguments about Genocide, 1966–70," *Journal of Genocide Research* 16, nos. 2–3, 205–225.

Bangarth, Stephanie. "The Politics of African Intervention: Canada and Biafra, 1967–70." In Michael K. Carroll and Greg Donaghy (eds.), *From Kinshasa to Kandahar: Canada and Fragile States in Comparative Perspective*. University of Calgary Press, 2016, 53–72.

Blacker, John. "The Demography of Mau Mau: Fertility and Mortality in Kenya in the 1950s: A Demographer's Viewpoint." *African Affairs* 106 (2007), 205–227.

Bush, Peter. "Biafra and the Canadian Churches, 1966–70." *Historical Papers 2003: Canadian Society of Church History*, 129–147.

Crowley, Daniel J. "Politics and Tribalism in the Katanga." *The Western Political Quarterly* 16, no. 1 (March 1963), 68–78.

de Waal, Alex. "Counter-Insurgency on the Cheap." *London Review of Books* 26, no. 15 (August 5, 2004), 25–27.

de Waal, Alex. "The Nuba Mountains, Sudan." In Samuel Totten and William Parsons (eds.), *Centuries of Genocide: Essays and Eye-witness Accounts*. New York: Routledge, 2013, 421–445.

Dedering, Tilman. "The German-Herero War of 1904: Revisionism of Genocide or Imaginary Historiography." *Journal of Southern African Studies* 19, no. 1 (March 1993), 80–88.

Degomme, Olivier and Guhu-Sapir, Debarati. "Pattern of Mortality Rates in Darfur Conflict." *The Lancet* 375, no. 9711 (January 2010), 294–300.

Doron, Roy. "Marketing Genocide: Biafran Propaganda Strategies during the Nigerian Civil War, 1967–70." *Journal of Genocide Research* 16, no. 2–3 (2014), 227–246.

Fournet, Caroline. "Reflection on the Separation of Powers: The Law of Genocide and the Symptomatic French Paradox." In Ralph Henham and Paul Behrens (eds.), *The Criminal Law of Genocide: International, Comparative and Contextual Contexts*. Aldershot, UK: Ashgate, 2007, 203–214.

Hintjens, Helen. "Explaining the 1994 Genocide in Rwanda." *Journal of Modern African Studies* 37, no. 2 (June 1999), 241–286.

Hitchcock, Robert K. and Babchuk, Wayne A. "Genocide of Khoekhoe and San Peoples of Southern Africa." In S. Totten and R. Hitchock (eds.), *Genocide of Indigenous Peoples: A Critical Bibliographic Review*, vol. 8. London: Transaction Publishers, 2011, 143–172.

Hohenhaus, Peter. "Commemorating and Commodifying the Rwandan Genocide: Memorial Sites in a Politically Difficult Context." In Leanne White and Elspeth Frew (eds.), *Dark Tourism and Place Identity: Managing and Interpreting Dark Places*. London: Routledge, 2013, 142–155.

Howard-Hassmann, Rhoda E. "Genocide and State-Induced Famine: Global Ethics and Western Responsibility for Mass Atrocities in Africa." *Perspectives on Global Development and Technology* 4, no. 3–4 (2005), 487–516.

Ibreck, Rachel. "The Politics of Mourning: Survivor Contributions to Memorials in Post-genocide Rwanda." *Memory Studies* 3, no. 4 (2010), 330–343.

Kabanda, Marcel. "Kangura: The Triumph of Propaganda Refined." In Allan Thompson (ed.), *The Media and the Rwanda Genocide*. London: Pluto Press, 2007, 62–72.

Kagwanja, P. "Courting Genocide: Populism, Ethno-nationalism and the Informalization of Violence in Kenya's 2008 Post-election Crisis." In P. Kagwanja and R. Southall (eds.), *Kenya's Uncertain Democracy: The Electoral Crisis of 2008*. New York: Routledge, 2010, 106–128.

Kisangani, Ezimet. "The Massacre of Refugees in Congo: A Case of UN Peacekeeping Failure and International Law." *The Journal of Modern African Studies* 38, no. 2 (2000), 163–202.

Korieh, Chima. "Biafra and the Discourse on the Igbo Genocide." *Journal of Asian and African Studies* 48, no. 6 (2013), 727–740.

Kress, Claus. "The Darfur Report and Genocidal Intent." *Journal of International Criminal Justice*, 3 (2005), 562–578.

Kuperman, Alan. "Provoking Genocide: A Revised History of the Rwandan Patriotic Front." *Journal of Genocide Research* 6, no. 1 (2004), 61–84.

Laband, John. "Zulu Civilians during the Rise and Fall of the Zulu Kingdom, c.1817–1879." In J. Laband (ed.), *Daily Lives of Civilians in Wartime Africa: From Slavery Days to Rwandan Genocide*. Westport, CT: Greenwood, 2007, 51–84.

Lafargue, Jerome and Katumanga, Musambayi. "Kenya in Turmoil: Post-Election Violence and Precarious Pacification." In Jerome Lafargue (ed.), *The General Elections in Kenya, 2007*. Dar es Salaam: Mkuki na Nyota Publishers, 2009, 13–32.

Lemarchand, Rene. "Burundi 1972: Genocide Denied, Revised and Remembered." In Rene Lemarchand (ed.), *Forgotten Genocides: Oblivion, Denial and Memory*. Philadelphia: University of Pennsylvania Press, 2011, 37–50.

Lieven, Michael. "'Butchering the Brutes All over the Place': Total War and Massacre in Zululand, 1879." *History* 84, no. 276 (October 1999), 614–632.

Madley, Benjamin. "From Africa to Auschwitz: How German South West Africa Incubated Ideas and Methods Adopted and Developed by the Nazis in Eastern Europe." *European Historical Quarterly* 35, no. 3 (2005), 429–464.

Mahoney, Michael R. "The Zulu Kingdom as a Genocidal and Post-Genocidal Society, c.1810 to the Present." *Journal of Genocide Research* 5, no. 2 (2003), 251–268.

Marineau, Josiah. "Securing Peace in Burundi: External Interventions to End the Civil War, 1993–2006." In Toyin Falola and Charles Thomas (eds.), *Securing Africa: Local Crises and Foreign Interventions*. New York: Routledge, 2014, 229–248.

Mayersen, Deborah. "Deep Cleavages That Divide: The Origins and Development of Ethnic Violence in Rwanda." *Critical Race and Whiteness Studies* 8, no. 2 (2012), 1–17.

Meierhenrich, Jens. "Topographies of Forgetting and Remembering: The Transformation of Lieux de Memoire in Rwanda." In Scott Strauss and Lars Waldorf (eds.), *Remaking Rwanda: State Building and Human Rights after Mass Violence*. Madison: University of Wisconsin Press, 2011, 283–297.

Newbury, Catherine and Newbury, David. "The Genocide in Rwanda and the Holocaust in Germany: Parallels and Pitfalls." *Journal of Genocide Research* 5, no. 1 (2003), 135–145.

Njoku, Carol Ijeoma. "A Paradox of International Criminal Justice: The Biafra Genocide." *Journal of Asian and African Studies* 48, no. 6 (2013), 710–726.

Plotnicov, Leonard. "An Early Nigerian Civil Disturbance: The 1945 Hausa-Ibo Riots in Jos," *The Journal of Modern African Studies* 9, no. 2 (August 1971), 297–305.

Rettig, Max L. "Transnational Trials as Transitional Justice: Lessons from the Trials of Two Rwandan Nuns in Belgium." *Washington University Global Studies Law Review* 11, no. 2 (2012), 365–414.

Rodt, Annemarie Peen. "The African Mission in Burundi: The Successful Management of Violent Ethno-Political Conflict." *Ethnopolitics Papers* 10 (May 2011), 1–31.

Roessler, Phillip and Prendergast, John. "Democratic Republic of Congo." In William J. Durch (ed.), *Twenty-First Century Peace Operations*. Washington, D.C.: United States Institute of Peace, 2006, 229–318.

Russell, Aidan. "Rebel and Rule in Burundi, 1972." *International Journal of African Historical Studies* 48, no. 1 (2015), 73–97.

Schabas, William A. "Has Genocide Been Committed in Darfur? The State Plan or Policy Element in the Crime of Genocide." In Ralph Henham and Paul

Behrens (eds.), *The Criminal Law of Genocide: International, Comparative and Contextual Aspects*. Aldershot, UK: Ashgate, 2007, 39–47.

Schaller, Dominik J. "Genocide and Mass Violence in the 'Heart of Darkness': Africa and the Colonial Period." In D. Bloxham and D. A. Moses (eds.), *The Oxford Handbook of Genocide Studies*. Oxford University Press, 2010, 345–364.

Schaller, Domink J. "Raphael Lemkin's View of European Colonial Rule in Africa: Between Condemnation and Admiration." *Journal of Genocide Research* 7, no. 4 (2005), 531–538.

Smith, Karen. "The UK and 'Genocide' in Biafra." *Journal of Genocide Research* 16, no. 2–3 (2014), 247–262.

Solway, Jacqueline. "Human Rights and NGO 'Wrongs': Conflict Diamonds, Culture Wars and the 'Bushman Question.'" *Africa: The Journal of the International African Institute* 79, no. 3 (2009), 321–346.

Tiba, Firew Kebede. "The Mengistu Genocide Trial in Ethiopia," *Journal of International Criminal Justice*, 5 (2007), 513–528.

Wagner, Michele. "Burundi to c. 1800" and "Burundi: Nineteenth Century: Pre-Colonial." In Kevin Shillington (ed.), *Encyclopedia of African History*, vol. 1. New York: Fitzroy Dearborn, 2005, 185–188.

Wagner, Michele. "Burundi: Colonial Period: German and Belgian." In Kevin Shillington (ed.), *Encyclopedia of African History*, vol. 1. New York: Fitzroy Dearborn, 2005, 188–190.

Waldorf, Lars. "Goats and Graves: Reparations in Rwanda's Community Courts." In Carla Ferstman, Mariana Goetz, and Alan Stephens (eds.), *Reparations for Victims of Genocide, War Crimes and Crimes against Humanity*. Leiden: Martinus Nijhoff, 2009, 515–539.

Webb, Stewart Tristan. "Mali's Rebels: Making Sense of the National Movement for the Liberation of Azawad Insurgency." In S. N. Romaniuk and S. T. Webb (eds.), *Insurgency and Counter-insurgency in Modern War* (London: CRC Press, 2016), 135–144.

Weisbord, Robert G. "The King, The Cardinal and the Pope: Leopold II's Genocide in the Congo and the Vatican." *Journal of Genocide Research* 5, no. 1 (2003), 35–45.

THESES

Jansohn, Uwe F. "Operation Amaryllis: French Evacuation Operation in Rwanda 1994—Lessons Learned for Future German Noncombat Evacuation Operations," Master of Military Art and Science Thesis, Fort Leavenworth, Kansas, U.S. Army Command and General Staff College, 2000.

Maser, Genevieve. "The Pursuit of Hutu Power: The Forces Armees Rwandaises, 1960–94," MA Thesis, Dalhousie University, 2010.

Odom, Thomas P. "Dragon Operations: Hostage Rescues in the Congo, 1964–65," Fort Leavenworth, Kansas: Combat Studies Institute, 1988.

Odom, Thomas P. "Shaba II: The French and Belgian Intervention in Zaire in 1978," Fort Leavenworth, Kansas: U.S. Army Command and General Staff College, Combat Studies Institute, 1993.

REPORTS

"Annual Report of the Secretary General on the Work of the Organization, June 16, 1960–June 15, 1961." United Nations, New York 1961, Supplement 1 (A/4800); http://dag.un.org/handle/11176/173474

"Broadcasting Genocide: Censorship, Propaganda and State-Sponsored Violence in Rwanda, 1990–94." https://www.article19.org/data/files/pdfs/publications/rwanda-broadcasting-genocide.pdf

"The Counting of the Genocide Victims: Final Report." Ministry for Local Government, Department for Information and Social Affairs, BP 3445, Kigali, Rwanda, November 2002.

"Final Report on the African Union Commission of Inquiry on South Sudan." Addis Ababa, October 15, 2014. http://www.peaceau.org/uploads/auciss.final.report.pdf

"Germany Refuses to Acknowledge Herero Massacres as Genocide." *Deutsche Welle*,March23,2012.http://www.dw.de/germany-refuses-to-acknowledge-herero-massacres-as-genocide/a-15830118

"Human Security Report, 2009: The Shrinking Costs of War." Human Security Report Project, Simon Fraser University, January 2010.

"International Commission of Inquiry for Burundi." United Nations Security Council, S/1996/682. http://www.usip.org/sites/default/files/file/resources/collections/commissions/Burundi-Report.pdf

"Ituri: Covered in Blood: Ethnically Targeted Violence in Northeastern DR Congo." *Human Rights Watch* 15, no. 11 (A), (July 2003), https://www.hrw.org/reports/2003/ituri0703/

Joensen, Vagn to UN Security Council. "Report on the Completion Strategy of the International Criminal Tribunal for Rwanda as of May 5, 2015." May 15, 2015, http://www.unictr.org/sites/unictr.org/files/legal-library/150515-completion-strategy-en.pdf

Lemarchand, Rene. "Rwanda: The State of Research." *Online Encyclopedia of Mass Violence,* May 27, 2013, 14–15. http://www.massviolence.org/rwanda-the-state-of-research,742.

"Operation Artemis: The Lessons of the Interim Emergency Multi-national Force." United Nations, Peacekeeping Best Practices Unit, Military Division, October 2004.

"Report of the International Commission of Inquiry on Darfur to the United Nations Secretary General, Pursuant to Security Council Resolution 1564 of September 18, 2004." Geneva, January 25, 2005. http://www.un.org/news/dh/sudan/com_inq_darfur.pdf

"Repression and Genocidal Dynamics in Burundi." International Federation for Human Rights, November 2016. http://www.responsibilitytoprotect.org/burundi%20report%20fidh.pdf

"Rwanda: Justice After Genocide—20 Years oO." *Human Rights Watch,* March 28, 2014. https://www.hrw.org/news/2014/03/28/rwanda-justice-after-genocide-20-years

United Nations. "Report of the Secretary General's Investigative Team Charged with Investigating Serious Violations of Human Rights and International

Humanitarian Law in the Democratic Republic of Congo." S1998/581, 7. https://documents-dds-ny.un.org/doc/UNDOC/GEN/N98/177/22/IMG/N9817722.pdf?OpenElement

Van Grasdorff, Eric, Roeschert, Nicolai, and Manji, Firoze. "Germany's Genocide in Namibia: Unbearable Silence or How Not to Deal with Your Colonial Past." *Pambazuka News* 577, March 20, 2012, http://www.pambazuka.org/en/category/features/80911

"Weapons and Ammunition Airdropped to SPLA-IO Forces in South Sudan," Conflict Armament Research, June 2015, http://www.conflictarm.com/wp-content/uploads/2015/06/Weapons_and_ammunition_airdropped_to_SPLA-iO_forces_in_South_Sudan.pdf

Index

About the Author

TIMOTHY J. STAPLETON is a professor in the Department of History and a senior research fellow at the Centre for Military, Security, and Strategic Studies (CMSS) at the University of Calgary. He has taught in South Africa and held research appointments in Zimbabwe and Botswana. His most recent books include *African Police and Soldiers in Colonial Zimbabwe, 1923–80* (2011), a three-volume *Military History of Africa* (2013), and *Warfare and Tracking in Africa, 1952–90* (2015).